ARAB
STATES

BUSINESS LAW HANDBOOK

VOLUME 1
ARAB COUNTRIES INVESTMENT LAWS AND REGULATIONS

International Business Publications, USA
Washington DC, USA

ARAB STATES

BUSINESS LAW HANDBOOK

VOLUME 1 ARAB COUNTRIES INVESTMENT LAWS AND REGULATIONS

UPDATED ANNUALLY

Cover Design: International Business Publications, USA

We express our sincere appreciation to all government agencies and international organizations which provided information and other materials for this handbook

2016 Updated Reprint International Business Publications, USA
ISBN 1-4330-0174-8

This handbook provides basic information for starting or/and conducting business in the country. The extraordinary volume of materials covering the topic, prevents us from placing all these materials in this handbook. For more detailed information on issues related to any specific investment and business activity in the country, please contact Global Investment Center, USA
Please acquire the list of our business intelligence and marketing reports and other business publications. We constantly update and expand our business intelligence and marketing materials. Please contact the center for the updated list of reports on over 200 countries.

in the USA: **Global Investment Center, USA.**
P.O.Box 15343, Washington, DC 20003
Phone: (202) 546-2103, Fax: (202) 546-3275, E-mail: rusric@erols.com

For additional analytical, marketing and other information please contact Global Investment Center, USA

Printed in the USA

ARAB STATES BUSINESS LAW HANDBOOK

VOLUME 1

ARAB COUNTRIES INVESTMENT LAWS AND REGULATIONS

TABLE OF CONTENTS

ARAB COUNTRIES: STRATEGIC AND ECONOMIC INFORMATION ... 9

ARAB LEAGUE: IMPORTANT INFORMATION AND ACTIVITIES ... 9
Economy of the Arab League COUNTRIES ... 10
Demographics ... 12
RELIGION ... 13
ISLAM AND MARKETS ... 14
JOINT DEFENCE AND ECONOMIC CO-OPERATION TREATY ... 16
Economic and Social Council ... 16
Arab Economic and Social Development summits ... 17
ARAB ORGANIZATION FOR INDUSTRIALIZATION ... 17
Arab British Helicopter Company ... 18
Egyptian isolation ... 18
Organisation ... 18
AOI Aircraft Factory ... 19
AOI Engine Factory ... 19
Other factories and enterprises ... 19

FREE TRADE AREAS AND ZONES ... 21

BASIC INFORMATION ... 21
MIDDLE EAST FREE TRADE AREA ... 21
GREATER ARAB FREE TRADE AREA ... 22
Members: ... 22
Progress ... 23
MIDDLE EAST FREE TRADE INITIATIVE ... 23
U.S.-Middle East Free Trade Efforts ... 24

ARABIC COUNTRIES: STRATEGIC PROFILES ... 26

ALGERIA STRATEGIC ECONOMIC AND BUSINESS INFORMATION ... 26
BAHRAIN STRATEGIC PROFILE ... 27
COMOROS STRATEGIC PROFILE ... 27
DJIBOUTI STRATEGIC PROFILE ... 28
EGYPT STRATEGIC PROFILE ... 29
IRAQ STRATEGIC PROFILE ... 29
JORDAN STRATEGIC PROFILE ... 31
KUWAIT STRATEGIC PROFILE ... 31
LEBANON STRATEGIC PROFILE ... 32
LIBYA STRATEGIC PROFILE ... 33
MAURITANIA STRATEGIC AND BUSINESS PROFILES ... 34
MOROCCO STRATEGIC AND BUSINESS PROFILES ... 34
OMAN STRATEGIC PROFILE ... 35
STATE OF PALESTINE) WEST BANK AND GAZA) STRATEGIC PROFILE ... 36
QATAR STRATEGIC PROFILE ... 36

SAUDI ARABIA STRATEGIC PROFILE 37
SOMALIA STRATEGIC PROFILE 38
SUDAN STRATEGIC PROFILE 38
SYRIA STRATEGIC PROFILE 39
TUNISIA STRATEGIC PROFILE 40
UNITED ARAB EMIRATES STRATEGIC PROFILE 41
YEMEN STRATEGIC PROFILE 41

IMPORTANT LAWS RELATED TO INVESTMENT ACTIVITY 43

ISLAMIC LAW MYTHS AND REALITIES 43
No Separation of Church and State 43
Judge (Qadi) 44
Elements of Sharia Law 44
Crimes in Islam 45
Had Crimes 45
Ta'zir Crimes 46
Qisas Crimes and Diya 47
Conclusions 48

ALGERIA 49

ALGERRIA INVESTMENT LAW 49
TITLE I NAME - OBJECT - HEADQUARTERS 49
TITLE II ORGANISATION - MANAGEMENT - FUNCTIONING 50
TITLE Ill FINANCIAL PROVISIONS 55
TITLE IV SPECIAL PROVISIONS 55
TITLE V MISCELLANEOUS PROVISIONS 56

BAHRAIN 57

ESTABLISHMENT & ORGANISATION OF INDUSTRIAL ESTATE LAW 57
CHAPTER ONE DEFINITIONS 57
CHAPTER TWO ESTABLISHMENT OF INDUSTRIAL AREAS 58
CHAPTER THREE UTILISATION OF INDUSTRIAL AREAS 59
CHAPTER FOUR CONSTRUCTION IN INDUSTRIAL AREAS 61
CHAPTER FIVE OBLIGATIONS AND RIGHTS OF INDUSTRIAL AREAS LESSEES 61
CHAPTER SIX PENALTIES 63
CHAPTER SEVEN GENERAL 63
INVESTMENT INCENTIVES 63
Agreements 64
Customs 64
INVESTMENT AND PRIVATIZATION REGULATIONS 65
Privatization 65
INVESTMENT OPPORTUNITIES 65
Build Operate Transfer 65
Best INVESXTMENT Prospects 66
LEGISLATIVE DECREE NO. 6 FOR 1984 RESPECTING THE ORGANISATION OF INDUSTRY 66
MINISTERIAL RESOLUTION MINISTRY OF DEVELOPMENT AND INDUSTRY 70

EGYPT 74

INVESTMENT REGULATIONS AND INCENTIVES 74
Investment Law 74
Tax Incentives 74
Free Trade Zones 75
AGREEMENTS 75
CUSTOMS 75
SECTORS FOR INVESTMENT 76
Industry 76
Agriculture 76
Tourism 77

Energy ... 77
Trade ... 77

IRAN ... **77**

FOREIGN INVESTMENT PROMOTION AND PROTECTION ACT (FIPPA) ... 77
Chapter One: Definitions ... 77
Chapter Two: General Criteria for Admission of Foreign ... 78
Chapter Three: Competent Authorities ... 79
Chapter Five: Provisions on Admission, Importation and Repatriation of Foreign Capital ... 80
Chapter Six: Settlement of Disputes ... 81
Chapter Seven: Final Provisions ... 81
WHAT ARE THE PRIVATIZATION ACHIEVEMENTS IN IRAN? ... 82
Privatization Statistics ... 83
Privatization in the Third Development Plan ... 83
Impacts of Stock Transfer ... 84

IRAQ ... **85**

LEGAL SYSTEM DEVELOPMENT ... 85
IRAQ INVESTMENT LAW ... 87
Chapter One Definitions ... 87
Chapter Two The National Commission for Investment and the Investment Commission in the Regions and Governorates ... 88
Chapter Three Privileges and guarantees ... 91
Chapter four Investor Obligations ... 92
Chapter Five Exemptions ... 93
Chapter Six Procedures for Granting investment and project Establishment License ... 94
Chapter Seven General Provisions ... 94

JORDAN ... **98**

THE INVESTMENT PROMOTION LAW ... 98
Regulation No.(54) for the Year 2000 Regulating Non-Jordanian Investments Regulation Issued Pursuant to Article (24) of the Investment Promotion Law No. (16) for the Year 1995 ... 106
Regulation No. (2) of 1996 The Regulation of the Investment Areas And Sectors Issued pursuant to Article (4) Of the Investment Promotion Law No. (16) of 1995 ... 108
INVESTMENT INCENTIVES ... 110
Encouragement of Investment Law ... 110
Restrictions on Foreign Investment ... 111
Encouragement of Foreign Investment ... 111
Investment Tax Incentives ... 111
Free Trade Zones ... 112
Qualifying Industrial Zone ... 112
Customs ... 113
Customs Procedures ... 113
PRIVATIZATION ... 113
Sale ... 114
Incorporation ... 114
Licensing ... 114
Stock Exchange ... 114

KUWAIT ... **115**

FOREIGN INVESTMENT LAW IN STATE OF KUWAIT ... 115
Chapter1 In Relation to Investment of Foreign Capital ... 115
Chapter2 Investment Committee of Foreign Capital ... 115
Chapter 3 Guaranteed Warranties for Foreign Investment ... 116
Chapter 4 Settled Advantages for Foreign Investment and Its Obligations ... 116
Chapter 5 Penalties ... 117
Chapter 6 Concluding Judgments ... 117
LAW DECREE NO.(8) OF 2001 REGARDING ORGANIZATION OF DIRECT INVESTMENT OF FOREIGN CAPITAL IN THE STATE OF KUWAIT ... 118
Law Regarding Organization Of Direct Investment Of Foreign Capital ... 118

Definitions *118*
Chapter 1 Foreign Capital Investment *119*
Second Chapter Foreign Capital Investment Committee *119*
FOURTH CHAPTER FOREIGN INVESTMENT PRIVILEGES AND OBLIGATIONS *120*
FIFTH CHAPTER Penalties *121*
SIXTH CHAPTER Final Provisions *121*
INVESTMENT INCENTIVES 122
Investment Laws *122*
Trade Agreements *122*
PRIVATIZATION 123
Stock Exchange *123*
PRACTICAL INFORMATION FOR INVESTING AND BUSINESS ACTIVITY 123

LEBANON **128**

INVESTMENT 128
Public Finance *128*
Privatization *128*
Stock Exchange *128*
Barriers to Trade and Investment *129*
Customs *129*
Work Permits *129*

LYBIA **130**

LIBYA INVESTMENT LAW 130
THE LEGAL ENVIRONMENT FOR INVESTMENT IN LIBYA 133

MAROCCO **136**

INVESTMENT 136
Investment Incentives *136*
Investment Promotion Fund *137*
Foreign Trade *137*
Free Trade Agreements *138*
Free Trade Zone *138*
Privatization *138*
Stock Exchange *138*

OMAN **140**

FOREIGN INVESTMENT REQUIREMENTS 140
Licensing Requirements *140*
Investment Incentives *140*
Government Loans *141*
Other Incentives and Provisions *141*
Investment from Gulf Co-Operation Council States *142*
Privatization *142*
Stock Exchange *142*
PRACTICAL INFORMATION FOR INVESTING AND BUSINESS ACTIVITY 143
FORMS OF ENTRY *144*
OMANI COMPANIES *144*
JOINT VENTURES *144*
PUBLIC SECTOR *145*
INDUSTRIAL PROJECTS *146*
TAX *146*

PALESTINE (WEST BANK AND GAZA) **148**

LAW ON THE ENCOURAGEMENT OF INVESTMENT IN PALESTINE 148
Chapter One *148*
Chapter Two *150*
Chapter Three *151*
Chapter Four *154*

Chapter Five ... 158
Chapter Six ... 158

SAUDI ARABIA ... **160**

SAUDI DOMESTIC AND FOREIGN CORPORATE LAWS ... 160
FOREIGN INVESTMENT ... 164
Privatization ... 165
Saudiization ... 165
Stock Exchange ... 166
INVESTMENT INCENTIVES ... 166
Other Incentives ... 167
Trade Agreements ... 167
Imports and Exports ... 167
Imports ... 167
Exports ... 167
Protective Tariffs and Non-Tariff Trade Barriers ... 167
Trade Barriers ... 167
INVESTING IN SAUDI ARABIA PRACTICAL INFORMATION ... 168
FOREIGN INVESTMENT IN SAUDI ARABIA ... 168
INDUSTRIAL PROJECTS ... 169

QATAR ... **171**

LAW NO. (13) OF THE YEAR 2000 ON ORGANIZATION OF FOREIGN CAPITAL INVESTMENT IN THE ECONOMIC ACTIVITY. ... 171
JASIM BIN HAMAD AL – THANI DEPUTY EMIR OF THE STATE OF QATAR ... 175
FOREIGN INVESTMENTS INVCENTIVES ... 175
Trade Agreements ... 175
Import and Export Restrictions ... 175
Exports ... 176
Privatization ... 176
Stock Exchange ... 176
Principal Growth Sectors ... 177
Best INVESTMENT Prospects ... 177

SYRIA ... **177**

ENCOURAGEMENT OF INVESTMENT LAW ... 177
Incentives for the Tourism Industry ... 178
Trade Regulations ... 178
Free Trade Zones ... 178
Trade Agreements ... 179
Customs ... 179
Private Sector Investment ... 179
BEST PROSPECTS FOR INVESTMENTS ... 180
Industry ... 180
Agriculture ... 180
Tourism ... 180
Franchising ... 180

TUNISIA ... **182**

INVESTMENT LAW ... 182
INVESTMENT INCENTIVES ... 184
Trade Agreements ... 185
Free Trade Zones ... 185
Customs ... 185
PRIVATIZATION ... 186
Stock Exchange ... 187
Price Controls and Competition Policy ... 187
INVESTMENT Prospects ... 187

UNITED ARAB EMIRATES ... **188**

INVESTMENT 188
Free Trade Zones *188*
Trade Agreements *188*
Customs *189*
Real Estate Investment *189*
Collaterization of Loans *189*
PRIVATIZATION 189
Stock Exchange *190*

YEMEN 191

INVESTMENT LAW 191
Section I PRELIMINARY PROVISIONS *191*
Section II GUARANTEES AND BENEFITS ACCORDED TO PROJECTS *194*
Section III CUSTOMS DUTY AND TAX EXEMPTIONS ACCORDED TO PROJECTS, PROMOTING OF LOCAL PRODUCTION AND INCRESING EXPORTS *197*
Section IV GENERAL INVESTMENT AUTHORITY *201*
Section V PROJECT REGISTRATION AND EXEMPTION PROCEDURES *205*
Section VI INVESTMENT COMPANIES *206*
Section VII ADMINISTRATIVE APPEALS AND SETTLEMENT OF INVESTMENT DISPUTES *209*
Section VIII OBLIGATION OF INVESTORS AND PROJECT SPONSORS: VIOLATIONS AND SUBSEQUENT PENALTIES *210*
Section IX TRANSITIONAL PROVISIONS *212*
Section X GENERAL PROVISIONS *213*

SUPPLEMENTS 215

PRINCIPAL ISLAMIC BANKS 215
ISLAMIC EQUITY FUNDS 221
OPIC FUNDS 226
SELECTED INVESTMENT AND BUSINESS CONTACTS 229
BAHRAIN *229*
EGYPT *232*
JORDAN *241*
LEBANON *246*
MAURITANIA *248*
MOROCCO *250*
OMAN *254*
QATAR *257*
SAUDI ARABIA *264*
SYRIA *269*
TUNISIA *273*
UNITED ARAB EMIRATES *276*
WEST BANK – PALESTINE *278*
YEMEN *285*
ISLAMIC LAW GLOSSARY 287

ARAB COUNTRIES: STRATEGIC AND ECONOMIC INFORMATION

ARAB LEAGUE: IMPORTANT INFORMATION AND ACTIVITIES

Administrative center	Cairo[a]
Official languages	• Arabic
Membership	22 members
Leaders	
- Arab League Secretariat	Nabil el-Araby
- Arab Parliament	Ali Al-Daqbaashi
- Council Presidency	Lebanon
Legislature	Arab Parliament
Establishment	
- Alexandria Protocol	22 March 1945
Area	
- Total area	13,333,296 km^2 5,148,048 sq mi
Population	
- 2012 estimate	400,652,486
- Density	24.33/km^2 63/sq mi
GDP (PPP)	2011 estimate
- Total	$1.898 trillion
- Per capita	$11,895
GDP (nominal)	2011 estimate
- Total	$3.526 trillion
- Per capita	$4,239
Currency	21 currencies
Time zone	(UTC+0 to +4)
Website	
www.lasportal.org	

The **Arab League** officially called the **League of Arab States**, is a regional organisation of Arab states in North and Northeast Africa, and Southwest Asia. It was formed in Cairo on 22 March 1945 with six members: Egypt, Iraq, Transjordan (renamed Jordan after 1946), Lebanon, Saudi Arabia, and Syria. Yemen joined as a member on 5 May 1945. The Arab League currently has 22 members and four observers. The main goal of the league is to "draw closer the relations between member States and co-ordinate collaboration between them, to safeguard their independence and sovereignty, and to consider in a general way the affairs and interests of the Arab countries."

Through institutions such as the Arab League Educational, Cultural and Scientific Organization (ALESCO) and the Economic and Social Council of the Arab League's Council of Arab Economic Unity (CAEU), the Arab League facilitates political, economic, cultural, scientific and social programs designed to promote the interests of the Arab world. It has served as a forum for the member states to coordinate their policy positions, to deliberate on matters of common concern, to settle some Arab disputes, and to limit conflicts such as the 1958 Lebanon crisis. The League has served as a platform for the drafting and conclusion of many landmark documents promoting economic integration. One example is the *Joint Arab Economic Action Charter* which sets out the principles for economic activities in the region.

Each member state has one vote in the *League Council*, while decisions are binding only for those states that have voted for them. The aims of the league in 1945 were to strengthen and coordinate the political, cultural, economic, and social programs of its members, and to mediate disputes among them or between them and third parties. Furthermore, the signing of an agreement on *Joint Defense and Economic Cooperation* on 13 April 1950 committed the signatories to coordination of military defense measures.

The Arab League has played an important role in shaping school curricula, advancing the role of women in the Arab societies, promoting child welfare, encouraging youth and sports programs, preserving Arab cultural heritage, and fostering cultural exchanges between the member states. Literacy campaigns have been launched, intellectual works reproduced, and modern technical terminology is translated for the use within member states. The league encourages measures against crime and drug abuse, and deals with labour issues—particularly among the emigrant Arab workforce.

The current members of the Arab League are listed below:

ECONOMY OF THE ARAB LEAGUE COUNTRIES

Rank	Country	GDP (billions of USD)
-	World	73,982.3
-	Arab League	2,836.4
1	Saudi Arabia	745.3
2	United Arab Emirates	396.2
3	Egypt	271.4
4	Iraq	229.3
5	Algeria	206.1
6	Qatar	202.6
7	Kuwait	185.3
8	Morocco	105.1
9	Oman	80.6
10	Sudan	70.1
11	Libya	67.1
12	Syria	64.7(2010)
13	Tunisia	47.4
14	Lebanon	44.3
15	Yemen	39.2
16	Jordan	33.9
17	Bahrain	32.2
18	Palestine	6.7
19	Mauritania	4.2
20	Somalia	2.5

21	Djibouti	1.5
22	Comoros	.7

Rank	Country	Population	Density (/km²)	Density (sq mi)
1	Egypt	83,550,000	93	241
2	Algeria	37,100,000	16	41
3	Morocco	32,064,173	77	199
4	Iraq	31,234,000	71	184
5	Sudan	30,894,000	16	41
6	Saudi Arabia	28,146,658	12	31
7	Yemen	23,580,000	45	117
8	Syria	21,906,000	118	306
9	Tunisia	10,673,800	65	168
10	Somalia	9,133,000	14	36
11	United Arab Emirates	8,264,070	99	256
12	Libya	6,733,620	3.8	9.8
13	Jordan	6,316,000	71	184
14	Lebanon	4,224,000	404	1,046
15	Palestine	4,136,540	687	1,779
16	Kuwait	3,566,437	200	518
17	Mauritania	3,291,000	3.2	8.3
18	Oman	2,845,000	9.2	24
19	Qatar	1,699,435	154	399
20	Bahrain	1,234,596	1,646	4,263
21	Djibouti	864,000	37	96
22	Comoros	691,000	309	800
Total	Pan-Arab States	313,147,329	30.4	78.7

The Arab League is rich in resources, with enormous oil and natural gas reserves. It also has great fertile lands in the south of Sudan, an area usually referred to as the food basket of the Arab World. The region's instability has not affected its tourism industry, which is considered the fastest growing sector in the region, with Egypt, the UAE, Lebanon, Tunisia and Jordan leading the way. Another industry that is growing steadily in the Arab League is telecommunications. Within less than a decade, local companies such as Orascom and Etisalat have managed to successfully compete internationally as global power players.

Economic achievements among member states have been low in the League's history. Other smaller Arab organizations, such as the GCC, have achieved more than the League has. However, lately there has emerged several major economic projects that slated to be completed soon that appear promising. Of these, the Arab Gas Pipeline, a project which hopes to funnel Egyptian and Iraqi gas to Jordan, Syria and Lebanon, and then to Turkey and Europe, is scheduled to reach completion by the year 2010. The GAFTA free trade agreement is to be completed by the January 1, 2008, effectively rendering 95% of all Arab products free of customs tax.

The economic development in the Arab League exhibits a great diversity. There is a significant difference between, on the one hand, the rich oil states of the UAE, Qatar, Kuwait, and Bahrain, and on the other hand, the poor countries like the Comoros, Mauritania and Djibouti. For instance, the GDP per capita of the wealthiest Arab Country and the wealthiest in the world, Qatar, is 73 times higher than that of Mauritania

Country	GDP (PPP) US$M	GDP (PPP) US$ per capita
Arab League	2,765,867	7,682
Saudi Arabia	618,744	23,701
Egypt	496,604	6,347
Algeria	252,189	7,104
Morocco	193,150	5,866
United Arab Emirates	182,876	40,175
Kuwait	140,589	38,984
Iraq	111,500	3,570
Syria	105,238	5,043
Qatar	102,147	90,149
Sudan	98,926	2,464
Libya	96,138	14,884
Tunisia	86,086	8,254
Oman	74,431	25,109
Lebanon	58,576	14,988
Yemen	58,218	2,457
Jordan	35,300	5,956
Bahrain	28,275	27,214
Palestine	11,950	2,900
Mauritania	6,326	2,037
Somalia	5,731	600
Djibouti	2,101	2,549
Comoros	772	1,159

DEMOGRAPHICS

The Arab League is a culturally and ethnically diverse association of 22 member states, although the overwhelming majority of the League's population identifies as Arab (either on a cultural basis, or on an ethno-racial basis). As of 1 January 2007, about 340,000,000 people live in the states of the Arab League. Its population grows faster than in most other global regions. This threatens to diminish the slow economic expansion expected in the league's developing countries.

The most populous member state is Egypt, with a population of about 77.5 million. The least populated is the Comoros, with over 0.6 million inhabitants.

Since large parts of the Arab countries are desert, the population is concentrated in and around cities where most the trade and industry are located. The largest Arab city is Cairo, followed by Baghdad, Khartoum, Giza, Damascus, Riyadh, and Casablanca.

Pos	Country	Population
1	Egypt	79,089,650
2	Sudan	43,939,598
3	Algeria	35,423,000
4	Morocco	32,200,000

5	Iraq	31,234,000
6	Saudi Arabia	27,136,977
7	Yemen	23,580,000
8	Syria	22,505,000
9	Tunisia	10,432,500
10	Somalia	9,359,000
11	Libya	6,420,000
12	Jordan	6,407,085
13	United Arab Emirates	4,975,593
14	Lebanon	4,224,000
15	Palestinian territories	4,136,540 (Disputed)
16	Kuwait	3,566,437
17	Mauritania	3,291,000
18	Oman	2,845,000
19	Qatar	1,696,563
20	Bahrain	1,234,596
21	Djibouti	864,000
22	Comoros	691,000
Total	Arab League	355,251,539

RELIGION

Muslims	91%
Christians	5%
Others	4%

Judaism, Christianity, and Islam were all founded in or near areas that are now Arab League countries. Today, consequently, the vast majority of the Arab League's citizens are Muslim, with Christianity being the second largest religion. Prior to the establishment of the State of Israel, significant number of Jews also lived in Arab counties, but these communities are nearly extinct since the Jewish exodus from Arab and Muslim lands. The members of the Arab League host several holy cities and other religiously significant locations, including Bethlehem, Alexandria, Mecca, Medina, Najaf, Kirkuk, Arbil, and Baghdad. Sunni Muslims make up the majority of the Arab League's citizens. However, large numbers of Shi'a Muslims make up the majority in areas of Lebanon, Iraq, Bahrain, and Kuwait.

Christianity is the second largest religion in the League, with over 20 million Christians living in countries such as Iraq, Lebanon, Egypt, Sudan, Syria, and Jordan. There are smaller Jewish populations living mainly in the western part of the Arab League. States such as Morocco, Algeria, and Tunisia all have Jewish populations. However, most Jews living in the Arab World immigrated or were expelled to Israel after its creation in 1948. Other minor religions such as the Bahá'í Faith are practiced on a much smaller scale.

- Muslim population - 311,093,951
- Total population - 339,510,535

Religious percentages of the Arab League

N	Country	Islam	Christians	Others
_	Arab League	91%	5%	4%
1	Algeria	98%	1%	1%
2	Bahrain	81.2%	9%	8.81%
3	Comoros	99%	1%	n/a
4	Djibouti	94%	5%	1%

5	Egypt	90%	9%	1%
6	Iraq	95%	4.3%	0.7%
7	Jordan	93%	6%	1%
8	Kuwait	85%	10%	5%
9	Lebanon	59.7% (Druze represent 5%)	40%	0.3%
10	Libya	97%	0%	3%
11	Mauritania	100%	0%	0%
12	Morocco	95%	5%	0%
13	Oman	92.5%	5%	2.5%
14	Palestinian Authority	92%	8%	-
15	Qatar	77.6%	11%	11.4%
16	Saudi Arabia	100%	0%	0%
17	Somalia	100%	0%	0%
18	Sudan	70%	5%	25%
19	Syria	87% (Druze represent 3%)	10%	3%
20	Tunisia	98%	1%	1%
21	United Arab Emirates	76%	9%	15%
22	Yemen	99%	0.2%	0.8%

ISLAM AND MARKETS[1]

The relationship between Islam and trade is not well appreciated in the West. The Prophet Muhammad (peace be upon him) and his wife Khadija were both merchants. The Qur'an, the Muslim scripture, is filled with parables using the language of trade. It was merchants, not soldiers, who were mainly responsible for the spread of Islam throughout the world.

Conversely, the rise of the Islamic civilization contributed to the progress of economic development and economic theory. In his history of economics, Murray Rothbard noted the more advanced understanding of markets found among the Scholastics and in the 16th century school of Salamanca, compared to that of the ancient Greeks. The Muslim influence on these schools is expected. The Scholastics inherited Greek knowledge from Arabic translations and commentaries, and the Spanish of the 16th century had recently conquered the land upon which rested the universities of the Moors.

The rising tide of Islam today is in part a reaction against the Arab socialism that has destroyed the markets of the Muslim world. That the rejection of secularism and of socialism should come hand-in-hand should not be surprising. One cannot be a Muslim and opposed to freedom of enterprise, as we shall show.

Opposition to free markets can come from a number of directions. It may be rooted in an ideological objection to private property (socialism), in a disdain for material prosperity itself (asceticism), in an antipathy to the variations in wealth that must accompany market mechanisms (economic egalitarianism), or in a mistaken belief that a command economy can better provide economic benefits (authoritarianism). Islam refutes all of these.

In contrast to socialism, Islam enshrines private property as a sacred trust. Everything belongs to God, and it is Man that God has created as His *khalîfah*, or His agent on earth (Qur'ân 2:30). Each person is individually responsible directly to the Almighty for the faithful execution of this awesome trust (36:54). Therefore that concept of private property well-established among the Semitic peoples is taken as a given by the Qur'an. Rather than modify the concept of property, the Qur'an specifies the terms for its wholesome and just enjoyment and employment. It should neither be used wastefully nor in a way that will deprive others of their justly acquired property (2:188). When one holds the property of others in trust, for example for orphans, one should not divert it to one's personal benefit (2:2; 4:10), but one should not turn over one's own property to those incapable of managing it (2:5). When orphans mature they should be given control of their own

[1]by Imad A. Ahmad

property (2:6). Inheritance rights are not only respected (4:33), but expanded to include women (4:7). Property rights of women are as sacred as those of men in other cases as well (4:24, 4:32) and the treatment of women as chattel is prohibited (4:19).

The Prophet emphasized the importance of property rights in his farewell pilgrimage by declaring to the assembled masses "Nothing shall be legitimate to a Muslim which belongs to a fellow Muslim unless it was given freely and willingly." The Qur'an mandates the respect for property rights be extended to all human beings regardless of religious faith (3:75).

Islam rejects both monastic asceticism that glorifies poverty and suffering and the Calvinistic variety discussed by Max Weber that esteems the accumulation of wealth at the expense of its enjoyment. Neither poverty nor wealth are proofs of virtue. Rather both are trials of one's commitment to the higher spiritual order. The Islamic view of the material world is as a neutral stage in which the individual demonstrates submission to the will of God by his choices, including the lawful acquisition and use of God's bounties. Profit may be pursued even on the day of congregational prayer (62:10).

The rejection of asceticism is not an invitation to hedonistic consumption, however. Moderate in all things, Islam emphasizes the importance of commerce and productivity: "O ye who believe! eat not up your property among yourselves in vanities: but let there be amongst you traffic and trade by mutual good-will: nor kill (or destroy) yourselves: for verily God hath been to you Most Merciful." (4:29)

Upon encountering Islamic social thought, some Westerners are so impressed by the detailed treatment Islamic law gives obligatory charity, they presume that Muhammad set out to impose a leveling of the wealth. There is no foundation for such a belief. On the contrary, the Qur'an denounces envy of the wealth of others: "And in no wise covet those things in which God hath bestowed his gifts more freely on some of you than on others: to men is allotted what they earn and to women what they earn: but ask God of His bounty: for God hath full knowledge of all things" (4:32).

The *zakat*, as this obligatory charity is called, basically set at 2.5% of accumulated wealth beyond the subsistence level which would qualify one to be a recipient, tools of the trade and current inventories of stock in trade exempted. It is thus an assessment against wealth, not an income tax (although farmers and miners pay a portion of their gross product instead of a percentage of their capital). Insofar as it is not an assessment against income, it does not discourage productivity, but rather discourages idle wealth. Further, the levels of the assessment are not confiscatory, so while it provides a safety net for the poor, it in no way "levels" the wealth nor penalizes the rich.

Finally, the term *zakat,* itself, comes from the root word meaning "to purify." The return of a small portion of one's wealth to the general community therefore purifies the rest from any taint that an initial inequality of assets might suggest. The needs of the unfortunate are met without impairing the productivity of those God has blessed materially.

The fallacy that the command economy can better provide for the material needs of a society has suffered a severe setback with the fall of the Soviet Union. But the command economy was unpopular with Muslim economists from the beginning. There are numerous traditions that demonstrate that the Prophet Muhammad turned to the marketplace to determine the just price of commodities. On learning that his companion Bilal had traded poor quality dates for high quality dates, the Prophet advised him that buying and selling at market prices over barter avoided the dangers of overcharging (*ribâ*) inherent in barter.

As might be expected from this respect for the market's ability to set just prices, Muhammad dislike price controls and limited his interventions to the prohibition of practices like fraud and *ribâ*. After the caliphs of the early Umayyid dynasty had departed from the Prophet's practices, the reformer Umar II ordered his governors to leave prices to the market with this advice: "God has made land and waters for seeking His bounties. So let traders travel between them without any intervention. How can you intervene between them and their livelihood?"

The Islamic analysis of markets reached the level of economic science by the time of the great fourteenth century historian Ibn Khaldun. He rejected the utopianism of the Greek-influenced philosophers. To him, the fact that the policies mandated by God could be scientifically demonstrated as the best social policies was the natural consequence of the fact that the laws of economics and the laws of good living had the same Creator. His understanding of the harmfulness of the command economy can be seen from the titles of the section headings in his magnum opus, the *Muqaddimah* (Introduction to History), *e.g.*, "Commercial activity on the part of the ruler is harmful to his subjects and ruinous to the tax revenue."

Markets antedate the mission of Muhammad. They are especially strong in the Semitic world. Like their cousins, the Jews, the early Arabs had a strong commitment to trade and bargaining. The rise of Islam did not change, nor did it seek to change, the centrality of trade and commerce to the Arab way of life. On the contrary, the establishment of commercial law, the expansion of property rights for women, the prohibition of fraud, the call for the establishment of clear standards of weights and measures, and the uncompromising defense of property rights (even while calling for a greater responsibility for alleviating the plight of the poor and needy) pushed the Islamic civilization to the front of the world's economic stage and made the Muslim world the defining force in international trade for over 800 years. The Islamic activists throughout the Muslim world can help to usher in a new Renaissance if they avoid the temptation to yield to political pragmatism and hold fast to the pro-market principles of Islam.

[Dr. Imad Ahmad is president of the Minaret of Freedom Institute, an Islamic public policy research institute and author of *Signs in the Heavens: A Muslim Astronomer's Perspective on Religion and Science*.]

JOINT DEFENCE AND ECONOMIC CO-OPERATION TREATY

The Treaty of Joint Defence and Economic Co-operation of the League of Arab States (commonly, the Joint Defence and Economic Co-operation Treaty) is a treaty among the member states of the Arab League signed on 18 June 1950 in Cairo, Egypt.

The Treaty created two of the principal institutions of the Arab League:

- the Joint Defence Council
- the Economic Council (renamed *Economic and Social Council* in 1980)

Both councils report to the Council of the Arab League

ECONOMIC AND SOCIAL COUNCIL

The **Economic and Social Council of the Arab League** (ESC) originally the **Economic Council**) is an institution of the Arab League that co-ordinates its economic integration. The ESC was established as the *Economic Council* under the terms of the Joint Defence and Economic Co-operation Treaty (1950). and held its first meeting in 1953. In 1957, the ESC established the Council of Arab Economic Unity (CAEU) and, in February 1997, the ESC adopted the *Agreement to Facilitate and Develop Trade Among Arab Countries* (1981) in pursuit of the Greater Arab Free Trade Area (GAFTA).

The establishment of the *Economic Council* of the Arab League under the terms of the Joint Defence and Economic Co-operation Treaty (1950) was the fulfilment of the promise made in articles II and IV of the Arab League's Charter (1945), which required the establishment of a council to co-ordinate close co-operation of member-states in economic affairs.

The *Economic Council* was renamed the *Economic and Social Council* in 1980.

RESPONSIBILITIES

The ESC continues to administer the Greater Arab Free Trade Area and the Arab Fund for Economic and Social Development, as well as supervising the Council of Arab Economic Unity and other subsidiary institutions.

ARAB ECONOMIC AND SOCIAL DEVELOPMENT SUMMITS

The **Arab Economic and Social Development summits** are summits of the Arab League, held at the head of state level to address issues of economic and social development among member-states. The inaugural summit was held in 2009 in Kuwait, and the second summit is planned to be held in Egypt in 2011.

On 29 March 2007, resolution 365, proposed by Egypt and Kuwait and calling for a summit to address exclusively the economic and social development issues facing the Arab world, was passed at the Arab League summit in Riyadh, Saudi Arabia.

In June 2007, the secretary-general of the Arab League convened an extraordinary session of the ESC, which had been tasked with organising the summit under the terms of resolution 365, and it was agreed that the responsibility of preparing for the first summit would fall to a preparatory committee, consisting of Saudi Arabia, Sudan, Syria, the chair of the ESC for the time being, and the two member-states that had proposed resolution 365, Egypt and Kuwait.

In October 2007, the secretary-general appointed Egyptian ambassador Mervat Tellawi the co-ordinator-general for the upcoming summit and established a management committee within the framework of the general secretariat of the Arab League, later renamed the *Development Summit Management Committee*, that included the newly appointed co-ordinator-general, Mervat Tellawi, and various assistant secretaries-general of the Arab League.

The summit was conceived as an opportunity to involve the private sector, and preparatory meetings were held by the Development Summit Management Committee with, *inter alia*, the Arab Banks Federation (November 2007), the General Union of Chambers of Commerce, Industry and Agriculture for Arab Countries (December 2007) and the Economic and Financial Affairs Committee of the Arab Parliament (May 2008).

By the 2008 Arab League summit in Damascus, Syria, advanced progress had been reported by the preparatory committee to the eighty-first session of the ESC, and having received an offer to host the summit from the emir of Kuwait, USD 2 million was approved by the Arab League for financing.

2009 SUMMIT

On 19–20 January 2009, the first Arab Economic and Social Development Summit was duly held in Kuwait. Coming almost immediately after the Gaza War, the Arab media praised the summit for its success in reconciling the Arab world, and various resolutions were passed "in solidarity with Gaza". Among the other resolutions passed, there was a call for adopting necessary measures to establish an Arab customs union as of 2010, to be fully operational by 2015, to ultimately establish an Arab common market.

2011 SUMMIT

Leaving the 2009 summit, Ahmed Nazif, the former Egyptian prime minister, announced that Egypt would hold the next summit in 2011. Among the issues to be discussed is the proposed *Arab Plan of Action for Science and Technology*, adopted at the 2009 summit, the implementation of which is being led by UNESCO and its Arab equivalent, the Arab League Educational, Cultural and Scientific Organization (ALECSO

ARAB ORGANIZATION FOR INDUSTRIALIZATION

Abbreviation	AOI
Formation	1975
Type	State-owned company
Purpose	Defence industry
Location	Cairo, Egypt
Region served	Arab world
Membership	Egypt

	Qatar (until 1993) Saudi Arabia (until 1993) United Arab Emirates
Official language	Arabic
Chairman	Abd El Aziz Seif-Eldeen
Main organ	Supreme Committee
Staff	~16,000
Website	http://www.aoi.com.eg/

The **Arab Organization for Industrialization** (AOI) is an Egypt-based Arab military organisation established in 1975 by Egypt, Qatar, Saudi Arabia and the United Arab Emirates (UAE) to supervise the collective development of the Arab defence industry. Following a gradual deterioration in relations between the AOI member-states, Egypt became sole owner of AOI in 1993. As well as meeting the requirements of the Egyptian military, AOI directs spare capacity to civilian programmes, including civilian transport and sanitation equipment, and has stated its intention of entering the wind power sector.

Initially an institution of pan-Arabism, Saudi Arabia and the United Arab Emirates returned their shares in AOI, valued at US$ 1.8 billion, to Egypt in 1993, leaving AOI wholly owned by the Egypt. AOI has approximately 16,000 employees, out of which 1,250 are engineers. AOI fully owns 10 factories and shares in 2 joint-ventures, besides the Arab Institute for Advanced Technology.

AOI was established by its four member-states - Egypt, Qatar, Saudi Arabia and the UAE - in response to the threat posed by the advanced Israeli defence industry. The initial capitalisation of AOI was USD 1 billion, contributed in equal part by the four member-states, although with the understanding AOI would be based in Egypt.

ARAB BRITISH HELICOPTER COMPANY

In 1978, AOI and Westland Helicopters, a British aerospace company, established the *Arab British Helicopter Company* as a joint venture, but a year later AOI announced the company's liquidation. In ensuing arbitration, the International Chamber of Commerce made an award, on grounds of breach of the principles of natural law and good faith, in favour of Westland Helicopters and against AOI's four member-states. This award was later annulled by the Court of Justice of Geneva, which annulment was upheld by the Swiss Federal Supreme Court, on grounds that the arbitrators had jurisdiction over AOI but not over the organisation's member-states.

EGYPTIAN ISOLATION

Following the signing of the Egypt-Israeli peace treaty (1979), Egypt had its membership to the Arab League suspended and a policy of economic isolation implemented against it. It was in this atmosphere that the three AOI member-states other than Egypt - Qatar, Saudi Arabia and the UAE - withdrew from the AOI, causing its collapse.

In 1983, the Egyptian chief-of-staff restated his interest in the joint manufacture of weapons, but it was only after the 1987 Arab League summit in Amman, Jordan, when the Arab League re-admitted Egypt and the other Arab states normalised relations with Egypt, that the possibility of renewed co-operation among the AOI member-states seemed possible.

The UAE seemed similarly eager to reinvigorate the AOI: in 1988, Egypt and the UAE held talks with Qatar about its re-entry into the AOI, at which an agreement for closer co-operation between Egypt and Qatar in the fields of culture and communication was signed.

ORGANISATION

AOI is one of the largest industrial organisations in Egypt with significant international relationships both in the defence and civilian transport sectors. The AOI is wholly state-owned by Egypt and administered by a

Supreme Committee, the chairman of which is the Egyptian president and which includes several cabinet ministers, and is considered a division of the *Ministry of Military Production*

AOI AIRCRAFT FACTORY

The AOI's *Aircraft Factory* also written *Air Craft Factory* and abbreviated *ACF*) was established in 1950 as the Helwan Aircraft Factory and is a key aerospace manufacturer in Egypt. It is located in Helwan.
The AOI Aircraft Factory manufactures and assembles aircraft for the Egyptian air force, including:

- the Helwan HA-200 Al Kahirah subsonic trainer;
- the prototype Helwan HA-300 supersonic fighter;
- the Alpha Jet;
- the Tucano turboprop trainer; and
- the K-8E jet trainer.

The K-8E is an Egyptian variant of the Chinese Hongdu JL-8, exported as the Karakorum-8 (or K-8) to (among others) Pakistan, Zambia and Myanmar. The K-8E's manufacture at the AOI Aircraft Factory began in 2000, under an agreement between the AOI and CATIC, the Chinese state-owned aerospace manufacturer, to produce a total of 60 K-8s over five years. The contract, valued at US$ 347.4 million, was signed in 1999 in connection with the state visit by Chinese president Jiang Zemin that year. Initially, most of the parts were manufactured in China and the aircraft were assembled in Egypt, but by the end of the programme the manufacture was to be carried out entirely at the AOI Aircraft Factory. In the end, 98% of each K-8E was locally-manufactured.
The AOI Aircraft Factory also manufactures aircraft parts for the Egyptian Civil Aviation Authority (ECAA), Dassault Aviation and SAGEM, and has received certification from the ECAA for its welding, painting, testing and calibration operations. The AOI Aircraft Factory also engages in civilian and technological projects.

AOI ENGINE FACTORY

In 1960, the *Engine Factory* was established by the Egyptian military with German technical assistance as a base to design, develop and produce aircraft engines. The first engines produced at the Engine Factory were:

- the E-200 for the Helwan HA-200 Al Kahirah subsonic trainer; and
- the E-300 for the Helwan HA-300 supersonic fighter.

In 1975, the Engine Factory was affiliated to AOI, since when it has focused its activities on the manufacture, assembly, repair and overhaul of gas turbines and accessories. The AOI Engine Factory has established maintenance facilities for auxiliary power units and SNECMA Atar 09C, T56, CT64, PT6-25 and -64, Larzac 04, R-13 and R-25 engines.
The AOI Engine Factory directs spare capacity to civilian projects, including the manufacture of fuel injectors for Robert Bosch GmbH, air brake systems for Knorr-Bremse and rail fastening clips for Pandrol.

OTHER FACTORIES AND ENTERPRISES

AOI Electronics Factory
Sakr Factory for Development Industries (AOI)
Kader Factory for Development Industries (AOI)
Arab British Engine Co. (ABECO) (AOI)
Arab British Dynamics Co. ABD (AOI)
Arab American Vehicle (AAV

FREE TRADE AREAS AND ZONES

BASIC INFORMATION

A **free trade zone** (FTZ) or **Export processing zone** (EPZ) is one or more areas of a country where tariffs and quotas are eliminated and bureaucratic requirements are lowered in order to attract companies by raising the incentives for doing business there. Free trade zones can be defined as labor intensive manufacturing centers that involve the import of raw materials or components and the export of factory products.

Most FTZs are located in developing countries. They are special zones where some normal trade barriers such as import or export tariffs do not apply, bureaucracy is typically minimized by outsourcing it to the FTZ operator and corporations setting up in the zone may be given tax breaks as an additional incentive. Usually, these zones are set up in underdeveloped parts of the host country, the rationale being that the zones will attract employers and thus reduce poverty and unemployment and stimulate the area's economy. These zones are often used by multinational corporations to set up factories to produce goods (such as clothing or shoes).

Free trade zones in Latin America date back to the early decades of the twentieth century. The first free trade regulations in this region were inacted in Argentina and Uruguay in the 1920s. However, the rapid development of free trade zones across the region dates from the late 1960s and the early 1970s.

In 2002 there were 43 million people working in about 3000 FTZs spanning 116 countries producing clothes, shoes, sneakers, electronics, and toys. The basic objectives of EPZs are to enhance foreign exchange earnings, develop export-oriented industries and to generate employment opportunities.

MIDDLE EAST FREE TRADE AREA

On May 9, 2003, President George W. Bush "proposed a plan of graduated steps for Middle Eastern nations to increase trade and investment with the United States and others in the world economy. The first step is to work closely with peaceful nations that want to become members of the World Trade Organization (WTO) in order to expedite their accession. As these countries implement domestic reform agendas, institute the rule of law, protect property rights (including intellectual property), and create a foundation for openness and economic growth, the United States will take a series of graduated steps with countries in the region tailored to their level of development. The U.S. will expand and deepen economic ties through Trade and Investment Framework Agreements (TIFAs), Bilateral Investment Treaties (BITs), and comprehensive Free Trade Agreements (FTAs), and will enhance the Generalized System of Preferences (GSP) program for eligible countries."

Middle East Free Trade Area (MEFTA) within a decade, "which would link 22 Arab nations, Israel and the United States by 2013."

> "Across the globe, free markets and trade have helped defeat poverty, and taught men and women the habits of liberty. So I propose the establishment of a U.S.-Middle East free trade area within a decade, to bring the Middle East into an expanding circle of opportunity, to provide hope for the people who live in that region." --President George W. Bush, May 9, 2003.

The **U.S. MEFTA** initiative started in 2003 with the purpose of creating a U.S. Middle East Free Trade Area by 2013.

The U.S. objective with this initiative has been to gradually increase trade and investment in the Middle East, and to assist the Middle East countries in implementing domestic reforms, instituting the rule of law, protecting private property rights (including intellectual property), and creating a foundation for openness, economic growth, and prosperity.

- Actively supporting WTO membership of countries in the Middle East and Maghreb
- Expanding the Generalized System of Preferences (GSP's) that currently provides duty-free entry to the U.S. market for some 3,500 products from 140 developing economies
- Negotiating Trade and Investment Framework Agreements (TIFA's) that establish a framework for expanding trade and resolving outstanding disputes
- Negotiating Bilateral Investment Treaties (BIT's) with interested countries by obligating governments to treat foreign investors fairly and offering legal protection equal to domestic investors
- Negotiating comprehensive Free Trade Agreements (FTA's) with willing countries that demonstrate a commitment to economic openness and reform
- Helping to target more than $1 billion of annual U.S funding and spur partnerships with private organizations and businesses that support trade and development

U.S. - Middle East Free Trade Efforts

Country	FTA	TIFA	BIT	WTO	GSP
'Israel	√	√	√	√	'
Jordan	√	√	√	√	√
Morocco	Ratified by U.S.	√	√	√	√
Bahrain	Signed	√	√	√	√
'Egypt	'	√	√	√	√
'Lebanon	'	'	'	Negotiating Accession	√
Algeria	'	√	'	Negotiating Accession	√
'Tunisia	'	√	√	√	√
Saudi Arabia	'	√	'	Negotiating Accession	Not Eligible
'Oman	Announced	√	'	√	√
Kuwait	'	√	'	√	Not Eligible
'UAE	Announced	√	'	√	Not Eligible
Yemen	'	√	'	Negotiating Accession	√
Qatar	'	√	'	√	Not Eligible
Syria	'	'	'	'	Not Eligible
Iraq	'	√	'	Observer Status	Not Eligible
'Libya	'	'	'	Negotiating Accession	Not Eligible
Iran	'	'	'	'	Not Eligible

GREATER ARAB FREE TRADE AREA

As of 1 January 2005, the Greater Arab Free Trade Area (also referred to as GAFTA) has come into existence. GAFTA is a pact made by the Arab League to achieve a complete Arab economic bloc that can compete internationally. GAFTA is perhaps the beginning of a strong self sufficient Arab economy, and is relatively similar to ASEAN. The Project was adopted in the Arab League Summit of Amman in 1997, with 17 Arab League members signing the pact.

MEMBERS:

- Jordan
- Bahrain
- United Arab Emirates
- Tunisia
- Saudi Arabia

- Syria
- Iraq
- Oman
- Qatar
- Kuwait
- Lebanon
- Libya
- Egypt
- Morocco
- Sudan
- Yemen
- Palestine

Possible future members:

- Comoros
- Djibouti
- Mauritania
- Somalia

PROGRESS

The Greater Arab Free Trade Area was a project adopted in 1997, when 17 Arab League members agreed on decreasing the customs on local production and to make an Arab Free Zone for exports and imports between members. The members participate in 96% of the total internal Arab trade, and 95% with the rest of the world by applying the following conditions:

1-Instruct the inter-customs fees: To reduce the Customs on Arab products by 10% annually, the 14 Arab states reported their custom tariff programs to the Security Council of the Arab League to coordinate them with each others, except for Syria that is still using the Brussels tariffs system.
2-Applying the locality of the Arab products: All members have shared their standards and specifications to help their products move smoothly from one country to another. The League also created a project to apply the Arab Agriculture Pact: which is to share the standards of the agricultural sector and inject several more restrictions and specifications where all members have involved in them. The Arab league granted exceptions, which allow a customs rate for certain goods, to six members for several goods, however rejected requests by Morocco, Lebanon and Jordan for additional exceptions.

3-Private sectors: The League created a database and a service to inform and promote for the private's sectors benefits, and how there work would be in the GAFTA treaty is needed.
4-Communication: The Arab Economic and Social Council in its 65th meeting agreed on pointing a base for communication to ease communication between member states, and also to work to ease communication between the Private and public sectors to apply the Greater Arab Free Trade Area between members.

5-Customs Duties: In the 67th meeting the Arab Economic and Social Council agreed that the 40% decrease on customs on goods in the past 4 years of the GAFTA will continue and following the decisions of the Amman Summit of the Arab League, the members will put more efforts to eliminate all customs duties on local Arab goods.

MIDDLE EAST FREE TRADE INITIATIVE

In May 2003, the President proposed a plan of graduated steps for Middle Eastern nations to increase trade and investment with the United States and others in the world economy. The first step is to work closely with peaceful nations that want to become members of the World Trade Organization (WTO) in order to expedite their accession. As these countries implement domestic reform agendas, institute the rule of law, protect property rights (including intellectual property), and create a foundation for openness and economic growth, the United States will take a series of graduated steps with countries in the region tailored to their level of development. The U.S. will expand and deepen economic ties through Trade and Investment Framework Agreements (TIFAs), Bilateral Investment Treaties (BITs), and comprehensive Free Trade Agreements (FTAs), and will enhance the Generalized System of Preferences (GSP) program for eligible countries.

Active Support for WTO Accession

Working on accession to the World Trade Organization with:
- Lebanon
- Algeria
- Yemen

Robust Trade and Investment Framework Action Plans

TIFAs promote the establishment of legal protections for investors, improvements in intellectual property protection, more transparent and efficient customs procedures, and greater transparency in government and commercial regulations. TIFAs in place:
- Algeria
- Egypt
- Iraq
- Kuwait
- Qatar
- Saudi Arabia
- Tunisia
- Yemen

Free Trade Agreements
- U.S.-Israel Free Trade Agreement (in force)
- U.S.-Jordan Free Trade Agreement (in force)
- U.S.-Morocco Free Trade Agreement (in force)
- U.S.-Bahrain FTA: signed September 2004, entry into force in 2006
- U.S.-Oman FTA: negotiations concluded September 2005
- U.S.-UAE FTA: launched negotiations March 2005

U.S.-MIDDLE EAST FREE TRADE EFFORTS

Country	FTA	TIFA	BIT	WTO	GSP
Israel	√	√	√	√	Not Eligible
Jordan	√	√	√	√	√
Morocco	√	√	√	√	√
Bahrain	Ratified	√	√	√	Not Eligible
Egypt		√	√	√	√
Lebanon				Negotiating Accession	√
Algeria		√		Negotiating Accession	√
Tunisia		√	√	√	√
Saudi Arabia		√		√	Not Eligible
Oman	Signed	√		√	√
Kuwait		√		√	Not Eligible

UAE	Negotiating	√		√	Not Eligible
Yemen		√		Negotiating Accession	√
Qatar		√		√	Not Eligible
Syria					Not Eligible
Iraq		√		Negotiating Accession	√
Libya				Negotiating Accession	Not Eligible
Iran				Negotiating Accession	Not Eligible

NOTE: The Palestinian Authority participates in the U.S.-Israel FTA

ARABIC COUNTRIES: STRATEGIC PROFILES

ALGERIA STRATEGIC ECONOMIC AND BUSINESS INFORMATION

Capital	Algiers 36°42'N 3°13'E
Largest city	Algiers
Official language(s)	Arabic (national languages: Arabic and Tamazight)
Government	Democratic Republic
- President	Abdelaziz Bouteflika
- Prime Minister	Abdelaziz Belkhadem
Independence	From France
- Declared	July 5, 1962
Area	
- Total	2,381,740 km² (11th)
	919,595 sq mi
- Water (%)	negligible
Population	
- est.	32,854,000 (35th)
- 1998 census	29,100,867
- Density	14/km² (196th) 33.6/sq mi
GDP (PPP)	2005 estimate
- Total	$237,684 million (38th)
- Per capita	$7,189 (86th)
HDI	0.722 (103rd) – medium
Currency	Algerian dinar (DZD)
Time zone	CET (UTC+1)
- Summer (DST)	CET (UTC+1 does not observe)
Internet TLD	.dz
Calling code	+213

BAHRAIN STRATEGIC PROFILE

Capital (and largest city)	Manama 26°13′N 50°35′E26.217°N 50.583°E
Official language(s)	Arabic
Demonym	Bahraini
Government	Constitutional Monarchy
- King	Hamad ibn Isa Al Khalifa
- Crown Prince	Salman ibn Hamad ibn Isa Al Khalifa
- Prime Minister	Khalifa ibn Salman Al Khalifa
Independence	
- From Persia	1783
- Termination of special treaty with the United Kingdom	August 15, 1971
Area	
- Total	750 km^2 (184th) 290 sq mi
- Water (%)	0
Population	
- 2010 estimate	1,234,596 (158th)
- Density	1,646.1/km^2 (10th) 4,257.2/sq mi
GDP (PPP)	2009 estimate
- Total	$28.275 billion
- Per capita	$27,214
GDP (nominal)	2009 estimate
- Total	$20.590 billion
- Per capita	$19,817
HDI (2010)	▲0.801 (very high) (39th)
Currency	Bahraini dinar (BHD)
Time zone	(UTC+3)
Drives on the	Right
ISO 3166 code	BH
Internet TLD	.bh
Calling code	973

COMOROS STRATEGIC PROFILE

Capital (and largest city)	Moroni 11°41′S 43°16′E11.683°S 43.267°E
Official language(s)	Comorian, Arabic, French
Demonym	Comorian(s)
Government	Federal republic
- President	Ahmed Abdallah Mohamed Sambi
- President-elect	Ikililou Dhoinine
Independence	from France
- Date	July 6, 1975
Area	
- Total	2,235 km^2 (178th (incl. Mayotte)) 863 sq mi
- Water (%)	negligible
Population	
- 2010 estimate	691,000 (163th)

- Density	275/km^2 (25th) 712.2/sq mi
GDP (PPP)	2009 estimate
- Total	$772 million
- Per capita	$1,159
GDP (nominal)	2009 estimate
- Total	$532 million
- Per capita	$798
HDI (2007)	▲0.576 (medium) (139th)
Currency	Comorian franc (KMF)
Time zone	EAT (UTC+3)
- Summer (DST)	not observed (UTC+3)
Drives on the	right
ISO 3166 code	KM
Internet TLD	.km
Calling code	+269

DJIBOUTI STRATEGIC PROFILE

Capital (and largest city)	Djibouti 11°36′N 43°10′E11.6°N 43.167°E
Official language(s)	Arabic and French
Demonym	Djiboutian
Government	Semi-presidential republic
- President	Ismail Omar Guelleh
- Prime Minister	Dileita Mohamed Dileita
Independence	from France
- Date	June 27, 1977
	Area
- Total	23,200 km^2 (149th) 8,958 sq mi
- Water (%)	0.09 (20 km² / 7.7 sq mi)
	Population
- 2009 estimate	864,000 (160th)
- 2009 census	818,159
- Density	37.2/km^2 (168th) 96.4/sq mi
GDP (PPP)	2010 estimate
- Total	2.101 billion
- Per capita	2,549
GDP (nominal)	2010 estimate
- Total	1.128 billion
- Per capita	1,369
Gini (2009)	40.0
HDI (2007)	▲0.520 (medium) (155th)
Currency	Franc (DJF)
Time zone	EAT (UTC+3)
- Summer (DST)	not observed (UTC+3)
Drives on the	right
ISO 3166 code	DJ
Internet TLD	.dj
Calling code	253

EGYPT STRATEGIC PROFILE

Capital (and largest city)	Cairo 30°2′N 31°13′E30.033°N 31.217°E
Official language(s)	Arabic
Ethnic groups	99% Egyptians 0.9% Nubians 0.1% Greeks
Demonym	Egyptian
Government	Military junta
- Chairman of the Supreme Council of the Armed Forces	Mohamed Hussein Tantawi
- Prime Minister	Essam Sharaf
Establishment	
- Unified state	c. 3100 BC
- Independence from the United Kingdom	28 February 1922
- Became republic	18 June 1953
- Adoption of Constitution	11 September 1971
- Transfer of power to interim junta	11 February 2011
Area	
- Total	1,002,450 km^2 (30th) 387,048 sq mi
- Water (%)	0.632
Population	
- Sept, 2010 estimate	79,089,650
- 2006 census	76,699,427
- Density	82.3/km^2 (120th) 214.4/sq mi
GDP (PPP)	2010 estimate
- Total	$496.604 billion
- Per capita	$6,347
GDP (nominal)	2010 estimate
- Total	$215.845 billion
- Per capita	$2,758
Gini (1999–00)	34.5 (medium)
HDI (2010)	▲0.620 (medium) (101st)
Currency	Egyptian pound (EGP)
Time zone	EET (UTC+2)
- Summer (DST)	EEST (UTC+3)
Drives on the	right
ISO 3166 code	EG
Internet TLD	.eg, مصر.
Calling code	+20

IRAQ STRATEGIC PROFILE

Capital (and largest city)	Baghdad 33°20′N 44°26′E33.333°N 44.433°E
Official language(s)	Arabic, Kurdish
Demonym	Iraqi
Government	Federal parliamentary republic
- President	Jalal Talabani
- Prime Minister	Nouri al-Maliki
Independence	

- from the Ottoman Empire	1 October 1919
- from the United Kingdom	3 October 1932
- Republic	14 July 1958
- Current constitution	15 October 2005
	Area
- Total	438,317 km^2 (50th) 169,234 sq mi
- Water (%)	1.1
	Population
- 2009 estimate	31,234,000 (39th)
- Density	71.5/km^2 (125th) 184.6/sq mi
GDP (PPP)	2009 estimate
- Total	$111.5 billion
- Per capita	$3,570
GDP (nominal)	2009 estimate
- Total	$65.838 billion
- Per capita	$2,108
Currency	Iraqi dinar (IQD)
Time zone	GMT+3 (UTC+3)
- Summer (DST)	not observed (UTC+3)
Drives on the	right
ISO 3166 code	IQ
Internet TLD	.iq
Calling code	964

JORDAN STRATEGIC PROFILE

Capital	Amman 31°57′N 35°56′E31.95°N 35.933°E
Official language(s)	Arabic
Spoken languages	Jordanian Levantine, English, French, Egyptian, Mesopotamian, Greek , Circassian, Chechen, Turkish and Tagalog
Demonym	Jordanian
Government	Constitutional monarchy
- King of Jordan	Abdullah II
- Prime Minister	Marouf al-Bakhit
	Independence
- End of British League of Nations mandate	25 May 1946
	Area
- Total	92,300 km^2 (112th) 35,637 sq mi
- Water (%)	0.8
	Population
- July 2010 estimate	6,407,085 (102nd)
- July 2004 census	5,611,202
- Density	68.4/km^2 (131st) 138.8/sq mi
GDP (PPP)	2010 estimate
- Total	$95.3 billion
- Per capita	$5,956
GDP (nominal)	2010 estimate
- Total	$99.129 billion
- Per capita	$4,435
Gini (2002–03)	38.8 (medium)
HDI (2010)	▲0.681 (high) (82nd)
Currency	Jordanian dinar (JOD)
Time zone	UTC+2 (UTC+2)
- Summer (DST)	UTC+3 (UTC+3)
Drives on the	Right
ISO 3166 code	JO
Internet TLD	.jo
Calling code	962

KUWAIT STRATEGIC PROFILE

Capital (and largest city)	Kuwait City 29°22′N 47°58′E29.367°N 47.967°E
Official language(s)	Arabic
Ethnic groups	33.4% Kuwaiti 34.8% Other Arabs 24.3% Asian 2.1% Iranian 5.4% Europeans and Americans
Demonym	Kuwaiti
Government	Constitutional hereditary emirate

- Emir	Sabah Al-Ahmad Al-Jaber Al-Sabah
- Crown Prince	Nawaf Al-Ahmad Al-Jaber Al-Sabah
- Prime Minister	Nasser Mohammed Al-Ahmed Al-Sabah
- Speaker of the National Assembly	Jassem Mohammed Abdulmohsen Al-Kharafi
	Establishment
- First Settlement	1613
- Anglo-Ottoman Convention	1913
- Independence from the British	19 June 1961
	Area
- Total	17,820 km^2 (157th) 6,880 sq mi
- Water (%)	negligible
	Population
- 2010 estimate	3,566,437 (130th)
- Density	167.5/km^2 (68th) 433.8/sq mi
GDP (PPP)	2010 estimate
- Total	$140.589 billion
- Per capita	$38,984
GDP (nominal)	2010 estimate
- Total	$135.062 billion
- Per capita	$37,451
HDI (2010)	▲0.771 (high) (47th)
Currency	Kuwaiti dinar (KWD)
Time zone	AST / KSA (UTC+3)
- Summer (DST)	(not observed) (UTC+3)
Date formats	dd/mm/yyyy (CE)
Drives on the	Right
ISO 3166 code	KW
Internet TLD	.kw
Calling code	965

LEBANON STRATEGIC PROFILE

Capital (and largest city)	Beirut 33°54′N 35°32′E33.9°N 35.533°E
Official language(s)	Arabic, French (conditional)
Ethnic groups	95% Arab 4% Armenian, 1% other
Demonym	Lebanese
Government	Confessionalist, parliamentary republic
- President	Michel Suleiman
- Prime Minister	Saad Hariri (acting) Najib Mikati (designate)
- Speaker of Parliament	Nabih Berri
Sovereignty	End of French League of Nations Mandate
- Declared	26 November 1941
- Recognized	22 November 1943
	Area
- total	10,452 km^2 (166th) 4,036 sq mi
- Water (%)	1.6
	Population
- 2009 estimate	4,224,000 (124th)

- Density	404/km^2 (25th) 1,046/sq mi
GDP (PPP)	2010 estimate
- Total	$58.576 billion
- Per capita	$14,988 (54th)
GDP (nominal)	estimate
- Total	$37.040 billion
- Per capita	$9,479
Currency	Lebanese pound (LBP)
Time zone	EET (UTC+2)
- Summer (DST)	EEST (UTC+3)
Drives on the	right
ISO 3166 code	LB
Internet TLD	.lb
Calling code	961

LIBYA[2] STRATEGIC PROFILE

Capital (and largest city)		Tripoli 32°54′N, 13°11′E
Official languages		Arabic
Demonym		Libyan
Government		Jamahiriya
-	Leader and Guide of the Revolution	Muammar al-Gaddafi
-	Head of State	Zenati Muhammad az-Zenati
-	Prime Minister	Baghdadi Mahmudi
Independence		
-	relinquished by Italy	February 10, 1947
-	from France/UK under UN Trusteeship	December 24, 1951
Area		
-	Total	1,759,540 km² (17th) 679,359 sq mi
-	Water (%)	negligible
Population		
-	estimate	5,670,688 (105th)
-	2006 census	5,670,688[1]
-	Density	3.2 /km² (218th) 8.4 /sq mi
GDP (PPP)		2006 estimate
-	Total	$74.97 billion (67th)
-	Per capita	$12,700 (58th)
HDI		□0.798 (medium) (64th)
Currency		Dinar (LYD)
Time zone		EET (UTC+2)
-	Summer (DST)	not observed (UTC+2)
Internet TLD		.ly
Calling code		+218

[2] currently suspended

MAURITANIA STRATEGIC AND BUSINESS PROFILES

Capital	Nouakchott 18°09′N 15°58′W
Largest city	Nouakchott
Official language(s)	Arabic, French de-facto
Government	Military junta
- President	Ely Ould Mohamed Vall
- Prime Minister	Sidi Mohamed Ould Boubacar
Independence	From France
- Date	November 28, 1960
Area	
- Total	1,030,700 km² (29th) 397,954 sq mi
- Water (%)	Negligible
Population	
- 2005 est.	3,069,000 (135th)
- 1988 census	1,864,236
- Density	3.0/km² (221st) 7.8/sq mi
GDP (PPP)	2005 estimate
- Total	$7.159 billion (144th)
- Per capita	$2,402 (132nd)
HDI	0.477 (152nd) – low
Currency	Ouguiya (MRO)
Time zone	GMT (UTC+0)
- Summer (DST)	not observed (UTC+0)
Internet TLD	.mr
Calling code	+222

MOROCCO STRATEGIC AND BUSINESS PROFILES

Capital		Rabat 34°02′N, 6°51′W
Largest city		Casablanca
Official languages		de jure: Arabic additional de facto: French and Spanish.[1]
Demonym		Moroccan
Government		Constitutional monarchy
-	King	Mohammed VI
-	Prime Minister	Driss Jettou
Independence		
-	from France	March 2, 1956
-	from Spain	April 7, 1956
Area		

-	Total	446,550* km² (57th) 172,414 sq mi
-	Water (%)	250km²
Population		
-	2005 estimate	33,241,259 (37th)
-	Density	70 /km² (122nd) 181 /sq mi
GDP (PPP)		2006 estimate
-	Total	$152.5 billion (54th)
-	Per capita	$4,600 (109th)
HDI		□0.640 (medium) (123rd)
Currency		Moroccan dirham (MAD)
Time zone		UTC (UTC+0)
Internet TLD		.ma
Calling code		+212

OMAN STRATEGIC PROFILE

Capital (and largest city)	Muscat 23°36′N 58°33′E23.6°N 58.55°E
Official language(s)	Arabic
Demonym	Omani
Government	Islamic absolute monarchy
- Sultan	Qaboos bin Said Al Said
- Deputy Prime Minister	Fahd bin Mahmoud al Said
Establishment	
- Imamate established	751
- Constitution	1966
Area	
- Total	309,550 km^2 (70th) 119,498 sq mi
- Water (%)	negligible
Population	
- 2009 estimate	2,845,000 (139th)
- 2003 census	2,341,000
- Density	9.2/km^2 (219th) 23.8/sq mi
GDP (PPP)	2009 estimate
- Total	$74.431 billion
- Per capita	$25,109
GDP (nominal)	2009 estimate
- Total	$53.395 billion
- Per capita	$18,013
HDI	▲0.846 (high) (56th)
Currency	Rial (OMR)
Time zone	(UTC+4)
- Summer (DST)	(UTC+4)
Drives on the	left
ISO 3166 code	OM
Internet TLD	.om
Calling code	968

STATE OF PALESTINE) WEST BANK AND GAZA) STRATEGIC PROFILE

Capital	Jerusalem (proclaimed) Ramallah, Gaza (administrative)
Largest city	[1] Gaza
Official language(s)	Arabic
Government	Semi-presidential; Parliamentary democracy
- President	Mahmoud Abbas
	Establishment
- Declared	November 15, 1988
	Area
- Total	[1] 6,020 km^2 (West Bank: 5,660 km^2, Gaza Strip: 360 km^2) [1] 2,230 sq mi
	Population
- 2010 (July) estimate	[1] 4,260,636 (124th)
GDP (PPP)	[1] 2008 estimate
- Total	[1] $11.95 billion (–)
- Per capita	[1] $2,900 (–)
HDI (2007)	[1] ▼0.731 (medium) (106th) 1
Currency	Jordanian dinar Egyptian Pound Israeli shekel (JOD, EGP, ILS)
Time zone	(UTC+2)
- Summer (DST)	(UTC+3)
Internet TLD	.ps
Calling code	+970[2]

[1] Population and economy statistics and rankings are based on the Palestinian territories

[2] +972 is also used as well.

QATAR STRATEGIC PROFILE

Capital (and largest city)	Doha 25°18′N 51°31′E25.3°N 51.517°E
Official language(s)	Arabic
Demonym	Qatari
Government	Absolute monarchy
- Emir	Hamad bin Khalifa AlThani
- Crown Prince	Tamim bin Hamad AlThani
- Prime Minister	Hamad bin Jassim AlThani
	Independence[1]
- National Day	December 18, 1878
- Independence from the Ottoman Empire	1913
- Termination of special treaty with the United Kingdom	September 3, 1971
	Area
- Total	11,437 km^2 (164th) 4,416 sq mi
- Water (%)	negligible
	Population

- 2010 census	1,696,563 (148th)
- Density	123.2/km^2 (123rd) 319.1/sq mi
GDP (PPP)	2010 estimate
- Total	$102.147 billion
- Per capita	$90,149
GDP (nominal)	2010 estimate
- Total	$110.844 billion (55th)
- Per capita	$81,963 (1st)
HDI (2010)	▲0.803 (very high) (38th)
Currency	Riyal (QAR)
Time zone	AST (UTC+3)
- Summer (DST)	(not observed) (UTC+3)
Drives on the	Right
ISO 3166 code	QA
Internet TLD	.qa
Calling code	974

SAUDI ARABIA STRATEGIC PROFILE

Capital (and largest city)	Riyadh 24°39′N 46°46′E24.65°N 46.767°E
Official language(s)	Arabic
Spoken languages	Arabic, English
Demonym	Saudi, Saudi Arabian
Government	Islamic absolute monarchy
- King and Prime Minister	Abdullah bin Abdul Aziz
- Crown Prince	Sultan bin Abdul Aziz
Legislature	None - legislation by royal decree
	Establishment
- Kingdom founded	23 September 1932
	Area
- Total	2,149,690 km^2 (14th) 830,000 sq mi
- Water (%)	0.7
	Population
- 2010 estimate	27,136,977 (46th)
- Density	12/km^2 (215th) 31/sq mi
GDP (PPP)	2010 estimate
- Total	$618.744 billion
- Per capita	$23,701.260
GDP (nominal)	2010 estimate
- Total	$438.009 billion
- Per capita	$16,778.112
HDI (2010)	▲0.752 (high) (55th)
Currency	Saudi Riyal (SR) (SAR)
Time zone	AST (UTC+3)
- Summer (DST)	(not observed) (UTC+3)
Drives on the	Right
ISO 3166 code	SA
Internet TLD	.sa, السعودية.
Calling code	+966

SOMALIA STRATEGIC PROFILE

Capital (and largest city)	Mogadishu 2°02′N 45°21′E2.033°N 45.35°E
Official language(s)	Somali, Arabic
Ethnic groups	Somalis (85%), Benadiris, Bantus and other non-Somalis (15%)
Demonym	Somali; Somalian
Government	Coalition government
- President	Sharif Ahmed
- Prime Minister	Mohamed Abdullahi Mohamed
- Speaker of Parliament	Sharif Hassan Sheikh Aden
	Formation
- British Somaliland	1884
- Italian Somaliland	1889
- Union and independence	1 July 1960
	Area
- Total	637,657 km^2 (42nd) 246,200 sq mi
	Population
- 2010 estimate	9,359,000 (89th)
- Density	14/km^2 (209) 36/sq mi
GDP (PPP)	2009 estimate
- Total	$5.731 billion (155th)
- Per capita	$600 (224th)
HDI (2009)	N/A (Not ranked)
Currency	Somali shilling (SOS)
Time zone	EAT (UTC+3)
- Summer (DST)	not observed (UTC+3)
Drives on the	right
ISO 3166 code	SO
Internet TLD	.so
Calling code	252

SUDAN STRATEGIC PROFILE

Capital (and largest city)	Khartoum 15°38′N 032°32′E15.633°N 32.533°E
Official language(s)	Arabic, English
Ethnic groups	Black 52%, Arabs 39%, Beja 6%, foreigners 2%, other 1%
Demonym	Sudanese
Government	Federal presidential democratic republic
- President	Omar al-Bashir (NCP)
- Vice President	Salva Kiir Mayardit (SPLM)
- Vice President	Ali Osman Taha (NCP)
Legislature	National Legislature
- Upper House	Council of States
- Lower House	National Assembly
	Establishment
- Kingdoms of Nubia	2000 BC
- Sennar dynasty	1504
- Unification with Egypt	1821

- Independence from Egypt, and the United Kingdom	1 January 1956
- Current constitution	9 January 2005
Area	
- Total	2,505,813 km^2 (10th) 967,500 sq mi
- Water (%)	6
Population	
- 2009 estimate	43,939,598 (31st)
- Density	16.9/km^2 (194th) 43.7/sq mi
GDP (PPP)	2010 estimate
- Total	$99.926 billion
- Per capita	$2,464.90
GDP (nominal)	2010 estimate
- Total	$65.742 billion
- Per capita	$1,638.07
HDI (2007)	▲0.531 (medium) (150th)
Currency	Sudanese pound (SDG)
Time zone	East Africa Time (UTC+3)
- Summer (DST)	Not observed (UTC+3)
Drives on the	right
ISO 3166 code	SD
Internet TLD	.sd
Calling code	249

SYRIA STRATEGIC PROFILE

Capital (and largest city)	Damascus 33°30′N 36°18′E33.5°N 36.3°E
Official language(s)	Arabic[1]
Demonym	Syrian
Government	Presidential single party republic under Emergency Law since 1963.
- President	Bashar al-Assad
- Prime Minister	Muhammad Naji al-Otari
- Speaker of Parliament	Mahmoud al-Abrash
Independence	
- from the Ottoman Empire	1918
- Evacuation from French mandate	April 17, 1946
Area	
- Total	185,180 km^2 (88th) 71,479 sq mi
- Water (%)	1.1
Population	
- 2011 estimate	22,457,763 (53rd)
- Density	118.3/km^2 (101st) 306.5/sq mi
GDP (PPP)	2011 estimate
- Total	$105.238 billion
- Per capita	$5,043
GDP (nominal)	2010 estimate
- Total	$60.210 billion
- Per capita	$2,958

HDI (2010)	▲0.712 (medium)
Currency	Syrian pound (SYP)
Time zone	EET (UTC+2)
- Summer (DST)	EEST (UTC+3)
Drives on the	Right
Internet TLD	.sy
Calling code	963[2]

TUNISIA STRATEGIC PROFILE

Capital	Tunis 36°50′N 10°9′E
Largest city	Tunis
Official language(s)	Arabic
Government	Republic
- President	Zine El Abidine Ben Ali
- Prime Minister	Mohamed Ghannouchi
Independence	
- from France	March 20, 1956
Area	
- Total	163,610 km² (92nd)
	63,170 sq mi
- Water (%)	5.0
Population	
- July 2005 est.	10,102,000 (79th)
- 1994 census	8,785,711
- Density	65.5/km² (133rd) 169.6/sq mi
GDP (PPP)	2005 estimate
- Total	$ 76.91 billion (63rd)
- Per capita	$7,400 (71st)
HDI	0.753 (89th) – medium
Currency	Tunisian Dinar (TND)
Time zone	CET (UTC+1)
- Summer (DST)	CEST (UTC+2)
Internet TLD	.tn
Calling code	+216

UNITED ARAB EMIRATES STRATEGIC PROFILE

Capital	Abu Dhabi 22°47′N 54°37′E
Largest city	Dubai
Official language(s)	Arabic
Government	Constitutional monarchy
- President	Khalifa bin Zayed Al Nahayan
- Prime Minister	Mohammed bin Rashid Al Maktoum
Establishment	December 2, 1971
Area	
- Total	83,600 km² (116th) 32,278 sq mi
- Water (%)	negligible
Population	
- 2006 est.	2,602,713 (140th)
- Density	54/km² (143rd) 139/sq mi
GDP (PPP)	2006 estimate
- Total	$111.3 billion (59th)
- Per capita	$27,957 (23rd)
HDI (2003)	0.849 (41st) – high
Currency	Dirham (AED)
Time zone	GMT (UTC+4)
Internet TLD	.ae
Calling code	+971

YEMEN STRATEGIC PROFILE

Capital (and largest city)	Sana'a 15°21′N 44°12′E15.35°N 44.2°E
Official language(s)	Arabic
Demonym	Yemeni, Yemenite
Government	Presidential democracy
- President	Ali Abdullah Saleh (GPC)
- Vice President	Abd Al Rab Mansur Al Hadi
- Prime Minister	Ali Mohammed Mujur (GPC)
- Deputy Prime Minister	Abdulkarim Ismail Al Arhabi
Establishment	
- North Yemen independence from the Ottoman Empire	November 1, 1918
- South Yemen independence from the United Kingdom	November 30, 1967
- Unification	May 22, 1990
Area	
- Total	555,000 km^2 (49th) 203,849 sq mi
- Water (%)	negligible
Population	
- 2009 estimate	23,580,000 (51st)
- July 2007 census	22,230,531
- Density	44.7/km^2 (160th) 115.7/sq mi

GDP (PPP)	2009 estimate
- Total	$58.218 billion
- Per capita	$2,457
GDP (nominal)	2009 estimate
- Total	$25.131 billion
- Per capita	$1,061
HDI (2007)	▲0.575 (medium) (140th)
Currency	Yemeni rial (YER)
Time zone	(UTC+3)
Drives on the	right
ISO 3166 code	YE
Internet TLD	.ye
Calling code	967

IMPORTANT LAWS RELATED TO INVESTMENT ACTIVITY

ISLAMIC LAW MYTHS AND REALITIES[3]

The general public and many academics have several preconceived notions about Islamic Law. One such notion is that Islamic judges are bound by ancient and outdated rules of fixed punishments for all crimes. This paper explores that idea and looks at other myths in an attempt to present Islamic Law from a non-biased view of Sharia Law.

Some contemporary scholars fail to recognize Islamic Law as an equal to English Common Law, European Civil Law and Socialist Law. A few academics have even attempted to place Islamic Law into the Civil Law tradition. Other writers have simply added a footnote to their works on comparative justice on the religious law categories of Islamic Law, Hindu Law, which is still used in some parts of India, and the Law of Moses from the Old Testament which still guides the current thought of the Israeli Knesset (Parliament) today. This survey will attempt to alter some of these inaccurate perceptions and treatments in both the contemporary literature and academic writings.

Mohammed Salam Madkoar explains the theoretical assumptions of Islamic Law:

> In order to protect the five important indispensables in Islam (religion, life, intellect, offspring and property), Islamic Law has provided a worldly punishment in addition to that in the hereafter. Islam has, in fact, adopted two courses for the preservation of these five indispensables: the first is through cultivating religious consciousness in the human soul and the awakening of human awareness through moral education; the second is by inflicting deterrent punishment, which is the basis of the Islamic criminal system. Therefore "Hudoud," Retaliation (*Qisas*)and Discretionary (*Ta'zir*) punishments have been prescribed according to the type of the crime committed.

Islamic Law and Jurisprudence is not always understood by the western press. Although it is the responsibility of the mass media to bring to the world's attention violations of human rights and acts of terror, many believe that media stereotyping of all Muslims is a major problem. The recent bombing at the World Trade Center in New York City is a prime example. The media often used the term "Islamic Fundamentalists" when referring to the accused in the case. It also referred to the Egyptian connections in that case as "Islamic Fundamentalists." The media has used the label of "Islamic Fundamentalist" to imply all kinds of possible negative connotations: terrorists, kidnappers and hostage takers. Since the media does not use the term "Fundamentalist Christian" each time a Christian does something wrong, the use of such labels is wrong for any group, Christians, Muslims, or Orthodox Jews.

A Muslim who is trying to live his religion is indeed a true believer in God. This person tries to live all of the tenets of his religion in a fundamental way. Thus, a true Muslim is a fundamentalist in the practice of that religion, but a true Muslim is not radical, because the Quran teaches tolerance and moderation in all things. When the popular media generalizes from the fundamentalist believer to the "radical fundamentalist" label they do a disservice to all Muslims and others.

NO SEPARATION OF CHURCH AND STATE

To understand Islamic Law one must first understand the assumptions of Islam and the basic tenets of the religion. The meaning of the word Islam is "submission or surrender to Allah's (God's) will." Therefore, Muslims must first and foremost obey and submit to Allah's will. Mohammed the Prophet was called by God to translate verses from the Angel Gabriel to form the most important book in Islam, the Quran, Muslims believe.

There are over 1.2 billion Muslims today worldwide, over 20% of the world's population. "By the year 2000, one out of every four persons on the planet will be a Muslim," Rittat Hassan estimated in 1990. There are 35

[3] By: Dennis J. Wiechman, Jerry D. Kendall, and Mohammad K. Azarian

nations with population over 50% Muslim, and there are another 21 nations that have significant Muslim populations. There are 19 nations which have declared Islam in their respective constitutions. The Muslim religion is a global one and is rapidly expanding. The sheer number of Muslims living today makes the idea of putting Islamic Law into a footnote in contemporary writings inappropriate.

The most difficult part of Islamic Law for most westerners to grasp is that there is no separation of church and state. The religion of Islam and the government are one. Islamic Law is controlled, ruled and regulated by the Islamic religion. The theocracy controls all public and private matters. Government, law and religion are one. There are varying degrees of this concept in many nations, but all law, government and civil authority rests upon it and it is a part of Islamic religion. There are civil laws in Muslim nations for Muslim and non-Muslim people. Sharia is only applicable to Muslims. Most Americans and others schooled in Common Law have great difficulty with that concept. The U.S. Constitution (Bill of Rights) prohibits the government from "establishing a religion." The U.S. Supreme Court has concluded in numerous cases that the U.S. Government can't favor one religion over another. That concept is implicit for most U.S. legal scholars and many U.S. academicians believe that any mixture of "church and state" is inherently evil and filled with many problems. They reject all notions of a mixture of religion and government.

To start with such preconceived notions limits the knowledge base and information available to try and solve many social and criminal problems. To use an analogy from Christianity may be helpful. To ignore what all Christian religions except your own say about God would limit your knowledge base and you would not be informed or have the ability to appreciate your own religion. The same is true for Islamic Law and Islamic religion. You must open your mind to further expand your knowledge base. Islamic Law has many ideas, concepts, and information that can solve contemporary crime problems in many areas of the world. To do this you must first put on hold the preconceived notion of "separation of church and state."

JUDGE (*QADI*)

Another myth concerning Islamic Law is that there are no judges. Historically the Islamic Judge (*Qadi*) was a legal secretary appointed by the provincial governors. Each Islamic nation may differ slightly in how the judges are selected. Some nations will use a formal process of legal education and internship in a lower court. For example, in Saudi Arabia there are two levels of courts. The formal Sharia Courts which were established in 1928 hear traditional cases. The Saudi government established a ministry of justice in 1970, and they added administrative tribunals for traffic laws, business and commerce. "All judges are accountable to God in their decisions and practices" (Lippman, p.66-68).

One common myth associated with Islamic Law is that judges must always impose a fixed and predetermined punishment for each crime. Western writers often point to the inflexible nature of Islamic Law. Judges under Islamic Law are bound to administer several punishments for a few very serious crimes found in the Quran, but they possess much greater freedom in punishment for less serious (non-*Had*) crimes. Common law is filled with precedents, rules, and limitations which inhibit creative justice. Judges under Islamic Law are free to create new options and ideas to solve new problems associated with crime.

ELEMENTS OF SHARIA LAW

Islamic law is known as Sharia Law, and Sharia means the path to follow God's Law. Sharia Law is holistic or eclectic in its approach to guide the individual in most daily matters. Sharia Law controls, rules and regulates all public and private behavior. It has regulations for personal hygiene, diet, sexual conduct, and elements of child rearing. It also prescribes specific rules for prayers, fasting, giving to the poor, and many other religious matters. Civil Law and Common Law primarily focus on public behavior, but both do regulate some private matters.

Sharia Law can also be used in larger situations than guiding an individual's behavior. It can be used as guide for how an individual acts in society and how one group interacts with another. The Sharia Law can be used to settle border disputes between nations or within nations. It can also be used to settle international disputes, conflicts and wars. This Law does not exclude any knowledge from other sources and is viewed by the Muslim world as a vehicle to solve all problems civil, criminal and international.

Sharia Law has several sources from which to draw its guiding principles. It does not rely upon one source for its broad knowledge base. The first and primary element of Sharia Law is the Quran. It is the final arbitrator and there is no other appeal. The second element of Sharia Law is known as the Sunna, the teachings of the Prophet Mohammed not explicitly found in the Quran. The Sunna are a composite of the teachings of the prophet and his works. The Sunna contain stories and anecdotes, called Hadith, to illustrate

a concept. The Quran may not have all the information about behavior and human interaction in detail; the Sunna gives more detailed information than the Quran.
The third element of Sharia Law is known as the Ijma. The Muslim religion uses the term Ulama as a label for its religious scholars. These Ulamas are consulted on many matters both personal and political. When the Ulamas reach a consensus on an issue, it is interpreted as a ijma. The concepts and ideas found in the ijma are not found explicitly in the Quran or the teachings of the Prophet (Sunna). Islamic judges are able to examine the ijma for many possible solutions which can be applied in a modern technical society. They are free to create new and innovative methods to solve crime and social problems based upon the concepts found in the ijma. These judges have great discretion in applying the concepts to a specific problem.
The Qiyas are a fourth element of Sharia Law. The Qiyas are not explicitly found in the Quran, Sunna, or given in the Ijma. The Qiyas are new cases or case law which may have already been decided by a higher judge. The Sharia judge can use the legal precedent to decide new case law and its application to a specific problem. The judge can use a broad legal construct to resolve a very specific issue. For example, a computer crime or theft of computer time is not found in the Quran or Sunna. The act of theft as a generic term is prohibited so the judge must rely on logic and reason to create new case law or Qiyas.

The fifth element of Sharia Law is very broad and "all encompassing." This secondary body of knowledge may be ideas contained in the other written works. The New Testament is an example of this area of information, and legal discourses based upon Civil Law or Common Law may be another example. All information can be examined for logic and reason to see if it applies to the current case. It also may be a local custom or norm that judge may find helpful in applying to the issue before him. The judge may also weigh the impact of his decision upon how it will effect a person's standing in the community.

CRIMES IN ISLAM

Crimes under Islamic Law can be broken down into three major categories. Each will be discussed in greater detail with some common law analogies. The three major crime categories in Islamic Law are:

1. *Had* Crimes (most serious).
2. *Ta'zir* Crimes (least serious).
3. *Qisas* Crimes (revenge crimes restitution).

Had crimes are the most serious under Islamic Law, and *Ta'zir* crimes are the least serious. Some Western writers use the felony analogy for *Had* crimes and misdemeanor label for *Ta'zir* crimes. The analogy is partially accurate, but not entirely true. Common Law has no comparable form of *Qisas* crimes. Fairchild, in her excellent book on comparative justice, makes the following observation of Islamic Law and punishment (Fairchild, p.41).

> Punishments are prescribed in the Quran and are often harsh with the emphasis on corporal and capital punishment. Theft is punished by imprisonment or amputation of hands or feet, depending on the number of times it is committed...

HAD CRIMES

Had crimes are those which are punishable by a pre-established punishment found in the Quran. These most serious of all crimes are found by an exact reference in the Quran to a specific act and a specific punishment for that act. There is no plea-bargaining or reducing the punishment for a *Had* crime. *Had* crimes have no minimum or maximum punishments attached to them. The punishment system is comparable to the determinate sentence imposed by some judges in the United States. If you commit a crime, you know what your punishment will be. There is no flexibility in the U.S. determinate model or in the punishment for *Had* crimes of Islamic Law.
No judge can change or reduce the punishment for these serous crimes. The *Had* crimes are:

1. Murder;
2. Apostasy from Islam

(making war upon Allah and his messengers);
3. Theft;
4. Adultery;

5. Defamation

(false accusation of adultery or fornication);
6. Robbery;
7. Alcohol-drinking.

The first four *Had* crimes have a specific punishment in the Quran. The last three crimes are mentioned but no specific punishment is found (Schmalleger, p.603).
Some more liberal Islamic judges do not consider apostasy from Islam or wine drinking as *Had* crimes. The more liberal Islamic nations treat these crimes as *Ta'zir* or a lesser crime.

Had crimes have fixed punishments because they are set by God and are found in the Quran. *Had* crimes are crimes against God's law and *Ta'zir* crimes are crimes against society. There are some safeguards for *Had* crimes that many in the media fail to mention. Some in the media only mention that if you steal, your hand is cut off. The Islamic judge must look at a higher level of proof and reasons why the person committed the crime. A judge can only impose the *Had* punishment when a person confesses to the crime or there are enough witnesses to the crime. The usual number of witnesses is two, but in the case of adultery four witnesses are required. The media often leaves the public with the impression that all are punished with flimsy evidence or limited proof. Islamic law has a very high level of proof for the most serious crimes and punishments. When there is doubt about the guilt of a *Had* crime, the judge must treat the crime as a lesser *Ta'zir* crime. If there is no confession to a crime or not enough witnesses to the crime, Islamic law requires the *Had* crime to be punished as a *Ta'zir* crime.

TA'ZIR CRIMES

Modern Islamic Society has changed greatly from the time of the Prophet. Contemporary Sharia Law is now in written form and is statutory in nature. Islamic concepts of justice argue that a person should know what the crime is and its possible punishment. For example, Egypt has a parliamentary process which has a formal penal code written and based upon the principles of Islamic Law, but Saudi Arabia allows the judge to set the *Ta'zir* crimes and punishments. Modern Islamic Law recognizes many differences between these two nations. It also allows for much greater flexibility in how it punishes an offender. The major myth of many people is that judges in Islamic nations have fixed punishments for all crimes. In reality the judges have much greater flexibility than judges under common law.

Ta'zir crimes are less serious than the *Had* crimes found in the Quran. Some common law writers use the analogy of misdemeanors, which is the lesser of the two categories (felony and misdemeanor) of common law crimes. *Ta'zir* crimes can and do have comparable "minor felony equivalents." These "minor felonies" are not found in the Quran so the Islamic judges are free to punish the offender in almost any fashion. Mohammed Salam Madkoar, who was the head of Islamic Law at the University of Cairo, makes the following observation (Ministry of the Interior, 1976,p.104):

> *Ta'zir* punishments vary according to the circumstances. They change from time to time and from place to place. They vary according to the gravity of the crime and the extent of the criminal disposition of the criminal himself.

Ta'zir crimes are acts which are punished because the offender disobeys God's law and word. *Ta'zir* crimes can be punished if they harm the societal interest. Sharia Law places an emphasis on the societal or public interest. The assumption of the punishment is that a greater "evil " will be prevented in the future if you punish this offender now.
Historically *Ta'zir* crimes were not written down or codified. This gave each ruler great flexibility in what punishments the judge was able to dispense. The judge under Islamic Law is not bound by precedents, rules, or prior decisions as in common law. Judges are totally free to choose from any number of punishments that they think will help an individual offender. The only guiding principle for judges under Sharia Law is that they must answer to Allah and to the greater community of Muslims. Some of the more common punishment for *Ta'zir* crimes are counseling, fines, public or private censure, family and clan pressure and support, seizure of property, confinement in the home or place of detention, and flogging.

In some Islamic nations, *Ta'zir* crimes are set by legislative parliament. Each nation is free to establish its own criminal code and there is a great disparity in punishment of some of these crimes. Some of the more common *Ta'zir* crimes are: bribery, selling tainted or defective products, treason, usury, and selling obscene pictures. The consumption of alcohol in Egypt is punished much differently than in Iran or Saudi Arabia because they have far different civil laws. Islamic law has much greater flexibility than the Western media portrays. Each judge is free to punish based upon local norms, customs, and informal rules. Each judge is free to fix the punishment that will deter others from crime and will help to rehabilitate an offender.

QISAS CRIMES AND *DIYA*

Islamic Law has an additional category of crimes that common law nations do not have. A *Qisas* crime is one of retaliation. If you commit a *Qisas* crime, the victim has a right to seek retribution and retaliation. The exact punishment for each *Qisas* crime is set forth in the Quran. If you are killed, then your family has a right to seek *Qisas* punishment from the murderer. Punishment can come in several forms and also may include "*Diya*." *Diya* is paid to the victim's family as part of punishment. *Diya* is an ancient form of restitution for the victim or his family. The family also may seek to have a public execution of the offender or the family may seek to pardon the offender. Traditional *Qisas* crimes include:

1. Murder (premeditated and non-premeditated).
2. Premeditated offenses against human life, short of murder.
3. Murder by error.
4. Offenses by error against humanity, short of murder.

Some reporters in the mass media have criticized the thought of "blood money" as barbaric. They labeled the practice as undemocratic and inhumane. *Qisas* crimes are based upon the criminological assumption of retribution. The concept of retribution was found in the first statutory "Code of Hammurabi" and in the Law of Moses in the form of "an eye for an eye." Muslims add to that saying "but it is better to forgive." Contemporary common law today still is filled with the assumptions of retribution. The United States federal code contains "mandatory minimum" sentences for drug dealing, and many states have fixed punishment for drugs and violence and using weapons. The United States justice system has adopted a retribution model which sets fixed punishments for each crime. The idea of retribution is fixed in the U.S. system of justice. *Qisas* crime is simple retribution: if one commits a crime he knows what the punishment will be.
Diya has its roots in Islamic Law and dates to the time of the Prophet Mohammed when there were many local families, tribes and clans. They were nomadic and traveled extensively. The Prophet was able to convince several tribes to take a monetary payment for damage to the clan or tribe. This practice grew and now is an acceptable solution to some *Qisas* crimes.

Today, the *Diya* is paid by the offender to the victim if he is alive. If the victim is dead, the money is paid to the victim's family or to the victim's tribe or clan. The assumption is that victims will be compensated for their loss. Under common law, the victim or family must sue the offender in a civil tort action for damages. *Qisas* law combines the process of criminal and civil hearings into one, just as the "civil law" is applied in many nations of the world. *Qisas* crimes are compensated as restitution under common law and civil law.
The *Qisas* crimes require compensation for each crime committed. Each nation sets the damage before the offense and the judge then fixes the proper *Diya*. If an offender is too poor to pay the *diya*, the family of the offender is called upon first to make good the *diya* for their kin. If the family is unable to pay, the community, clan or tribe may be required to pay. This concept is not found in common law or the civil law of most nations. It acts as a great incentive for family and community to teach responsible behavior. What happens to the debt if the offender dies and has not paid it? Historically, it was passed on to the offender's heirs; today, most nations terminate the debt if the offender left no inheritance.

One question that is often raised is "What happens if a victim takes the *diya* without government approval ?" The victim or family has committed a *Ta'zir* crime by accepting money which was not mandated by a judge: taking *diya* must be carried out through proper governmental and judicial authority.

Another concept of *Qisas* crimes is the area of punishment. Each victim has the right to ask for retaliation and, historically, the person's family would carry out that punishment. Modern Islamic law now requires the government to carry out the *Qisas* punishment. Historically, some grieving family member may have tortured the offender in the process of punishment. Now the government is the independent party that administers the punishment, because torture and extended pain is contrary to Islamic teachings and Sharia Law.

CONCLUSIONS

Contemporary treatment of Islamic Law and "Radical Muslims" is filled with stereotypical characterizations. Some in the Western media have used the "New York City bombings" as a way to increase hate and prejudice. They have taken the views of a few radicals and projected them onto all Muslims. This action has done a great disservice to the Muslim world. Some academic writings also have been distorted and not always completely accurate and some researchers have concluded that Islamic Law requires a fixed punishment for all crimes. These writers also have concluded that Islamic judges lack discretion in their sentences of defendants in the Sharia Court System. There are four *Had* crimes that do have fixed punishments set forth in the Quran, but not all the *Had* crimes are bound by mandatory punishment.

Islamic Law is very different from English Common Law or the European Civil Law traditions. Muslims are bound to the teachings of the Prophet Mohammed whose translation of Allah or God's will is found in the Quran. Muslims are held accountable to the Sharia Law, but non-Muslims are not bound by the same standard (apostasy from Allah). Muslims and non-Muslims are both required to live by laws enacted by the various forms of government such as tax laws, traffic laws, white collar crimes of business, and theft. These and many other crimes similar to Common Law crimes are tried in modern "Mazalim Courts." The Mazalim Courts can also hear civil law, family law and all other cases. Islamic Law does have separate courts for Muslims for "religious crimes" and contemporary non-religious courts for other criminal and civil matters.

ALGERIA

ALGERRIA INVESTMENT LAW

Executive decree No. 94-319

of 12 Joumada El-Ouma 1415 corresponding to 17 October 1994 pertaining to the functions, organisation and functioning of the agency for the promotion, support and follow-up of investment

TITLE I - NAME - OBJECT - HEADQUARTERS
TITLE II - ORGANISATION - MANAGEMENT - FUNCTIONING

Chapter 1 - BOARD OF DIRECTORS
Chapter 2 - THE DIRECTOR-GENERAL
Chapter 3 - THE ONE STOP FACILITY
Chapter 4 - MODALTIES OF GRANTING BENEFITS
Chapter 5 - FOLLOW-UP
Chapter 6 - APPEAL

TITLE III - FINANCIAL PROVISIONs
TITLE IV - SPECIAL PROVISIONS
TITLE V - MISCELLANEOUS PROVISIONS

TITLE I NAME - OBJECT - HEADQUARTERS

Article 1: In pursuance of the provisions of Article 7 of legislative decree No 93-12 of 5 October 1993 pertaining to investment promotion, the Agence de Promotion, de soutien et de suivi des investissements (APSI) (the Agency for the Promotion, Support and follow-up of Investments) hereinafter referred to as the "Agency" shall be a public, administrative establishment having the status of a corporate body and financial autonomy. The Agency shall be under the supervision of the Head of Government.

Article 2: The headquarters of the Agency shall be located in Algiers. It may be transferred to any other place within the country on the decision of the supervising authority.

Regional or local offices of the Agency shall be established throughout the country. The number, location and functions of such offices shall be decided on by the supervising authority on the proposal of the Director-General, after consultation with the Board of Directors of the Agency.

Article 3: The Agency shall operate in the field of investment and together with the administrations and bodies concerned:

- Support and assist investors within the framework of the implementation of their proposed investments;
- Promote investments;
- Decide, in application of the guidelines and criteria defined in the national economic policy, on the incentive package to be granted to investors within the context of legislative decree No 93-12 of 5 October 1993 mentioned above and regulation in force;
- Ensure that investors deliver on their commitments made to the administrations concerned.

Article 4: In this capacity, the Agency shall be responsible, among other things, for:

- Ensuring that investors are provided with all the economic, technical, legislative and regulatory informations relating to the exercise of their activities and to the modalities for the granting of the related benefits;
- Acknowledging receipt, in writing, of the investment proposal submitted by the investor and notifying him likewise in writing of the decision to grant or to refuse the benefits applied for;
- Assisting investors to complete the necessary formalities for making their investment by putting in place a "one-stop facility" in conformity with the provisions of Article 8 of the above-mentioned legislative decree No 93-12 of 5 October 1993;
- Acknowledging receipt, in writing, of investment proposals submitted by investors and notifying them likewise in writing of the decision either to grant or to refuse the benefits requested;
- Carrying out the required evaluation of investment proposals in order to formalise the decision to grant or to refuse the benefits requested by the investor;
- Publishing the decisions on investments that have been granted benefits;
- Identifying proposals of particular interest to the national economy by virtue of their size, the exceptional nature of the technology used, the high rate of technology transfer, high foreign exchange earnings or because of their long-term profitability, with a view to proposing the conclusion of an investment agreement to the Government in conformity with **Article 15:** of the above-mentioned legislative decree No 93-12 of 5 October 1993;
- Monitoring delivery by investors on commitments made with regard to realization of the investment;
- Working together with the concessionaires of export processing zones to coordinate activities in these zones;
- Enforcing all regulatory measures relating to investment;
- Ensuring that all decisions taken by the Agency affecting other administrations and bodies concerned with investment are binding on the latter and are executed accordingly.
- To carry out its functions, the Agency may:
- Set an expert groups to deal with specific issues relating to investment;
- Organise seminars, meetings, workshops and symposia on issues relating to its aims and objective;
- Maintain and develop co-operation with similar foreign agencies;
- Make use, in line with its objective, of all studies and data re ting to similar experiences in other countries.

The Agency shall be further obliged, within the limits of its functions, to report to or make proposals to the supervising authority on measures relating to the functioning, development and effectiveness of investment.

TITLE II ORGANISATION - MANAGEMENT - FUNCTIONING

Article 5: The Agency shall be governed by a board of directors chaired by the representative supervising authority.

Article 6: The organisation and rules of procedure of the Agency shall be proposed by the Director-General, adopted by the Board of Directors and enacted by decree of the supervising authority.

Chapter 1 BOARD OF DIRECTORS

Article 7: The Board of Directors shall comprise:

- The representative of the Ministry of Co-operation;
- The representative of the Ministry of the Interior and Local Government
- The representative of the Ministry in charge of the Budget;
- The representative of the Ministry in charge of Territorial Development;
- The representative of the Ministry in charge of Small-and Medium-sized Enterprises;
- The representative of the Ministry of Industry;
- The representative of the Banque d'Algérie (Central Bank);

- The President of the National Chamber of Commerce;
- The representative of professional and/or public employer's associations;
- The representative of professional and/or private employer's associations.

The office of the Director-General of the Agency shall serve as secretariat of the Board of Directors.

Article 8: The members of the Board of Directors and their alternate members shall be appointed by decree of the supervising authority on the proposal of the bodies to which they belong for a period of three years renewable.

Members of the Board of Directors shall have the rank, at least, Director of the central administration.

Representatives of professional and/or employer's associations all be designated in accordance with the statutory provisions governing their associations.

The mandate of members designated by virtue of their functions shall end when such functions cease. In case of interruption in the mandate of one of the members, his replacement shall be designated in the same way. The newly appointed member shall succeed the outgoing member until the end of his mandate.

Article 9: Administrators shall receive compensatory allowance for costs incurred in accordance with regulation in force.

Article 10: The Chairman of the Board of Directors shall convene a meeting at least once every three months.

The Board may also meet in special session, convened by the Chairman or on the proposal of two-thirds of its members, if the amount of dossiers to be considered or circumstances so demand.

Article 11: The Chairman of the Board shall be responsible for sending each member of the Board an invitation to the meeting together with the full agenda, 15 days prior to the date of the meeting.

The notice period may be reduced in the case of special sessions, but this should not be less than eight days.

Article 12: Deliberations of the Board of Directors can only proceed with a minimum of 2/3 two-thirds of its members present. If this quorum is not reached, the meeting shall be postponed and convened a second time when the Board shall meet whether the quorum is reached or not;

Decisions of the Board of Directors shall be made by majority vote of the members present.

In the case of a tie, the Chairman shall cast the deciding vote.

Article 13: Minutes of all deliberations of the Board of Directors shall be taken, numbered and listed in an ad hoc register and signed by the Chairman.

The minutes of the Board of Directors shall be transmitted to the supervising authority during the week after their adoption.

The deliberations shall be considered as approved one month after their transmission to the supervising authority, with the exception of those referred to in Article 39 of this decree.

Article 14: The Board of Directors shall deliberate among other things on:

- The draft rules of procedure;
- Adoption of the general work programme of the Agency;
- The draft budget and the accounts of the Agency;
- Acceptance of gifts and requests in conformity with laws and regulations in force;
- Plans for the purchase, assignment or exchange of real estate within the context of current regulation;
- Approval of the annual activity report as well as the administrative accounts.

The Board of Directors shall also deliberate on:

- The setting up of organs bound to sustain the Agency's investment activities;
- Analytical scales and schedules to be used for evaluating investment proposals submitted with a view to obtaining the benefits provided for in laws and regulations in force;
- Establishment of regional or local offices of the Agency.

CHAPTER 2 THE DIRECTOR-GENERAL

Article 15: The Director-General shall be appointed by executive decree, and shall be removed from office in the same manner.

The Director-General shall be assisted in his management duties by a Secretary-General, who shall have the rank of research director. He shall be appointed by executive decree on the proposal of the Director-General. He Shall be removed from office in the same manner.

Article 16: In the exercise of the duties of the Agency, the Director-General shall be assisted by research directors and directors appointed by executive decree. They shall be removed from office in the same manner.

Article 17: The Director-General shall be responsible for the functioning of the Agency within the framework of the provisions of this decree and the general rules on the administrative and financial management of public administrative establishments.

He shall administer all the departments of the Agency. He shall act on behalf of the Agency and shall appear for the Agency in the court of law and in all civil transactions.

He shall exercise hierarchical authority over all the staff of the Agency and shall make appointments for all posts for which an alternative mode of appointment is not provided for.

He shall be responsible for implementing decisions of the Board of Directors.

Article 18: The Director-General shall be empowered, after consultation with the Board of Directors, to set up any working or decision-making group, whose establishment in necessary for improving or strengthening the Agency's activity with regard to the promotion, support and follow-up of investment or evaluation of investment projects.

In this context, the Director-General may, if need be, call upon the services of local and foreign consultants and experts.

Article 19: The Director-General shall prepare a quarterly report for submission to the Board of Directors, indicating investment applications submitted and the decisions made to grant or to deny the benefits requested.

Article 20: The Director-General in entitled to organise the Agency's budget funds in accordance with laws and regulations in force.

Article 21: The Director-General shall conclude all transactions, agreements and contracts relating to the functions of his agency.

CHAPTER 3 THE ONE STOP FACILITY

Article 22: The one-stop facility referred to in Article 8, paragraph 2 of the legislative decree No 93-12 of 5 October 1993 mentioned above, shall comprise the offices of the Agency itself, as well as those of the customs administrations, the Banque d'Algérie, the Trade Registry, Land Registry, taxes, territorial development, environment, employment and the office of the Municipality of the Agency's headquarters.

With the exception of the submission of the investment proposal and the application for benefits, requests for one-stop services shall be up to investors themselves.

Article 23: The representatives of the ministries and bodies that are part of the one-stop facility shall be duly and mandated to provide administrative services directly within the facility.

The Agency shall provide on behalf of the relevant administrations the documents legally required for carrying out the investment, within a maximum period of 60 days from the date of deposit of the investment proposal and application for benefits.

Article 24: The documents issued by the Agency shall be opposable to all the relevant administrations.

Article 25: The officials of the one-stop facility as well as their alternate members shall be appointed by decree of the Agency's supervising authority on the proposal of the administration or body which they represent.

They shall be duty bound to respect the rules procedure of the Agency and its rules of general discipline.

Officials of the one-stop facility shall receive the current allowance within the Agency when the latter is higher than what pertains in their original administrations and bodies.

Article 26: The Director-General of the Agency may take all practical and organisational measures necessary for the functioning of the one-stop facility, including those aimed at making it easier for investors to fulfil the requirements for and obtain the legally required documents within the stipulated time limit.

In this connection, he may also consult any administration or body concerned in one way or another with the investment.

CHAPTER IV MODALTIES OF GRANTING BENEFITS

Article 27: The benefits provided for in the schemes enacted in the legislative decree No 93-12 of 5 October 1993 referred to above shall be granted on the decision of the Agency after preliminary evaluation of proposals by the Agency's departments on the basis of the analytical scales and schedules approved by the Agency's Board of Directors.

Article 28: The scales and schedules of analysis shall be drawn up in accordance with criteria established in reference to the economic policy on investment, and published in the official bulletin of legal notices.

Article 29: The decisions to grant or to deny the benefits shall appear in a report from the Director-General to the supervising authority and the members of the Board of Directors within a maxi mum period of eight days from the date the decision is made.

A decision shall be made on all investment proposals in accordance with Article 11 of the legislative decree No 93-12 of 5 October 1993 mentioned above, signed by the Director-General of the Agency and delivered to the investor within a maximum period of 60 days from the date of deposit of the investment proposal and the application for benefits.

CHAPTER V FOLLOW-UP

Article 30: Follow-up of the investments as envisaged in Article 46 of the legislative decree No 93-12 of 5 October 1993 above shall consist of:

1. In the case of the investor: ensuring that he/she meets no obstacles in making his investment and assist him/her, if need be, in his/her dealings with the administrations and bodies concerned in one way or another with the implementation of the investment.

2. In the case of the public authorities: ensuring respect of the rules and reciprocal commitments made with the investor in exchange for the benefits granted.

Article 31: The follow-up of investments that have been granted the said benefits shall be carried out by the competent departments of the Agency duly authorised for that purpose, together with the administrations which are responsible for monitoring adherence to the terms on which the benefits were granted.

Article 32: For the purpose of following up the investment, the investor who has been granted benefits shall be bound to submit an annual progress report on his commitments to the Agency in the format attached hereto.

This status report may include any other information relating to implementation of the investment.

CHAPTER VI APPEAL

Article 33: The appeal referred to in Article 9 (paragraph 2) of legislative decree No. 93-12 of 5 October 1993 shall be addressed to the Head of government in writing, signed by the investor and sent by mail and an acknowledgement of receipt obtained.

The said appeal shall be accompanied by the Agency's decision which is the subject of the appeal and any other documentary evidence against this decision.

Article 34: The above-mentioned appeal shall be introduced, among other things, in the case of refusal of the benefits requested; granting of an exemption period less than that requested; granting of an incentive me other than that which was requested; or failure of the Agency to reply within the established maximum timeframe of 60 days.

Article 35: If the Head of Government upholds the appeal made by the investor, the Agency shall immediately communicate to the investor the decision to grant the benefits requested.

Should the appeal be overruled, the Agency's decision shall be as final and shall not be susceptible of recourse in conformity with the provisions of Article 9 of legislative decree No 93-12 of 5 October 1993.

Article 36: The investor and the Agency shall be notified of the decision of the Head of Government within a maximum period of 15 days from the date of receipt of the appeal.

TITLE ILL FINANCIAL PROVISIONS

Article 37: The draft budget of the Agency, prepared by the Director-General, shall be submitted, after approval by the Board of Directors, for approval to the supervising authority and to the Minister of Finance.

Article 38: The Agency's budget shall consist of one heading for income and another for expenditure

Income shall comprise:

- Equipment and operating subsidies granted by the State, local governments or public bodies or establishments;
- Subsidies from international bodies, after authorisation by the authorities concerned;
- Grants and requests;
- Income generated from services rendered in connection with its object;
- Miscellaneous income;

Expenditure shall comprise:

- Operating expenditure;
- Equipment expenditure.

Article 39: The administrative accounts and the annual activity report for the year ended shall be sent to the supervising authority, the Minister of Finance as well as to the State Audit office.

Article 40: In his capacity as the person authorised to pass accounts, the Director-General shall commit or make expenditure within the limit of credits planned for in the Agency's budget and keep a record of income to the Agency.

Article 41: Keeping of the books and handling of funds shall be assigned to an accountant appointed by the Minister of Finance who will carry out his/her duties in conformity with applicable regulation.

Article 42: The Agency's accounts shall be kept in conformity with the rules of public accounting.

Article 43: Preliminary auditing of the expenditure of the Agency shall be carried out, under conditions laid down by legislation and regulation in force, by a financial controller appointed for that purpose by the Minister of Finance.

TITLE IV SPECIAL PROVISIONS

Article 44: The function of Director-General of the Agency shall be remunerated and ranked in reference to the senior public office of the "official representative" attached to the Head of Government.

Article 45: The functions of Research Director and Agency Director shall be remunerated and ranked in reference to the senior public office of Research Director and Director within the departments under the Head of Government.

Article 46: The positions of Head of Department at the Agency shall be remunerated and ranked in reference to the senior public office of Deputy Director within the departments under the Head of Government.

Article 47: The other staff who are needed for the functioning of the Agency shall be determined, if need be, by joint decision of the Minister of Finance and the authority responsible for the civil service.

Article 48: The Agency personnel shall enjoy the same allowance scheme existing within the departments under the Head of Government.

TITLE V MISCELLANEOUS PROVISIONS

Article 49: The Director-General of the Agency may, after having consulted the Board of Directors and the supervising authority, conclude any agreements or contracts, in line with the Agency's objective, with national or foreign bodies.

Article 50: In conformity with Article 10 of legislative decree no 93-12 of 5 October 1993, the decision of the Agency shall be published in the official bulletin of legal notices.

The decision to grant benefits shall stipulate the following about the investor:

- Corporate name;
- Address of headquarters;
- Status of the enterprise;
- Branch of activity envisaged by the project in question;
- Main activities envisaged;
- The benefits scheme granted;
- Duration of the benefits granted;
- Investor's obligations.

Article 51: All provision contrary to the present decree are hereby abrogated, particularly executive decree No 91-131 of 11 May 1991.

Article 52: The present decree shall be published in the Gazette of the Democratic People's Republic of Algeria.

Done in Algiers on 14 Joumada El-Oula 1415 corresponding to 17 October 1994.

BAHRAIN

ESTABLISHMENT & ORGANISATION OF INDUSTRIAL ESTATE LAW

In Pursuance of the constitution. Amiri Order No. (4) for 1975, Decree-Law No. (7) for 1970 with respect of the Provisional Law of the Organisation and Development of Land,

Decree-Law No. (13) for 1977 with respect to the Regulation of Building, as amended,

Decree-Law No. (18) for 1983 with respect to the Requirement for Owners of Land to Incur the Expenses of the Reclamation of Their Land,

Decree-Law No. (6) for 1984 with respect to the Regulation of Industry,

Decree-Law No. (11) for 1985 with respect to the Support and Protection of National Industries, as amended

Decree-Law No. (6) for 1989 with respect to the Protection of Industries of National Origin,

Decree-Law No. (9) for 1994 with respect to the Issue of the International Business Arbitration Law,

Decree-Law No. (2) for 1994 with respect to Urban Planning and the Implementation Regulations thereof,

Decree-Law No. (16) for 1996 with respect to the Regulation of Governorates,

Decree-Law No. (21) for 1996 with respect to the Environment,

Decree No. (23) for 1997 with respect to the Reorganisation of the Ministry of Oil and Industry.

(Cabinet Resolution No. (3) for 1998 with respect to the Specification of the Regulatory Conditions for Construction Throughout Bahrain, and In accordance with recommendation by the Minister of Oil and Industry, Consulting Shura Council, and after the approval of. Cabinet Council

WE HEREBY enact the following Law:

CHAPTER ONE DEFINITIONS

Article 1

In this Law, except where the context otherwise requires, the following terms shall have the meanings duly assigned to each of them:

"the Ministry", means the Ministry of Oil & Industry.

"the Minister", means the Minister of Oil & Industry.

"the Authorities concerned", means the Ministries or other authorities concerned with the development of industrial area and the provision of such Area with services and utilities.

"Industrial Areas Directorate", means the organisation entrusted with implementation of this Law within the implementation rules, regulation and instructions issued by the Minister.

"Industrial Areas", means the areas, including the land, the installations and the utilities erected thereon, which are allocated for industrial purposes and which are defined by a resolution of the Cabinet the recommendation of the Minister.

"Industrial, Craft & Related Activities", means the activities defined by a decision of the Minister.

"Movable and Immovable Industrial Installations", means the Installations erected in the industrial Areas under statutory terms and conditions.

"Industrial Area Committee", means the Committee set up under the provisions of this Law and the Implementation regulations thereof.

CHAPTER TWO ESTABLISHMENT OF INDUSTRIAL AREAS

Article 2

Industrial areas shall be established and defined by a Prime Ministerial Edict on a recommendation of the Minister, in co-ordination with the authorities concerned.

Article 3

The industrial areas shall be divided into two sub-areas and the sub-areas into plots. Such division shall be pursuant to the provisions of Cabinet of Resolution No. (3) of 1998 with respect to the Specification of the Regulatory regulations thereof. An investor may be allocated with the necessary plot of land in the light of the estimation by Industrial Areas Directorate based on the relevant study submitted.

Article 4

Maps in the scales determined by the implementation regulation of this Law shall be made. The maps shall define the boundaries of the industrial areas, the sub-areas, the plots within each area, the space occupied by installations indicating the required service facilities, development plans and the reclamation required of such Lands.

Article 5

The industrial areas shall be utilised for the Industrial, craft and other activities related to industry as may be determined by a decision of the Minister. An investor shall undertake to commence his project for which a licence has been issued within a year from receiving the plot. Implementation, however, shall be in accordance with the specifications, conditions and drawings on the basis of which the licence has been issued. Under no circumstances shall, without prior written consent of the Ministry, the investor change or alter his approved project.

Article 6

The Ministry, in co-operation with the authorities concerned, will be responsible for the management of and investment in the industrial areas.

Article 7

The Industrial Areas Directorate shall maintain appropriate records of the industrial lands as may be specified by the implementation regulations. Any person concerned may have access to the maps and records and may have true copies thereof after paying the fees determined by a decision of the Minister upon approval of the Cabinet.

Article 8

Industrial Lands granted to an investor will not be cancelled or reallocated nor may any industrial installation and equipment thereon be acquired without a Cabinet Resolution and against payment of fair compensation to the investor.

CHAPTER THREE UTILISATION OF INDUSTRIAL AREAS

Article 9

There shall be set up in the Ministry and Industrlal Areas Committee which shall be responsible for the various affairs of the industrial areas, including the supervision of the implementation of construction or expansion plans. Such responsibility shall be exercised in the manner set forth in this Law and in implementation regulations.
The committee shall be formed by a decision of the Minister which decision shall form the Committee and shall specify the functions and the terms of reference thereof.

Article 10

The utilisation of land in the industrial areas shall be effectived by a decision of the Minister on the recommendation of the Industrial Areas Committee. Such utilisation shall be under the terms and conditions set forth in the implementation regulations hereof. The rent of and industrial plot shall be effective only from the day the land is delivered to the lessee. Article

Article 11

Applications for industrial plots shall be made on the forms specifically designed by the Industrial Areas Directorate at the Ministry. Application's must be forward with supporting documents. The Industrial Areas Directorate shall, after examining the documents, refer the applications for industrial plots to the Industrial Areas Committee. The Industrial Areas Committee shall, within a period of thirty days from the date of such referral, consider the applications and issue its recommendations in the respect of each application and forward it to the minister for approval or rejection of such applications.

Article 12

Entrepreneurs may apply for provisional reservation of industrial plots against a monthly charge determined by a decision of the Minister. However, such reservation may not exceed three months, extendable for a similar period once only. An application for reservation shall become invalid at the end of such period should no licence have been obtained.
The implementation regulations shall specify the reservation procedure, conditions and the monthly charge. A special register shall be maintained for the purpose of reservation and priority thereto. The form and details to be entered in register records shall be specified in the implementation regulations.

Article 13

Banks or investment institutions and companies may, upon the approval of the Industrial Areas Committee be permitted to construct industrial complexes at the Industrial Areas for rental to private sector investors. The implementation regulations shall specify the terms and conditions for the construction of such complexes and the manner in which they may be invested.

Article 14

The land located within the industrial areas is Government property and shall be utilised in the manner specified herein.
No natural of juristic person may possess or otherwise acquire any property within the industrial areas save under provisions of this Law
Any act of disposal or determination of any right in rem in contrary to the provisions of this law shall deem to be null and void and may not be notarised.

Article 15

The utilisation of the industrial areas shall be by leasing subject to this Law and in accordance with the terms and conditions specifies in the implementation regulations.
The lease agreement of such areas shall be concluded through the Industrial Areas Directorate at the Ministry on the forms specifically made under the provisions of the implementation regulations.
A lease agreement must provide for the referral of and dispute arising therefrom for arbitration with the consent of both parties.
The Minister, where required, may conclude lease agreement of special terms within the provisions of the implementation regulations.
The implementation regulations shall specify the formula to be used in assessing the rent of such industrial plots, the duration of lease, manner in which the rent is payable, restraints in respect of lease agreements of special terms and any other leasing terms.
Under no circumstances shall the duration of a lease be more than (50) years unless otherwise agreed.

The Minister may issue provisional licences for the utilisation of industrial plots for an extendable period of one year for the purposes and under the terms and conditions specified in the implementation regulations.
Except for provisional licences, the lease agreements must be registered with the Notarisation Office at the Ministry of Justice & Islamic Affairs.
The lessee shall pay the notarisation fees.

Article 16

Subject to the provisions of Decree-Law No. (7) for 1970 with respect to the Provisional Law, of the Organisation and Development of Land, and Decree Law No. (18) for 1983 with respect to the Requirement for Owners of Land to incur the Expenses of the Reclamation of Their Land, the Minister may exempt a lessee from the rent for an appropriate period if it is established that the lessee had reclaimed or improved his land in the manner approved by the technical committees concerned.

Article 17

The Ministry may, on a temporary basis, exempt lessees from the rent for the purpose of encouraging certain types of industries. Such exemption shall be under the terms and conditions specified in the implementation regulations. Such exemption shall be effected only from the date of production.

Article 18

The land with plots shall be delivered to a lessee pursuant to the provisions hereof, together with the relevant easements, without any right of claim of compensations for such easements.

Article 19

Rentals payable to the Government in respect to property subject to the provisions hereof shall have lien and priority over any other preference save excluding those wages and benefits payable to workers arising from employment contracts and judicial expenses and fees.

Article 20

A lessee shall undertake to procure comprehensive insurance coverage for his installations. Such insurance must be in his favour or in favour of those who have rights therein. It shall be established to the Industrial Areas Directorate that such insurance has been made and that the lessee is in regular payment of the insurance premiums.

Article 21

A lessee may, with the consent of the Ministry, assign the lease to a third party. However, the lessor shall remain jointly liable with the lessee for and financial obligations prior to such assignment.
The industrial plots may not be subleased without the written approval of the Ministry.
The occupation of property by a subsidiary, for change in corporate entity, expansion or merger with another organisations, shall not be deemed to be subleasing. In all circumstances, any assignment, lease or sublease shall be effective against the Ministry of a third party only from the date of registration of such transaction with the Notarisation Office at the Ministry of Justice & Islamic Affairs.

CHAPTER FOUR CONSTRUCTION IN INDUSTRIAL AREAS

Article 22

No movable or immovable industrial installations may be constructed in the areas subject to the provisions hereof except with permission from the authorities concerned after approval of the Ministry, subject the terms and conditions specified in the implementation regulations.

Article 23

No demolition, alteration or improvement may be made to and industrial installation without the written consent of the Industrial Areas Directorate and in subject to the Building Regulation Law and its implementation regulations.

Article 24

Special buildings for use as warehouses and showrooms for the relevant industrial project products may by constructed in the industrial areas.
No residential buildings for workers may by constructed, However, the Industrial Areas Committee may exceptionally allow the construction of such buildings in respect of certain projects of a special nature, as set forth in the implementation regulations.
A lessee who is permitted to construct such buildings shall abide by the special decisions with respect to the conditions governing the obtainment of permits for demolition and construction on such plots and by the conditions of construction under the Building Regulations Law.

Article 25

Buildings constructed as industrial installations, for workers, residence of for the display of products shall be subject to the regulatory requirements for construction in industrial Areas as provided for in Resolution No. (3) for 1998 with respect to the Specification of the Regulatory Conditions for Construction Throughout Bahrain.

CHAPTER FIVE OBLIGATIONS AND RIGHTS OF INDUSTRIAL AREAS LESSEES

Article 26

A lessee of industrial plots shall undertake to:

pay the prescribed rent on time Repeated failure to observe this obligations, may lead to asking for a deposit in cash equivalent to the rent for a period not exceeding one year after the settlement of any outstanding

rents;
construct a fence and erect direction signs at the entrance as provided for in the implantation regulations;
provide car parking spaces and landscaping compatible with the purposed of the project. The implementation regulations shall specify the areas required for each project and the specifications of car parking spaces;
maintain the installations and the land in question. The Ministry, where required, may interfere to enforcing such maintenance and repairs and may appoint appropriate experts to perform such repairs. The Ministry, in case of necessity, may also request the Courts of Instant Matters to require the lessee concerned or to permit the Ministry to carry out such repairs at the lessee's expense and to recover such expenses in the manner provided for herein;
commence the construction of installations within the period specified in the lease agreement and to complete such construction and supply equipment within the time schedule predicated by the lessee and approved by the Ministry;
remove debris regularly and abide by the Environment Law; and, Abide by the rules and regulations of occupational health and safety within his installations.

Article 27

Any natural resources such as petroleum, natural gas, underground water, etc. emerging from or thought to be hidden under and industrial plot, shall be the property of the Government. Where the Government interferes to exploit such natural resources, the lessee shall be indemnified for any loss, partly or wholly, resulting from inability to exercise his usufruct. The lessee may, with special permission from the Ministry, utilise the natural quarry resources within his leased land for the purposed of the construction of his project areas against the charge levied for similar quarries in the state of Bahrain.

Article 28

The Industrial Areas Committee may, in its own discretion or at the request of a lessee, reserve adjacent plots for future expansion or for and industrial integration with other projects. Such reservation shall be subject to a charge and for the duration required for the land to remain reserved for the purpose.

Article 29

No industrial area investor shall bury underground or throw at seashores, roads, squares or in front of any public or private building or allow the leakage of any of the following materials:

debris of building destruction or any other industrial waste;
discharge of sewers, rubbish or and other material that is inflammable, toxic or detrimental to health.

Article 30

A lessee, where justifiable, may request that his plot be replaced.
The implementation regulatory shall specify the conditions and procedure for such replacement.

Article 31

In the event of any lessee being declared bankrupt , the Ministry may request that the lease agreement be terminated. The trustee of the bankruptcy may chose to terminate or carry on with the lease agreement. If it is decided by the trustee to continue with the agreement then he shall pay any rental arrears and give a sufficient guarantee for the payment of any future rents. Where such a guarantee is insufficient, the Ministry, within fifteen days from being notified of the trustee's desire to continue with the agreement, may request the Court to terminate the lease agreement.

CHAPTER SIX PENALTIES

Article 32

The lease agreement of plots shall be terminated in the following circumstances:

If the lessee fails to pay the rent or refrain from procuring the insurance coverage provided for in Article (26) (i) here of.
If the lessee, without any reason acceptable to the industrial areas Committee, fails to commence construction of the licensed project within one year from the date of receiving the plot.
If the lessee, without any reason acceptable to the Industrial Areas Committee, suspends work in the installation for a period of one year.
If the lessee, after being warned, has used the land for purposed other than those allocated thereto.
If, without the approval of the Ministry, the lessee has subleased the land, assigned the rent thereof or mortgaged any right in rem.
If the lessee dies before the termination date of the lease agreement and his heirs or any one of them does not desire to continue the agreement with the Ministry.
If the duration of the lease agreement expires without being renewed. The termination of the agreement and the evacuation of the lessee from the property shall be effected by a decision of the Minister on recommendation of the Industrial Areas Committee. The lessee may appeal against such decision before the Civil High Court within a period of not exceeding forty-five days from the date of serving the Minister's decision by registered letter with recorded delivery.

Unless otherwise agreed, the Ministry, in the event of the cancellation or termination of the agreement without being extended, may maintain the buildings and installations against compensations to the lessee, to be determined in accordance with the relevant formulas prescribed in the implementation regulations.

Article 33

Subject to the provisions of Article (32) of this law, if the Ministry finds no justification for terminating the agreement, the Minister may, by administrative procedure, order the closure of the installation for a period not exceeding three months.

CHAPTER SEVEN GENERAL

Article 34

The Minister may, be a decision, authorise certain staff of the Industrial Areas Directorate to have access to the industrial areas for the purposes of inspection and of ensuring that the provisions of this Law and any decisions issued in implementation thereof are properly enforced. Such staff shall be authorised to record andy contravention to the provisions of this Law and make the appropriate reports in this respect. Reports of this nature will be forwarded to the Industrial Areas Committee for review and for recommending and appropriate action to the Minister.

Article 35

The Minister of Oil & Industry shall issue the implementation regulations and the necessary decision required for the enforcement of this Law.

INVESTMENT INCENTIVES

The Bahraini government actively promotes foreign investment and, in recent years, has promulgated regulations permitting 100 percent foreign ownership of new industrial establishments and for the establishment of representative offices or branches of foreign companies without local sponsors. Most other commercial investments, however, are subject to government approval and generally must be made in partnership with a Bahraini national controlling 51 percent of the equity. Foreign nationals are not permitted to purchase land in Bahrain with certain exceptions made for GCC nationals. The government encourages the employment of local nationals by setting local-national employment targets in each sector and by restricting the issuance of expatriate labor permits.

Investment Incentives Applying to Both Foreign and Bahraini Firms

The Government of Bahrain, in recent years, introduced an industrial incentive program for private companies to employ locals and special measures to support new and existing small and medium-sized industries. These incentives include:

- ***Labor***: A subsidy of US$ 11,925 per year for the first three years, for each Bahraini employed by companies setting up factories in pioneering industries; US$ 7,950 per year for downstream industries, and US$ 2,650 per year for companies setting up factories in existing industries.
- ***Electricity Charges***: A 50 percent rebate for the first five years in all industries.
- ***Land Rental***: A 100 percent rebate of rental fees in Government industrial areas for the first five years, for all industries.
- ***Customs Duties***: A 100 percent rebate of customs duties for the first five years, for all industries.
- ***Export Credit Facility***: Available to all industries.
- ***Tariff Protection***: Subject to the approval of the National Committee on Tariff Protection, 10 to 20 percent protection may be given to pioneering downstream industries.

AGREEMENTS

The Basic Statute of the Gulf Cooperation Council (GCC) was signed in 1981 and the signatories thereto are Saudi Arabia, Oman, Kuwait, the United Arab Emirates, Qatar and Bahrain. The GCC aims to attain cooperation in all fields, to draw up comparable legislation in finance, trade, education, health, tourism and administration, to establish research centers and to encourage scientific development in industry. The ministers from the GCC countries are cooperating with a view towards unifying customs tariffs, establishing a regional stock market and allowing Gulf companies to open representative offices in other Member States.

The Uniform Economic Agreement was executed on 11 November 1981. It sets out various objectives which are to be realized by domestic legislation in the Member States. The Agreement deals with the free movement of goods within the Member States and exemption of goods from customs and other duties imposed by States on imports. It contemplates uniform customs tariffs for goods entering the area of the GCC from outside. It also deals in general terms with the issue of free movement of workers between Member States, leaving the practical realization of these goals to separate legislation to be agreed upon by Member States. The Agreements also cover development programs, oil policy, scientific policy and cooperation on technology transfer agreements with third parties.

The Member States have formed a customs union and have adopted a unified customs schedule based on the Brussels Tariff Nomenclature, the international standard for the classification of goods for customs.

CUSTOMS

Bahrain is, in some respects, a free port. There is no regulation restricting foreign trade with the exception that all goods imported into or exported from Bahrain must comply with certain requirements. Anyone wishing to import goods into Bahrain for sale or consumption must obtain a general license from the Customs and Ports Directorate of the Ministry of Finance and National Economy.

Customs duties are levied only on goods imported for sale in Bahrain. The rates of duty include the following: 5 percon foodstuffs and non-luxuries; 10 percent on general luxuries; 20 percent on vehicles; 50 percent on cigarettes and tobacco; and 125 percent on alcoholic drinks.

The Government of Bahrain permits the duty-free importation of raw material inputs for incorporation into products for export and the duty-free importation of equipment and machinery for newly established export industries. Except under special license, the private importation of weapons is generally prohibited, and only one private company is authorized to import explosives. The Government of Bahrain provides indirect export subsidies in the form of preferential rates for electricity, water and natural gas to select industrial establishments.

Imported and exported goods are classified according to the Standard International Trade Classification (SITC), Revision 1.

INVESTMENT AND PRIVATIZATION REGULATIONS

PRIVATIZATION

Privatization as a tool for reducing government expenditure, turning around unprofitable state-owned businesses and encouraging investment locally is an up-and-coming reality in the Gulf States including Bahrain. In the Gulf, privatization is often used to fund new developments of needed infrastructure, i.e., the use of private sector funding for new projects that, in the past, would have been commissioned and paid for by the government from its public sector account. This is in contrast to the approach known in Western countries as the "selling-off" of State assets.

In order to implement the "project-financing" approach, privatization regulation tends to develop through contractual negotiation rather than through comprehensive legislation, as it would be difficult to legislate in a manner that would suit the varied characteristics of financed projects. As a result, regulatory systems for privatized infrastructure projects in the Gulf region are relatively *ad hoc*, based on regulation mechanisms set forth in individually negotiated contract documentation.

A challenge facing the privatization process is the conflict between the realization of the benefits awarded by privatization and the past policy and culture of protecting one's own. In the not too distant past, only GCC nationals were permitted to trade freely in Bahrain. Non-GCC nationals were restricted to investing in four main financial houses. Restrictions on foreign investment and participation are gradually being relaxed. In 1994, Bahrain allowed non-GCC investors access to its markets provided they had a history of at least three-years residency in Bahrain. This requirement has been modified to one year, and it is expected that it will soon be lifted entirely thereby allowing all non-residents access to Bahrain's financial markets. A continuing restriction still hampering foreign participation in privatization schemes is the statutory limitation on foreign ownership by individuals of Bahraini companies' capital.

INVESTMENT OPPORTUNITIES

Bahrain is rapidly approving new industrial projects in an attempt to diversify its production base. During the first three months of 1996 alone, the Oil and Industry Ministry approved sixteen new projects worth US$ 16 million. Additional projects valued at US$ 14.5 million were approved in principle and are currently waiting for final licenses.

During 1996, approved projects include a US$ 600 million power and water plant, a port and a bridge to connect the new industrial and free trade zone area at Hidd with Bahrain's Salman Port. Additionally, a number oflocal and international banks have committed to finance a major portion of a proposed sponge iron plant, and the Korean conglomerate Hyundai is in negotiations to establish a pipe unit.

BUILD OPERATE TRANSFER

Use of the build-operate-transfer (BOT) method on power and water schemes was under active consideration during 1995-1996, but due to a dispute with the potential provider, the government decided against the project. Instead, the government will remain a buffer between the provider and the population, buying the water from the private operator and then passing it on to the consumer. The government intends to maintain subsidies, and, thus, expectations that the injection of private sector competition would expose true costs, push up tariffs and push down budget deficits are unlikely to remain realized.

FRANCHISING

Fast food franchises are highly sought after by local contacts. Many of the major food franchise companies are operating presently in Bahrain. There is also an increasing interest in non-food, service-sector franchises with proven international attractiveness. A local sponsor is required to set up a franchise in Bahrain.

BEST INVESXTMENT PROSPECTS

Rank	Sector
1	Electrical Power Systems
2	Water Resources Equipment / Services
3	Port / Shipbuilding Equipment
4	Automotive Products
5	Airport / Ground Support Equipment
6	Telecommunications Equipment and Services
7	Computer Products
8	Oil Support and Exploration Equipment
9	Air Conditioning / Refrigeration Equipment
10	Furniture

LEGISLATIVE DECREE NO. 6 FOR 1984 RESPECTING THE ORGANISATION OF INDUSTRY

CHAPTER ONE
INDUSTRIAL LICENCES

Article 1

For the purposes of enforcing this Act, an industrial establishment is defined as every establishment having the principal objects of converting raw materials into fully manufactured or semi manufactured products or turning the latter products into fully manufactured products. This shall also include the blending, assembly, packing or packaging of products through the use of mechanical power.

Article 2

It shall not be permitted to set up or manage and industrial establishment to which the provisions of this Act apply or to enlarge it, to move it or alter its principal objects except after obtaining a licence from the Ministry of Development and industry, in which he shall specify the terms and conditions under which the licence is granted.

Article 3

As from the effective date of this Act. the licences referred to in the preceding Article shall not be granted except to Bahraini persons and companies incorporated in accordance with the provisions of the Commercial Companies Law.

Non-Bahrainis who own industrial establishments existing on the effective date of this Act shall satisfy the conditions provided for in this Article by obtaining a licence according to the provisions of this Act during the period set forth in Article 15, otherwise, they shall be required to liquidate their business activities within two years form the effective date of this Act.

Article 4

An application for a Licence shall be filled with the Directorate of Industry at the Ministry of Development and Industry on the form to be prescribed by order of the Minister of Development and Industry accompanied by such necessary drawings and documents evidencing the validity of the details required under the terms of the resolutions to be issued for the implementation of this Act. If the applicant is an already established company such company shall provide evidence of its incorporation in accordance with the provisions of the Commercial Companies Law.

Article 5

The Ministry of Development and Industry shall, upon the recommendations of the Directorate of Industry, make a decision on the application for the licence referred to in Article 2 within sixty days from the date of filling the application and completing all documents and studies relating thereto.

Article 6

Subject to the conditions to made by any other government authority with the intention of preserving security, public health and environment, the Minister of Development and Industry shall by ministerial resolutions determine the conditions applicable to each type of such establishments.

Article 7

The Directorate of industry may introduce technical modifications it deems fit to the drawings and specifications before issuing the licence. The applicant shall be bound to effect such modifications at its own expenses on the specified date. If one year elapses from the specified date without effecting the said modifications, the applicant shall be deemed to have relinquished his application.

Article 8

A licence issued for an establishment shall specify a period of time for commencing execution of the works, which period shall not be more than one year and may be extended by a resolution from the Minister of Development and industry for such period as he deems fit at the request of the applicant concerned should the latter give acceptable reasons for the delay.

Article 9

For issuing a licence, the following shall be taken into consideration:

a. The country's economic needs and the possibility of local consumption and export.
b. Requirements of the Country's development programmes.
c. The objects of the establishment shall not be contrary to public order or public interest.
d. The capacity of the local market as regards the setting up of an establishment similar to existing establishments.
e.

Article 10

No modifications shall be made to licensed establishment without the consent of the Ministry of Development and Industry. An example of such modifications shall include everything affecting the establishments facilities whether inside or outside the establishment, or the method of operating its machinery, or the kind of know-how used therein, method of manufacture, addition of a new activity or increasing the mechanical power used.

Article 11

In case of sale, lease of assignment of all or part of the establishment and in the case of fully or partially ceasing to operate, the person concerned shall be bound to give notice thereof to the Ministry of Development and industry stating the reasons for the situation. Failure to comply with such procedures shall result in depriving the establishment of all or some the privileges granted by the State to such industrial establishment.

Article 12

The Minster of Development and Industry may, upon a recommendation from the Undersecretary of the Ministry of Development and Industry, terminate any industrial licence or close the establishment by an administrative order at the occurance of the following events.

a. Setting up, expanding, relocating or altering the principal objectives of an industrial establishment without a licence.
b. Cessation of the establishments operations for one year without justifiable reasons.

c. Notifying the Directorate of Industry by a registered letter of the desire of the establishments proprietor to cease the operations of the establishment.
d. Demolition of the establishment premises, even if they are rebuilt.
e. Modification of the establishment without obtaining the consent of the Ministry of Development and Industry.
f. Contravening the conditions of the licence.
g. Failure to start construction within the period specified in the licence.

Cancellation of the licence pursuant to the events referred to in this Article shall not prevent the person concerned from seeking the issuance of a new licence should the conditions thereof be fulfilled.

Article 13

An applicant for a licence or a licensee shall have the right to appeal against the decision rejecting his application for a licence, cancellation thereof or closure of the establishment before the High Civil Court within sixty days from the date of notifying it/him of such decision.

Article 14

The provisions of this Chapter shall apply to the industrial establishments which are specified by the Minister of Development and Industry's resolutions.

Article 15

Industrial establishments already in existence on the effective date of this Act shall, within 3 months from its coming into effect, apply to the Ministry of Development and Industry for the registration thereof in accordance with the required terms and conditions.

CHAPTER TWO
INDUSTRIAL REGISTRY

Article 16

A Registry shall be established at the Ministry of Development and Industry for the registration of various types of industrial establishment which are subject to the provisions of this Act.

Article 17

Proprietors of establishments which are subject to the provisions of this Act shall apply to the Ministry of Development and Industry for registration in the Industrial Registry within two months from the date of commencing actual production, and such Registration shall be renewed within thirty days after the elapse of one year from the date of registration or the last renewal thereof.

The Executive Regulations shall determine the particulars to be recorded in the aforesaid Registry and the requirements of applications for registration and renewal and manner of filling them.

Article 18

The Ministry of Development and Industry shall deliver to the establishment a certificate of registration with the Industrial Registry, renewal of registration or altering particulars thereof within 30 days from filling an application and completing its particulars.

Article 19

Proprietors of industrial establishment and officers responsible for the management thereof shall notify the Ministry of Development and Industry in writing of any alteration to the particulars registered in the Industrial Registry within 90 days from the date of such alteration subject to the terms and conditions to be determined by the Executive Regulations.

Article 20

In the event of contravening the provisions of Articles 17 and 19, the Minister of Development and Industry may, upon a recommendation from the Directorate of Industry, close the establishment by an administrative order.

Article 21

An establishment shall be struck off the Registry in any of the following events:

a. Upon an application from a concerned party owing to the liquidation thereof.
b. If it finally ceases production.
c. Issuance of a judicial decree for the removal thereof.

Article 22

A concerned party may appeal to the Minister of Development and Industry against the decisions taken pursuance of the provisions of this Chapter within 60 days from his notification of the decision appealed against.

Article 23

A committee shall be formed by a resolution from the Minister of Development and Industry, he membership of which may include representatives from relevant ministries and other governmental departments. The said committee shall be responsible for deciding on the appeals referred to it by the Minister of Development and Industry pursuant to the preceding Article. The committee shall decide on the appeal within 60 days from the date of reference thereof and its decision shall be supported by reasons. Once confirmed by the Minister of Development and Industry, the committee's decisions shall be final, and the appellant shall be notified in writing of the committee's confirmed decision. The Executive Regulations shall determine the committee's terms of reference and the procedures to be followed for handling the appeals.

Article 24

A person whose appeal has been dismissed may re-appeal against the resolution dismissing his appeal before the High Civil Court within 60 days from the date of receiving notice of the said resolution.

Article 25

The Ministry of Development and Industry shall publish a statistical bulletin for the registered industrial establishments. The bulletin shall contain particulars determined by Executive Regulations.

Article 26

The Ministry of Development and Industry shall register the industrial establishments the proprietors of which have failed to apply for registration thereof with the industrial registry and shall update and alter the particulars contained in the said Registry.

Article 27

Save for the particulars contained in the statistical bulletin provided for in Article 26 :

a. The officers in charge of enforcing the provisions of this Act shall maintain the confidentiality of the particulars contained in the Industrial Registry.
b. Third parties may obtain registration certificate of the particulars contained in the Industrial Registry pursuant to a resolution from the Minister of Development and Industry to that effect.

CHAPTER THREE
GENERAL AND FINAL PROVISIONS

Article 28

The authorised officers of the Ministry of Development and Industry who are designated by a resolution form the Minister of Development and Industry shall have the right to inspect the establishment which are subject to the provisions of this Act and have access to their records and documents to ascertain their fitness to operate in accordance with the licence granted thereto and the accuracy of the particulars recorded in the Industrial Registry.

Article 29

Without prejudice to any severe penalty specified under any other law, any person who contravenes the provisions of Articles 2, 11, 15, 17 and 19 of this Act shall be punished with a fine of not less than BD 100 and not more than BD 500. In the event of the second contravention, the court shall order the closure of the establishment for a period not exceeding three months. For the contravention, the court shall order the establishment to be closed finally.

Article 30

Without prejudice to any severe penalty specifies under any other law, any person who provides or gives false information with the intent to obtain an industrial licence or registration with the Industrial Registry shall be punished with imprisonment for a period not exceeding one month and with a fine not less than BD 100 or with any of them.

Article 31

Without prejudice to any severe penalty specified under any other law, every civil servant who is in charge of enforcing the provisions of this Act and who contravenes Article 27(a) thereof shall be subject to disciplinary penalties prescribed under the civil service regulations.

Article 32

The Minister of Development and Industry shall issue Executive Regulations and resolutions required for the implementation of the provisions of this Act.

Article 33

The Minister, each in his respective capacity, shall implement the provisions of this Act which shall come into force after six months from the date of its publication in the Official Gazette.

Signed: Hamad bin Isa Al-Khalifa,
the Amir of the State of Bahrain
Issued at Riffa Palace
on 22 Rajab, 1404, Hijra
corresponding to 23 April 1984

MINISTERIAL RESOLUTION MINISTRY OF DEVELOPMENT AND INDUSTRY

MINISTERIAL RESOLUTION NO. 1 OF 1986 WITH RESPECT TO PROMULGATING THE IMPLEMENTING REGULATIONS OF THE LEGISLATIVE DECREE NO. 6 OF 1984 GOVERNING THE ORGANISATION OF INDUSTRY

The Minister of Development and Industry,
having examined legislative Decree No. 6 of 1984 governing the Organisation of Industry,
and upon the submission of the Undersecretary of the Ministry of Development and Industry,
HEREBY RESOLVES THE FOLLOWING :

Article 1

The provisions of the Implementing Regulations attached to the Act governing the organisation of Industry shall come into force.

Article 2

This resolution shall be published in the Official Gazette and be enforced from the date of its publication.

Signed: Yousuf Ahmed Al Shirawi
Minister of Development and Industry
Dated: 6 April 1986

MINISTRY OF DEVELOPMENT AND INDUSTRY

IMPLEMENTING REGULATIONS TO THE ACT GOVERNING THE ORGANISATION OF INDUSTRY

Article 1

Any person wishing to set up a new industrial establishment or effect any change in an existing industrial establishment as regards its capacity, output, location or industrial objectives shall obtain a licence for this purpose from the Ministry of Development and Industry.

Article 2

The Owner of the project or establishment, or whoever deputises for him by a special power of attorney, shall submit the application for a permit to the Directorate of Industry, at the Ministry of Development and Industry, which shall examine the matter and issue the necessary recommendations in respect thereof.

Article 3

An application for a permit to set up a new industrial establishment shall down contain the details recorded on Form No. AS/1 or Form No. AS/2, as the case might be.

The application for a permit to effect any alteration in an industrial establishment as to its capacity, output, location or industrial objectives shall include the particulars recorded on the above mentioned two forms as the case might be.

Article 4

Before making a recommendation concerning the permit, the Directorate of Industry may hear the views and statements of the applicant or his attorney, and may instruct him to submit any particulars clarifications or documents necessary for examining his application.

Article 5

Upon approving the application, the permit shall be issued to concerned persons including the terms and conditions of granting such permit, which terms and conditions shall be written on the prescribed licence certificate according to Form AS/3.

Article 6

A Register shall be established at the Ministry of Development and Industry wherein industrial establishments already in existence in Bahrain and all the particulars set forth in these implementing Regulations shall be recorded. This Register shall be maintained by a special section to be called Industrial Register Section.

Article 7

Every proprietor or manager of an industrial establishment, whether already in existence or under formation on the effective date of the Organisation of Industry Act 1984, (Act No. 6) must apply to the Industrial Register Section at the Ministry of Development and Industry within 3 months from the effective date of enforcing the Act for the registration of his establishment in the Industrial Register according to the conditions specified in the Act and in these implementing Regulations pursuant to Forms Nos. AS/4 and AS/5. As regards establishments set up after the enforcement of the Act, registration thereof shall be effected within two months from the date of actually going on stream.

Article 8

Following the final approval of the application for the permit, the Industrial Register Section shall enter the particulars of the application in the Industrial Register in addition to the licence number concerning the setting up on an industrial establishment and date thereof.

Article 9

The owner of an industrial establishment or his heirs, as the case may be shall apply according to registration for the cancellation of the establishments registration in the following events:

1. Relinquishing the establishment by the owner thereof.
2. Death of owner.
3. Liquidation of the establishment.

The application must be filled within one from the date of the occurance involving cancellation of registration. Should the concerned percons fail to submit the application, the Industrial Register Section shall, on its own accord, cancel the registration.

Article 10

A separate page shall be set aside in the Industrial Register for each industrial establishment. The pages of the Register shall have serial numbers, and they shall be endorsed with the official seal of the Industrial Register Section.

Article 11

Applications for registration, entry in the Industrial Register or cancellation therefrom shall be written on the forms designed for this purpose which shall be accompanied by the supporting documents.

Article 12

Registration and entry particulars must be noted down in legible handwriting without any abbreviation, alteration, insertion or deletion. The applicant shall sign on every addition or correction on the margin thereof. He shall count the number of words added or deleted, which words shall be entered in by the Industrial Register Section to prove that checking has been made.

Article 13

Accepted applications shall be given serial numbers according to the date of filling them, and the Industrial Register Section shall write down one each application the serial number thereof and the date of depositing it. A receipt to this effect shall be given to the applicant.

Article 14

The applications referred to in the preceding Article shall be entered in the Industrial Register according to the succession of approving them. This shall be effected by noting down the particulars thereof in the relevant columns of the Industrial Register. Entries in the Register shall always be given serial numbers.

Article 15

In case an application for registration or entry is rejected, the Industrial Register Section shall notify the applicant of the reasons for rejection.

Article 16

Any person who has registered his establishment in the Industrial Register may obtain a copy of the details thereof which have been recorded in the Register in accordance with Form No. AS/6.

Article 17

In the event of entering particulars which may cause alteration or amendment to the details recorded in the Industrial Register, such details shall be deleted and the new particulars shall be entered in the same relevant column, and the date of entry thereof and the document supporting such amendments and its date shall be noted in the margin of the Register.

Article 18

The following recorded details or any amendments thereof in the Industrial Register shall be published in the Official Gazette:

1. Date of registration and number thereof.
2. Name of industrial establishment, type and name of owner.
3. Location of the industrial establishment

Article 19

Registration with the Industrial Register shall be renewed within thirty days after one year from the date of registration or the last renewal thereof in accordance with the applicable terms and conditions of registration.

Article 20

The Ministry of Development and Industry may publish a statistical bulletin of the registered industrial establishment. Such bulletin shall contain the following particulars:

1. Name of the industrial establishment.
2. The legal status of the establishment.
3. Location.
4. Address.
5. Capital of the establishment.
6. Production capacity.
7. Kinds of products.
8. Manager in charge of the project.

Article 21

Appeals against the decisions provided for in Article 22 of the Organisation of Industry Act 1984 (Act No. 6) shall be filled with the Minister of Development and Industry or mailed to him by a registered letter with an acknowledgement slip within sixty days from the date of giving notice to the appellant of the decision appealed against.

Article 22

The appeal must include the following details:

1. Name of the appellant, designation and address.
2. Date of the decision appealed against and date of notifying the appellant of the said decision.
3. Subject of the decision appealed against and the reasons for the appeal. The appeal shall be accompanied by the documents which the appellant deems necessary.

Article 23

The committee referred to in Article 23 of Legislative Decree No. 6 of 1984 shall receive the appeals and enter them under serial numbers in a special register wherein the date of filling or receipt thereof shall be indicated. A receipt showing the appeal number and date of filling thereof shall either be given to the appellant or sent to him by a registered letter.

Article 24

After completion of the documents, the Committee shall examine them and decide on the appeal. The decision shall be submitted to the Minister of Development and Industry for confirmation within a period of thirty days from the date of placing the appeal before the Committee.

Article 25

Appellant shall be notified by a registered letter of the confirmed decision taken in respect of the appeal and the reasons for taking thereo.

EGYPT

INVESTMENT REGULATIONS AND INCENTIVES

INVESTMENT LAW

On May 11, 1997, Egypt's new Investment Incentives and Guarantees Law (Law No. 8 of 1997), which repeals and replaces Investment Law No. 230 of 1989, was legislated. The new law aims to boost production and foreign and domestic investment and offers potentially good incentives for investors, including:

- The prohibition of nationalization, confiscation, and freezing of assets;
- The right to own buildings and land for project purposes regardless of investors' nationality and place of residence;
- The right to maintain foreign currency bank accounts;
- The exemption of manufacturing projects from price controls or profit limitations;
- The right to repatriate capital and profits;
- The right of 100 percent foreign ownership of ventures.

In addition, the new law provides extended tax holidays for projects in target areas. It allows companies, once established, to gain their tax incentives automatically without receiving the prior approval of any administrative authority. It also provides incentives for exporters. Whereas the previous law extended tax incentives for any capital increase or any project expansions, however, the new law provides no such tax concessions.

The law specifies a list of priority sectors that automatically benefit from its guarantees and incentives. These sectors include land reclamation, manufacturing and mining, transport, software and computer systems development and production, medical services, certain financial services, oil field services, agriculture and tourism. For these and for most other projects, investments are automatically approved.

The new law expressly preserves the benefits and incentives, as well as investment guarantees granted under law No. 230 for companies established under that law or existing prior to the promulgation of the new law under Law No. 230, all foreign investment projects are exempted from taxes and duties applied in Egypt for a period of five years which may be extended by another five years, regardless of the location of the project.

The new law has also abolished the highly bureaucratic General Authority for Investment (GAFI). The entity that will replace GAFI and its functions are to be determined by a presidential decree. Pending issuance of the decree, GAFI will remain the authorized administrative agency.

TAX INCENTIVES

Law No. 8 of 1997 grants the projects working under its rubric a tax holiday that includes provisions of interest to investors.
Profits on projects and shareholder shares are exempted from the tax on industrial and commercial profits and from the corporate tax for a period of five years starting from the first fiscal year following the beginning of production or activity. The exemption may be extended to ten years for projects established in new industrial zones, new urban communities, remote arand those projects financed by the Social Fund for Developmen.

Profits on projects operating outside the Old Valley and profits of shareholder shares shall be exempted from tax on industrial and commercial profits and from the corporate tax for a period of twenty years starting from the first fiscal year following the beginning of production or activity.
An amount equivalent to a percentage of the capital paid in, to be determined by the Egyptian Central Bank for Lending, and discount rates, for the year of fiscal treatment, shall be exempted from the corporate tax, provided that the company is a JSC and its stocks are registered at one of the stock exchanges.

Yields of bonds, finance share warrants and incomes of the other similar securities portfolios as issued by the JSCs shall be exempted from the tax on revenues of movable capitals, providing they are placed for public subscription and registered at one of the stock exchanges.
A customs tax at a unified rate of 5 percent of the value is levied on the value of all imports (machines, equipment and instruments) imported by such projects.

The profits resulting from the merger, division or the change of the legal entity of a project are exempted from the taxes and duties payable on the merger, division or change of legal entity. Such projects shall enjoy the exemptions prescribed before the merger, division or change of legal entity, until the relevant exemption periods expires. The merger, division or change of the project's legal entity shall not result in any new fiscal exemptions.

The result of assessing the in-kind portions forming the foundation of JSCs, Partnership Limited by Shares and LLCs shall b exempted from the tax on revenues of commercial and industrial activities or the tax on corporate companies' profits according to each case.

FREE TRADE ZONES

Projects set up in one of the active free zones enjoy certain benefits that may be of interest to foreign investors. Such projects are not subject to exchange-control regulations nor are they subject to any customs duties on imported goods or equipment. In addition, they are exempt from taxes for an unlimited period. These projects, however, are subject to annual duty of 1 percent of the value of products entering or leaving the free zone or on the annual value added to the project, as the case may be. Licenses to operate in free zones may be granted for the following activities: storage of goods in transit from one port to another; storage of Egyptian goods intended for export (provided taxes have been paid); storing, mixing, blending and repackaging operations; manufacturing, assembly and processing; and ancillary activities or services required by companies operating in the free zones.

The existing free zones are located in Nasr City, Alexandria, Port Said, Suez, and Ismailia. In addition, new free zones are being established in Damietta, Cairo Airport, Safaga, Al Arissh and in Sinai east to Port Said.

AGREEMENTS

Egypt is not a signatory to any free trade agreement. Egypt, however, has been negotiating with the European Union (EU) to realize a free trade agreement which will replace the earlier agreement concluded in 1977 that gave Egyptian industrial products free access to the European market. Negotiations have focused on the abolition of quotas on oil, textiles and other manufactured products and a relaxation of restrictions on agricultural produce.

While Egypt is a member of the Arab Common Market, along with Syria, Jordan, Iraq and Libya, this endeavor has not produced notable trade relations.
Egypt has entered into extra-regional trade relations with the EU and the US, among other countries, relating to the preferential treatment of certain specified goods. Egypt has pursued similar kinds of preferential treatment trade agreements with the Czech Republic, Greece, Jordan, Kuwait, Malta, Poland, Saudi Arabia and Syria. In March of 1995, Egypt and China entered into a trade accord. Egypt has also recently signed an Economic Treaty with Russia.
Egypt and Israel signed the Agreement on Trade and Commerce in May of 1980. The peace between the two countries, until recently, may best be described as "cold". In the wake of the peace process with the Palestinian Authority, the Joint Committee on Trade of Egypt and Israel met in November 1994, and issued the Taba Declaration in February 1995; it is hoped this step will lead to a new chapter in the trade relations between the two countries.

CUSTOMS

Egypt has complex tariff and non-tariff barriers. The latter include: a banned import list, quality control inspection standards, prior approval list, quotas, Egyptian selling prices imposed on imported goods for customs valuation purposes and government procurement practices. Tariffs range from 5 percent to 55 percent, with certain rare exceptions such as automobiles (up to 135 percent).

The current tariffs are a result of a presidential decree issued in 1996 which lowers Egypt's highest customs tariffs by 10 to 15 percent across the board. In early 1996, the government also announced the reduction of tariffs on a wide variety of capital goods needed for industrial investment to 10 percent from previous rates that ran as high as 70 percent. The government, however, has levied a 3 percent to 4 percent surcharge on the value of imported shipments as a fee paid for the inspection, listing, classification and re-examination of the shipment.

Overall, high tariffs have not crimped trade by foreign countries because the tariffs apply to all imports equally, and clever importers have been successful in discovering where exceptions and loopholes exist in the system. Exemptions to the banned import list are available for many sectors including the petroleum, tourism and military industries.

The list of banned import items was created to protect domestic industry and to reduce foreign exchange expenditures on luxury goods (called provocative items under customs terminology). Goods on the list include passenger cars, textiles, apparel, leather, steel pipes, PVC and batteries. Exemptions to the ban may be granted by the Ministry of Economy and Foreign Trade if no equivalent product exists in the local market or if the banned item is required for the survival of an industry. As the Egyptian Government has been rapidly reducing the items contained on the banned list, it has become less of a barrier to trade. A number of years ago the list covered 37 percent of all imports. Today, this percentage is lower and eventually is expected to be reduced to 5 percent of imports.

Egypt's quality control inspection standards adversely affect certain products, particularly food items. The Government has expanded the list of products subject to inspection to include many manufactured products, in addition to the previously monitored foodstuffs. Quality control is seen as a moral issue by policy makers who point to the need to protect consumers from fraud and counterfeits. The major hurdle for foreign suppliers is that these quality standards often are ill defined or not written at all. The restrictive features of this system are in the process of revision.

Egypt's 1996 agreement with the IMF provides for the reduction of the maximum tariff rate to 40 percent, a reduction of certain rates to 30 percent, and the limitation of the number of tariff bans to seven by 1998. This is also, according to the agreement, the deadline for the reduction of the current 4 percent and 3 percent import surcharge rates to a uniform 1 percent and for the government to eliminate all remaining non-tariff barriers.

SECTORS FOR INVESTMENT

INDUSTRY

The most important products of Egyptian industry include cotton yarn, jute yarn and fabrics, wool yarn, refined sugar, sulfuric acid nitrogenous fertilizers, paper, cement, motor-vehicle tires and television receivers. Other industrial activities include the manufacture of iron and steel the assembling of motor vehicles and the refining of oil (at several locations). Smaller-scale industrial enterprises of significance to the economy include tanning, brewing, and the manufacture of pottery, perfumes, handicrafts, cottonseed oil, flour and other processed foodstuffs, and asphalt. Most industrial activity is centered around Cairo and Alexandria.

AGRICULTURE

Agriculture, which accounts for 20 percent of GDP and 36 percent of total employment, is the area in which the Government has pushed economic reform the farthest. As a result, production has increased steadily in recent years. Impressive growth has been achieved both in terms of increases in cultivated areas and in production levels. According to official figures, the value of agricultural production increased by 74 percent over the five year period 1988-1994, from US$ 7 billion in 1988 to US$ 12.2 billion in 1994 and value added in agriculture reached US$ 9.6 billion in 1994.

Cultivation is concentrated in the Nile and Delta regions, and less than 3 percent of total land area is cultivated. The yields of Egyptian farmlands are now among the highest in the world. Egypt is the world's most important producer of long-staple cotton. Other leading crops include rice, tomatoes and wheat. Also produced are sugarcane, watermelons, millet, barley, onions, vegetables, citrus fruits, mangoes, dates, figs and grapes.

TOURISM

The Egyptian tourism industry is one of the most important sectors in the economy, in terms of high employment and incoming foreign currency. Egypt offers tremendous attractions in terms of cultural heritage and of natural beauty, but since 1992, intermittent terrorist actions have damaged this sector. Tourism receipts tumbled following fundamentalist attacks which killed twelve western tourists, but government efforts to crack down on terrorism have countered this trend.

Tourism officially became the country's second largest foreign currency earner in 1996, when revenues reached US$ 3 billion, an increase of US$ 710 million over 1995 figures. The increase was due in large part to development along the Red Sea coast. For 1997, hotel occupancy is expected to increase by 12 percent over 1996, to twenty-nine million tourist nights for the year. Egypt's goal is draw six million tourists annually by the year 2000. Meanwhile, accommodation capacity will expand to 75,000 hotel rooms, facilitated by the addition of 7,300 rooms during 1997-98. Related construction by German, French and Italian investors will create about 17,500 new jobs. Foreign marketing campaigns are expected to draw a large number of foreign tourists.

ENERGY

Egypt produces approximately 800,000 to 900,000 barrels of oil a day (approximately forty-five million tons per year). Natural gas accounts for approximately 28 percent of total energy consumption in the country. In the next three years, production of natural gas and its derivatives is expected to increase by 5.2 percent annually. During 1997, Egypt hopes to have sufficient LNG production for export. Egypt's electrical capacity has grown substantially over the last decade, reaching 11,910 MW. Hydroelectric power represents about 8.3 percent of the total annual energy production in the country.

TRADE

Egypt offers an import market exceeding US$ 10 billion annually. The United States is the largest foreign supplier, capturing approximately 30 percent annually of Egypt's imports, hovering around US$ 3 billion for several years.

The principal imports of Egypt are agricultural products, foodstuffs, transportation equipment, chemicals, mining and quarrying machinery and metal products. The country has become more and more dependent on imports and food grants, especially for wheat, flour and meat, because of rapid population growth.

The major exports of Egypt are crude petroleum, raw cotton, cotton yarn, fabrics and rice. The chief customers for these and other exports are Italy, the US, Germany, France, the former USSR, Japan and Great Britain.

IRAN

FOREIGN INVESTMENT PROMOTION AND PROTECTION ACT (FIPPA)

CHAPTER ONE: DEFINITIONS

Article (1)
The terms and expressions used in this Law shall have the following meanings:
Law: The Law for the Promotion and Protection of Foreign Investments.
Foreign Investor: Non-Iranian natural and/or juridical persons or Iranians using capital of foreign source, who have obtained the investment license referred to in Article (6).
Foreign Capital: All types of capital, being cash or non-cash, brought into the country by foreign investors and includes the following:

a) Cash funds in the form of convertible currency imported into the country through banking system or other methods of transfer, acceptable to the Central Bank of the Islamic Republic of Iran;
b) Machinery and equipments;
c) Tools and spares, CKD parts and raw, addable, and auxiliary materials;
d) Patent rights, know-how, trade marks and names, and specialized services;
e) Transferable dividends of foreign investors;
f) Other permissible species approved by the Council of Ministers.

Foreign Investment: Application of foreign capital in a new or existing economic entity after obtaining the investment license.

Investment License: The license issued for every foreign investment in accordance with Article 6 of this Law.

Organization: The Organization for Investment, Economic and Technical Assistance of Iran, subject matter of Article (5) of the Law establishing the Ministry of Economic Affairs and Finance ratified on July 15, 1974.

High Council: The High Council for Investment, subject matter of Article (7) of the Charter of the Organization for Investment, Economic and Technical Assistance of Iran ratified on June 2, 1975.

Board: The Foreign Investment Board, subject matter of Article (6) of this Law.

CHAPTER TWO: GENERAL CRITERIA FOR ADMISSION OF FOREIGN

Article (2)

Admission of foreign investment shall be made, in accordance with the provisions of this Law and with due observance of other prevailing laws and regulations of the country, subject to the following criteria:

a. Help create economic growth, upgrade technology, enhance ,development of the quality of products, increase employment opportunities, exports, and penetrate into international markets;

b. Does not threaten the national security and public benefits, and deteriorate the environment; does not distort the country's economy and impose unfair implication on products based on local investments;

c. Does not involve granting of concessions by the Government to foreign investors. The word concession as used herein means special rights which place the foreign investors in a monopolistic position.

d. The ratio of the value of the goods and services produced by the foreign investments, subject matter of this Law, to the value ,t of the goods and services supplied to the local market at the time of issuance of the investment license, shall not exceed 25% in each economic sector and 35% in each field (sub- sector). The fields and investment ceilings in each field shall be determined in the by-law to be approved by the Council of Ministers.

Foreign investment for the production of goods and services specifically for export purposes other than oil, shall be . exempted from the aforementioned ratios.

Note. The Law for the Ownership of Immovable Properties by Foreign Nationals ratified on June 6, 1921 shall remain enforceable.Ownership of land of any type and at any scale in the name of foreign investors is not permissible within the framework of this Law.

Article (3)

Foreign investments admitted in accordance with provisions of this Law shall enjoy the incentives and protections available under this Law. Such investments may be admitted under the following two categories:

a) Foreign direct investment in areas where the activity of private sector is permissible;

b) Foreign investments in all sectors within the framework of "civil participation", "buy-back" and "build-operate-transfer" arrangements where the return of capital and profits accrued is solely emanated from the economic performance of the r project in which the investment is made, and such return of capital and profit shall not be dependent upon a guarantee by the Government, state-owned companies or banks.

Note1. So long as the foreign investment subject matter of "build-operate-transfer" arrangements referred to in Para (b) of this Article, and its incurred profits thereon are not amortized, the exercise of ownership right by the foreign investor over the unamortized capital in respect of the recipient economic entity is permissible.

Note 2. With respect to investments subject matter of Para (b) of this Article, if, as a result of promulgation of laws or Government resolutions, the execution of approved financial agreements within the framework of this Law is prohibited or : interrupted, the accrued losses, to a maximum of due installments shall be committed and paid by the Government. The scope of ac:ceptable commitments shall be approved, within the framework of this Law, by the Council of Ministers.

Article (4)
The investment by a foreign government or foreign governments in the Islamic Republic of Iran shall have to be approved by the Islamic Consultative Assembly on a case by case basis. The investment by foreign state-owned companies is considered to be private.

CHAPTER THREE: COMPETENT AUTHORITIES

Article (5)
The Organization is the only official authority for the promotion of foreign investments in the country, and for Investigation of all Issues pertaining to foreign Investments. Applications of foreign investors in respect of issues such as admission, importation, employment and repatriation of capital shall have to be submitted to the Organization.

Article(6)
For the purpose of investigation and making decision on applications subject matter of Article (5), a Board under the name of the "Foreign Investment Board" shall be established under the chairmanship of the Vice Minister of Economic Affairs and Finance who is ex-officio the President of the Organization Vice Minister of Foreign Affairs, Deputy Head of the State Management and Planning Organization, Deputy Governor of the Central Bank of the Islamic Republic of Iran and vice ministers of relevant ministries, as the case requires.

In relation to applications for admission, the investment license shall, after the approval of the Board, be issued upon confirmation and signature by the Minister of Economic Affairs and Finance.

At the time of admission of foreign investments, the Board is required to observe the criteria referred to in Article (2) of this Law.

Note. The Organization, after preliminary appraisal, is required to take the investment applications, along with its own considerations, to the Board within a maximum period of 15 days as from the date of receipt of the applications. The Board is under obligation to review the applications within a maximum period of one month from the date of submission, and announce its final decision in writing.

Article (7)
In order to facilitate and accelerate issues related to the admission and activity of foreign ,investments in the country, all relevant bodies Including the Ministry of Economic Affairs and Finance, Ministry of Foreign Affairs, Ministry of Commerce, Ministry of labor and Social Affairs, Central Bank of the Islamic Republic of Iran, Costumes Administration of the Islamic Republic of Iran, Directorate General for Registration of Companies and Industrial property, and the Organization for Environment Protection are required to introduce to the Organization a fully authorized representative whose designation is signed by the highest authority of the body. The representatives so introduced are recognized to act as medium and coordinator for all issues related to their respective body vis-a-vis the Organization.

CHAPTER FOUR: GUARANTEE AND TRANSFER OF FOREIGN CAPITAL

Article (8)

Foreign investments under this law shall equally enjoy all , rights, protections, and facilities provided for domestic investments.

Article (9)
Foreign Investments shall not be subjected to expropriation or nationalization, unless for public purposes, in accordance with due of law, in a non-discriminatory manner, and upon payment of appropriate compensation on the basis of the real value of the investment immediately before the expropriation.

Note1. Application for compensation shall have to be submitted to the Board within one year from the date of
r-' expropriation or nationalization.

Note 2. Disputes arising from expropriation or nationalization shall be settled by virtue of the provisions of Article (19) of this Law.

Article (10)
Ceding the whole or part of the foreign capital to domestic investor and/or, upon approval of the Board and confirmation of the Minister of Economic Affairs and Finance, to other foreign investor is permissible. In case of ceding to another foreign investor, the cedee shall, at least, have the same qualifications as the initial investor, and shall replace and/or become a partner to the former investor from the standpoint of this Law.

CHAPTER FIVE: PROVISIONS ON ADMISSION, IMPORTATION AND REPATRIATION OF FOREIGN CAPITAL

Article (11)
Foreign capital may be imported into the country by way of one or a combination of the following manners to be protected by this Law:

a) Sums of cash to be converted into Rials;
b) Sums of cash not to be converted into Rials but to be used directly for purchases and orders related to foreign investment;
c) Non-cash items after evaluation by the competent authorities.

Note. Arrangements related to the manner of evaluation, and registration of foreign capital shall be determined in the Implementing Regulations of this Law.

Article (12)
The rate of conversion of foreign exchange applicable at the time of importation or repatriation of foreign capital as well as the rate for all transfers, in case of applicability of a unified rate of exchange, shall be the same rate prevailing in the country's official network; otherwise, the applicable rate shall be the free-market rate as acknowledged by the Central Bank of the Islamic Republic of Iran.

Article (13)
The original foreign capital and the accrued profits, or the balance of capital remaining in the country subject to a three month prior notice, after fulfillment of all obligations and payment of legal deductions, and upon confirmation by the Minister of Economic Affair and Finance, shall be transferable abroad.

Article (14)
Dividends of foreign investments after deduction of taxes, dues and statutory reserves, upon the approval of the Board, and confirmation by the Minister of Economic Affairs and Finance, shall be transferable abroad.

Article (15)
Payments related to the installments of the principal of the financial facilities of foreign investors and relevant expenses,agreements for patent rights, know-how, technical and engineering assistance, trade marks and names, management as well as similar agreements within the framework of the relevant foreign investment, upon the approval of the Board and confirmation by the Minister of Economic Affairs and Finance, are transferable abroad.

Article (16)
Transfers referred to in Articles (13) , (14) and (15), shall be made subject to the provisions of Para (b) of Article (3) of this Law.

Article (17)

Foreign exchange required for the transfers referred to in Articles (14), (15) and (16) of this Law may be secured by way of the following methods:
a) Purchase of foreign currency from the banking system;
b) Out of the foreign exchange earnings from the export of the products and/or out of the foreign exchange earnings from service activities of the economic entity in which the foreign capital is employed;
c) The export of permissible goods subject to the relevant laws and regulations.

Note1. Application of one or a combination of the above methods shall be specified in the investment license.

Note 2. The Central Bank of the Islamic Republic of Iran is under obligation, to make available to the foreign investor the equivalent foreign currency for the transferable sums referred to in Para (a), upon agreement of the Organization and confirmation by the Minister of Economic Affairs and Finance.

Note 3. In case the investment license expressly refers to Para (b) and/or (c) of this Article, this license is regarded as an export license.

Article (18)
Transfer abroad of the portion of the foreign capital imported into the country within the framework of the investment license but remains unused, is released from all foreign exchange, and export and import laws and regulations.

CHAPTER SIX: SETTLEMENT OF DISPUTES

Article (19)
Disputes arising between the Government and the foreign investors in respect of the mutual obligations within the framework of investments under this Law, if not settled through negotiations, shall be referred to domestic courts, unless another method for settlement of disputes have been agreed under the Law for Bilateral Investment Agreement with the respective Government of the foreign investor.

CHAPTER SEVEN: FINAL PROVISIONS

Article (20)
The relevant executive bodies are required to take , measures, upon the request of the Organization, for the issuance of entry visa, residence permit, work and employment permit, as the case may be, for foreign investors, managers and experts working for the private sector involved in foreign investments under this Law, as well as their immediate relatives.

Note. Differences of opinions between the Organization and executive. bodies. will be settled upon the opinion of the Minister of Economic Affairs and Finance.

Article (21)
The Organization is required to provide for the public to have access to all information related to investments, foreign investors, investment opportunities, Iranian partners, fields of activity and other information available to the Organization.

Article (22)
All Ministries, state-owned companies and organizations as well as public institutes to whom the applicability of law is required to be stipulated by name, are under obligation to provide the Organization with reports on foreign investments implemented as we,ll a.s information requir~d for foreign in~estors I so that the Organization can proceed In accordance with the above Article.

Article (23)
The Minister of Economic Affairs and Finance is required to provide, every six months, the relevant committees in Islamic Consultative Assembly with a report on the performance of the Organization with respect to foreign investments under this Law.

Article (24)
As from the date of ratification of this Law and its t Implementing Regulations, the Law for the Attraction and Protection of Foreign Investments ratified on November 28, 1945 - as well as its Implementing Regulations

are repealed. The provisions of this Law shall be repealed or altered by subsequent laws and regulations in the event that repeal or alteration of this Law would have been stipulated in those laws and regulations.

Article (25)
The Implementing Regulations of this Law shall be Prepared by the Ministry of Economic Affairs and Finance and shall be subsequently approved by the Council of Ministers within two months.

The above Law comprised of 25 Articles and 11 Notes has been approved by the Islamic Consultative Assembly in its session .

WHAT ARE THE PRIVATIZATION ACHIEVEMENTS IN IRAN?[4]

Summary: Some 25 years have elapsed since the first law on expansion of transfer of production units to the private sector. However, there has not been much improvement in this effort due to various legal problems as well as lack of experience and absence of a custodian agency. One of the achivements of the privatization plan during the third plan has been the transfer of shares worth over 648 billion rial from 180 manufacturing units to 359,270 workers from 300 workplaces.
Text: Privitization has been among President Mohammad Khatami's goals in the past few years in an effort to create a suitable environment for attracting stray capitals toward the manufacturing sector.

The history of privatization in Iran in general, dates back to the law ratified in 1975 pertaining to the expansion of transfer of manufacturing units. The above law provided that up to 99 percent of the government's ownership in nonbasic industries, as well as 49 percent of the stocks of the private sector be transferred to the blue-collar workers as well as other segments of the population. The sub-article 32 of the First Development Plan in 1368 (1989) was the first legal fulcrum for adopting privatization policies in the country.

The essence of this sub-article which was derived from the context of the relative articles and the description of the guidelines contained in part one of the above law, was the separation of the governments' authoritative duties from its executive responsibilities.

The execution of the sub-article 32 led to the centralization of the related matters at the office of deputy minister of economy and finance handling the issues related to government companies.

The next step was the cabinet decree issued in June 1991. This decree was aimed at increased productivity of various activities, and a reduction of government responsibilities in nonessential economic and service related activities, creation of an economic balance by transferring government owned stocks in government organizations and companies.

According to item 3 of the above decree, guidelines for transfer of 33 percent of transferable stocks to the blue-collar workers at a median price, were established. In January 1992, the cabinet issued a new decree which established the organization charged with the privatization plan, the method for calculating the value of the stocks and pricing, as well as the transfer secretariat.

The laws governing the procedures for transfer of the government owned stocks to Isargaran (volunteers fighting for the cause of the state and revolution) and the blue-collar workers ratified in August 1994, were the subsequent steps in the collection of laws and regulations relating to privatization. This law which was instated within a different framework and applied conventional methods employed in privatization was ratified by the Islamic Parliament.

The sub-article 35 of the national budget bills for the years 1998 and 1999 covered all the remaining issues and regulations relating to the privatization program which were approved by appropriate authorities prior to the start of the Third Development Plan. Based on the sub-article 35, a committee headed by the President and consisting of the minister of economy and finance, the governor of the Central Bank, the head of the Plan and Budget Organization, three parliamentarians as observers, as well as the relevant minister in connection to establishing privatization policies and procedures pertaining to his ministry were formed. The finance organization for the expansion of transfer of manufacturing units, was assigned as secretariat of the

[4] Ettela'at (Afternoon Daily) Jan 27, 2001, No. 22118 Page: 5

sub-article committees 35 and was to be the headquarters for the relative executive activities in 1999.

Paragraph F of the sub-article 2 of the 2000 national budget bill, authorizes the implementation of the above mentioned article 35, until the establishment of a privatization organization which is anticipated to be concluded by the end of the year (March 20, 2001). The paragraph concludes regulations in this area prior to the implementation of the Third Development Plan.

PRIVATIZATION STATISTICS

Beginning in 1990 when the idea of privatization was first initiated in Iran, the absence of an organization in charge of the issue, shortage of legal basis and lack of necessary resolve and experience of the transferring organizations are elements that have prevented the expansion of privatization within a statistical scope. 6100 billion rial in revenues from sale of government owned stocks in the above years for most part must be attributed to the ministry of industry.

PRIVATIZATION IN THE THIRD DEVELOPMENT PLAN

The law governing Iran's 3rd economic, cultural and social development plan, in its second and third chapters, includes 23 articles that deal with the reorganization and efficiencies of government companies and the transfer of stocks owned by ministries, government organizations, and government owned companies, also referred to as the privatization program.

The content of these two chapters sets guidelines for appointment of organizations that would be charged with drawing up policies and procedure and implementation, in connection with restructuring of government owned companies as well as the offering and sale of their stocks. The cabinet and the high council of transfer (subject of the article 12 of the above law) including the minister of economy and finance (the council chairman), the head of the management and planning organization, the governor of the Central Bank, minister of relevant ministries, minister of justice, members of Majlis economic, planning and budget, and auditing commissions, as policy-makers, and the salient specialized state-run companies and the privatization organization are appointed to be in charge of the affairs relating to reorganizations and transfer of stocks.

In the light of the above mentioned law and its implementation regulations, it has been resolved that the state-run companies be reorganized within the specialized mother companies and managed under the relevant ministries and within the framework of relevant constitutions.

Following the restructuring and establishment of the base price, the privatization organization based on the article 15 of the law, will emerge as a result of change of function of expansion of transfer of manufacturing units, which will have power of attorney for the transfer stages.

Unlike its earlier counterparts, the new law introduces a privatization organization, which as an independent guardian institution in turn should execute policies instated by the cabinet and the high council of transfer through controlling the transfer of stocks.

The transfer law in the Third Development Plan has been anticipated to encompass prioritizing a few individuals and groups including employment generators, competent directors, the blue-collar, specialized groups, etc, undertaking the management and task of renting state companies, expending procedures of the stock sale revenues, an arbitration panel, commenting and judging individual complaints at the transfer, safeguarding the transfer authorities against any of their unintentional mistakes.

The Finance Department for Promoting Ownership of Manufacturing Units (FDPOMU) titled Privatization Organization in the 3rd economic, social and cultural development plan, was initially kicked off in 1975 as a state enterprise affiliated to the ministry of economy and finance and treasury subject to the Note 4 of the single article concerning promotion of ownership of manufacturing units. By large, it targeted participation of workers in their factories' ownership granting funds and pioneering measures (listed below) to hit the goal.

1. Paving the way for the workers and farmers to possess manufacturing units through the concerned law ratified in 1975
2. Transfer of stocks to manufacturing units' personnel to execute the note of paragraph 3 in a bill approved by the cabinet in June 1991

3. Transfer of stocks to manufacturing units' staff after note 3, article 6 declaring the transfer procedure to the Isargaran and workers
4. Fulfilling note 35, paragraph `J' of the budget bill passed in 1999, the secretariat of the note 35 committee manages and runs the FDPOMU.
5. Subject to Article 15 of the Third Development Plan, the charter shake-up in FDPOMU breeds its title switch to `Privatization Organization'.

To hit the set targets, thanks to the steps taken by the organization including granting loans and funds, a portion of manufacturing units in various industries namely foodstuff, pharmaceutical, developing chemicals, textiles, home appliances, entertainment, vehicles and nonmetallic mining items have been traded. The steps brought about the transfer of shares worth over 648 billion rial from 180 manufacturing units to 359,270 workers from 300 workplaces.

IMPACTS OF STOCK TRANSFER

The workers welcomed the ownership scheme by using the grants offered by this organization. The striking impacts of such a measure readily stand out in workplaces. According to the statistical studies conducted by FDPOMU the leading outcomes are the following:

- Workers get down to business more decisively and enthusiastically due to their sense of ownership
- Establishing motivation resulting in a boost of manufacture, output, and efficiency
- All-out curb of waste
- Drastic cooperation with the management (in most cases) in airing efficient comments which are to improve manufacturing units' status and tackle their issues
- Growing process of manufacturing units' economic boom and further profitability

IRAQ

LEGAL SYSTEM DEVELOPMENT

1.1. In spite of the transfer of formal sovereignty to a new Interim Iraqi Government at the end of June 2004 and other major developments, that will be briefly referred to blow, the lack of essential security and local instability remains predominant factor in Iraq. It is expected that the escalation of violence will persist until substantial Iraqi security and armed forces can be reorganized and become effective in imposing law and order. To achieve the restructuring of the armed forces the new Interim Government recently announced that it will rescind the order to dissolve the Iraqi army.

1.2. The above mentioned prevailing lack of security remains the main obstacle to achieving the stability which is essential for economic progress in the different sectors including oil production and exports, production of refined products, electricity supply, water purification, medical care and other essential services.

1.3. One of the first steps taken by the Interim Government was the issue of the Law for the Defence of National Security (Emergency Law) allowing for the declaration of emergency measures for specific periods and in specific areas as and when is deemed necessary.

2. **Transfer of Sovereignty**

2.1. Prior to the transfer of sovereignty important measures were taken. The issue in March 2004 of the Transitional Administrative Law (TAL) (colloquially referred to as the interim Constitution) by the Governing Council is considered as one of the major developments on the ground in Iraq. The TAL will be the supreme law in Iraq during the transitional period and provides the detailed mechanism for the selection, election and running the country until a permanent constitution is adopted and a Government is accordingly formed.

2.2. The formation of the Interim Government, referred to above, on 1st June 2004, was a major new development in the process for the transfer of sovereignty. This was the culmination of a lengthy joint process involving the UN representative, the CPA and the Governing Council for the transfer of sovereignty to an Iraqi Government. The Governing Council, which until then had assisted in running the country, declared that it was dissolved.

2.3. On 8th June 2004, the UN Security Council unanimously adopted Resolution 1546 welcoming the termination of the Coalition's formal occupation of Iraq and the transfer of sovereignty to the Interim Government that will take place on 30th June 2004. While the termination of the occupation will lead to the dissolution of the CPA, the new interim Iraqi Government is expected to agree the new status for the US led multinational forces presently in Iraq.

2.4. The above mentioned UN Resolution 1546 provided the details and timetable for the political transition to a democratic government in Iraq.

3. **The Interim Government**

3.1. On 28th June 2004 sovereignty was formally transferred to new Iraqi Government referred to in 2.2 above which included the President, two Vice Presidents, the Prime Minister, two Deputy Prime Ministers and thirty Ministers.

3.2. Consequently, from that date, the CPA ceased to exist in accordance with the provisions of UN Security Council Resolution 1546 referred to in 2.4 above.

4. **Economy and Finance**

4.1. The trend for economic liberalization and free market approach adopted by the CPA is expected to be continued by the Interim Government. Important Orders (laws), some of which are referred to below, were issued by the CPA prior to its dissolution. These Orders in accordance with Paragraph (C) of Article 26 of TAL will remain valid until changed or amended by new laws.

5. **Banking**

5.1. In addition to the important step of issuing the new Central Bank of Iraq (CBI) Law, on 6 March 2004 which we had referred to in a previous update, further steps were taken for the liberalization of the previously strictly controlled banking sector. Initially a Bank Law was issued on 19 September 2003 which rescinded and replace by a new Banking Law on 07 June 2004. The Bank Law primarily aims to maintain public confidence in the banking system, promoting better understanding and information and more importantly providing an appropriate degree of depositors protection.

5.2. Foreign banks that were reportedly given licenses to operate branches in Iraq will probably be able to establish and expand such branches when the security situation improves.

6. **Investments & Company Law**

6.1. In a previous update we reported on the Order issued by the CPA to encourage foreign investment in Iraq, Order (39), and anticipated that even though this Order will have major ramifications on the business environment in Iraq, to be effectively applied the relevant laws had to be accordingly amended. One of the important laws that had to be amended was the Company Law. Consequently, Order 64 was issued on 05 March 2004 providing the requisite extensive amendments to the Company Law No. (21) of 1997.

6.2. To implement the provision in the above Order provides that foreign investors may, to implement foreign investment using freely convertible currencies and Iraqi legal tender, establish a wholly foreign-owned business entity in Iraq including a subsidiary, the Company Law now allows the incorporation of Iraqi companies by foreign individuals and corporate entities. The Department of the Companies Registrar of the Ministry of Trade has issued the requisite forms for the registration of these companies.

7. **Intellectual Property**

7.1. Very important Orders were issued by the CPA amending the protection of intellectual property laws to make them compatible with current internationally-recognized standards of protection of such property, extend the scope of geographical protection and to demonstrate the current Iraqi interest to become a full member in the international trading system, known as the World Trade Organization. While Order (80) was issued amending the Trademarks and Descriptions Law No. 21 of 1957, Order 81 was issued amending the Patent, Industrial Design, Undisclosed Information, Integrated Circuits and Plant Variety Law No. 65 of 1970 and Order 83 was issued to amend the Copyright Law No. 3 of 1971.

8. **Labor**

8.1. Another important Order Number 89 was issued to amend the provisions of the Labor Code Law No. (71) of 1987 to improve conditions of work, technical skills, improve work opportunities and fight unemployment.

CAVEAT

The above update is a guideline not intended to be considered as a legal opinion or advice. For such opinion and/or advice on specific legal aspects, matters or developments in Iraq, kindly contact GLS for detailed advice required.

IRAQ INVESTMENT LAW

No. (13) of 2006

Pursuant to what was approved by the Council of Representatives in accordance with provisions of Para (first) of Article (61) of the constitution and elapse of the legal period given in Para 5/A of Article 138 of the constitution ,the following law is promulgated

CHAPTER ONE DEFINITIONS

Article (1)

The following terms, wherever mentioned in this Law, shall have the following specific meanings unless the context indicates otherwise:

A: The Council :the Council of Ministers

B: National Commission for Investment: the commission established in accordance with this law responsible for drawing up the national policy and laying out its guidelines and monitoring the implementation of these guidelines and instructions in investment. It shall specialize in investment projects of a federal nature exclusively.

C: Region's Commission: The investment commission of the region responsible for investment planning and granting investment licenses in the region.

D: Governorate Commission : The investment commission of the governorate not organized in a region responsible for investment planning and granting investment licenses in the governorate.

E: The commission: The National commission for Investment or the Region's commission or the Governorate Commission as the case.

F: Chairman of the Commission: the Chairman of the National Commission for Investment.

G: The Project: the economic activity subject to the provision of this law.

H: The Assets: the tools, apparatuses, equipments, machineries, transportation means and office furnishings and appliances to be used for the project exclusively and the furniture and appliances of the hotels, tourist cities, hospitals, schools and colleges.

I: The foreign Investor: is the investor who does not hold the Iraqi nationality in the case of real person, and is registered in a foreign country in the case of a juridical or legal person.

J: The Iraqi investor: is the investor who holds Iraqi Nationality in case of real person, and registered in Iraq in case of a juridical or legal person.

K: Taxes and duties: all kinds of taxes and duties imposed according to applicable laws.

L: The designed production capacity: is the production capacity designed within a specific unit of the time (hour, day.....etc) in accordance to what is fixed in the documents incoming with the machine of the supplier and the feasibility study of the project.

M: Investment Portfolio: A collection of investments in shares and bonds.

N: Investment: is the investment of capital in any economic activity or project that results in a legitimate benefit for the country.

Goals and Means

Article(2)

This law aims at the following:-

First: To promote investment and transfer modern technologies in order to contribute to the process of the developing and enhancing Iraq, and expanding and diversifying its production and service base.

Second: To encourage the Iraqi and foreign private sector to invest in Iraq by providing the required facilities for establishing investment projects and enhancing its competitive capacities in the local and foreign markets for projects covered by this law.

Third: To develop human resources based on market demands and provide work opportunities for the Iraqis.

Fourth: To protect the rights and properties of investors.

Fifth: To expand exports and improve the balance of payments and balance of trade of Iraq.

Article 3

The following means shall be adopted to realize the objectives of this law:

First: To grant projects covered by provision of this law the necessary privileges and guarantees for its continuation and development by providing support in a way that enhances the competitive capacities of these projects in the local and foreign markets.

Second: To grant projects that obtained an investment license from the Commission, additional facilities and exemptions from taxes and duties in accordance with the stipulations of this law.

CHAPTER TWO THE NATIONAL COMMISSION FOR INVESTMENT AND THE INVESTMENT COMMISSION IN THE REGIONS AND GOVERNORATES

Article 4

First: A Commission shall be established and called the "The National Commission for Investment".it shall enjoy a juridical personality and shall be represented by the Chairman of the Commission or the person authorized by him. It shall be responsible for drawing up the national policies for investment and drawing up it's Plans, regulations as well as monitoring the implementation of these guidelines and instructions in investment. It shall specialize in strategic investment projects of a federal nature exclusively.

Second: The National Commission for Investment shall be managed by Board of Director comprised of nine member who must be competent, specialized, and hold a college degree that suits the specialty of the Commission. They must not have been sentenced for a felony or misdemeanor of moral turpitude or have declared their bankruptcy.

Third:

A. Upon a request by the prime Minister, the Council of Ministers shall nominate a Chairman of the Commission at a grade of Minister and a Deputy Chairman at a grade of Deputy – Ministry for a period of five years and present them to the Council of Representative for approval.

B. The prime Minister shall appoint four member for a period of five years at a Grade of Director General.
C. The Prime Minister shall select three members from the private sector for five years after their nomination by Chairman of the Commission and specifying their compensations according to the bylaws.

D. At the conclusion of the membership of any member of the Commission referred to in Paragraph (A and B) of this Article in cases not involving dismissal and resignation, the Prime Minister shall assign them to any governmental entity at the same grade. Those mentioned in (A) of this article shall be retired on pension when not assigned to a government position equivalent to their grade.

E. The Council of Representatives may directly dismiss the Chairman of the National Commission for Investment and his Deputy, or upon a request by the Prime Minister for compelling reasons.

F. The Council of Ministers may dismiss or replace any member of the Commission or replace him with others in case he does not adhere to the standards and regulations of the Commission.
G. The Board of Directors of the National Commission for Investment shall meet at the invitation of its Chairman. The quorum of convening and adopting resolutions and recommendation shall be determined by absolute majority. The conduct of work shall be organized by by- laws issued by the commission.
H. The National commission for Investment shall be connected to the prime Minister.
I. The salary scale and entitlements of the Commissions employees shall be determined by a decision of the Prime Minister based on a proposal from the Chairman of the National Commission for Investment.

Fourth:

The Commissions headquarters shall be in Baghdad and it may appoint representatives in the regions and governorates.

Fifth:

The National Commission for investment shall draw up an overall national strategic policy for investment identifying the more important sectors and shall prepare a map of investment projects in Iraq in the light of the information it receives from the regions and governorates. It shall also prepare lists of investment opportunities in strategic and federal investment projects with initial information about these projects and making it available to those wishing to invest.

Article 5

First: The regions and governorates not organized in a region may form investment commissions in their areas. The latter shall enjoy the powers of granting the investment licenses, investment planning ,promoting investment and opening branches in their areas within the provisions of this law in consultation with National Commission for Investment to guarantee the availability of the legal conditions.

Second: The Investment Commission of the regions and governorate shall be composed of at least seven members including the chairman and the vice chairman of at least seven years of experience and competence and with a university degree appropriate to the specialization of the commission and not convicted in a felony or a misdemeanor involving turpitude or has declared his bankruptcy.

Third: The regions and governorates not organized in a region shall establish a mechanism of forming the investment commission of the region and the governorate and dismissing the Commission member in case of not adherence to the Commission regulations and standards.

Fourth: The Investment Commissions of the regions and governorate shall coordinate their work with the National Commission for Investment, and shall coordinate and consult with local governments regarding investment plans and facilities.

Fifth: The regions and governorates Commissions shall draw up their investment plan in a way that dose not contradict with the federal investment policy and shall prepare list of the investment opportunities in the areas that are subject thereto, with initial data about these projects and offer it to those wishing to invest.

Sixth: The regions Commissions shall be connected to the prime Minister of the region and is subject to the scrutiny of the regions Council. The governorate commission shall be connected to the Governor and is subject to the scrutiny of the governorate council in a way that does not contradict with the provisions of this law.

Seventh: Regions and Governorates Commissions board of directors shall convene upon an invitation from their chairman . The quorum of convening and adopting resolutions and recommendations shall be determined by absolute majority. The conduct of work shall be organized by by – laws issued by the Commission.

Article 6 :

In addition to ordinary correspondence, the Commission may adopt electronic mail with the official entities connected with the work and activity of the Commission through local networks or the Internet according to guidelines set by the Commission.

Article 7 :

A- The Commission shall accept investment license requests for projects whose capital is not less than the minimum amount determined by the Council of Ministers or the Council of Ministers of region as the case, by a regulation issued based on a proposal by the Commission.
B- The Commission must obtain the approval of the Council of Ministers before granting the license if the value of the investment project is more than two hundred and fifty million dollars.
C- The Commission shall make its final decision concerning the requests of investment license within a period not exceeding (45) forty five days from the date of filing a request.
D- The decisions of the Commission regarding the approved investments projects shall be obligatory for the purposes of this law.

Article 8 :

The Commission shall have an independent annual budget whose revenues shall be made up of its allocated amount in the State General Budget.

Article 9 :

The Commission shall promote investment through the following:-

First: Building confidence in the investment environment, identifying investment opportunities, and promoting and stimulating investment in them.

Second: Simplifying the procedures for registration, issuing of investment projects licenses, and following up existing projects and giving them priority in processing with the official entities. Completing the procedures of answering investor requests and obtaining the required approvals for the investor and the project.

Third: Establishing one window at the National Commission for investment and the Regions and Governorates Commissions, which includes authorized representatives from the ministries, and members nominated by the Councils of the regions and governorates as the case and the concerned authorities to undertake issuing licenses and obtain the approvals of other authorities in accordance with the law.

Fourth: Providing advice, information, and data to investors and issuing special manuals in this regard.

Fifth: Setting forth and implementing programs to promote investment in different areas of Iraq in order to attract investors.

Sixth: Facilitating the allocation of the needed lands and renting them out for establishing projects for a sum to be determined by the Commission in coordination with the concerned authorities.

Seventh: Establishing secure and free investment areas with the agreement of the Council of Ministers.

Eighth: Encouraging Iraqi investors through providing them with easy loans and financial facilities in coordination with the Ministry of Finance and with the assistance of Banking Institutions, provided that the investor obtaining the loan shall employ a number of unemployed Iraqis proportional with the volume of the loan.

Ninth: Any other tasks related to its work and assigned by the Council of Ministers.

CHAPTER THREE PRIVILEGES AND GUARANTEES

Article 10:

The Investor irrespective of his /her nationality shall enjoy all privileges, facilitations and guarantees and shall be subject to the obligations stated in this law. The Iraqi and foreign investor shall have the right for the purposes of housing projects, the use of the land for a sum to be determined between him and the land owner without land speculation according to conditions set forth by the National Commission of investment and the approval of the Council of Ministers. The Commission shall facilitate the allocation of the required lands for the housing projects. The housing units shall be allocated for ownership by the Iraqis after the completion of the project.

Article 11:

The investor shall enjoy the following benefits:-

First: the investor shall have the right to take out the capital he brought into Iraq and its proceeds in accordance with the provision of this law and pursuant to the instructions of the Central Bank of Iraq in an exchangeable currency after paying all his taxes and debts to the Iraqi Government and all other authorities.

Second: The foreign investor shall have the right to :

A. Exchange shares and bonds listed in the Iraqi Stock Exchange
B. Form investment portfolios in shares and bonds

Third: Renting or leasing land needed for the project for the term of the investment project, provided that it dose not exceed 50 years renewable with the agreement of the Commission, and provided that the nature of the project and its benefit for the national economy is taken into consideration when determining the period.

Fourth: Insuring the investment project with any foreign or national insurance company it deems suitable.

Fifth: Opening accounts in Iraqi or foreign currency or both at a bank inside or outside Iraq for the licensed project.

Article 12:

This law shall guarantee the following for the investor:-

First: The right to employ and use non- Iraqi workers in case it is not possible to

employ an Iraqi with the required qualifications and capable of performing the same task in accordance with guidelines issued by the Commission.

Second: Granting the foreign investor and non –Iraqis working in the investment projects the right for residence in Iraq and facilitate inter and departure from Iraq.

Third: Non- seizure or nationalization of the investment project covered by the provisions of this law in whole or in part, except for projects on which a final judicial judgment was issued.

Fourth: Non Iraq technicians and administration employees working in any project shall have the right to transfer their salaries and compensations outside Iraq in accordance with the law after paying their dues and debts to the Iraqi government and all other entities.

Article 13:

Any amendment to this Law shall not have any retroactive affect regarding the guarantees, exemptions, and rights recognized by this Law.

CHAPTER FOUR INVESTOR OBLIGATIONS

Article 14:

The Investor shall observe the following:-

First: To notify the National Commission for Investment , the Region or Governorate Commission in writing immediately after the installation and equipping of the fixed assets for the purposes of the project and the date of the beginning of commercial activity.

Second: To keep proper records audited by a certified accountant in Iraq in accordance with the law.

Third: To provide an economic and technical feasibility study for the project and any information, data or documents required by the Commission or other competent authorities regarding the budget of the project and the progress made in its execution.

Fourth: To keep records of the projects duty- free imported materials in accordance with the provisions of this Law and specifying the depreciation periods of these materials.

Fifth: To protect the safety of the environment and to adhere to the valid quality control norms in Iraq and International regulations in this field also adhere to laws connected to security and health and to public order and Iraqi social ethics.

Sixth: To adhere to the valid Iraqi laws regarding salaries, vacations, work hours, work conditions and others as a minimum.

Seventh: Commitment to the correspondence of the work progress schedule submitted by the investor with reality provided that the time difference shall not exceed six months, the National Commission for Investment shall set forth punitive conditions in case of exceeding the six –month period and the Commission shall have the right to withdraw the license.

Eighth: To train and rehabilitate its Iraqi employees as well as raising their efficiency, skill and capabilities. Priority in employment and recruitment shall be given to the Iraqis.

CHAPTER FIVE EXEMPTIONS

Article 15:

First: The project that has obtained an investment license from the Commission shall enjoy exemption from taxes and duties for a period of (10) ten years as of the date of commencing commercial operations in accordance with the areas of development defined by the Council of Ministers at the suggestion of the National Commission for Investment based on the degree of economic development and the nature of the investment project.

Second: To Council of Ministers shall have the right to propose draft laws to extend or grant exemptions in addition to the exemptions stipulated in paragraph (First) of this Article, or provide incentives, guarantees or other benefits to any project or sector or region and for the periods and percentages it deems appropriate in accordance with the nature of the activity, its geographical location and its contribution to manpower employment and its effect on driving the economic development, for considerations of national interest.

Third: The National Commission for Investment has the right to increase the years of tax and duties exemption in a way directly proportional to the increase in the Iraqi Investor share in the project to reach fifteen years if the Iraqi Investor share in the project was more than 50% .

Article 16:

In case the project is moved from one development area to another during the exemption period, the project – for the purpose of exemption stipulated in(First) of Article 15- shall be treated during the remaining term the treatment of the project in the development areas it is moving to, provided that the Commission is informed of such move.

Article 17:

The project that obtains an investment license shall also enjoy the following:-

First: Assets imported for the purposes of the investment project shall be exempted from duties provided that their entry to Iraq is made within(3) three years from the date of granting the investment license.

Second: The imported assets required for the expansion, development or modernization of the project shall be exempted from duties in case they led to an increase in the designed capacity, provided they are brought in within three years from the date of notifying the Commission of the expansion or development. Expansion, for the purposes of this law, shall mean adding fixed capital assets aimed at increasing the designed capacity of the project in commodities or services or materials by a percentage exceeding (15%)fifteen percent. Development, for the purposes of this law, shall mean replacing project machines with more developed ones, totally or partially or making a development on the standing devices and equipments of the project by adding new machines and devices or parts thereof with the aim of raising the productive efficiency or improving and developing the quality of the products and services.

Third: Spare parts imported for the purposes of the project shall be exempted from duties if the value of these parts does not exceeded(20%) twenty percent of the fixed assets value, provided that they are not be used for any other purpose.

Fourth: Hotels, tourist institutions, hospitals, health institutions, rehabilitation centers and educational and scientific organizations project shall be granted additional exemptions from duties and taxes on their imports of furniture, furnishings and requisites for renewing and updating purposes at least once every four years, provided that these items are brought into Iraq or used in the project within (3) three years from the date of the approval decision of the Commission on the import lists and their quantities, and provided that these items are not used for purposes other than the imported purposes.

Article 18:

In case it is found that the project assets totally or partially exempted from customs and duties, are sold, in contrary to the provisions at this law or used not for the project, or used not for the declared purpose then the investor must pay the taxes and fines incurred pursuant to the law.

CHAPTER SIX PROCEDURES FOR GRANTING INVESTMENT AND PROJECT ESTABLISHMENT LICENSE

Article 19:

First: The investor shall obtain the license in addition to obtaining the rest of the licenses for the purpose of enjoying the privileges and exemptions provided by the Commission.

Second: To Commission shall grant the license for investment or project establishment based on a request submitted by the investor according to conditions facilitated and prepared by the Commission. The request submitted by the investor shall include the following:-

A- Filling a request form prepared by the Commission.
B- Financial competency from an accredited bank.
C- Projects performed by the investor inside or outside Iraq.
D- Details of the project intended to invest in and its economic feasibility.
E- A timetable for completing the project.

Article 20:

First: The Commission must issue the establishing license through establishing one window in the region or the governorate not organized in a region that includes authorized representatives of the ministries and relevant bodies. The Commission shall grant project establishment license and obtain approvals from the entities in accordance with the law.

Second: To Commission must help the investor to obtain licenses by approaching the competent authorities and exploring the opinions of the entities concerning the issuance of the establishment license. These entities must issue the decision to reject, approve or request amendment within 15 days from the date of being notified. The failure to reply from the entity from which the opinion is solicited shall be deemed as an approval and in case of a rejection there must be cause for it.

Third: In case of disagreement between the National Commission for Investment decision and the other entity related to granting establishment license other than the region commission the dispute shall be raised to prime Minister for settlement.

Fourth: In case the request for registration in rejected, the applicant may file a complaint to the Chairman of the region or the governorate Commission concerned within(15) fifteen days after receiving notification of the rejection decision. The Chairman of the Commission concerned shall take a decision concerning the complaint in question within a period of seven days. The petitioner may appeal the decision of the Chairman of the Commission concerned rejecting his complaint to the authority to which the Commission concerned is connected to within 15 days from the date the complaints rejection and its decision is deemed final.

CHAPTER SEVEN GENERAL PROVISIONS

Article 21:

The project capital subject to the provisions of this law shall be made up of the following:-

First: Cash transferred to Iraq through banks and financial companies or any other legal means with the aim of investing it for the purposes of this law.

Second: The in – kind assets and incorporeal rights imported to Iraq or purchased from the local markets by the cash transferred into Iraq:-

A- In- kind assets related to the project.

B- The machinery, tools, equipment, building , construction, transportation means, furniture and offices appliances required for establishing the project.

C- The incorporeal rights that include patents, registered trade marks, technical know- how, engineering services, administrative and marketing services and the similar.

Third: Profits, proceeds and reserves resulting from the capital invested in Iraq in the project if the capital of such a project was increased or was invested in another project covered by the provisions of this law.

Article 22:

The foreign investor shall enjoy additional privileges in accordance with international agreements signed between Iraq and his country or multilateral international agreements which Iraq has joined.

Article 23:

In case the property of the project during the exemption term is transferred to another investor the project shall continue to enjoy granted exemption facilities and guarantees until the end of that period provided that the new investor continue to work on the project in the same specialization or in another, with the approval of the Commission. The new investor must take the place of the former investor in the rights and obligations consequent to the provisions of this law.

Article 24:

First: The investor, with the approval of the Commission, may sell exempted fixed assets or relinquish it to another investor benefiting from the provisions of this law, provided that he uses them in his project.

Second: The investor, after informing the Commission, may sell the exempted fixed assets to any person or other project not subject to the provisions of this law after paying the outstanding duties and taxes.

Third: The investor, with the approval of the Committee, may re-export the exempted fixed assets.

Article 25:

In the event two or more companies or enterprises merge, the new company or entity resulting from the merger must set up separate accounts for each project before the merger in order to register and apply exemptions and facilitations stipulated in this law during the remaining period of the exemption.

Article 26:

Any project approved in accordance with the provisions of the previous applicable laws shall continue to benefit from all exemptions granted to it pursuant to that law and until the expiration of the exemption period and under the same terms.

Article 27:

Disputes arising between parties who are subject to the provisions of this law shall be subject to the Iraqi law unless otherwise agreed, save to the cases that are subject to the provisions of the Iraq law exclusively or the jurisdiction of Iraqi courts.

1- Disputes arising from the labor contract shall exclusively be subject to the provisions of the Iraqi law and the jurisdiction of the Iraq courts. Non –Iraqi labor shall be exempted if the work contract stipulated otherwise.
2- If parties to a dispute are non – Iraqis and in disputes not arising from a crime, the opponents may agree on the law to be applied, the competent court or any other agreement to resolve their dispute.
3- In case of dispute between partners or between the owner of a project subjected to the provisions of this law, and others that result stoppage of work for a period of more than three months, the Commission may withdraw the license and ask the owners of the project to settle the dispute within a period not exceeding three months. If such period elapsed without settling the dispute between the partners or between the owner of the project and others, the Commission may take legal measures to liquidate the project and notify the owner of the project or one of the partners of such action. The liquidation money shall be deposited in one of the banks after paying the dues of the State or any other dues after final judgment of their entitlement is rendered.
4- If the parties to a dispute are subject to the provisions of this law, they may, at the time of signing the agreement, agree on a mechanism to resolve disputes including arbitration pursuant to the Iraqi law or any other internationally recognized entity.
5- Disputes arising between the Commission or any governmental entity and any of those subject to the provisions of this law on matters not related to violations of one of the provisions of this law shall be subject to Iraqi law and courts on civil matters. As for commercial disputes, parties may resort to arbitration provided that such an arrangement is stipulated in the contract organizing the relationship between parties.

Article 28:

In case the investor violates any of the provisions of this law, the Commission shall have the right to warn the investor in writing to remove the violation within a specific period.

In case the investor dose not remove the violation within the specified period, the Commission shall summon the investor or who represent him to state his position and grant him other respite to settle the issue. Upon repeating or not removing the violation, the Commission shall have the right to withdraw the investors license it issued and order stoppage of work on the project and retain the state's right to deny the investor the granted exemptions and privileges from the date of the violation and allow other to retain their rights to demand compensation for the damage caused by this violation, without breaching any punishments or other compensations stipulated in the applicable laws.

Article 29:

All fields of investments shall be subject to the provisions of this law except:-

First: Investment in Oil and Gas extraction and production.

Second: Investment in banks and insurance companies sectors.

Article 30:

The council of Ministers may.

First: Issue regulations to facilitate the implementation of the provisions of this law.

Second: Issue bylaws defining the Commissions formations, divisions tasks, process of its work, its authorities, financial affairs, employee affairs and any others matters.

Article 31:

The Committee may issue instructions to facilitate the implementation of regulations issued by the Council of Ministers pursuant to the provisions of this law.

Article 32:

The Provisions of this law shall be applied to the existing and operating projects of the mixed and private sectors which have commenced before the issuance of this law and upon a request from its management and the approval of the Commission with no retroactive effect.

Article 33:

No text shall be valid which contradicts the provisions of this law.

Article 34:

The (dissolved) CPA Order No. 39 of 2003 shall be revoked.

Article 35:

The Arab Investment law No(62) of 2002 issued by the dissolved Revolution Command Council shall be annulled.

Article 36:

This law shall enter into force from the date of its publication in the Official Gazette.

Justifying Reasons

For the purpose of driving the process of economic and social development and bringing technical and scientific experience and developing human resources, and for creating work opportunities for the Iraqis by encouraging investments and supporting the process of establishing investment projects in Iraq and their expansion and development at various economic levels and by granting privileges and exemptions for these projects, this law is legislated.

JORDAN

THE INVESTMENT PROMOTION LAW

Article (1) This Law shall be named "The Investment Promotion Law of 1995", and shall come into effect as of the date of its publication in the Official Gazette[(1)].

Article (2) Wherever used in this Law, and unless the context otherwise provides, the following terms and expressions shall have the meaning ascribed there to hereunder:

* **The Council:** The Higher Council for Investment Promotion formed pursuant to this Law.

* **The Corporation:** The Jordan Investment Board established pursuant to this Law.

* **The Board:** The Board of Directors of the Corporation.

* **The Minister: The Minister of Industry and Trade.**

* **The Committee:** The Investment Promotion Committee formed pursuant to this Law.

* **The Director General:** The Director General of the Jordan Investment Board.

* **The Project:** Any economic activity to which the provisions of this Law and Regulations and Instructions issued hereunder shall apply.

* **Fixed Assets:** The machinery, apparatus(es), equipment, supplies and tools to be exclusively used in the Project, and the furniture and supplies for hotels and hospitals.

(1) This Law was published in the Official Gazette issue No.(4075) dated 16/10/1996, and amended in the Law No. (13) of 2000 published in the official Gazette issue No. (4423) dated 2/4/2000.

* **Fees:** Import Fees, Custom Duties and other fees imposed on Fixed Assets Items in accordance with the applicable laws, with the exception of Municipal Fees.

* **Taxes** Taxes imposed on Fixed Assets Items pursuant to the applicable laws, with the exception of Municipal Taxes.

* **The Investor:** The natural or legal person investing in the Kingdom in accordance with the provisions of this Law.

* **Production Capacity:** The designed or occupancy capacity of the Project.

Article (3) a) Any project falling within the following Sectors or Sub-sectors shall enjoy the exemptions and facilities provided by this Law:

1. Industry
2. The Agriculture Sector (without prejudice to any privileges provided by other laws).
3. Hotels.
4. Hospitals.
5. Maritime Transport and Railways.
6. Any other Sector or subsectors the Council of Ministers decide to add upon the Council's

(1) (2) recommendations.

b. The Council of Ministers may, upon recommendation of both the Minister and the Committee, offer any project established within the Sectors mentioned in this Law incentives or guarantees or other privileges for the number of years the Council of Ministers sees fit according to the nature of the project's activity, its geographic location, its contribution to increasing exports, creating jobs, exploiting national natural resources and accelerating economic development, in special cases and due to considerations determined by the Council of Ministers, and to be of national interest.

(1) The following two subsectors were added by virtue of the resolution of the Council of Ministers dated 28/10/1997: **a.** Leisure and Recreational Compounds **b**. Conventions and Exhibition Centers.

(2) The following sector has been added by virtue of the resolution of the Council of Ministers dated 28/5/2002: "Pipeline transportation and distribution services for water, Gas and Petroleum derivatives as well as its exploitation"

Article (4) a. For the purposes of this Law, the (geographical) areas which enjoy tax exemptions are classified into three development areas (A,B,C); subject to the degree of the economic development of such areas in each of the Sectors listed in Article (3) of this Law, pursuant to a regulation to be issued for this purpose.

b. The Subsectors and the investment activities listed in paragraph (a) of this Article, along with the eligibility conditions for the enjoyment of the privileges provided by this Law in each of the development areas designated hereunder, shall be specified in a regulation to be issued for this purpose.

Article (5) For the purposes of this Law, the expression: "Invested Foreign Capital" shall mean money invested in the Kingdom by a non-Jordanian, cash or in kind, or any rights having a financial value, including the following:

a. Cash transferred to the Kingdom via licensed banks and financial companies which is invested for the purposes of this Law.

b. The imported assets in kind whose cost has been paid from outside the Kingdom.

c. Profits, returns and reserves resulting from investing Foreign Capital in the Project, provided that such profits, returns or reserves are used to increase the capital of the Project or are invested in another Project covered by the provisions of this Law.

d. Intangible rights such as licenses, patents, trademarks and trade names registered in the Kingdom.

Article (6) a. The Fixed Assets of the Project shall be exempted from Fees and Taxes provided that they are imported into the Kingdom within a period of three years from the date of the Committee's decision approving the lists of fixed Assets of the Project. The Committee may extend this period if it deems that the nature of the Project and the size of work required that.

b. Imported spare parts for the Project shall be exempted from Fees and Taxes provided that the value of such spares does not exceed 15% of the value of the Fixed Assets for which they are required, and provided that they are imported into the Kingdom or used in the Project within a period of ten years from the date of commencement of production or work, in accordance with a decision taken by the Committee approving the lists of spare parts and their quantities.

c. The Committee shall exempt from Fees and Taxes Fixed Assets that are required for the expansion, development or modernization of the Project if such expansion, development or modernization shall result in an increase in the Production Capacity of the Project by not less than 25%.

d. The Committee shall exempt from Fees and Taxes any increase in the value of the Fixed Assets which are imported for the Project if such increase is a result of a rise in the prices of such assets in the country of origin, of a rise in the freight charges applicable thereto or of changes in the exchange rate.

Article (7) a. By a decision of the Committee, the Project that falls within one of the Sectors or Subsectors listed in Article (3) of this law shall be exempted from income and social services taxes, by the following percentages in accordance with the development area applicable thereto: 25% if the Project is in a class A development area. 50% if the Project is in a class B development area. 75% if the Project is in a class C development area. The Exemption period upon the committee's decision shall be

(10) ten years starting from the date of commencement of work for services projects, or from the date of commencement of production for manufacturing projects.

b. The Committee shall grant an additional exemption if the Project has been expanded, developed or modernized with the result of increasing it's Production Capacity. The additional exemption period shall be for one year per each increase in production capacity not less than 25%, and for a maximum of four years.

Article (8) Projects in the Hotel and Hospital Sectors shall be granted additional exemptions from Fees and Taxes once every seven years for their purchases of furniture and supplies required for modernization and renewal, provided that such items are imported into the Kingdom or used in the Project within four years from the date of the Committee's decision approving the list of purchases and their quantities.

Article (9) If the Project is transferred from one development area to another during the granted exemption period, then for the purposes of the exemption, and provided that the Jordan Investment Board is (duly) notified (of the transfer), the Project shall be afforded, for the remaining period of the exemption, the same treatment as Projects located in the (new development) area to which the Project has been transferred.

Article (10) Excluding the exemptions provided in Article (7) of this Law, any existing Project, whether approved as an "Economical Project" or as an "Approved Economical Project" pursuant to the provisions of the Encouragement of Investment Law No. (11) of 1987 and it's amendments or the proceeding laws, and any other project that did not benefit from the provisions of these laws, shall enjoy the exemptions and privileges provided by this Law if it meets the requirements of a regulation that will be issued for this purpose , and adjusts its status according to the provisions thereof.

Article (11) a. A council named "The Higher Council for Investment Promotion" shall be established. The Council shall be chaired by the Prime Minister, and with the membership of:

-Minister of Industry & Trade **Deputy Chairman**

-Minister of Finance **Member**

-Minister of Planning **Member**

- Minister of Tourism **Member**

-Minister of Transport **Member**

-Governor of the Central Bank **Member**

-Director general **Member/Rapporteur**

-Chairman of the Union of Jordanian Chambers of Commerce **Member** -Chairman of Amman Chamber of Industry **Member** -Three competent and experienced Persons from the private sector appointed by the Chairman upon recommendation of the Minister for two renewable years. **Members**

b. The Council shall hold its meetings whenever the need arises, pursuant to an invitation from its Chairman, or Deputy-Chairman in case of the Chairman's absence. The Council's meeting shall be considered legal if attended by two thirds of the Council's members, provided that the Chairman, or the Deputy-Chairman in case of the former's absence is present. Resolutions shall be reached unanimously or by a majority of votes of members attending the meeting. In the case of equal votes the side supported by the Chairman of the meeting shall prevail.

Article (12) The Council shall create a suitable environment for investment in order to achieve the comprehensive development goals. For that, the Council has the authority to assume the following responsibilities:

a. Approving a National Strategy for Investment including the development of production sectors, developing and following-up its implementation.

b. Approving investment policies.

c. Approving the Investment Promotion Policy, and following-up its implementation.

d. Reviewing investment regulations.

Article (13) a. According to the provisions of this law, a corporation named "The Jordan Investment Board (JIB)", shall be established which enjoys a legal personality with financial and administrative independence. Thus, the JIB may carry out all legal acts such as concluding contracts, acquiring movable and immovable property, borrowing, selling, mortgaging and accepting donations and grants. The Jordan Investment Board shall be represented in legal matters and judicial proceedings pertaining to or arising from its activities by the General Civil Lawyer or by any registered lawyer appointed by the JIB.

b. The JIB shall have a director General appointed by a decision of the Council of Ministers, upon a recommendation by the Minister; provided that the decision is endorsed by a Royal Decree.

c. The headquarters of the JIB shall be in the city of Amman. The JIB may establish branches in any place within or outside the Kingdom.

Article (14) The JIB shall aim at promoting investment in the Kingdom by

carrying out the following:

a. Enhancing confidence in the investment environment, identifying investment opportunities, promoting these opportunities and motivating investment therein.

b. Simplifying the registration and licensing procedures of investment projects, following-up existing Projects, and giving them priority in the finalization of applications at official authorities.

c. Establishing an investment window at the JIB which shall undertake licensing investment projects and obtaining approvals on such projects from other authorities pursuant to the legislations in force. The Minister has the right to issue a decision to license a certain Project if the relevant ministries or public authorities fail to issue a reasoned decision regarding the licensing (of that Project) within a period of thirty days from the date on which the investor submitted a request for licensing.

d. Giving advice, providing available information and data for investors and issuing related guides.

e. Setting and implementing investment promotion programs to attract investors to the Kingdom.

Article (15) The JIB shall have an independent annual budget, and its funds shall be constituted of the following sources:

a. Funds allocated by the Government.

b. Returns of services rendered by the JIB and other revenue received thereby.

c. Local or foreign loans, provided that the Council of Ministers approves the foreign loans.

d. Profits on the JIB's funds.

e. Grants, aids, gifts, and wills or other funds offered to the JIB and approved by the Council.

Article (16) a. The financial year of the JIB shall start on the first of January of each year and shall end on the thirty first of December of the same year.

b. Within the four months following the end of its financial year, the JIB shall prepare a comprehensive report on its activities, accompanied by its final accounts certified by the auditors, and shall submit such report to the Board for approval.

c. In organizing it's accounts and records, the JIB shall pursue the principles and basis of commercial accounting.

Article (17) a. The Jordan Investment Board shall be managed by a Board of Directors chaired by the Minister. The Board shall be formed pursuant to a decision of the Council with a number from the Council's members not exceeding (7) seven, provided that the Director General is among them. The Board shall select one of its members to be a Deputy Chairman.

b. Whenever the need may arise, the Board shall convene pursuant to an invitation from the Chairman. The Board meeting shall be considered legal if it is attended by the majority of members, provided that the Chairman, or Deputy Chairman, in the case of the Chairman's absence, is present. The Board shall reach its decisions unanimously or by a majority vote. In the event of equal votes the side supported by the chairman of the meeting shall prevail.

c. The Chairman of the Board may invite any expert and specialized person to attend the Board's meetings to offer consultations on the subject presented thereto without such person being entitled to vote.

d. The remuneration of the members of the Board shall be determined by the Council's decision and shall be paid according to the number of meetings attended by the relevant member.

e. The Chairman of the Board shall appoint one of the JIB's staff as secretary to the Board, in accordance with the Director general's recommendation. The secretary shall be responsible for organizing the administrative work of the Board, recording its resolutions and obtaining the signatures of the Chairman of the meeting and the other members on such resolutions.

Article (18) The Board shall carry out the duties and assume the authorities provided for in this Law including the following:

a. Supervising and following up the administrative affairs of the JIB.

b. Suggesting the investment policies of the Kingdom, determining its priorities, setting programs and plans, determining and submitting them to the Council for approval.

c. Approving the JIB's budget, the auditors' report and the final financial statements.

d. Approving the financial and administrative instructions of the JIB.

e. Determining returns of services rendered by the JIB.

f. Appointing licensed auditors for the JIB and determining their fees.

g. Establishing branches of the JIB anywhere within or outside the Kingdom.

Article (19) The Chairman of the Board shall represent the JIB in all its relations with others, and may delegate this representation to the Director General.

Article (20) The Director General shall carry out and assume the following duties and authorities:

a. Applying the general policy of the JIB, implementing decisions issued in accordance with the provisions of this law, and following up their implementation.

b. Administering the activities of the JIB, supervising its staff and its technical, administrative and financial affairs.

c. Laying down programs that achieve the goals and tasks of the JIB, submitting the related recommendations to the Board, and working towards their development.

d. Any other duties determined by the Board, or assigned to him pursuant to the regulations issued pursuant to this Law.

Article (21) a. A Committee named "The Investment Promotion Committee" shall be formed. The Committee shall be chaired by the Director General, and with the membership of :

1. The Director General of the Income Tax Department.
2. The Director General of the Customs Department.
3. A Representative of the Ministry of Industry and Trade appointed by the Minister.
4. A representative of the private sector appointed by the Chairman of the Council.

b. In the absence of the Committee's Chairman, the Director General of the Customs Department shall assume the chairmanship of the Committee.

c. The Committee shall convene pursuant to an invitation from its Chairman. The meeting shall be considered legal if four of its members are present, including the Chairman. The committee shall reach its decisions by a majority vote of three of its members.

d. The Director General may invite one or more persons from any entity from the relevant sector to attend the Committee's meetings in order to provide advice on the matter presented thereto, without such person being entitled to vote.

e. The Director General shall appoint one of the JIB staff to carry out the duties as secretary to the Committee to record and follow-up the Committee's decisions.

The Committee shall carry out the duties and assume the **Article (22)** authorities stated in this Law including the following:

a. Reviewing applications submitted by the Investors and reaching decisions thereon within a period of thirty days from the date of submittal of the application, and in case of disapproval, reasons shall be mentioned.

b. Approving additional exemptions pursuant to this Law.

c. Reviewing objections on the Committee's decisions that are raised by Investors. The decision of the Committee to dismiss an objection shall be subject to appeal to the Board within a period of thirty days from the date of notification of the decision.

Article (23) In the event that all or part of the exempted Fixed Assets have been sold in a manner contrary to the provisions herein, or have not been used in the Project, or have been used for purposes other than as declared, the due taxes, fees and fines shall be imposed on the Project in accordance with the provisions of the laws and regulations in force.

Article (24) Subject to the provisions of other Laws:

a. The Non-Jordanian Investor may invest in the Kingdom through ownership or partnership or shareholding, in accordance with the provisions of a regulation to be issued for this purpose. Said regulation shall clarify the project sectors or subsectors thereof in which the foreign Investor may invest and the maximum percentage of ownership and the minimum Foreign Capital allowed therein.

b. Subject to the provisions of paragraph (a) above, the Non-Jordanian Investor investing in any Project governed by this Law shall be afforded the same treatment as the Jordanian Investor.

c. The Investor has the right to manage the Project in the manner he deems appropriate and through the person(s) chosen by the Investor for its management. The competent authorities shall provide the required facilities.

Article (25) It shall not be permissible to expropriate any Project or to subject it to any measure that may lead to expropriation, unless such expropriation is done by way of compulsory purchase for the purposes of public interest, and in return for a just compensation to be paid to the Investor. The compensation paid to a Non-Jordanian Investor in such case shall be in a convertible currency.

Article (26) The Investor must carry out the following:

a. Notify the JIB in writing, upon completing the installation of the Fixed Assets and preparation for the Project, of the date of commencement of work or actual production.

b. Maintain regular books and records and have them audited by licensed auditors in the Kingdom.

c. Maintain a record of the Fixed Assets that are admitted to the Project where all details of such assets shall be entered.

d. Furnish any information, data or documents required by the JIB which are pertinent to the Fixed Assets of the Project. Any authorized employee of the JIB shall be allowed to have access to the Project to check the accuracy of such data and information.

Article (27) If the ownership of the project is transferred during the granted exemption period, the Project shall continue to enjoy the granted exemptions, facilities and guarantees till the end of such period, provided that the new investor continues to work in the Project and replaces the previous investor in the rights and obligations provided under the provisions of this Law.

Article (28) a. Upon obtaining the approval of the Committee, the Investor may sell the exempted Fixed Assets or relinquish them to another Investor benefiting from the provisions of this Law, provided that these assets are used in the Project of such Investor. Upon notifying the Committee, the investor may also sell the exempted Fixed Assets to any person or to another project not covered by the provisions of this Law after paying the fees and taxes due on such Fixed Assets.

b. Upon obtaining the approval of the Committee, the Investor may re-export the exempted Fixed Assets.

Article (29) If two or more companies or corporations merge, the new company or corporation resulting from the merger shall for the remaining period of the exemption, be obliged to maintain separate accounts for each Project that had enjoyed the exemptions and benefits provided for in this Law before the merger.

Article (30) The Non-Jordanian Investor shall be entitled to remit abroad without delay and in a convertible currency the Foreign Capital transferred to the Kingdom for investment pursuant to the provisions of this Law or any previous legislation, together with any returns and profits accrued thereon, and also, the proceeds of liquidation of the investment, or the proceeds of sale of all or part of his Project.

Article (31) Non-Jordanian technicians and administrators working in any Project may transfer their salaries and remunerations abroad in accordance with the legislation in force.

Article (32) a. The provisions of "The Investment Agreement of Arab Capital and their Transfer between Arab States" and the provisions of all treaties concluded with Arab States and their amendments shall be taken into consideration with respect to Arab Capital invested in accordance with the provisions of this Law.

b. Any Investor, whose investment is guaranteed by his country or by an official agency thereof, may assign to that country or agency any returns on his investment or other compensation to which he is entitled, so that the country or agency subrogates him.

Article (33) Investment disputes between an Investor of Foreign Capital and Jordanian governmental agencies shall be settled amicably. If no amicable settlement can be reached within a period not exceeding six months, either party may resort to litigation or may refer the dispute to "The International Center for the Settlement of Investment Disputes" (ICSID) for settlement by conciliation or arbitration in accordance with the provisions of the Agreement on the Settlement of Investment Disputes between states and Nationals of other states, which has been signed by the Kingdom.

Article (34) It shall be permissible to register mortgages on equipment and machinery that are part of the Fixed Assets of any Project as security for extended credit facilities. For the purposes of Implementing the provisions of this Article, the JIB shall, pursuant to instructions issued for this purpose by the Board and published in the Official Gazette, maintain an industrial register listing the equipment and machinery for every Project.

Article (35) Any project, which was approved pursuant to the provisions of the Encouragement of Investment Law No. (11) of 1987 and its amendments, shall continue to enjoy the exemptions granted thereto in accordance with that Law until the end of the exemption period and subject to its conditions.

Article (36) The JIB shall enjoy the same exemptions and benefits applicable to ministries and governmental departments.

Article (37) The Council of Ministers may issue the necessary regulations for implementing the provisions of this Law, including those pertinent to financial, procurement and employment affairs of the JIB.

Article (38) The following are cancelled:

a. The Encouragement of Investment Law No. (11) of 1987, its amendments, and the regulations issued pursuant thereto.

b. The Law Regulating Arab and Foreign Investments No. (27) of 1992 and the regulations issued pursuant thereto.

Article (39) The Prime Minster and the Ministers are entrusted to implement the provisions of this Law.

REGULATION NO.(54) FOR THE YEAR 2000 REGULATING NON-JORDANIAN INVESTMENTS REGULATION ISSUED PURSUANT TO ARTICLE (24) OF THE INVESTMENT PROMOTION LAW NO. (16) FOR THE YEAR 1995

Article (1) This Regulation shall be named the "Regulating Non-Jordanian Investments Regulation for the year 2000", and shall come into force thirty days after its publication in the Official Gazette[1]

Article (2) In the cases not mentioned in Articles (3) and (4) of this Regulation which specify the percentage of non-Jordanian ownership or participation in the sectors and activities cited therein, the non-Jordanian investor may own any project wholly or partially or may participate in it in any percentage.

Article (3) The Non-Jordanian investor ownership shall not exceed (50%) fifty percent of the capital of any project in the following sectors and activities:

a. The Following commercial activities:

1. Purchase of goods and other movable tangibles for purposes of leasing or renting for re-leasing thereof, including machinery and equipment, transport vehicles and other transport equipment, rent a car, aircraft (without operator) and ships, excluding financial leasing services conducted by banks, financial companies and insurance companies.
2. Purchase of goods and other movable tangibles for purposes of selling with profits.
3. Wholesale trade and retailing.
4. Import and export excluding importation up till the Kingdom's border outlets.
5. Distribution of goods and services within the Kingdom including distribution of audiovisual works.

(1) This Regulation was published in the Official Gazette issue No. (4465) dated 16/11/2000.

6. Supply services excluding food catering that is not conducted by restaurants, cafes and cafeterias, without prejedice to the provisions of item (12) of paragraph (B) of this Article.

b. The Following services:

1. Engineering services, including all engineering categories, urban planning and landscape architectural services.
2. Construction contracting including construction services and related engineering services.
3. Technical testing services concerning soil tests and geotechnical testing for construction purposes.
4. Maintenance and repair services of land transport equipment.
5. Maintenance and repair services of radio and television transmitters and broadcast equipment.
6. Photographic services including photocopying services and excluding motion picture and television photography services.
7. Placement and supply services of personnel.
8. Brokerage services excluding financial brokerage and intermediaries conducted by banks, financial companies and financial services companies.
9. Advertising services including advertising agencies and firms. 10 Commercial agents and intermediary services and insurance agents. 11 Money exchange services excluding those provided through banks or financial companies.

12 Restaurants, cafes and cafeterias excluding those that are provided within hotels, motels, and on board of ships and trains.

13 Travel Agencies and tour operators services (tourist and travel bureaus).

c. The following transport services:

1. Maritime transport and auxiliary services, including:

-Passenger and freight transportation excluding transportation over ships owned by non-Jordanians.

-Maritime survey and inspection. -Maritime freight forwarding. -Shipping agents' services. -Ships chandlers. -Ships brokers. -Ships management services.

    1. Air transport auxiliary services, including: -Ground Handling. -Freight Inspection. -Packing and unpacking. -Air Cargo Agents. -Freight Forwarders. -Cargo Terminals and Stores.
    2. Excluding : -Engine Overhaul. -Airports duty-free shops. -Simulators Training -Computer Reservation System (CRS).
2. Rail transport auxiliary services, including: -Cargo handling. -Inspection. -Packing and unpacking. -Storage & warehouse services. -Freight transport agency services. -Cargo Agents services.

Excluding: -Passenger and freight transportation. -Pushing and towing services. -Supporting services for rail transport such as rail passenger terminal services.

4. Road transport services, including: -Specialized tourist transportation services. -Supporting services of road transport such as bus station

services, parking services, services related to operating subways, bridges and highways.

- Auxiliary services to road transport including cargo handling services, storage and warehousing services, freight transport agency services, inspection services, packing and unpacking services and freight forwarders services.

d. Clearance services in cases where such clearance is linked to any of the services provided for in Paragraph (c) of this Article.

Article (4) The Non-Jordanian investor ownership shall not exceed (49%) forty nine percent of the capital of any project in the following sectors and activities:

a. Scheduled and non-scheduled passenger, freight and mail air transport services.

b. Rental services of aircraft with operator.

Article (5) The non-Jordanian ownership or participation in any of the sectors or activities not listed in Articles (3) and (4) of this Regulation, or the ones that are excluded therefrom, shall not be restricted unless the concerned legislation restricts such ownership or participation.

Article (6) Non-Jordanian investors are not allowed to own or to participate, wholly or partially in any of the following projects or activities.

a. Passenger and freight road transportation services including taxi, bus and trucks services.

b. Quarries for natural sand, dimension stones, aggregates and construction stones used for construction purposes.

c. Security and investigation services.

d. Sports clubs including the organization of sports events services, excluding health fitness clubs services.

e. Clearance services, without prejedice to paragraph (D) of Article

(3) from this Regulation.

Article (7) Subject to the provisions of this Regulation, the non-Jordanian investment shall not be less than (JD50,000) fifty thousand Jordanian Dinars or the equivalence thereof, with the exception of participating in public shareholding companies.

Article (8) The Council of Ministers may upon the recommendation of the Higher Council for Investment Promotion permit the ownership or participation in big development projects that enjoy special importance for any non-Jordanian investor in higher percentages than is provided by this regulation and according to the percentage in the Council's decision.

Article (9) The Minister may issue the necessary instructions for the implementation of the provisions of this Regulation.

Article (10) The Non-Jordanian Investment Promotion Regulation No. (39) for the year 1997 and its amendment shall be annulled.

REGULATION NO. (2) OF 1996 THE REGULATION OF THE INVESTMENT AREAS AND SECTORS ISSUED PURSUANT TO ARTICLE (4) OF THE INVESTMENT PROMOTION LAW NO. (16) OF 1995

Article (1) This Regulation shall be named "The Regulation of the Investment Areas and Sectors" of 1996 and shall come into effect as of the date of its publication in the Official Gazette. [1]

Article (2) Whenever used in this Regulation, and unless the context otherwise provides, the following terms shall have the meanings ascribed thereto hereunder:

-The Law: The Investment Promotion Law in force.

- **The Committee:** The Investment promotion Committee formed in accordance with the provisions of the Law.

Article (3) a. Subject to the provisions of paragraphs (c) , (d) and (f) of this Article, the Kingdom shall be divided for the purposes of ascertaining the development areas which shall enjoy the tax exemptions in accordance with the schedule shown below. The applicable administrative divisions system in force shall be relied upon to determine these development areas.

b. All areas of the Kingdom shall be classified under zone (c) for the sectors of Agriculture and Maritime Transport and Railways.

c. The Shore of the dead Sea area, with a 5 km depth from the sea line shall be classified under zone (A) for the hotel sector.

d. The provisions of paragraph (a) of this Article shall not be applicable to conservatories and environmental protection areas that already exist or will be established.

e. Leisure and Recreational Compounds, Convention and Exhibition Centers will be classified under category (A).

f. The Qualified Industrial Zones (QIZs) shall be classified under zone (B) unless already located under zone (C).

(1) This Regulation was published in the Official Gazette issue No. (4095) dated 16/1/1996, and amended in the Regulations No. (27) of 1997 published in issue No. (4205) of the Official Gazette dated 17/5/1997, and amended in the Regulation No. (60) of 1997 published in issue No. (4241) in the Official Gazette dated

16/11/1997, and amended by Regulation No. (88) of 2001 published in issue No. (4515) of the Official Gazette dated 1/11/2001.

THE SCHEDULE

The Governorate	District	Industry	*Hotels	Hospitals	Agriculture & Maritime Transport & Railways	Leisure and Recreational Compounds + Conventions and Exhibition Centers
The Capital	Amman Kasba	A	A	A	C	A
	Ras Al-Ain	A	B	A	C	A
	Marka	A	C	B	C	A
	Qweismeh	A	C	C	C	A
	University	A	A	A	C	A
	Wadi Al-Seer	A	A	B	C	A
	Marj Al-Hamam	A	C	B	C	A
	Iraq Al-Amir	A	C	B	C	A
	Remaining Districts	A	B	B	C	A
	Aljizah	B	C	C	C	A
	Umm Al-Rassas	C	C	C	C	A
	Al-Qunaitrah	C	C	C	C	A
	Dhab'ah	C	C	C	C	A
	Al-Amiriayya	C	C	C	C	A
	Zmeileh	C	C	C	C	A
	Sahab	A	C	C	C	A
	Muwagar	B	C	C	C	A
	Na'our	A	C	C	C	A
	Hisban	B	C	C	C	A
Irbid	Irbid Kasba	B	B	C	C	A
	Remaining Districts	B	C	C	C	A

*** For a hotel to obtain the exemption specified in the Law, the Project should not be classified less than three starts in zone (A).**

THE SCHEDULE

The Governorate	District	Industry	*Hotels	Hospitals	Agriculture & Maritime Transport & Railways	Leisure and Recreational Compounds + Conventions and Exhibition Centers
Balqa	Salt Kasba	B	C	C	C	A
	Deir-Allah	C	C	C	C	A
	South Shouneh	C	C	C	C	A
	Ain Al-Basha	A	C	C	C	A
Karak	All Districts	C	C	C	C	A
Ma'an	Wadi Mousa	C	A	C	C	A

	Remaining districts	C	C	C	C	A
Zarqa	All Districts	A	C	C	C	A
	Al-Azraq	B	C	C	C	A
	Berain	B	C	C	C	A
	Al-Hashemiyeh	B	C	C	C	A
	Ad Dulayl	C	C	C	C	A
	Qasr Al-Hallabat	C	C	C	C	A
Mafraq	All Districts	C	C	C	C	A
Tafileh	All Districts	C	C	C	C	A
Madaba	Madaba Kasba	B	C	C	C	A
	Dhiban	C	C	C	C	A
Jerash	All Districts	C	C	C	C	A
Ajloun	Ajloun	C	C	C	C	A
Aqaba	Aqaba Kasba	C	C	C	C	A
	Qwaireh	C	C	C	C	A

Article (4) a. For the purposes of this Regulation, "Industries" shall mean all sectors of industry and its subsectors including any whole or partial modification on the substance to produce a product different in description, shape, characteristics or formation, provided that such activities are conducted inside a relevant establishment in a continuous form.

b. For the purposes of this Regulation, "Agriculture" shall mean all sectors of agriculture and animal resources.

c. For the purposes of this Regulation, the term "Hotels" shall include touristic villages, compounds and resorts. For a hotel to obtain the exemption specified in the Law, the project should not be classified less than three stars in zone (A).

d. The expression "Leisure and Recreational Compounds" includes any tourist facility or establishment concerned with offering specialized entertainment and cultural services, open for domestic and foreign tourism. The facilities should have lobbies, restaurants and multi-purpose halls provided that their standard should not be less than those of a four star hotels.

e. The expression "Convention and Exhibition Centers" includes any establishment concerned with local, regional and international conferences and exhibitions specialized in economic information and cultural activities. These centers contain multi-purpose halls, theaters, press, information, translation and secretarial offices, in addition to supplementary services such as food, beverage and technical communication services as well as other facilities usual in such centers and exhibitions.

Article (5) The Minster may issue the necessary instructions for the implementation of this Regulation upon the recommendation of the Committee.

INVESTMENT INCENTIVES

ENCOURAGEMENT OF INVESTMENT LAW

The Investment Promotion Law No. (16) of 1995 repealed the Encouragement of Investment Law, No. 11 of 1987 and Law No. 27 of 1992 Regulating Arab & Foreign Investments. The new law opens the financial markto all investors and provides for the equal treatment of investors regardless of nationality.

The new law abolishes the distinction between *economic* and *approved economic* projects. Therefore, projects in the following sectors enjoy the special exemptions specified under the law: (1) Industry; (2) Agriculture; (3) Hotels; (4) Hospitals; (5) Maritime transport and railways; (6) Leisure and Recreation

Compounds; (7) Convention and Exhibition Centers; and (8) any other sectors or its branches that the Council of Ministers decides to add based on the recommendation of the Higher Council for Encouragement of Investment. These sectors are also subject to a revised tax rate of 15 percent under latest amendments to the Income Tax Law.

In addition, exemptions from taxes and fees extend to all imported fixed assets, imported fixed assets of the expansion of productive capacity over 25 percent, and imported spare parts.

Exemptions from income and social service taxes for a ten year period starting from the date of production is granted in ranging amounts according to the level of development of particular locales.

The Committee for Encouragement of Investment considers investors' applications from other sectors for inclusion under the Encouragement of Investment Law and makes the appropriate decisions within thirty days from receiving such applications. A rejected application that is returned must include the reasons for the rejection. A new government office is to be established to encourage investment and to speed procedures for registering and licensing new investments. The law also contains a commitment that all investment proposals will receive a response from the Higher Council for the Encouragement of Investment, a body made up of ministers and business representatives within thirty days of application.

The new law also allows direct entry into the Jordan stock market in order to help attract foreign capital. Furthermore, it makes it possible for a foreign investor to buy shares directly, provided that the total foreign ownership in the publicly traded company does not exceed 50 percent at the end of the close of trade on the official market.

RESTRICTIONS ON FOREIGN INVESTMENT

Special rules were issued specifying the sectors in which foreign investors are allowed to invest and the proportion of ownership foreign investors may maintain in addition to the minimum capital requirement for foreign investors. Until recently, such minimum capital requirements were set at a minimum of JD 100,000 with the exception of investments in the stock market, where such minimum was set at JD 1,000. On February 22, 1997 the Council of Ministers resolved to remove the minimum investment requirement of JD 100,000. Pursuant to said resolution, Jordanian and non-Jordanian investors are now afforded equal treatment with regard to their investment in Jordanian companies.

ENCOURAGEMENT OF FOREIGN INVESTMENT

The Encouragement of Foreign Investment Regulation of 1995 allows wider foreign ownership and direct entry of foreign nationals and companies into the Jordan stock market. This regulation is intended to enhance the opportunity for substantial foreign investment and, in conjunction with a reduced tax structure, to enhance returns on stock. The Regulation is intended to boost confidence in Jordan as an attractive emerging market and to help attract foreign capital.

The Regulation eliminates the cumbersome requirements requiring prior approvals by the Cabinet and the purchasing of permits through licensed brokers as well as the set limitations on ownership. It also provides tax exemptions for investment in less developed regions in Jordan.

The Regulations for the Promotion of Foreign Investment No. 39 of 1997 eliminated the 50 percent ceiling on foreign equity ownership in the Amman Financial Market, transportation, insurance, banking, telecommunications and agricultural sectors. The 50 percent ownership ceiling remains in the construction, trading, trade services and mining sectors. These Regulations also reduced the minimum amount of foreign investment from JD 100,000 to JD 50,000.

INVESTMENT TAX INCENTIVES

Exemptions from income tax and customs duties for projects are provided for under the Encouragement of Investment Law. All fixed assets for the project are exempt from customs duties and taxes. Fixed assets include the equipment, machinery apparatus and tools needed for the project. For hotels and hospitals, the definition includes furniture and other material specific to these industries. Imported spare parts for the project will be exempt from customs duties and taxes provided the value of these parts does not exceed 15 percent of the value of their related fixed assets.

Net profits of the projects are exempt from income tax for up to ten years starting from the commencement of commercial production or providing services in accordance with the rates set forth, in the Other Tax Exemptions section above.

Furthermore, additional incentives are granted if the project undergoes expansion, development or modernization resulting in an increase of its productive capacity. Hotels and hospitals may enjoy exemption from customs duties and taxes every seven years for the purchase of new furniture and other materials specific to these industries.

FREE TRADE ZONES

In order to encourage export-oriented industry, Jordan has set up a number of Free Zones. The first Free Zone was established at the Aqaba port along the Red Sea. Other free trade zones are located at Zarqa, the Sahab industrial estate and Irbid.

Free Zones come under the supervision of an autonomous body, the Free Zone Corporation and are governed by the Free Zone Corporation Law, No. 32 of 1984.

In order to qualify for licenses to operate within a free zone area, projects must meet the following criteria: (1) applying new technology and introducing new industries to the country; (2) using local raw materials or components; (3) raising the level of domestic labor skills; and (4) reducing Jordan's imports. Applications for a Free Zone license are filed with the Free Zone Corporation.

Projects granted a license in a Free Zone enjoy the following privileges: (1) exemption of profits from income tax for a period of twelve years; (2) exemption of non-Jordanian employees from income tax on their remuneration and from the social service tax; (3) exemption for goods imported into or exported from Free Zones from customs duties, import fees and any other fees and taxes; (4) exemption of lands, buildings and properties in free zones from licensing fees and taxes; and (5) freedom to repatriate capital investment and profits earned, subject to prevailing laws and regulation.

Furthermore, importers using the Free Zones to supply the local market, avoid import license fees amounting to 5 percent of cargo value, until the goods are actually cleared for release from the Zone.

QUALIFYING INDUSTRIAL ZONE

Pursuant to the United States - Israel Free Trade Area Implementation Act of 1995, the governments of Israel and Jordan have agreed to the creation of the Irbid Qualifying Industrial Zone (QIZ). This zone is located in the Irbid duty-free zone in Jordan in conjunction with the Israeli side of the border-crossing at the Sheikh Hussein - Nahar Hayarden Bridge. Pending American designation of the Irbid duty-free zone as a qualified industrial zone, this zone would provide duty-free treatment to products jointly produced by Israelis and Jordanians that meet the requirements of US legislation. The Israeli parliament's reconfirmation and American approval of this project are expected in 1998.

The agreement signed between the Israeli and Jordanian governments provides for the creation of a joint committee that will identify businesses whose products are eligible for duty-free treatment and will advise the US Customs Trade Compliance Office of such businesses. Qualifying businesses in the QIZ area must meet, *inter alia*, standards requiring substantial economic cooperation between the two countries.

Additional border free trade zones, including the Jordan Gateway Project and the Sahab Industrial Zone, intend to requeQIZ designation in the near future.

CUSTOMS

General

Taxes on imports are the chief source of domestic revenue. All imported goods are subject to custom duty, except those specifically exempted. Rates of duty vary according to the importance of the item to the national economy. Essential commodities and various raw materials attract relatively low rates of duty, while luxury goods attract high rates.

CUSTOMS PROCEDURES

Customs procedures in Jordan have historically been a major impediment to free trade. Overlapping areas of authority and excessive signature clearances on paperwork of shipments remain unchanged. Actual commodity appraisal and tariff assessment practices often differ from the written regulations. Discretionary decisions are sometimes made about certain cases that are subject to conflicting instructions and regulations.

It is anticipated that Jordanian customs legislation will be amended in the near future. The amendments provide the Customs Department with more powers regarding violations and confiscation and delegates part of the Minister of Finance's powers to the Director General of the Customs Department.

Under the prevailing Import Tariff Schedules, valid since 1989, a high tariff rate is imposed on luxury goods and on major categories of consumer goods. On automobiles, the tariff rate ranges from 110 percent to 310 percent. To stimulate export production, import tariffs are low on many raw materials, machinery and semi-finished goods. To secure tariff exemptions, businesses must document that the raw materials to be imported will be used in export production, maintaining at least 40 percent Jordanian value-added content.

The Director General of Customs may grant temporary admission status to certain goods such as heavy machinery and equipment used to implement Government projects or important projects which have obtained Government approval. Foreign construction companies operating alone or with a Jordanian partner can apply for this temporary admission status.

PRIVATIZATION

The government of Jordan has embarked on a privatization program that is to include most public sector enterprises. This program is supervised by the Cabinet Committee on Privatization, recently created by the Council of Ministers. The Committee is responsible for setting broad policy and guidelines for the privatization program.

The government of Jordan will carry out its privatization program through three distinct methods. The government will sell its shares in existing companies; it will incorporate existing state economic enterprises as a first step towards their privatization and the eventual sale of their shares; the government will also sanction the licensing of private investment in various activities, mainly utilities, that have previously been controlled by government monopolies.

The Telecommunications Law (No. 13 of 1995) created a committee with the authority to license private sector projects. In the electricity sector, the recently enacted General Electricity Law (No. 10 of 1996) permits the licensing of independent power producers and independent power distributors. The General Electricity Law also allows industrial enterprises to set up their own power generating facilities and allows them to exchange their electricity with other independent power producers.

Jordan's Telecommunications Corporation (TCC) and the Jordan Electricity Authority have both been commercialized. The government has already announced its intention to sell a 26 percent stake in the TCC, and new telecommunications services are open to the private sector. The Jordan Investment Corporation (JIC) plans to sell shares in a number of public companies, including a 33 percent stake in the Jordan

Cement Factories Company (JCFC). There has also been discussions regarding the privatization of Jordan's national airlines, Royal Jordanian.

In November 1996, the Jordanian Transport Ministry invited international consultants to submit detailed proposals to assist it in the privatization of the Aqaba Railways Corporation (ARC). Consultants on this project include Coopers & Lybrand and Booz, Allen & Hamilton, both of the US; Mercer Management Consultants of the UK; Canada's CPCS; and Padeco of Japan. Fourteen companies submitted preliminary proposals in September.

SALE

The JIC functions as the investment arm of the Jordanian government. It has already concluded a number of sales of its shareholding in Jordanian private and public shareholding companies, mostly in the hotel and tourism sector.

INCORPORATION

The 1989 Companies Law allows for the transformation of state economic enterprises into public shareholding companies. Initially, such companies are to be owned by the government. They may be sold at a later stage, in whole or in part.

The Jordan Electricity Authority which was incorporated in the form of a public shareholding company as of September 1996 was the first such enterprise to be incorporated. Next was the Telecommunications Corporation which was incorporated as of January, 1997. Similar plans are underway regarding the Royal Jordanian Airlines, Aqaba Railway Corporation, Public Transport Company, Aqaba Port and Queen Alia International Airport.

LICENSING

In order to license private investments in government controlled sectors, legislative amendments and reforms are required. This task has already been accomplished for the telecommunications and electricity sectors.

STOCK EXCHANGE

The Amman Financial Market (AFM) is a credible and regulated market that is one of the largest Arab stock markets. The AFM is open to foreign investors who may own up to 50 percent of any listed public shareholding company.

Bonds and shares of Jordanian public shareholding companies, government and municipal bonds may be traded on the AFM. Over-the-counter trades, options, futures and other derivative trading, however, are prohibited.

The new Securities Law, described above, provides for the establishment of a Securities Commission that would supervise all securities transactions. The new law would allow for the establishment of a Securities Market and Central Depository. In addition, it would relax some of the restrictions on futures and options trading.

KUWAIT

FOREIGN INVESTMENT LAW IN STATE OF KUWAIT

Law No.10 for year 1999

From encouraging foreign investment in state of Kuwait and its role in economic development projects, added to closing the gap in resources and possibilities to obtain more developed technology, marketing administrative experiences owned by international companies to expand the investment base together with limiting immigration of national capitals abroad to provide new opportunities for national employment in private sector with the manner that contribute to treating disability problem in the state balance sheets, the Kuwaiti legislators issued a law decree No.10 for year 1999 in relation to organizing direct investment for foreign capital in state of Kuwait and included the following chapters and terms:

CHAPTER1 IN RELATION TO INVESTMENT OF FOREIGN CAPITAL

Article 2
The Cabinet should determine the economic projects that the foreign investor may practice inside state of Kuwait whether in independent manner or by participation of national capital and with the manner that becomes in harmony with the public policy of state together with economic development plans.

Article 3
The license is issued for the foreign investor to practice one of the economic projects by decree from Minister of Commerce & Industry in accordance with recommendation from investment committee and after approval of the concerned authorities.
1

Article 4
It is allowed, by a decree from Minister of Commerce & Industry in accordance with a recommendation from investment license, to grant license for establishing companies in which the foreigners share amount to 100% of company capital in accordance with conditions and terms set by cabinet.

CHAPTER2 INVESTMENT COMMITTEE OF FOREIGN CAPITAL

Article 5
A new committee headed by Minister of Commerce & Industry is called investment committee of foreign capital where issuing its formation, work system, duration and its members' rewards is set by cabinet.

The head of foreign capital investment office assumes responsibility of undersecretary of this committee and the Minister of Commerce & Industry issues a decree in relation to committee work order.

Article 6
The investment committee is concerned with the following:

1. Studying investments applications and view recommendation involved
2. Promoting for available investment opportunities in the state added to taking initiative to attract foreign investments
3. Granting incentives to encourage foreign investor on investment as per article 12 of this article by coordination with the concerned authorities taking into consideration supporting Kuwaiti private sector
4. Facilitating procedures of project license added to registering it and surpassing obstacles that may face its construction

5. Putting machinery for observing foreign investments performance with the objective of recognizing any obstacles it may face together with fixing them
6. Searching for what the foreign investors together with others related to the same concern in terms of complaints or those aroused among them from disputes resulting from application of this article laws and raising their recommendation in this concern to the concerned authorities
7. Signing laid down penalties in article 14 of this law
8. Preparing projects of regulations required for performing rules of this law
9. Reviewing those referred to it from Minister of Commerce & Industry in relation to matters deny rules of this law

10. Preparing annual report about foreign investment movement inside added to the most obstacles it faces and the methods of facing them to be raised to cabinet

Article 7
A new office, called foreign capital Office, is set up to shoulder the task of administrative and technical body in investment committee, and this formation and work system involved is issued as per a decree form minister of commerce & industry.
The office assume responsibility of receiving license applications and fulfilling hem by the concerned authorities together with making studies and presenting suggestions required in this concern and offering them on investment committee.
The office also assumes responsibility of everything related to foreign capital investment especially the following:

1. Informing the international market with the raised projects for investment added to showing the advantages in which the foreign capital investment is characterized in state of Kuwait.
2. Offering information, clarifications and statistics required for foreign investors.
3. Follow up executing licensed projects added to overcoming difficulties and obstacles they face.
4. Coordinate with the concerned authorities to facilitate entry of foreign investor in state of Kuwait and to reside in together with his representative or dealers with him outside Kuwait.
5. Preparing periodical statistical reports related to foreign investment activity added to preparing annual report raised to investment committee in relation to licensed projects to be raised to cabinet.

CHAPTER 3 GUARANTEED WARRANTIES FOR FOREIGN INVESTMENT

Article 8
It is not allowed to attribute any licensed foreign project to the state in accordance with rules of this law except by indemnity equals its marketing value.
It is not allowed also to cause damage to obtained advantages and rights of the licensed foreign investor as per rules of law except by indemnity for these rights and advantages.

Article 9
This law is effective on established investments that are considered revenues to foreign capital with the amount that achieves goals of this law. This provided that the advantages, exemptions and guarantees granted to them do not lesser than its previous decided rules, and that the applications are offered by the foreign investor to make the best use of advantages laid down herein in this law and raised to foreign capital investment committee for review as mentioned in article 6.

Article 10
1. The foreign investor may have the right to transfer his investment to another foreign investor or to national investor or rather cede it in the event of participation provided that this occurs in accordance with regulations and laws in force in state of Kuwait together with licenses terms.
2. In the event that the ownership was transferred to another foreign investor, the dealing of investment continues as per laws of this law.

Article 11
The foreign investor may have the right to transfer his profits and capital abroad together with the indemnity laid down in article 8 of this law.
The non-Kuwaiti employees in this project and those who deal with him outside Kuwait may have the right to transfer their savings and dues abroad.

CHAPTER 4 SETTLED ADVANTAGES FOR FOREIGN INVESTMENT AND ITS OBLIGATIONS

Article 12
The investment committee shall have the right to grant foreign investment all or some of the following advantages in the light of scope of contribution of such project to performance of economic development plans in state of Kuwait:

1. Exempting from income tax or any taxes or other fees for a period not exceed ten years from the start of project effective operation. This added to exempting any new investment in this project from taxes and fees for an exemption period similar to this granted to original investment upon establishment of project.

2. Making the best use of advantages resulting from agreements of avoiding double taxation added to agreements of enco9raging and protecting investment.
3. exempting fully or partially from customs in relation to the following imports:
a. Machines, equipments and pieces required for construction, replacement, expansion and development
b. Raw materials, half manufactured goods and binding materials and packaging added to other materials required for productive purposes
4. Exempting from all or some restrictions imposed on exports and imports
5. Specifying lands and real estate required for their purposes in accordance with laws and regulations in force in state of Kuwait.
6. Recruiting foreign employment required for their purposes in accordance with laws and regulations in force in state of Kuwait.

Article 13
The foreign investor should adhere to the following:
1. Give priority to national employment in case of its availability added to working on training it with imparting it to required skills.
2. Keep safety and soundness of environment from pollution.
3. Keep public arrangement and public morals

CHAPTER 5 PENALTIES

Article 14
In the event that the foreign investor breaches any judgment of this law or any licenses terms or laws and regulations in force in state of Kuwait, the committee may have the right to force him one of the following penalties:

1. Warning
2. Notice
3. Deprival of licenses granted to him fully, and the foreign investor, in the event of deviating from breaching terms, may have the right to ask for review in the decision of deprival.
4. Stop Project administrative for specific period.
5. Cancel license and clearing investment.

The foreign investor and the concerned people shall have the right to offer complaint to cabinet due to these penalties laid down in terms 3,4 and 5 during thirteen days from the date of his notification with the decision of penalty, and in the event that the complaint was refused, the decision should be written and with a reason.
In case that sixty days of complaint passed without taking any final decision, this complaint will be considered refused.

CHAPTER 6 CONCLUDING JUDGMENTS

Article 15
It is agreed upon that any dispute arising between foreign investment projects and others should be referred to international or local arbitration authority.
Others here refer, in relation to application of these material judgments, to those government authorities and natural together with legal persons in general and private.

Article 16
The foreign investment, in accordance with rules of this law, has the benefit of principles of secrecy of information, equality and keeping investment initiatives as per related effective laws judgments.

LAW DECREE NO.(8) OF 2001 REGARDING ORGANIZATION OF DIRECT INVESTMENT OF FOREIGN CAPITAL IN THE STATE OF KUWAIT

LAW REGARDING ORGANIZATION OF DIRECT INVESTMENT OF FOREIGN CAPITAL

Having seen Having seen the Constitution: and
Decree No. (3) of 1995 regarding the Kuwaiti Income Tax and amending Laws thereto; to and
The Law of Chamber of Commerce of 1959
Law No. 15 of 1960 regarding the Commercial Companies law and the amending laws thereto; and Law No. 16 of 1960 penal code law and the amending laws thereto: and And Law Decree No. 4 of 1962 concerning patent rights, designs and industrial models, amended by Law No. 3 of 2001; and
Law No. 33 of 1964 on expropriation and temporary requisition in the Public Interest; and
Law No. 32 of 1968 on currency, Central Bank of Kuwait and organization of Banking profession, with all amending laws thereof; and
Law No. 32 of 1969 regarding organization of commercial shops licences and the amending laws thereto; and
Law Decree No. 68 of 1980 regarding promulgation of the Commercial Law and the amending laws thereto; and
Law No. 58 of 1982 ratifying the unified Economic Agreement among the Gulf Cooperation Council; and
Law No. 56 of 1996 regarding the promulgation of the Industry Law; and
Law No. 19 of 2000 regarding the support of the National manpower and its encouragement to work in non-government sectors; and
The National Assembly has passed the following Law which we hereby ratify and promulgate.

DEFINITIONS

Article 1

The following expression shall have the meaning assigned against each one of them

- The Minister

the Minister of Commerce & Industry

- Invested Foreign Capital

1. Foreign currency,securities and commercial papers transferred to Kuwait.
2. Machinery,equipment, transportation, vehicles, raw materials, commodities imported abroad for investment purposes.
3. Moral rights such as patents, trademarks licences, registered commercial names as well as engineering and technological designs.
4. Investment foreign capital profits and gains if the foreign capital is increased according or in case they are invested in new investment projects.

- Foreign Investor

A natural or who/which artificial person who which is a holder of a non-Kuwaiti Nationality.

- Foreign Investment

Investment of foreign capital in a licensed activity in accordance with the provisions of this Law.

- Project

Any economic activity to which the provisions of this law apply

- Investment Committee

The foreign Capital Investment Committee set up under the provision of Article (5) of this Law.

CHAPTER 1 FOREIGN CAPITAL INVESTMENT

Article 2

Without the prejudice to the provisions of Article 3 of this Law of Council of Ministers shall specify the economic activities and projects which may be practised by the foreign investor within the country whether independently or with national sharing capital in conformity with the State's general policy and confirmed and economic development plans.

Article 3

A licence shall be used to a Foreign Investor to practise any activities economic projects under a resolution issued by the Minister pursuant to a recommendation made by the Investment Committee after having secured the approval of the competent authorities.

The licence request shall be determined in a period not exceeding 8 months from the date of application, in case of rejecting request, the decision must be written and grounded with the reasons of rejection. The provisions of item 1 of Article (23) and the provisions of Article (24) of Law No. 68 of 1980 referred to herein before shall not apply to this licence.

Any commitment to invest any of the natural resources or any of the public utilities shall be only made under a law and for a specific period. A preliminary procedure shall undertake to facilitate the works of Exploration, publicity and competition.

Renewal or amendment of any of the agreements,contracts,or commitments concluded shall not be made before the enforcement of the constitution of this law save under law.

Article 4

In exception to the provisions of Article (68) of Law No. 15 of 1960 referred to herein before, a licence may be granted, under a resolution passed by the Minister on a recommendation made by the Investment Committee, to incorporate Kuwaiti companies foreigners shares of which may reach 100% of the company capital in accordance with the terms and conditions laid down by the Council of Ministers.

Article 5

SECOND CHAPTER FOREIGN CAPITAL INVESTMENT COMMITTEE

A committee called "Foreign Investment Committee shall be formed under a resolution passed by the Council of Ministers, provided that it shall be presided over by the competent Minister and comprising members representing experts from the Private Sector and Kuwait Chamber of Commerce and Industry. The Head of the foreign capital Investment referred to in article "7" hereof shall perform the duties of the Secretary General of the said Committee.

The Minister shall issue a resolution organizing the functions and duties of the said committee and the remunerations of its members shall be fixed under a resolution passed by the Council of Ministers.

Article 6

The Investment Committee shall be competent to perform the following duties and functions:

1. Studying investment applications and making the necessary recommendations.

2. Promoting investment opportunities available in the State of Kuwait and taking the initiative to attract foreign investments. 3. Granting privileges and advantages to encourage the foreign investor and Kuwait Private sector to make investments in accordance to Article (13) of this Law in coordination with the competent authorities taking into consideration the encouragement of Kuwaiti Private Sector.

4. Facilitating the licensing procedures for the project, its registration and overcoming any obstacles that any hinder establishment.

5. Setting up a mechanism for monitoring and follow up of the foreign investments with the aim of identifying and overcoming any obstacles that may be faced.

6. Discussing the complaints made by foreign investors and other concerned parties besides any disputes that may arise from the implementation of this law and presenting its recommendations in this respect to the competent authorities.

7. Imposing the penalties stipulated in Article (15) of this law.

8. Preparing the by law drafts and regulations required for the implementation of the provisions of this law.

9. Considering the issues referred to it by the Minister in respect of implementing the provisions of this law.

10. Preparing periodical statistic statements covering foreign investment activity, with an annual report on licensed investment projects activity and the obstacles confronting the movement of foreign investment into the country and the relevant means of dealing with. This report shall be presented to the Council of Ministers within a period not exceeding the end of March every year.

Article 7

An office called "Foreign Investment Office" shall be established. It shall perform the functions of the Executive Committee Staff. The office formation and procedure of work shall be made under a resolution issued the Minister; and its head shall be appointed by means of a Decree pursuant to the Minister's nomination.

The office shall be responsible for receiving the relevant applications and getting them completed by the concerned authorities. It shall conduct studies and submit pertinent proposals and present them to the Investment Committee to take an action in a period not exceeding 4 months from the date of application. The period may be extended for a similar by the Minister under a grounded resolution.

The office shall also carry out any duties related to the foreign capital investment, particularly:

1. Notifying the international market of the project offered for investment and stating the privileges enjoyed by the foreign capital investment in the country.
2. Providing the information, clarification and statistics required by the foreign investors.
3. Following up the execution of the licensed projects and overcoming any obstacles which may be encountered.
4. Coordinating with the concerned authorities to assist the foreign investor to enter the country and reside in together with those whom he deals from outside the Country.

THIRD CHAPTER

Foreign Investment Guarantees

Article 8

Any project licensed in accordance with the provisions of this law may not be confiscated or nationalized. It may only be expropriated in the event of public interest, in conformity with the applicable laws, against a consideration equivalent to the true actual value of the expropriated project at the time of expropriation, duly assessed and evaluated on the ground of ex economic situation prior to any intimation of expropriation. The due consideration shall be payable immediately without any delay.

Article9

Without prejudice to the provisions of Article 3 hereof, the provisions of this law shall be applicable to the existing investments of any foreign capital in accordance with the provisions of the law hereof, provided that the privileges, exemptions and the guarantees extended in conformity with its provisions shall not be less than what already determined in that respect.

A foreign investor for the purpose of benefiting from this law shall submit his application for the Investment Committee for consideration.

Article 10

A foreign investor duly licensed in accordance with the provisions of this law shall not be subject to any amendments of these provisions which may prejudice his/her interests or benefits, save any expansions of a current investment made after the operative date of such amendment.

Article 11

1. A foreign investor shall have the right to wholly or partially assign his/her investment to any other foreign or national investor, or to waive and/or assign his/her investment to a national investor in the event of sharing or partnership. All of which shall be made in conformity with the law provisions and relevant licences stipulations.
2. In the event of assigning a whole or partial foreign investment to another foreign investor, the later (assignee) shall subrogate the assignor to the extent of assigned amount, and the investment shall continue to deal with in accordance with the provisions of this law.

Article 12

A foreign investor may transfer his/her profits and capital abroad as well as the compensation stipulated in Article (8) of this law.

Moreover, the non Kuwaiti employees working on the project and those dealing with it from abroad may transfer their savings abroad.

FOURTH CHAPTER FOREIGN INVESTMENT PRIVILEGES AND OBLIGATIONS

Article 13

The Investment Committee may grant all or some of the following privileges to the foreign investments:
1. Exemption from the income tax or from any other taxes for a period not exceeding ten years as of the actual commencement of the project with exemption of any new investment in the project from the said taxes for a period similar to the exemption period granted to the original investment upon the establishment of the project.
2. Benefiting from the privileges constituted under the agreements of double taxation avoidance and investment encouragement and protection agreements.
3. Total or partial exemption from custom duties on the following imports.
One. Machinery, equipment and spare-parts required for construction, replacement, expansion and development.
Two. Raw materials, semi manufactured products, easing, packing and bottling materials deemed necessary for production purposes.
4. Allocation of lands and real estates required for investment purposes in accordance with the laws and regulations applicable in the country.
5. Employing the foreign manpower in required accordance with the country applicable laws and regulations. A resolution shall be issued by the Council of Ministers specifying the national manpower related to the projects under the provisions of this law.
The grant of the privileges referred to in this article shall be made in accordance with the economic development plans and the number of Kuwaitis employed in the project besides abiding by the provisions of law No. 19 of 2000 referred to hereof regarding the appointment of national manpower.

Article 14

The foreign investor shall abide by maintaining the safety of environment, observing the public order, public moral ethics and the instructions concerning the security and public health besides avoiding others to dangers.

FIFTH CHAPTER PENALTIES

Article 15

In case a foreign investor violates the provisions of this law or the licensing conditions or the rules and laws applicable in the country, the Investment Committee may impose the following penalties on him:
1. Warning
2. Deprivation of all or part of the privileges granted to him. In case the foreign investor has rectified such a violation he may apply reconsideration of the violation decision.
3. Administrative suspension of the project for a certain period of time.
The court may, upon the request of the investment committee render a judgement canceling the licence and liquidating the investment. Without prejudicing the rights of the foreign investor to resort to the court of law he may submit a grievance to the council of Ministers against the penalties provided for in clauses 3 and 4 herein before, within a thirty day period from the date of notification. In case the grievance request is rejected, the decision shall be made in writing the relevant reasons indicated.
The elapse of sixty days from the date of the submitted grievance receipt without a relevant reply in that respect shall be considered as rejected on of grievance.
The penalty application shall not prejudice the civilian or panel liability, whenever.

SIXTH CHAPTER FINAL PROVISIONS

Article 16

The Kuwaiti courts of Law shall alone jurisdiction overhearing and determining on any dispute whatsoever arising between the Foreign Investment Projects and Third Parties. However agreement may be reached to refer such dispute to Arbitration panel.

Article 17

Pursuant to the provisions of this law a foreign investor shall enjoy the principles of equality, secrecy of technical, economic and financial information related to the project, with preservation of investment initiatives in accordance with the country applicable laws, by-laws and regulations.
Without prejudice to any severer penalty provided for in any other law punishable by imprisonment for a term not exceeding one year and a fine not more that KD 10,000 or either of these two penalties, any person who discloses any information has come aware of by virtue of his office, and which relates to the Investment initiative or to the relevant technical, economic or financial aspects of the foreign investment in conformity with the provisions of this law, save the cases and circumstances determined under law.

Article 18

The competent Minister shall submit to the National Assembly a copy of the annual report, provided for in clause 10 of article 6 of this law, within thirty (30) days from the date of its presentation to the Council of Ministers, besides presenting to a comprehensive six month periodical statement, covering all the applications submitted in accordance with the provisions of articles 34 and 9 of this law and the resolutions adopted in respect of the said applications.

Article 19

The Foreign Investment shall be subject to State of Kuwait applicable laws, rules and regulations for any item not particularly provided for in this law, provided that it is not contradictory to its provisions.

Article 20

The provisions of this law shall apply to the economic activities and project which are practised by a national investor without a foreign sharing partner whenever they are within the activities and projected determined by the council of Ministers in conformity with article 2 of the law hereof.

Article 21

The Minister shall issue the by-laws, regulations and decisions required for the implementation of the provisions of this Law Decree.

Article 22

The Prime Minister, all Ministers each within his jurisdiction, shall implement this Law Decree.

INVESTMENT INCENTIVES

Recently, Kuwait adopted Law No. 56 of 1996 (Effective 15.1.97), creating an independent entity called the Industrial Authority, and abolishing the Shaubia Industrial Authority and the Industrial Committee. All industrial projects in the emirate, including those now in operation, will have to be licensed by the new authority.

INVESTMENT LAWS

A variety of incentives are offered to new manufacturing businesses under the investment laws. Industrial enterprises which are eligible to receive such investment incentives must first obtain a permit from the Minister of Commerce and Industry prior to being established. Prior to effecting any change in its capacity, location, or business, an approved industrial enterprise must obtain a modified permit from the Minister of Commerce and Industry. Eligible enterprises are businesses run by Kuwaiti individuals or companies established in Kuwait.

Approved industrial enterprises must provide the Ministry of Commerce and Industry with their annual financial statements and records of goods importduty-free under the incentivesprogram. The work force of an approved industrial enterprise must be composed of at least 25 percent Kuwaiti nationals, unless waived by the Ministry of Commerce and Industry because of the unavailability of sufficient qualified Kuwaiti labor.

TRADE AGREEMENTS

Kuwait is a member of the GCC and, as such, is subject to the GCC trade agreements. These agreements are described in the section on Trade Agreements in the chapter on Bahrain. Kuwait has been a member of GATT since 1963 and has signed the WTO agreement.

CUSTOMS

Only Kuwaiti nationals and entities in which Kuwaitis hold at least a 51 percent interest are permitted to import goods into Kuwait. Foreign business entities are required to use a Kuwaiti import agent. The standard customs duty is levied at 4 percent of the CIF value of the goods imported. Some items which are competitively produced in Kuwait are subject to an elevated customs duty of 15 percent.

The Ministry of Commerce and Industry was authorized to set up free trade zones by Law No. 26 of 1995. In June 1996 the Ministry accepted a proposal to manage a free trade zone at Shuwaikh Port. Many of the current restrictions on foreign investors will not apply to offices and plants located in that zone.

PRIVATIZATION

Kuwait's privatization program began in 1993. In 1994, the Kuwait Investment Authority (KIA) established a fund that would allow investors to buy into its holdings. Since that time, its shares in the Kuwait Land Transport Co., the Commercial Facilities Co., the National Industries Co. and the Kuwait Investment Project Co. have all been introduce successfully to the market. KIA's long-term goal is the sale of some 90 percent of its US$ 2.64 billion holdings in sixty-two companies. Other sectors such as health care, telecommunications, tourism, electric power and airlines are government-run but are intended to be privatized in the coming years.

As of mid-1997, the Kuwaiti government had successfully sold its holdings in sixteen private firms, but its privatization of government entities has been slower. In June 1997, the Kuwaiti National Assembly considered legislation which would establish a framework for privatizing public utilities.

STOCK EXCHANGE

The Kuwaiti Stock Exchange (KSE) was reopened after the Iraqi invasion. Presently, the KSE lists stocks of sixty-five Kuwaiti companies, ten companies from other Gulf states and Kuwaiti mutual funds. Foreigners are not allowed to trade in Kuwaiti stocks on the Kuwaiti stock exchange except through mutual funds.

PRACTICAL INFORMATION FOR INVESTING AND BUSINESS ACTIVITY

Articles 23 and 24 of the Kuwaiti Commercial Code state the basic premise for doing business in Kuwait. Article 23 provides that non-Kuwaitis cannot engage in commerce in Kuwait without having a Kuwaiti partner whose equity holding is at least 51 percent. Article 24 provides that a foreign company cannot establish a branch in Kuwait and it may not engage in commercial activities in Kuwait except through a Kuwaiti agent.

In an effort to attract foreign investment, Kuwait's Parliament recently passed Law No. 8 Regulating Foreign Capital Direct Investment in Kuwait (April 22, 2001). This law creates an exception to the general rules under which foreign investors conduct business in Kuwait by permitting up to 100% foreign ownership of business entities in certain approved sectors. Implementing regulations, which establish the guidelines for investment under the law, will be forthcoming.

A foreign person or entity may enter the Kuwaiti market and conduct business in the following ways:

- Establishment of a company;
- Entering into a joint venture agreement;
- Appointment of a local commercial agent; or
- Appointment of a commercial representative.

II. ESTABLISHING A KUWAITI COMPANY

Kuwaiti law permits foreign persons or entities to establish a permanent presence in Kuwait by forming and investing in the following Kuwaiti companies:

1) Limited Liability Company;
2) Closed Joint Stock Company;

3) Public Joint Stock Company.

A. Limited Liability Company ("WLL")

Both foreign individuals and corporate bodies may establish this type of entity. However, Article 191 of the Companies Law provides that a Kuwaiti must own at least 51% of the WLL shareholding. A WLL is simple to form and takes approximately three months to incorporate. The WLL provides the limited liability shield and is nontaxable since Kuwait has no individual income tax and its corporate tax applies only to non-Kuwaiti corporate bodies.

B. Closed Joint Stock Company ("KSC Closed")

A closed Kuwaiti joint stock company (KSC Closed) is the other type of company open to non-Kuwaiti entities. Articles 68 and 94 of the Companies Law provide for this type of company as an exceptional kind of Joint Stock Company. The general rule is that the shareholders of joint stock companies must be Kuwaiti nationals. As an exception, foreigners may own 49% of the share capital of a KSC Closed after obtaining the approval of the concerned authorities. The company's objects cannot be banking or insurance. The incorporation of a KSC Closed may take up to six months.

The limitation in using this form of business is that, over and above the tax levied on the profits made by the foreign company as a shareholder in KSC Closed Company, the KSC Closed Company is itself subject to the 5% contribution to the Kuwait Foundation for the Advancement of Science.

C. Public Joint Stock Company

In June of 1999, Kuwait passed a law permitting non-Kuwaitis, for the first time, to own shares in publicly traded shareholding companies. Pursuant to this law, the Minister of Commerce & Industry is to issue the implementing regulations setting forth the restrictions and conditions of this right, including the maximum amount of shares non-Kuwaitis may hold and the corresponding rights of the holder.

III. ENTERING INTO A JOINT VENTURE

Joint ventures are simple contracts that require no formal establishment procedures (Article 57 of the Kuwait Companies Law).

The Kuwaiti Companies Law refers to joint ventures as joint venture companies (Article 56). A joint venture company does not have a legal personality and may not transact business in its own name (Article 59). The joint venture may transact business with third parties only through one venturer, who is personally liable for the transactions he enters into with third parties. The transacting venturer's liability to third parties is unlimited. The liability of a non-transacting venturer is limited to his share in the joint venture. If the transacting venturer is a non-Kuwaiti, then the Kuwaiti venturer in the company must guarantee him in that transaction. If the joint venture were to deal with third parties in its own name, the effect would be to expose all of the joint venturers to unlimited joint and several liability, whether or not they were personally involved in the transaction.

IV. COMMERCIAL AGENCY

Law No. 36 of 1964 on the Regulation of Commercial Agencies, and the Kuwaiti Commercial Code, Articles 260-296 regulates commercial agencies. Non-Kuwaitis may not act as commercial agents in Kuwait (Article 1 of Law No. 36 of 1964), and those who violate the rule are subject to three months imprisonment and/or a fine (Article 10 of Law No. 36 of 1964).

The relationship between the Kuwaiti agent and the foreign principal must be direct. Article 2 of Law 36 provides that commercial agencies are not enforceable unless registered in the Commercial Register.

The Code's provisions set out the general rules governing commercial agencies and the types of commercial agencies.

The first type is a contracts agency (Article 271 of the Kuwaiti Commercial Code). In a contracts agency, the local agent, by contract, undertakes to promote the principal's business on a continuous basis in the territory and to enter into transactions in the name of the principal in return for a fee. The contract must be in writing and must include the territory covered, the agent's fee, the term, the product or service that is the subject of the agency, and any relevant trademarks. The term of the contract must be at least five years if the agent is required to set up showrooms, workshops, or warehouse facilities.

The second type of agency is a distributorship under which the local agent is the distributor of the principal's product in a defined territory in return for a percentage of the profit (Article 286 of the Kuwait Commercial Code). Distributorships are governed by the same general rules as contracts agencies if the distributor is the sole distributor for the whole country. These rules provide protection to both types of agents. The following protective measures are provided:

- Commercial agencies must be registered in order to be enforceable.
- Kuwaiti law is the governing law in matters pertaining to public policy.

- The principal may not terminate the agreement without proving breach of contract by the agent; otherwise, the principal is liable for paying compensation to the agent.
- The principal may not refuse to renew the agency agreement when it expires without paying the agent equitable compensation for nonrenewal if the agent proves that he committed no breach and that his activities led to the successful promotion of the principal's products.
- The agency may sue both the principal and any new agent the latter may appoint in Kuwait if the termination is proven to be the result of their concerted action.

The third type of commercial agency is the commission agency, which is provided for in Articles 287 through 296 of the Commercial Code. In this type of agency, the agent enters into contracts in his/its own name. The principal's name may not be disclosed without his permission.

V. COMMERCIAL REPRESENTATIVES

A commercial representative is a Kuwaiti individual or entity engaged by a foreign company pursuant to a contract called a "commercial representation agreement" to represent its business interests in Kuwait. The scope of authority of a commercial representative is usually more limited than the authority granted an agent. A commercial representative may be paid a set fee on a regular basis or a commission or percentage of profits. The duties and obligations of commercial representatives are governed by Articles 297 - 305 of the Commercial Code.

In executing documents on behalf of the foreign company, the commercial representative must sign his name as well as the name of the foreign company and indicate that he is a commercial representative. A foreign company is liable for all of the commercial representative's actions and liabilities, so long as they are conducted or incurred within the scope of representation.

Unlike an agency agreement, a commercial representation agreement cannot be registered with the Ministry of Commerce and Industry.

VI. TAXATION

Generally, individuals (Kuwaiti and foreign nationals) and Kuwaiti companies are not subject to taxes on income. However, a foreign corporate body engaged in commercial activities in Kuwait is subject to income tax. The tax rates range from 5% to 55%. These rates are applied progressively to income brackets.

VII. CONTRIBUTION TO THE KUWAIT FOUNDATION FOR ADVANCEMENT OF SCIENCE (KFAS)

KFAS was established to provide aid and assistance to science students and researchers for their education and training and for scientific research and development in general. Article 6 of the Memorandum of Association of KFAS provides that a source of KFAS's funding shall be from the payment by all Kuwait Shareholding Companies (a "KSC") of five percent of such companies' net profits to KFAS.

While, as a legal matter, a KSC is not strictly speaking obligated to pay five percent of its net profits to KFAS (under Article 48 of the Kuwait Constitution, taxes may be levied only by a duly promulgated law), it has become the general and accepted practice in Kuwait for KSC's to make such payments.

VIII. PUBLIC SECTOR PROCUREMENT

Procurement by the Kuwaiti Government and its agencies is regulated by Law No. 37 of 1964 (modified by Laws No. 13 and 31 of 1970 and 1977, respectively) concerning Public Tenders (the "Public Tenders Law"). The Public Tenders Law provides that any procurement made by the Kuwait Government with a value in excess of KD 5,000 (approximately $16,500) must be conducted through the Central Tenders Committee and in accordance with its procedures in order to ensure competitive pricing.

Article 5 of the Tenders Law provides that a tenderer for government contracts must:

1. "Be a Kuwaiti merchant, individual or company, registered in the Register of Commerce in the Chamber of Commerce and Industry of Kuwait; The tenderer may be a foreigner if he has a Kuwaiti merchant acting as a partner or agent pursuant to a deed duly executed by a notary, provided the Central Trading Committee shall set down a specific regulation for the participation of the foreign company in the tenders of large works.
2. Be registered in the Classification List of Contractors and Suppliers in conformity with the following Articles."

Thus, a foreign entity may act as a government contractor only through a Kuwaiti entity in which it has an ownership interest or by acting directly but with the assistance and support of a Kuwaiti agent or commercial representative.

There are two important exceptions to the application of the Public Tenders Law:

1. Ministry of Defense Procurement. The Public Tenders Law does not apply to the procurement of military items for the Ministry of Defense and Security Forces. "Military materials" is broadly defined by Kuwait law to include land, sea and air weapons, spare parts, military communications, detection equipment and related systems ("strategic military procurement").

There are no comprehensive laws or regulations that govern strategic military procurement by the Ministry of Defense ("MOD") Instead, the MOD has developed internal policies and procedures for such procurements, and such policies and procedures are not available to the public. In general, such policies are more flexible than those of the Public Tenders Law in an effort to accommodate MOD's specialized needs with respect to strategic military procurement.

2. Other Specialized Procurement. Kuwait government agencies may request permission of the Central Tenders Committee to conduct particular tenders outside the Public Tenders Law. However, such tenders are relatively rare.

IX. KUWAIT OFFSET PROGRAM

The Counter-Trade Offset Program (Offset Program), established by Decision No. 694/1994, requires all foreign contractors who meet certain criteria to participate in the Offset Program.

The guidelines issued by the Ministry of Finance for the Counter-Trade Offset Program define in Article 4 the terms "Offset obligation" and "foreign contractor". Offset obligations are triggered when the single cumulative value of supply contract(s) awarded to a foreign contractor is equal to or greater than KD 1 million. The offset obligation is effective as of the signature date of the supply contract and is equal to 30% of the monetary value of the said supply contract. 50% of the offset obligation must be completed in the first four years and 100% in eight years.

"Foreign contractors" are defined as business entities having all of the following characteristics, namely:

1. The entity does not exist or operate under Kuwait laws as per the Ministry of Commerce and Industry, Department of Corporations.
2. The entity has been awarded, as either prime contractor or sub-contractor, a supply contract by the government or any of its public sector institutions.
3. The goods and/or services to be provided under the supply contract are defined as foreign produced under Kuwaiti law.

Kuwaiti business entities acting on behalf of foreign businesses that are formed to circumvent the Offset Program will be deemed foreign contractors.

X. DISCLOSURE LAW

In August 1996, the Kuwaiti Government passed Law 25 of 1996 regarding the disclosure of commissions in connection with government contracts. This law effectively requires full transparency and accountability in all government contracts in excess of one hundred thousand dinars (approximately $300,000) in value. The law, which applies to all transactions entered into by the Kuwaiti Government or its agencies or instrumentalities, requires a stipulation by the contracting party as to whether it has paid or will pay a commission of any kind to a disclosed or concealed intermediary. Additionally, the law imposes an obligation on both the payor and the payee to disclose in a separate declaration, the amount of the commission, the type of currency, and the place and manner of the commission. The sanctions for non-disclosure or misinformation range from civil and criminal penalties equal to the value of the payment to imprisonment. However, it is important to remember that full compliance does not necessarily exonerate the parties in the event that the payment in question constitutes a violation of any other Kuwaiti law.

XI. INTELLECTUAL PROPERTY

Law No. 4 of 1962 governs patents in Kuwait. In order to obtain patent protection in Kuwait, the inventor must first register the patent with the Patents Office at the Trademark Control Department of the Ministry of Commerce & Industry (Article 4). The law permits foreigners who are nationals of or live in countries that give Kuwait reciprocity, as well as companies and other juristic personalities, to register patents in Kuwait (Article 5). Once registered, the owner of the patent is vested with the right to use that patent by any means

for 15 years from the date of the application (Articles 10 and 12). The patent may be renewed for an additional five-year term (Article 12).
Similarly, industrial designs must be registered in the Industrial Designs & Models Register and an application for registration is to be submitted to the Trademark Control Department (Articles 36 and 37). The registration is valid for five years and renewable for two additional consecutive terms (Article 42).

The Commercial Code (Law No. 68 of 1980) governs trademark registration and the penalties for infringement. Any person may apply to have his trademark registered at the Register of Trademarks (Article 64). Once the application is approved, the trademark will be protected for 10 years, and may be renewed for another ten years (Article 77).

Law No. 64 of 1999 governs copyrights and provides copyright protection and penalties for copyright infringement. With respect to non-Kuwaitis, the law applies to 1) works of foreign nationals that are published for the first time in Kuwait; 2) works of Arab authors who are nationals of member countries of the Arab Agreement for the Protection of Author's Rights and published in any of those countries; and 3) works of authors who are nationals of member states of the World Intellectual Property Organization that are published for the first time in one of those states (Article 43 of Law No. 64 of 1999).
The period of copyright protection is as follows:

1. 50 years from the death of the author (or last surviving author if joint work)
2. 50 years from the end of the calendar year of publication for (i) works published under a pseudonym or anonymously, (ii) works in which the owner of the copyright is a legal personality, (iii) cinematic and photographic works; and (iv) works published for the first time after the author's death
3. 50 years from the end of the calendar year in which the performance or recording took place, where applicable.
4. 20 years form the end of the calendar year in which the broadcast of a program occurred, where applicable.

(Article 17 of Law No. 64 of 1999)
Kuwait is a member of the World Trade Organization and a signatory to the Agreement on Trade Related Aspects of Intellectual Property Rights. As such, it is under an obligation to pass intellectual property laws meeting the minimum standards for the protection and enforcement of intellectual property rights set forth in this agreement. Kuwait is also a member of the World Intellectual Property Organization.

LEBANON

INVESTMENT

PUBLIC FINANCE

As noted, the government's budget deficit remains one of Lebanon's most important and pressing economic problems. The budget has been in chronic deficit throughout the last decade as the government continued to pay its employees and to supply goods, despite its inability to collect sufficient revenues. The deficit has been financed by borrowing from the banking sector.

As reconstruction takes off, capital expenditures are expected to increase dramatically, with a consequential sharp rise in the overall fiscal deficit in the absence of fiscal adjustment.

Since 1992, the government has taken a number of practical measures to reduce the deficit and to maintain a stable budget. These include the regulation of public expenditure and steps to increase internal revenues.

The huge structural imbalance in Lebanon's trade has also restricted growth. The manufacturing sector is not sufficiently developed to provide an alternative to imported consumer goods or production input. The result is that economic activity remains almost entirely dependent on imports.

1993 - 2003 Budgetary Allocations

Transportation	US$ 2,969 billion	Water Supply	US$ 930.0 million
Electricity	US$ 1,645 billion	Government Buildings	US$ 270.0 million
Education	US$ 1,530 billion	Solid Waste	US$ 180.0 million
Housing and Resettlement	US$ 1,050 billion	Tourism	US$ 188.7 million
Telecommunications	US$ 715.0 million	Social Affairs	US$ 130.0 million
Agriculture and Irrigation	US$ 650.0 million	Management and Implementation	US$ 150.2 million
Public Health	US$ 500.3 million	Private Sector Services	US$ 100.6 million
Wastewater Treatment	US$ 500.3 million	Information	US$ 50.0 million
Industry	US$ 394.9 million	Environment	US$ 35.0 million

PRIVATIZATION

The Lebanese government habeen making fairly modest steps towards privatization. One project that seems likely to get off the ground is the expansion and management of the port of Sidon. Consideration is also being given to the private management of the port of Beirut. Plans are being drawn for the private operation of the postal service under a twelve year concession. The US$ 50 million opwill cover the entire country and will entail mail handling, gathering, sorting, distribution, the installation of postal boxes, express mail, facsimile services and stamp sales.

STOCK EXCHANGE

The Beirut Stock Exchange (BSE) was reopened in the beginning of 1996, after more than eleven years of inactivity. The BSE is considered to be an important financial tool which will assist in stimulating the

Lebanese economy by attracting capital to the country. Currently, there are only a few securities traded on the BSE, and it does not meet international stock exchange standards. In addition, the BSE faces fierce competition from the Tel-Aviv Stock Exchange. The Lebanese government intends to increase the level of trade on the BSE by developing its exchange standards, enhancing technological support, and offering attractive tax rates and liberal currency regulations to foreign investors.

BARRIERS TO TRADE AND INVESTMENT

Lebanon is a country of free trade. There are certain goods, however, such as computer hardware and software, and firearms and munitions that require an import license. Lebanon adheres to the Arab league boycott of Israel, and, therefore, the importing of goods from Israel is officially prohibited, although this ban is not fully enforced.

CUSTOMS

Lebanon levies most customs duties on an *ad valorem* basis, the average being 25 percent calculated on the CIF value of the goods converted to local currency by reference to the official dollar rate. Special low rates apply to certain imports from member countries of the Arab League, and many agricultural products are exempt from customs duties. Importation of a few specified commodities require an import license that must be obtained prior to shipment. Free zones offering facilities for re-packaging and processing merchandise, assembling and manufacturing are located in the Beirut Port and the Tripoli Port.

WORK PERMITS

To reside and work in Lebanon, a foreigner is required to have a work permit issued by the Ministry of Social Affairs, a residence permit issued by the Ministry of Interior. In addition, foreign nationals that wish to carry on business in Lebanon must have a commercial register. Broadly speaking, work permits are granted to persons having skills not readily found in Lebanon and to management personnel (usually up to three people on the management staff of foreign firms).

LYBIA

LIBYA INVESTMENT LAW.

As the new law no, 7 of the year 2003, which was issued as an amendment to law no,5 of the year 1997, and which has been in force since 13 June 2003, introduced the concept of shared or joint ownership of the investment enterprise between local and foreign investors. Therefore reference shall be made to the formula of joint venture, provided for under the Libyan commercial code, as an investment vehicle which enables the parties to carry on business with the required flexibility, without the need of legal formalities. In particular, the above-mentioned new law no, 7 of 2003 has not specified the legal form of partnership that may be entered into between local and foreign investors, and delegates that task to executive regulations to be issued there under, which regulations have not yet been issued.

Regardless of the legal form of the investment enterprise through which the investment activity is carried out, the responsibilities and liabilities of the manager of the said enterprise remain the same.

Summary of the general principles regarding the joint Venture Agreement under Libyan Law. In order to ascertain the rights and obligations of the parties to a joint venture, one should first shed some light on the general principles of Libyan Law applicable to the joint venture agreement:

Article 681 of the Libya commercial code (L.C.C) defines the joint venture as "a contract, not subject to the formalities of registration, as in the case of commercial companies and partnerships, where by a merchant gives to another person a specific share of the profit of his commercial undertaking or of one or more transactions, against an agreed contribution by the person to whom the share is granted."

Therefore the joint venture, as any other partnership, is an agreement between two or more parties, one of whom is engaged in commercial undertakings, whereby each of the parties must contribute a share of money or labour to an economic enterprise, for the purpose of sharing the profit or loss resulting there from.

The parties in a joint venture could be either natural persons or corporate entities, such as companies or corporations.
The basic characteristic of the joint venture is that, unlike commercial companies, it is neither subject to publicity, nor to registration formalities. Therefore the joint venture has no legal personality separate from that of the partners involved therein. It has no legal domicile, nor a separate patrimony.

In other words a joint venture has no separate legal existence in relation to third parties. However as far as its parties are concerned, the joint venture constitutes a binding agreement in the fullest sense, and is considered as an existing partnership between them, capable of creating rights and obligations for parties, which rights and obligations are applicable in terms of law.

Intrinsic Features of the Joint Venture:
1. A partnership.
The joint venture formula is usually chosen because of the confidence and trust which the partners place in one another partner to the joint venture cannot assign his share to a third party without the consent of the other partners, unless the joint venture agreement stipulates otherwise.

2. A non disclosed and covert partnership.
The joint venture has no exterior legal existence in respect of third parties, and therefore has no legal personality of its own.

However if the partners sign documents under the partnership's name, or otherwise undertake any other action similarly indicating its legal existence, such covert feature would cease to exist, and the joint venture would automatically be transformed into a de facto general partnership with uncompleted registration formalities. Consequently each of the partners will jointly and severally liable for the obligations of the partnership towards third parties.

3. Limits of the liability of the partners.
In general, the liability of each partner for the obligations of the joint venture is limited according to his respective share in the partnership.

However, this limit could be raised by agreement between the partners, provided that the partners would in on circumstance be liable for an amount equal to their total assets. In such case the joint venture would automatically be transformed into a general partnership.

On the other hand, given the fact that the joint venture is a covert partnership, the manager of such joint venture, be it a natural person or a corporate entity, and should alone be liable towards third parties for whatever undertakings such manager performs on behalf of the joint venture (Article 683 of the L.C.C).

In such circumstance, on legal relationship would exist between the other partners and the third party concerned, provided that the third party is aware of the existence of the joint venture not by virtue of any action in this respect taken by the partners.

4. The commercial nature of the joint venture.
The joint venture is considered as a commercial partnership if it is set up for a commercial objective. However, as the joint venture is a covert partnership, any partner, thereof not having the status of a merchant dose not acquire such status simply because he becomes a partner in a commercial joint venture.

5. Title to the contributions of the partners.
The basic obligation of a partner is to contribute to the capital of the partnership. However, given the fact that the joint venture has no corporate nature and no separate patrimony, it is necessary to designate the owner of the capital of the joint venture.

As a rule it is up to the partners to decide this matter. They can agree to designate the main partner of the joint venture as the owner of all the capital of the partnership. As a consequence such partner would act on their behalf, and would invest such capital in the common objective targeted by them, as set out in the joint venture agreement. He will also be responsible for the distribution of the joint venture's profits and losses among all the partners according to their respective contribution towards the capital of the joint venture.

In the absence of an agreement regulating the ownership of the contributions to the capital of the joint venture, each partner would maintain the title to his capital contribution, since the joint venture has no separate patrimony and therefore does not own such capital.

When applying the foregoing principles to the joint venture agreement that may be reached between the local investor and the foreign investor, the following points should be highlighted:

1- The motive behind entering into the joint venture is undoubtedly that of optimising the benefit of merging the expertise, technical capabilities and financial resourced of both parties. This would typically enable the joint venture to exploit the local partner's potential and experience in Libya, his understanding of the investment climate in the chosen field of the investment enterprise in Libya, the resources and infrastructure readily available to it as a national investor entitled to government support and assistance, together with the technical and other resources available to the foreign partner. This is especially the case where the role of managing the joint venture operations is assigned to the local partner, and the technical support and assistance is assumed by the foreign partner.

2- Once the partners express their intention to disclose the joint venture, the joint venture would start operating under an identifiable name, and would have a legal domicile of its own. In such a situation the joint venture would be actually transformed into a general partnership lacking registration formalities. The two parties would as a consequence be jointly and severally liable for the obligations of the joint venture, and they would be obliged to settle the debts of the joint venture, even when such debts exceed the total value of its assets. Any creditor of the joint venture would have the right to claim all amounts due to him from either party, without the need to apportion such debt between the partners according to their respective share of the contributed capital.

3- If the local partner assumes the role of joint venture operator on behalf of parties, his right and obligations in this regard would be limited to the rights and obligations of an agent in respect of his principal. This means that local partner will neither make a profit nor a loss when undertaking the management of the joint venture operations. However in return for his contribution towards the operations of the joint venture, the local partner should get a fair remuneration and should also be reimbursed for all expenses incurred whilst discharging such duties.

4- If it is the intention of the parties to benefit from the tax exemptions and other privileges available under law no 5 of the year 1997, as amended by law no 7 of the year 2003, regarding the encouragement of foreign capital investment in Libya, the draft of the joint venture agreement should be submitted to the foreign investment board (FIB) for approval. Such board has the authority to supervise the percentage contribution to the capital of the joint project, and the terms of investment to be undertaken by the parties.

However, by virtue of article 13 of law no. 5 of the year 1997 as amended, investment enterprises operating under the above-mentioned law are not subject to registration at the commercial register.

Obligations of the manger of the investment enterprise under law no, 5 of 1997 as amended:
1- The obligation not to dispose of the assets of the enterprise: The manager of the investment enterprise should not dispose of any assets imported by the enterprise for its operations including, but not limited to, machinery, equipment, apertures, spare parts and raw material, without the prior approval of the FIB, and after payment of the customs duties and other taxes for their importation. Nor shall the said imported items be used for purposes other than those for which they were licensed.

2- The obligation to maintain books and prepare a balance sheet:
The manager of the investment enterprise or any other commercial company manager, as representative of the investor, is responsible for:
a. Maintaining regular books of account and such other financial records for the enterprise;
b. The preparation of an annual balance sheet and profit and loss account audited by a chartered accountant in accordance with the terms of the commercial code, and the submission of the final statement of account and general budget of the enterprise to both the FIB, and to the tax department within the times and dates prescribed by the commercial code and the tax law;
c. The submission of quarterly reports on the activity of the enterprise to the FIB.
3- The obligation to start carrying on the enterprise within the prescribed period of time.
The manager of the investment enterprise must initiate the operations of the enterprise within six months from the date of notification of the FIB approval of the enterprise. Failure to carry out this obligation may result in the cancellation of such approval.

4- The obligation to adhere to approved feasibility studies.
The manager of the investment enterprise is responsible for carrying on the enterprise in accordance with the feasibility studies on the basis of which the permit would have been issued. It is also imperative that there be no amendments thereto unless such changes are made by virtue of a decision taken by the respective competent secretary, and upon a recommendation by the people's committee of the board, based on substantive facts exigencies.

5- The obligation to give priority when recruiting employees for the enterprise. Another obligation is to give priority to Libyan nationals over expatriates in cases where local and foreign prospective employees hold comparable qualifications.

Liabilities of the manager of the investment enterprise: If the investor violates any rule of the investment law, or the executive regulation thereof, the FIB would first warn the manger to rectify the violation committed within a specified period of time. Should the investor, or indeed its representative, fail to abide by such warning, the secretary may, upon the recommendation of the board, impose one or more of the following penalties:
1- Depriving the enterprise from some of the benefits provided for under the investment law.
2- Obliging the investor to pay double the value of the exemptions granted to the investment enterprise.

However the foreign investor may at any time make recourse to the competent court in Libya to seek settlement of any dispute that might arise with the board in respect of the activity of the enterprise.

Settlement by arbitration rather then by the court can be another option, provided that an agreement in the respect is concluded between the investor and the board.

THE LEGAL ENVIRONMENT FOR INVESTMENT IN LIBYA[5]

Libya is embarking on a new era of world relations and is opening up to foreign investment, but finds itself in a position where it has to undo a great deal of what was done during the "Great Revolution". Indeed, it finds itself in need of a great deal of catching up in all aspects, but especially in the field of legal reform.

Prior to its revolution, Libya had adopted a legal system based on the Egyptian civil law model. This was the order of the day for most Arab countries and these systems worked to create a secular legal system with a general Islamic flavor. In the 1970s, Libya adopted a new approach to government which had a great impact on its legal system. It changed its name to "Jamahiriya" [People's Republic] and established what is referred to as the direct rule of the people through a system of pyramidal conferences. The lowest level is a Basic People's Congress and at the top of the pyramid the General People's Congress (a parliament-like annual conference comprised of representatives and officials of Popular Committees, appointed by the Basic People's Congresses and Municipal Congresses, and representatives of popular associations and trade unions). This conferences system was based on the theory that every person of age regardless of gender should participate through direct consultation and consensus building otherwise known in Islamic jurisprudence as 'Shura'. Each conference/congress at all levels has a committee – a mini government- and a secretariat. At the top of the pyramid of committees is the General People's Committee (The Cabinet). The Cabinet does not enjoy the normal authorities a government would. It has the authority to recommend to and implement the decisions of General People's Congress.

In 2000, all executive and legislative authority was decentralized to 26 municipal congresses with the exception of economy, finance, energy, defense and security, infrastructure, foreign affairs, social security and trade. Each local government was given its own budget.
The declared new form of government required that class differences to be eliminated, outside influence to be severed, health and education and all basic amenities to be provided by the state. Women must be given equal opportunity. As everyone was expected to protect the revolution, no regular army should be needed. Each citizen was expected to keep an eye on public funds. Property law as we know it was abolished. Labor as a "master-servant" relationship was eliminated. In the realm of foreign investment, nationalization was the fashion of the day. Commercial agencies were abolished as only the public sector can act in that capacity. In fact all private property rights as we understand them were eliminated with the exception of small self-employed service providers who were not deemed exploitive by their very nature.

As a result of these policies and the international sanctions in place, Libya developed deep-seated problems that require serious and concerted reform efforts.

Against this background Libya has embarked on a series of legal reforms. Of course, legal reforms are only as good as the policies behind them. Polices must be coherent and part of a concerted effort; they cannot be reactive and sporadic. Libyans agree on one thing, the principles of the revolution were great, but the implementation went awry. As a result, there appears to be determination this time to follow good policy with robust implementation.

As part of this reform policy, Libya began enacting various laws in the late 1990s and has continued in the past few years. Chief among these has been Foreign Investment Law No. 5 of 1997, and its amendments and implementing regulations, ("Foreign Investment Law") which together create the most liberal legal framework for attracting foreign direct investment ever adopted by this Libyan government.

The Foreign Investment Law attempts to cover not only pure foreign investment, but also Libyan private capital abroad. It opens up many sectors that were previously closed to the private sector and to foreign investment. Although it takes a conservative approach and adopts a list of those sectors that are allowable – rather than a negative list which simply opens up all sectors with certain specific exceptions- the list is growing and suggestions continue to be made and viewed with favor. The current list covers Industry, Health, Tourism, Agriculture, Oil related services but not drilling and exploration (these are covered by the

[5] By Reema Ali Ali & Partners *www.mideastlaw.com*

Petroleum Law) and any other sector specified by the GPC upon recommendation of the Secretary of the GPC for Planning Economy and Commerce.

The Foreign Investment Law provides the opportunity for 100% foreign equity ownership of companies licensed under the law. It provides for various preferences for licensed projects such as an exemption from corporate income tax for 5 years with a possible extension of 3 years provided net profits are reinvested in the project. It provides for an exemption from customs duties on imports of machinery, tools, and equipment needed for the execution of the project and will continue for a period of 5 years during the operation of the project. It also provides for an exemption from excise taxes on exported goods.

Investors are permitted to open an account in convertible currency, to repatriate profits, to employ expatriates when there is no qualified local labor and to own and lease property. They are protected against expropriation and permitted access to arbitration.

Yet despite these incentives and the great opportunities in Libya, foreign direct investment remains low. Those who have seen businessmen return from travel to Libya can see the confusion on their faces. More importantly, statistics show that few projects have been licensed and of those licensed, fewer still are operational.

The problems are multifaceted. The simplest to identify are the flaws in the policy behind the Foreign Investment Law. More difficult are those that result from long-standing policies that cannot easily be reversed. A foreign investor must address these regardless of the form of entry into the market; every investor must proceed with a comprehensive strategy.

Under the Foreign Investment Law, the licensing process is actually a lengthy approval process rather than one in which the Foreign Investment Board verifies compliance of applicants with a list of requirements. It includes an in-depth analysis based on criteria that is unclear to the investor. The minimum capital needed is left to the discretion of the public officials and is not specified in the law. The Board often requires a minimum of Euros 600,000.

In support of this process, the foreign investor must submit an application to the Foreign Investment Board with a detailed feasibility study and a 5 year financial plan which will be reviewed by the Board. The Board, in turn, will make recommendations to the Secretary on the application and the minimum capital required for the company to be formed. This process is uncertain and the investors are given no guidance as to the requirements they are expected to meet to ensure approval.

The sectors that remain closed are the very ones that are attractive to foreign investors. Telecommunications and the financial sector, for example, remain government monopolies. Retail and wholesale operations are restricted to Libyan nationals.

The Law does not afford 'national treatment' to Foreign Investment projects. This has a significant impact when these projects have to compete with state enterprises and may have serious indirect implications in the context of dispute resolution in the judicial system. Furthermore Libyan courts would not concede jurisdiction to the foreign courts and Libya is not a member of the New York Convention on Enforcement of Foreign Arbitral Awards, although local courts may defer to arbitral proceedings if there is proof that they will proceed in a timely fashion.

The real problems and obstacle are those that arise from the former policies. These policies go to the root of the ease with which business can be conducted in Libya. As a result of abolishing real property ownership for investment purposes, the commercial real estate market has been completely distorted. There exists now a private land market and a public land market with a price gap that creates considerable uncertainty for both foreign and local investors. Compounding the problem, the Foreign Investment Law is not clear as to whether real property can be used as collateral or even can be freely transferred without government approvals. The government has announced plans to reform the laws governing property and rentals, but their scope is uncertain.

Labor Law and the scarcity of skilled technicians present another serious problem. There are plans to reform the Labor Code to allow a labor relationship that conforms to international labor standards. The Foreign Investment Law currently provides that foreign companies investing in Libya must train local workers to replace their own technically qualified staff, although it allows them to hire foreign labor if there are no qualified local alternatives.

Perhaps the biggest obstacle to a predictable investment environment is the large public administration machinery, with its broad discretionary powers, minimal checks and balances and lengthy approval process. The tedious and discretionary administrative practices often undermine the very solid guarantees afforded by the law. This is particularly true in the light of the committee system adopted in Libya where everyone must agree and, even when they do, their decision is only a recommendation to yet another committee.

Libya has demonstrated its clear intention to reform. It is embarking on accession to the WTO which means that most of it laws will remain in a state of flux as they are reviewed in the context of WTO requirements. It is in the process of dismantling a great deal of its public sector through a vast privatization effort and of providing greater predictability to investors. Whether good policy and good intentions will be accompanied by effective implementation remains to be seen.

High rewards often accompany high risk. In the case of Libya, investors can benefit now if they:

1. appoint as an agent, consultant or partner a qualified Libyan who has in-country experience. The emphasis should be on knowledge of the market and the rules, rather than on political influence; and

2. seek legal advice and guidance from a local law firm with experience and knowledge of the system.

The most lucrative opportunities are usually those seized in times of transition.

MAROCCO

INVESTMENT

INVESTMENT CHARTER

Resident or non-resident foreign nationals are entitled to invest freely in Morocco, no investment operation in Morocco requires any prior authorization from the Control Exchange Office. Prior to 1996, Morocco offered foreign investors a package of investment incentives contained in various investment codes in different areas of business such as exports, tourism, industrial, mining, maritime, handicraft and real estate investments. Those codes have been replaced by a new Investment Charter, promulgated by Decree No.1-95-213 of November 8, 1995. Effective as of January, 1996, the new Charter set up as a framework the main objectives regarding the promotion and development of investments in Morocco within the next ten years. It also codified several existing regulations some of which have been implemented through their inclusion in the Corporate Tax Law in 1996. Further, the Charter establishes that benefits for investors under previously existing laws will be maintained until expiration of their term and of the conditions for which they had been granted.

INVESTMENT INCENTIVES

The Charter gives the same preference to all sectors except for agriculture. The top five sectors Morocco is trying to develop are: banking, industry, holdings, real estate and trade. Special incentives have been made available to attract these industries, these incentives differentiate between the installation phase and the operational phase of a company.

Incentives offered for the Installation Phase are:

- Exemption from formalities for land acquisition;
- Application of a registration fee of 2.5 percent for acquisition formalities for land;
- Application of 0.5 percent registration fee for inputs in capital formation of companies or increases in capital;
- Reduced import dues (between 2.5 percent and 10 percent maximum *ad valorem*);
- Exemption from import tax levy (PFI);
- Patent tax: suppression of the variable tax and exemption dufirst five years of operation;
- Exemption of urban tax for first five years after the completion or installation of new buildings;
- Exemption of reimbursement of VAT for equipment, material and tools acquired locally or imported.

Incentives for the Operational Phase are:

- Profits and income liable to corporate tax are not subject to the National Solidarity Contribution (PSN);
- Profits and income completely exonerated from corporate tax pay a contribution at a rate of 25 percent of the normal corporate tax;
- Exemption from corporate tax for exporting enterprises for five years;
- 50 percent reduction in corporate tax or income tax during the first five years thereafter;
- Enterprises are allowed to create an annual investment reserve free of tax;
- Application of sliding scale amortization for equipment;
- Exemption from real estate profits tax when premises are first ceded for use as accommodation.

In addition, special incentives are available to encourage companies to comply with environment protection laws or to install environment protection equipment.

Administrative Proceedings

Apart from serving as an outline for various changes in tax law, the Charter also promotes facilitation and reduction of administrative procedures involving the carrying out of investments. To that end, a special administrative body for the promotion of investments was instituted and charged with assisting investors. In addition, in all cases where approval of an administrative authorization for the granting of advantages proves to be necessary, this authorization is deemed to be granted when the administration has kept silent regarding the result of the request during a period of sixty days after the date the request has been filed.

Public Sector Investment Contracts

The Charter also offers special contracts with the state to enterprises whose investment programs are important due to their size, the number of stable jobs created, the region in which they will be carried out, the technology they transfer or their level of environmental protection. Under these contracts, the state can grant a partial exemption from the following expenses:

- Costs of purchasing the land necessary for carrying out the investment;
- Costs of external infrastructure;
- Costs of professional training.

The Charter explicitly mentions that these contracts can include provisions, stipulating that the method regarding the settlement of disputes arising between a foreign investor and the Moroccan state will be in accordance with international agreements ratified by Morocco with respect to international arbitration.

INVESTMENT PROMOTION FUND

The Charter creates an Investment Promotion Fund, a special appropriation account designed to be used for the operations relating to the responsibility of the state for the cost of advantages granted to investors under the framework of the investment contract regime. The Charter, however, does not stipulate how the fund will be financed.

FOREIGN TRADE

As a member of GATT, Morocco has gradually removed most restrictions for imports originating from other member countries. According to the law of November 9, 1993 relating to foreign businesses, all goods and services can be imported without a licensing requirement. In the event that imports are deemed to have a negative impact on national production, however, an import license may be required. In addition, the following duties can be imposed:

- Compensatory duties, in the event that the product imported benefits from manufacturing or export bonuses or subsidies in its country of origin;
- An anti-dumping duty, in the event that the import value is lower that the normal value of the item.

In order to import into Morocco, some documentation procedures are required. A person or entity must be registered in a register of importers and must obtain the authority to import from the Ministry of Commerce and Industry. An import registration form (*engagement d'importation*) should be obtained from a Moroccan Schedule A Bank for all imports into Morocco. This form facilitates both custom formalities and the payments of the invoice.

In recent years, export regulations have undergone a substantial amount of liberalization. Export licenses are not required, and export sales are not subject to export tax. The sole obligation on the part of the exporter is the repatriation of export benefits. The repatriation should be performed in a 120 day period, however, the deadline can be extended in case the trade obligations require do so. Settlements relating to exports can now be made in foreign currency, and the exporter is no longer required to produce the customs declarations justifying the import of foreign currency. Similarly, the financial regulations pertaining to investment operations are now directly handled at the level of the banking institutions.

FREE TRADE AGREEMENTS

In 1995 Morocco entered into a Free Trade Agreement with the European Union which gives preferential treatment to Moroccan goods exported to the EU. Under the agreement, industrial products can be exported to the EU duty-free and without quantitative restrictions, only for agricultural products. Some quotas and restrictions remain.

Recently, the country has signed an additional trade agreement with Ministers from four EFTA States (Switzerland, Norway, Iceland and Liechtenstein), due to come into force in early 1998. Whereas the EFTA members will eliminate all restrictions on imports of industrial products, processed agricultural goods, fish and other marine products, Morocco has agreed to phase out tariffs and quotas over twelve years, while retaining the right to introduce restrictions to protect nascent or restructuring industries.
Morocco has also signed free trade arrangements with members of the Maghreb Arab Union (UMA). For all practical purposes, however, the UMA is dormant, and regional economic integration has been stalled. Another bilateral free trade arrangement has been established with Saudi Arabia.

FREE TRADE ZONE

There is a Free Trade Zone in Tangier which is open to both Moroccan and foreign companies. The sixty-five companies located in the zone may import goods duty free and are exempt from other takes. The only requirement is that all local workers be paid directly in foreign exchange, which they are then obliged to exchange for MDh at Moroccan commercial banks operating in the zone.

PRIVATIZATION

Morocco boasts what many have termed the Arab world's most ambitious privatization program, with 112 firms worth US$ 2 billion mandated for sale by mid-1996. As a result of a rough economic performance in 1995, however, the government raised less than half the US$ 400 million that had been forecast from selling state-owned assets that year.

Already released for public offering, 35 percent of Sonasid (the state-run steel company) through 1.35 million shares at approximately US$ 38 per share were called on 1.6 times per share. Most of the remainder will be sold to a strategic investor. A group led by Shell du Maroc bought 56 percent of Somas oil company for US$ 8.9 million. Morocco is also working on a scheme to split up the state power company into separate agencies.

Morocco announced that it will soon issue privatization bonds in banks, accredited stock exchange companies and the General Treasury. The bonds will have a nominal value of US$ 117 and will be worth US$ 12 billion. They will be negotiable on the Casablanca Bourse for the coming three years and will give holders preferential options on shares. These bonds will also give the holder the right to convert them into shares in enterprises that could be privatized or to sell them at the 8 percent interest rate a year on the Casablanca Bourse.

Bonds not exchanged by the end of December 1998 will be reimbursed on the basis of their nominal value with a bonus of 8.5 percent a year. Subscriptions will be opened to any individuals or companies regardless of nationality, except public insurance and credit companies, which are barred from participating in the subscriptions. During 1996, eight mutual funds were allowed to operate on the Bourse for the first time, including Wafabank, Banque Centrale Populaire, CFG stockbroker and Societe Generale Marocaine de Banques. Wafabank and CFG stockbroker were authorized to operate on the Bourse with three mutual funds each.

STOCK EXCHANGE

The Moroccan securities market is in the process of modernization. The single stock exchange in Morocco, situated in Casablanca, has been regarded as rather inactive. In October 1993 Morocco passed a law aiming at turning thstock exchange into a private company, with stock held by brokers and monitored by a special commission. The effect of this law after full implementation should provide investors with a new and important investment facility making Morocco more attractive to foreign capital. It is notable, however, that there are no markets in Morocco yet for trade in financial futures or other types of derivatives. Privatization measures, as discussed above, have also had an effect on the operation of the stock exchange.

OMAN

FOREIGN INVESTMENT REQUIREMENTS

The Foreign Capital Investment Law of 1994 provides the legal framework within which foreigners may invest and carry on business in the Sultanate of Oman. The following address procedural requirements and investment vehicles of which prospective investors should be aware.

LICENSING REQUIREMENTS

Foreigners cannot conduct any commercial, industrial or tourist business or otherwise participate in an Omani company unless a license is obtained from the Ministry of Commerce and Industry. A license is granted upon the fulfillment of the following conditions:

- The business must be conducted by an Omani company with a capital of at least RO 150,000;
- The foreign share therein must not exceed 49 percent of the company's total capital, unless authorization to increase participation up to 65 percent is given by the Minister of Commerce and Industry. In instances where the project contributes to the development of the economy, the project's capital exceeds RO 500,00 and an approval is given by Development Council, foreign participation may be increased up to 100 percent.

Exemptions from the above requirements may be granted under the following circumstances:

- The company conducts a business under a special contract with the government or a contract established pursuant to a Royal Decree;
- The company conducts a business which is declared by the Cabinet as necessary for the country.

The following information and certified documents must accompany a license application:

- The objects of the proposed business;
- Articles of association or constitutive agreement;
- Details of each proposed shareholder or partner;
- The aggregate interest in the capital to be owned by foreigners;
- A certificate from the Commercial Registrar Secretariat of the Ministry of Commerce and Industry that no other company is engaged in Oman under the proposed name;
- Power of attorney to at least one individual;
- Financial reports;
- The foreigner's major activities and projects;
- Approvals from other government departments where relevant;
- Operation through a Branch of a foreign Company or through a Commercial Agency.

It is possible for foreigners to carry on business in Oman without direct Omani participation in ownership and management. For example, foreigners may set up a branch office to perform specific contract awarded by the government or by an oil company holding a concession granted by the government. Registration of such a contract with the Ministry of Commerce and Industry and the appointment of an Omani agent allows lawful performance of the contract, including ancillary activities, without the need to set up a company of the types described above. In addition, certain professional consultants, in areas where there is a critical shortage, are allowed to set up a branch office in Oman subject to the satisfaction of certain requirements.

INVESTMENT INCENTIVES

Investment incentives granted by the Ministry of Commerce and Industry are provided pursuant to Royal Decrees and the Foreign Capital Investment Law of 1994:

GOVERNMENT LOANS

Under Royal Decree 40/87, foreign investors may be eligible for interest-free soft loans from the Ministry of Commerce and Industry, provided that not more than 25 percent of the equity in the company is owned by non-Omani persons. Such attractive loans are given for the following purposes:

- Acquisition of fixed assets for new projects;
- Acquisition of machinery and equipment for expansion of existing projects;
- Infusion of finance into a 'failing' industry, provided that the entity has been in existence for at least one year, losses have not been caused by mismanagement and that it can be established that the loan would convert the entity into a viable enterprise.

The granting of such loans is linked to priority areas as determined by the Ministry of Commerce and Industry. There are two priority areas which are encouraged in the Sultanate. The first concerns the following industrial projects or entities:

- Export-oriented projects;
- Food processing industries;
- Projects using at least 20 percent local raw materials;
- Projects employing at least 35 percent Omani employees;
- Joint stock companies with at least 40 percent of public subscription.

The second priority area concerns the following tourism projects or entities:

- Projects outside the capital area assisting in regional development;
- Projects involving a new tourism activity;
- Projects with at least 30 percent Omani work force;
- Projects with foreign investment that will transfer management techniques to Oman;
- Projects that promote traditional industry or that market their products;
- Joint stock companies with at least 40 percent of public subscription.

The amounts of the loans are determined in accordance with the following guidelines:

- Up to 100 percent of the paid-up capital for projects in the capital area;
- Up to 125 percent of the paid-up capital for projects in other areas;
- Joint stock companies may be granted a loan not exceeding RO 3 million;
- Non- joint stock companies may be granted a loan not exceeding RO 250,000;
- Tourism projects may be granted a loan not exceeding RO 500,000.

Loans given for new and expansion projects can be repaid over fifteen years, with the first installment paid after a grace period of five years. For tourism projects and 'failing' industries, the repayment period is thirteen years, with a grace period of three years. Delayed installments may attract an annual 10 percent interest charge, calculated for the period of delay. As to securities, all fixed assets of the project are mortgaged under a first priority charge to the government for the term of the loan.

OTHER INCENTIVES AND PROVISIONS

Tax-related incentives and government loans are the major incentives given to foreign investors. Additional incentives and provisions are provided under Royal Decrees and the Foreign Capital Investment Law.

Foreign investors are specifically allowed to resolve disputes with third parties by way of local or international arbitration. The importation of any production materials, machinery, parts, and the like does not require to registration in the Importers Registrar. Foreign investors are free to conduct the licensed activity and to transfer abroad the imported capital along with the profits accrued in the project. Their projects may not be confiscated or expropriated unless for the public interest and against equitable compensation.

Foreign businesses may be entitled to preferential allocation of government land. They may be given a free survey of industrial investment opportunities, a reduction in charges for electricity, and priority in government purchases.

INVESTMENT FROM GULF CO-OPERATION COUNCIL STATES

Oman is a member of the Gulf Co-Operation Council States (GCC), which also includes Saudi Arabia, United Arab Emirates, Bahrain, Qatar and Kuwait. Under the United Economic Agreement of the GCC states of 1981 and the resolution of the Supreme Council of GCC states, Oman permits GCC nationals to conduct certain economic activities in specified fields in the Sultanate upon the same terms and conditions as applicable to Omanis. The fields are determined periodically by Ministries of Commerce and Industry and of Finance and Economy. Activities currently permitted include industry, agriculture, animal resources, fisheries, construction, management of hotels and restaurants, retail and wholesale trade, law, medicine, accountancy, engineering, pharmaceutical, craft and computer programming.

The government's emphasis on income diversification has opened the country to foreign participation in the economy, particularly in the form of joint ventures. Oman is actively seeking private foreign investors, putting specific emphasis in the industrial field. Those investors who allow technology transfer and provide employment and training for Omanis are particularly welcome.

Oman's labor law and the Oman tax law also affect a foreigner's ability to do business in Oman. Since there is no complete body of regulations codifying these laws and many government decisions are made on an *ad hoc* basis, investors should consider engaging local counsel. Recent changes in the tax law have, for the first time, required Omani companies to pay taxes on profits. The taxes levied on foreign companies and joint ventures were recently changed, and companies with foreign ownership of less than 90 percent are subject to the same tax as Omani firms.

Foreign investment in Oman is allowed only through joint stock companies or joint ventures. In both forms, majority Omani ownership is generally required, although joint venture industrial projects may be up to 65 percent foreign and up to 100 percent in special cases.

PRIVATIZATION

Royal Decree 42/96, which became effective on June 15, 1996, authorized the creation of a Privatization Committee charged with the task of establishing a privatization program, particularly with respect to service and utility sector businesses. The Foreign Capital Investment Law applies to the participation of foreign investors in the privatization of such entities.

The Decree acknowledges that the government has set a course of slow and careful privatization in order to encourage economic growth. Priority is to be given to the service and utility industries, and special considerations must be made with regards to environmental protection in implementing privatization plans. The Decree encourages investment from abroad. Foreign investment, however, must be licensed according to the Foreign Capital Investment Law.

The first schemes to be offered will include electricity, water, road and telecommunications projects. Coopers & Lybrand of the UK have conducted a study for the government on privatization.

Oman also intends to initiate the selling of existing state assets, including holdings in a number of banks, the General Telecommunication Organization (GTO), Gulf Air and possibly the Oman Mining Co. As GTO is the second highest government revenue earner, it will not be easy for the government to let it go.

STOCK EXCHANGE

The Muscat Securities Market was established in 1989 pursuant to the Law of Muscat Securities Market and Amendments (Royal Decree 53/88) and Ministerial Decision 112/88. The Exchange was modeled after exchanges in Taiwan, Malaysia and New York. The framework of the statute and regulation is rather comprehensive and sets out provisions regarding members, brokers, dealers, administrative organization, market finance, disclosure, control, disciplinary actions and the like. The Muscat Securities Market is active and sophisticated. It has acquired a good reputation in terms of management and administration. A well-known fund-raising exercise associated with the National Bank of Oman was conducted through the Muscat Securities Market, and local companies have raised funds through that market. Modifications to the Law adopted in 1994 allow foreign investors to invest in approved investment funds, up to 49 percent of the shares, and such investment funds are treated as 100 percent Omani entities and can freely invest elsewhere in the economy as such.

The capitalization markets, or volume of investments, listed on the Muscat Securities Market totals US$ 4.16 billion, of which overseas contributions account for 10.55 percent, or US$ 444.86 million. This is the result of Oman's continued economic reforms and strong performance of trading institutions world-wide for 1996. The year 1989 saw US$ 24.7 million in turnover; 1990 saw US$ 122.2 million; 1994 reached US$ 327.6 million; and 1995 ended with US$ 283 million.

At the end of 1995, fifty-two of the eighty-four listings on the market were open to non-Omanis. More foreign investment is sought and expected for 1997 and onward. Presently, there are eighty-nine companies listed on the exchange. December 1996 saw the listing of Shell Marketing Group with paid up capital of RO 50 million, 40 percent of which is to be raised through public conscription.

Oman's Information Technology (IT) plan, initiated at the beginning of 1996, includes the gradual introduction of electronic trading to the stock market (to take approximately two years) and involves new hardware to assist in the clearance, settlement, depositing and finance. Oman does not need the electronic upgrading for many years, even under the most positive growth assumptions. Thus, the move towards high technology is seen as a sign of the country's commitment to sustained growth in the future.

PRACTICAL INFORMATION FOR INVESTING AND BUSINESS ACTIVITY

The Commercial Code of Oman ("The Code") (Royal Decree No. 55 / 90) provides that foreign nationals may not engage in commerce in the Sultanate of Oman except after obtaining "permission to do so in accordance with the applicable Laws" (Article 24). Article 25 of the Code provides that foreign companies may not establish a branch in the Sultanate or engage in Commerce except through an Omani local agent who is a merchant and in accordance with the rules set forth by the Law.

Royal Decree No. 102 / 94 relating to the Regulation of Foreign Capital Investment (Repealing Royal Decree No. 4 / 74) provides the general framework for foreign investment in Oman. In particular, it provides:

1. Foreign nationals may not conduct any business activities or participate in an Omani company without obtaining a license to that effect from the Ministry of Commerce and Industry
2. Licenses to conduct business in Oman are granted to Omani entities whose share capital is not less than OR 150,000 and in which the foreign participation is not more than 49%. The percentage of foreign ownership may be increased in certain situations.
3. Foreign investors are permitted to own up to 100% of an entity provided it is engaged in a national economic development project that is approved by the National Development Council, and that it has a minimum capital investment of Omani Rial (OR) 500,000 (Article 2 of Decree 102/94).
4. Foreign companies that have special contracts with the government, or provide services that are needed in Oman, are exempted from the requirement of obtaining a license (Article 3 of Decree 102/94).
5. All license applications are to be submitted to the Foreign Capital Investment Committee (Article 4 of Decree 102/94).

FORMS OF ENTRY

The following forms of entry into the Sultanate's market are available to foreign nationals and foreign entities:

1. Participation in a local commercial company
2. Formation of a joint venture with a local partner
3. Appointment of a local commercial agent
4. Contracting with the public sector

OMANI COMPANIES

The Commercial Companies Code provides that commercial companies with non-Omani partners must comply with the Foreign Capital Investment law (Article 7 of the Commercial Companies Code). The following types of commercial companies are open for foreign participation under the Commercial Companies Code.

A. Limited Liability Companies "LLC"

An LLC must have at least two partners (national or juristic persons). Their share capital may not be less than Omani Rial (OR) 10,000 when all partners are Omani and OR 150,000 if there is foreign participation. The capital is divided into equal parts that are not available for public subscription. The partners' liability is limited to their share of the capital. An LLC may not engage in banking, financial guarantees, or commercial aviation activities. LLC's are popular since they are relatively easy to form.

B. Joint Stock Companies

There are two types of joint stock companies permitted in Oman:

1- Closed joint stock companies whose shares are not publicly traded (minimum capital OR 50,000)

2- Public joint stock companies whose shares are publicly traded (minimum capital OR 150,000)

The minimum capital is set at OR 150,000 for both types of joint stock companies if there is foreign participation. The minimum par value per share is OR 1 and the maximum is OR 5. Joint stock companies may not be incorporated without the prior approval of the Ministry of Commerce and Industry and issuance of a license to that effect.

JOINT VENTURES

Joint ventures are regulated by the Commercial Companies Code (Royal Decree 4/74, as amended by Royal Defense Decrees 13/89; 83/94; 16/96). Joint ventures are not considered juristic persons under the law (Articles 3 and 52). Joint venture agreements are private arrangements, and thus, do not require public recording (Articles 6 and 52). An Omani partner must hold at least 51% ownership of the joint venture project (Article 7).
If the joint venture conducts business with third parties as a joint venture, the transactions will be subject to the provisions of Al-Tadamon Company and the provisions of the general partner in a Tadamon Company (Article 54). Tadamon companies are very similar to general partnerships in common law legal systems.

COMMERCIAL AGENCIES

Commercial agencies are utilized as vehicles for importing products and/or services into the Sultanate and not to establish a business presence. Commercial agencies are governed by the Commercial Code (the "Code") (Royal Decree 55/90), the Commercial Agencies Law (Royal Decree 26/77 as amended by Royal Decree 82/84 and Royal Decree 73/96), and the Commercial Register Law (Royal Decree 3/74 as amended by the Royal Decree 88/86).

The Commercial Agencies Law defines a commercial agency as "Any agreement through which a merchant or a commercial company in the Sultanate is assigned to promote or distribute the products or services of a foreign person or entity in consideration for profit or commission".

Only Omani nationals (or a naturalized person who has been a citizen at least three years) who is eighteen years age or older and who is registered as a member of the Oman Chamber of Commerce, or companies duly established in accordance with the laws of Oman and with at least 51% Omani ownership may be appointed as commercial agents.

Commercial agency agreements need not be exclusive. This means that the principal is free to appoint more than one agent in Oman. The commercial agency agreement must be in writing and must be duly certified and authenticated. The agency agreement must include at least the following essential elements (Article 6):

- The names of the agent and principal and their nationality;

- The products or services subject matter of the agency;

- The term and the territory.

The agreement must be directly between the provider of the services or the manufacturer of the products and the agent. Furthermore, during the term of the agency, the principal may not engage in the sale of the products and services in the territory, whether directly or through any other intermediary. The agent will be entitled to his/her commission/share of profit for any such sales (Article 7).

An agency agreement must be registered at the Commercial Agencies register at the Ministry of Commerce and Industry to be enforceable. No claim may be heard regarding any agency that is not duly registered (Article 11 (D)).

Omani law provides substantial protection to commercial agents, especially in the context of termination. If the principal terminates an unlimited term commercial agency without cause, the principal must compensate the agent. With respect to limited term agencies, the principal is free to cancel registration at the end of the term. However, an agent may seek compensation where the principal has abused this right to terminate. The most common example is where the principal unjustly terminates or fails to re-new.

The Dispute Resolution Authority has jurisdiction over commercial agency disputes (Article 18). The Dispute Resolution Authority was formed by Royal Decree 79/81 and is the sole body responsible for hearing Commercial disputes in the Sultanate. The Authority has sole discretion in determining the appropriate amount of compensation to be paid in disputed cases.

Types of Commercial Agencies:

1- Contracts agency: The principal compensates the agent for promoting the principal's services/products in the territory. The agent remains independent and may or may not have the authority to sign on behalf of the principal. Principals wishing to contract with the public sector usually use this type of agency.

2- Commission Agents: This type of agency is usually used when the principal is concealed and the agent contracts in his/her name but for the benefit of the principal.

3- Trade Representatives: This is a type of employment contract whereby the principal sends representatives to Oman.

4- Brokers: This is an agency agreement whereby the principal entrusts the agent to locate and identify possible buyers in consideration for a commission.

PUBLIC SECTOR

The Public Tenders Law governs public procurements in the Sultanate (Royal Decree 86/84 and the amendments thereto). Article 1 of the Public Tenders Law provides that all government procurement and public works contracts are to be governed by the Tenders Law and shall be conducted via a public tender with the exception of:

1. *Defense contracts and projects:* The Ministry of Defense oversees defense procurement through an internal tenders committee.

2. *Specific exceptions provided for by the law:* The law provides that, upon meeting certain criteria,

Ministries may form their own internal tenders committees, contract directly with the supplier, or sole source.

The Tenders Committee is responsible for overseeing all government tenders (Article 2). Persons who reside in the Sultanate and have an address to which a valid notice may be served are permitted to submit bids. Furthermore, the bidder must have a local agent or a sponsor who must be named in the bid. Tenders may also be submitted through local agents who must present a proper power of attorney duly authenticated from the bidder's country.

INDUSTRIAL PROJECTS

Royal Decree No. 1/79 and the amendments thereto relating to the Encouragement and Regulation of Industrial projects provide various incentives for local industrial projects. These include tax holidays for five years; exemptions from export and import taxes and provision of utilities at reduced rates. Furthermore, the government gives preference to local products in its procurements.

TAX

There are no personal income taxes in Oman. Corporate income tax in Oman is regulated by the Corporate Income Tax Law (Royal Decree 47/81 and the amendments thereto) (The "Tax Law"). All corporate entities as defined in Article 2 of the Omani Commercial Companies Law are subject to corporate income tax. The law also applies to Omani joint ventures and any entity which has a "permanent presence" in Oman and is supported by a foreign entity, or which the Director of Taxes deems to be supported by a foreign entity (Article 2(4) of the Tax Law). The Tax Law defines the words "Entity with Permanent Presence" in Article 2(11) as: "An entity that has a fixed place of activity in which the project conducts all or part of its business" and it includes in particular:

- **a place for selling;**
- **a place for management;**
- **a branch;**
- **an office;**
- **a manufacturing facility;**
- **a mine, quarry, or any other place for natural resources;**
- **a construction site or place or an assembly plant.**

The Law also carves out certain exclusions to the above definition.

Income is defined in Article 8 in the broadest possible terms. Article 13 defines the allowable deductions. Ministerial Decision No. 91/84 defines further the deductions that should be taken into account when calculating the corporate income tax of Omani branches of foreign corporations. These include corporate headquarters expenses that are actually incurred and are attributable to the branch. If determination of actual expenses is difficult, the law provides various formulas for the purpose of accounting for headquarters expenses. The applicable tax rates vary depending on whether or not the company is wholly owned by Omani nationals, the percentage of Omani participation in the company's share capital if it is "a mixed company" (i.e., includes Omani and foreign shareholders) and the activity in which the company is engaged. In all cases, the applicable rates apply to slices of income on a progressive scale.

A. Tax Rates

- Purely Omani entities & Mixed Public Joint Stock Entities are taxed between 0%-7.5%
- Other Mixed Corporate entities:
    - 0-99% Omani participation (i.e., 1-90% foreign ownership): taxes range from 0% to 25%
    - 9% or less Omani participation (i.e., 91% or more foreign ownership): taxes range from 0% to 50%

B. Exemptions and Tax Holidays

Corporations whose main object is manufacturing, agriculture, fishery, tourism, exportation of local products, public utility projects and infrastructure projects, as well as companies whose activities are deemed essential for economic development, may be exempted from tax for five years (Royal Decrees 125 / 94; 102 / 94; 75 /

21). These corporations may carry forward losses incurred during the five-year exemption period for as many years needed until the losses are set off against taxable income.

C. Withholding Tax

Royal Decree No. 89/96 provides that foreign companies without a permanent presence in Oman and who receive fees/income from management contracts, royalties, leases of equipment and machinery, technical expertise and/or research and development, will be subject to a withholding tax amounting to 10% of the total fees/income received.

PALESTINE (WEST BANK AND GAZA)

LAW ON THE ENCOURAGEMENT OF INVESTMENT IN PALESTINE

Law No. (1) of1998

The President of the Palestine Liberation Organization

The President of the Palestinian National Authority

Reconsidering Law No. (6) of 1995 on the Encouragement of Investment

Considering the Proposed law submitted by the Council of Ministers

and its adoption by the Palestinian Legislative Council,

We promulgate this Law.

CHAPTER ONE

DEFINITIONS AND GENERAL PROVISIONS

Article1 .0

Unless the context otherwise states, this Law on the Encouragement of Investment in Palestine defines the words and phrases as follows:

"National Authority" shall be defined as the Palestinian National Authority.

"Council of Ministers" shall be defined as the Council of Ministers of the National Authority.

"Ministry" shall be defined as the Ministry of Economy and Trade.

"Minister" shall be defined as the Minister of Economy and Trade

"Agency" shall be defined as the Palestinian Investment Promotion Agency

"Board of Directors" shall means the Agency's Board of Directors.

"Director General" shall mean the Agency's Director General.

"Confidential Information" shall be defined as all information, of whatever kind, received by the Agency from any Investor in connection with any interaction between the Investor and the Agency pursuant to the operation of the Investment Law, excluding information about the Investor that the Investor has already publicly disclosed voluntarily, under this Law, or under other Palestinian laws.

"Enterprise" shall be defined as any entity constituted and properly registered for profit, including any company, branch, partnership, sole proprietorship, joint venture, or other association.

"Investment" shall be defined as actual monetary investmentof capital (fixed capital assets) by an Investor in an Enterprise, whether a newly-created or an existing enterprise.

"Confirmation of Investment" shall be defined as the document issued by the Agency to an Investor in accordance with the provisions of this Law.

"Incentive" shall be defined as the exemptions and benefits granted in accordance with of this Law.

"Investment Law" shall mean the Law on the Encouragement of Investment in Palestine.

"Investor" shall be defined as any natural or legal person, domestic or foreign, who seeks to invest in Palestine or who has invested in Palestine under the Investment Law.

"Registry of Investments" shall be defined as the public registry created and maintained by the Agency that lists the Investments confirmed by the Agency.

"Incentives Committee" shall be defined as the committee of the Board of Directors that reviews and evaluates Investor requests for Confirmation of Investment pursuant to this Law.

Article (2)

The Investment Law aims to achieve the development objectives and priorities in Palestine by promoting investment through the following:

(A) Establishing the Agency, an institution responsible for encouraging and

promoting investment in Palestine.

(B) Providing guarantees to all Investors and Investments operating in Palestine;

(C) Granting the Incentives to Investors.

(D) Providing the appropriate environment for encouraging investment in Palestine.

Article (3)

Any Investor may invest in any sector of the Palestinian economy; unless it contravenes other laws.

Article (4)

Enterprises in all sectors shall enjoy the exemptions and incentives provided for in this Law unless otherwise provided below such investment require the approval by the Council of Ministers before becoming eligible:

1. Manufacturing and distribution of weapons, ammunition or their parts;

2. Aviation industries, including airports;

3. Electrical power generation and distribution;

4. Processing of petroleum and its derivatives;

5. Reprocessing of refuse and solid waste;

6. Communications and telecommunication services; and

7. Radio and television.

Article (5)

To be eligible under this Law, all Investments in Palestine must be registered.

CHAPTER TWO

GENERAL GUARANTEES

Article (6)

(A) No Investor will be discriminated against on any basis whatsoever in the application of the incentives provided for under this Law.

(B) The National Authority may grant preferential treatment to Investors on the basis of nationality under bilateral or multilateral trade and/or investment agreements with other statesthat the National Authority may enter into in the future.

Article (7)

The Authority prohibits the nationalization of any Investment in Palestine and may not expropriate any investment except by operation of the law.

Article (8)

There shall be no expropriation of an Investment or part, thereof save and except in exceptional cases for a public purpose, with due process of law accorded to the Investor subject to an expropriation, who shall be compensated the fair market value and for losses suffered because of such expropriation.

Article (9)

Notwithstanding the instances when the Agency may cancel the confirmation of Investment in accordance with the provisions of this Law, no other administration may cancel the permits issued in relation to real property, as licensed, for the purposes of enjoying the benefits by the Enterprise in whole or in part unless the Agency is consulted. The Agency may give its opinion within seven days from the date of the request. The permits may not be canceled unless for legal reasons or public purpose on the basis of non-discrimination. The injured Investor shall, through the judicial system, have the right to request compensation for losses incurred as a result of the cancellation.

Article (10)

Without prejudice to Article **(11)** and in furtherance of free market principles, the National Authority shall guarantee to all Investors free transfer of all financial resources out of Palestine, including capital, profits, dividends, capital gains, wages and salaries, interest and principal payments on debts, royalty payments, management fees, technical assistance and other fees, compensation payments for expropriations or unilateral termination of contracts for non-commercial reasons, judicial and arbitral awards and judgments, and any other kind of financial payment or resource. Investors may freely transfer all financial resources out of Palestine, at the applicable market currency exchange rates in effect the time of transfer, in a convertible currency acceptable to the Investor.

Article (11)

The National Authority may limit the transfer of financial resources by any Investor when any of the following apply to the Investor:

(A) Palestinian bankruptcy, insolvency, and other laws for the protection of the rights of creditors;

(B) Palestinian laws relating to issuing, trading, or dealing in securities;

(C) Palestinian criminal or penal laws;

(D) Palestinian tax laws;

(E) Palestinian laws relating to reports of transfers of currency or other monetary instruments; or

(F) Ijunctive orders or final judgments rendered in Palestinian judicial or arbitral proceedings.

CHAPTER THREE

THE AGENCY

Article (12)

The Palestinian Investment Promotion Agency ("Agency") shall be established under this Law. The Agency shall be an autonomous institution of the Authority, competent in respect of any obligation, right, or legal act. The Agency's operations shall be governed by this Law.

Article (13)

The principle venue of the Agency shall be the city of Jerusalem. The National Authority shall specify any other temporary location.

Article (14)

The Agency's Board of Directors shall consist of thirteen (13) voting members:

(1) The Minister of Economy and Trade, Chairman of the Board of Directors;

(2) A representative of the following ministries and authorities:

(a) Finance, Deputy Chairman of the Board of Directors;

(b) Industry;

(c) Agriculture;

(d) Tourism;

(e) Housing;

(f) Planning and International Cooperation; and

(g) Monetary Authority.

(3) (A) five representatives from the Palestinian private sector. These representatives, in the exercise of their functions on the Board of Directors, shall act independently, without conflicts of interest and within the objectives of this Law.

(B) The Council of Ministers shall appoint the five private sector representatives upon the recommendation of the Board of Directors.

(C) The private sector members of the Board of Directors shall serve terms as provided in the Regulations.

Article (15)

The functions of the Board of Directors shall convene to:

(1) Oversee and evaluate policies and Investments.

(2) Submit recommendations to the Council of Ministers and propose needed changes in the criteria for granting the incentives and exemptions.

(3) Attract investors to Palestine.

(4) Advise the Minister of Economy and Trade and the Minister of Finance on Palestinian investment policies.

(5) Issue confirmations of Investment.

(6) Create and maintain the Registry of Investments.

(7) Supervise enterprises benefiting from the Incentives.

(8) Appoint independent auditors to audit the financial statements of the Agency.

(9) Implement decisions of the Council of Ministers concerning changes in the criteria for granting the Incentives.

(10) Monitor the implementation of the Investment Law and recommend changes to the Council of Ministers and the Palestinian **Legislative** Council.

(11) Monitor any Palestinian law or regulation that may restrict, limit, or prejudice any of the rights and guarantees provided in the Investment Law, and propose changes to such laws and regulations to the Council of Ministers for adoption.

(12) Assist the Authority in complying with any investment agreement that the Authority may enter into with another State or international organization.

(13) Develop a close working relationship with the concerned Palestinian authorities to assure a unified national investment promotion strategy.

(14) Monitor the performance of the Agency, which shall include preparing an annual report on the Agency's activities and the Agency's audited financial statements.

(15) Look into proposing and modernizing laws related to investment and adopting policies and programs that contribute to providing an environment conducive to investment.

(16) Issue an annual guide for investment opportunities in Palestine.

(17) Suspend the confirmation of exemptions and incentives in the event the Investor is found in violation of this Law; the Investor has the right to appeal within thirty (30) days.

(18) Create a one-stop shop to facilitate all procedures for the Investor concerning the investment including the issuance of permits and reduction of routine administrative procedures at various official offices.

(19) Adopt the necessary procedures for the Agency staff in accordance with the Civil Servants Law.

(20) Appoint consultants and experts as deemed necessary by the Agency and in accordance with the conditions set by the Board of Directors.

Article (16)

(A) The Board of Directors shall convene a regular meeting at least once a month called for by the Chairman or, in his absence, the Deputy Chairman. Quorum of one-third is required.

(B) The Board of Directors may convene, within a five-day notice, at the written request of two-thirds of the members. If necessary, it may convene by shorter notice.

(C) Resolutions by the Board shall be made by majority vote. In the event of a tie, the Chairman's vote shall be decisive.

(D) The deliberations of the Board shall be closed, unless the members agree otherwise.

Article (17)

(A) The Agency shall have a Director General appointed by the Board of Directors.

(B) The Director General shall be a non-voting member of the Board.

(C) The Director General shall have the following responsibilities:

(1) Execute the policies of the Agency as determined by the Board of Directors.

(2) Organize and oversee the day-to-day operations of the Agency.

(3) Report to the Board of Directors regularly on the Agency's operations and performance.

(4) Participate in activities designed to promote domestic and foreign investment in Palestine.

(D) The Board of Directors shall determine the compensation and terms of employment for the Director General.

(E) The Director General may not have any interest or be party, directly or indirectly, in an investment.

Article (18)

The Agency shall be funded by:

(A) Revenues generated by the Agency's provision of services to Investors; all revenues generated by the Agency shall remain at the disposal of the Agency.

(B) Stamp duties paid in the investment process.

(C) Penalties collected pursuant to this Law.

(D) Grants from countries, international organizations, and domestic and foreign non-governmental organizations.

Article (19)

All income and revenue generated by the Agency shall be deposited in a special account at the Ministry of Finance constituting part of the Treasury. The Agency shall have a regular appropriation under the National Authority's budget.

Article (20)

(A) The Agency shall have one or more independent auditor(s) appointed by the Board who shall conduct audits of the Agency's income and expenditures.

(B) The independent auditor(s) shall have the right to examine all books, records, ledgers and request any necessary documentation in the conduct of the audit including the right to verify the Agency's assets.

(C) The independent auditor shall submit the annual financial report to the Board of Directors who shall submit it to the Council of Ministers.

Article (21)

(A) The Agency shall protect all Confidential Information, except for information made public in the Registry of Investments or that is made public through the registration of Enterprises pursuant to this Law.

(B) The Agency shall prohibit the disclosure of Confidential Information to any person or entity by any employee, officer, or member of the Board of Directors, or the Agency staff.

(C) The Agency shall not disclose Confidential Information to any governmental entity or official or any private entity or person without obtaining:

(1) The Investor's informed and written consent of the investor; or

(2) A court order from a Palestinian court of competent jurisdiction that compels the disclosure of Confidential Information.

CHAPTER FOUR

INVESTMENT INCENTIVES

Article (22)

The fixed assets of the Enterprise shall receive the following exemptions:

(A) The fixed assets of the Enterprise shall be exempt from customs duties provided that they are brought in or imported within the period set by the Agency when it approved the list of the fixed assets; the Agency may extend this period if the nature and size of the investment so require.

(B) Spare parts imported by the Enterprise shall be exempt from customs duties provided that their value does not exceed15 % of the fixed assets and, so long as, they are brought in or used by the Enterprise within the period set by the Agency commencing from the date of production or investment start-up and pursuant to a decision by the Agency approving the list and quantity of spare parts.

(C) The fixed assets of the Enterprise required for enlarging, developing, or upgrading the Investment shall be exempt from customs duties if the Agency determines that they increase the productive capacity of the Investment.

(D) A price increase in the value of fixed assets shall be exempt from customs duties if the increase in value was caused by a rise in prices at the country of origin or as a result of an increase in the cost of shipping or change in the price of transformation.

Article (23)

The Agency shall grant Incentives to Investments that meet the requirements of this Law as follows:

(A) Any Investment between One Hundred Thousand and One Million dollars shall entitle the Enterprise to an exemption from income taxation for a period of five (5) years as of the date of production or commencement of activity. The Enterprise shall be subject to the payment of income tax on net profitat the nominal rate of10 % for a period of eight (8) additional years.

(B) Any Investment between One Million dollars and Five Million dollars shall entitle the Enterprise to an exemption from income taxation for a period of five (5) years as of the date of production or commencement of activity. The Enterprise shall be subject to the payment of income tax on net profitat the nominal rate of10 % for a period of twelve (12) additional years.

(C) Any Investment exceeding Five Million dollars shall entitle the Enterprise to an exemption from income taxation for a period of five (5) years as of the date of production or the commencement of activity. The Enterprise shall be subject to the payment of income tax on net profitat the nominal rate of10 % for a period of sixteen (16) additional years.

(D) Any special Investment in type and capital may, as approved by the Council of Ministers, upon the recommendation of the Agency, entitle the enterprise to an exemption from income taxation for a period of five (5) years as of the date of production or the commencement of activity. The Enterprise shall be subject to the payment of income tax on net profitat the nominal rate of10 % for a period of twenty (20) additional years.

Article (24)

(A) The Council of Ministers may decide, upon the recommendation of the Agency and for public purpose, to extend the exemption period(s) up to a maximum of five (5) additional years depending on the nature and location of the Enterprise, increase in exports, job creation opportunities and advancement of development.

(B) The investment period for Enterprises operating in the industrial zones, areas that are remote or under the threat of settlement may be limited by the Council of Ministers

who may designate new industrial zones or remote areas or those under threat of settlement.

(C) The exemption period for Enterprises may be increased for two additional years if the local input in equipment, machines and fixtures exceeds60 %. The Agency shall make these determinations. Capital investment inland is excluded..

(D) The National Authority may give preferential treatment, special guarantees or incentives to the national investor.

Article (25)

(A) Upon submission by the Investor of the requested information mentioned in the regulations relating to the project, the Agency shall access the information, and if the Agency does not decide upon the application for the enjoyment of the incentives provided in this law within thirty (30) days from the date of filing of the application, the project shall qualify to the incentives provided in this law.

(B) The decision of the Agency for approval of the project should be issued after the expiration of the thirty (30) days intended for the assessment of the information without rejecting the project.

Article (26)

The regulations shall specify the methods by which the Agency's Incentive may require information for the Confirmation of incentives.

Article (27)

A nominal10 % income tax rate shall be assessed on enlargements of existing Enterprises for capital investments made subject to Article (24) provided that the Board of Directors of the Enterprise approves the enlargements commencing either on the date of production or the commencement of activity. Enlargement shall mean the increase in the stated capital or capital injection to acquire fixed assets intended to increase the productive capacity of the Investment be it goods, services or production or for the purposes of a new line of production or service or activity.

Article (28)

Income tax on profits distributed by the project shall be exempted at the rate of10 % from the original capital of the investor in the project and this shall take place after the expiration of the period of the exemption mentioned in Articles22 , 23 and the exemption mentioned in the previous paragraph shall be20 % from nominal value of the shareholders share in the capital value of the project which shall be in the form of a Public Liability Company formed in accordance with this law provided that at least40 % of its capital shall be covered.

Article (29)

(A) An enterprise benefiting from the Incentives may be transferred freely to a new owner in its entirety; provided that the new owner continues to operate the enterprise as a going concern.

(B) The new owner of a transferred enterprise can benefit from the Incentives as long as the new owner continues to operate the enterprise as a going concern.

Article (30)

Companies, merged and companies that have been split or whose legal structure is altered shall enjoy the exemption granted prior to the merger or splitting or the altering of the legal structure until the expiration of the period of exemption, and no new tax incentives shall be granted for such mergers or splitting or altering of legal structure.

Article (31)

The Agency may grant additional exemptions to enterprises engaged in export activity provided that the input is not less than30 % of the total value of its output. This additional exemption may be granted for a period not exceeding three years.

Article (32)

(A) The Agency may cancel a Confirmation of Investment in the event that the Agency finds, that the Investor supplied the Agency with information about the Investment that was not true at the time the Investor supplied it, or withheld from the Agency information about the proposed Investment that was material to the Agency's decision to confirm the Investment as an Investment eligible for the Incentives. The Regulations shall specify the procedure for the cancellation.

(B) In the event this Law or its conditions and requirements are violated, the Board of Directors shall have the right to take by either reducing the period for exemption or canceling the exemptions.

(C) An Investor may appeal the Agency's decision to cancel the Confirmation of Investment under the procedures specified in the Regulations.

Article (33)

In the event that the Incentives are modified, Enterprises benefiting from the Incentives prior to the date on which the modification became effective shall have a choice to opt for the relevant incentive provided in the modification or continue to benefit from the incentive in effect for that Enterprise prior to the effective date of the modification which ever is better.

Article (34)

If the Enterprise moves from one area to another during the period of the exemption, the Enterprise shall continue to receive the exemptions provided that the Agency is notified.

Article (35)

(A) The furniture imported for hotels **and hospitals** shall be exempt from customs duties.

(B) The electrical appliances and electronics imported for tourism Enterprises shall be exempt from customs duties.

(C) The electrical appliances and electronics imported for hotel and hospital Enterprises shall be exempt from customs duties.

(D) Hotel and hospital Enterprises shall be granted additional exemptions from customs duties at least once every **five (5)** years for purchases of furniture and electrical appliances and electronics required for modernization and renovation, provided that they are brought into or imported into Palestine or used by the Enterprise within (2) years from the date of approval.

Article (36)

If it becomes clear that the exempt fixed assets, in whole or in part, have been sold or used for an unauthorized purpose, the Enterprise shall pay all customs duties and taxes owed in accordance with the provisions of this Law.

Article (37)

(A) The Investor must inform the Agency in writing once the fixed assets have been installed and production has actually started.

(B) The Investor must submit any information or records related to the fixed assets of the Enterprise at the request of the Agency and permit Agency staff to enter the premises of the Enterprise.

Article (38)

(A) The Investor may sell the fixed assets that are exempt or assign them to another Investor enjoying the benefits of this Law provided that the approval of the Agency is obtained.

(B) The Investor may sell the fixed assets that are exempt to any person or any business concern that is not benefiting from the exemptions and incentives of this Law provided that the Agency is notified and all due taxes and fees are paid.

CHAPTER FIVE

DISPUTE SETTLEMENT

Article (39)

The provisions in this Chapter shall apply to disputes between Investors and the National Authority that relate to rights and obligations provided for in the Investment Law.

Article (40)

(A) When either an Investor or the Authority believes that a dispute between them has arisen, it may request that good faith negotiations begin according to procedures established in the Regulations. Either party to a dispute must request good faith negotiations before it may have access to the dispute settlement procedures provided for in paragraph (B) of this Article. .

(B) If good faith negotiations fail to resolve the dispute in the period of time specified in the Regulations, either party shall have the right to take the dispute to:

(1) binding, independent arbitration as provided in the Regulations.

(2) Palestinian courts.

CHAPTER SIX

FINAL PROVISIONS

Article (41)

The Agency may at any time if it finds that any or all information provided by the Investor is false or fraudulent, immediately terminate all approvals granted to the Enterprise.

Article (42)

Nothing in the Investment Law shall adversely affect the approvals and incentives provided to Investors and enterprises under all prior relevant laws. Those approvals and incentives shall remain valid and enforceable under the Investment Law until they terminate or expire under the terms of the laws under which they were issued.

Article (43)

All Investment Enterprises shall enjoy the Incentives provided in this Law except:

Commercial enterprises, insurance, real property (except development enterprises), banks, money changers and any financial institution (except housing mortgage companies only).

Article (44)

Unless a more aggravated penalty is prohibited for in any other legislature, any investor giving false information or entries in his books or accounts such false information or provides false information as a result of which the investor was granted the incentives or benefits in accordance with this law, should be fined with an amount not less than (2000) two thousand (2000) Jordanian Dinars, and not exceeding five thousand (5000) Jordanian Dinars, and all exemptions and incentives awards as a result shall be withdrawn as of the date such incentives were awarded.

Article (45)

Without prejudice to Article (43) of this Law, the Investment Law supersedes and replaces all prior laws dealing with investment in Palestine.

Article (46)

The Board of Directors shall issue the regulations to implement this Law which shall be adopted by the Council of Ministers and published in the *Official Gazette.*

Article (47)

All concerned shall implement this Law which shall go into effect thirty days after its publication in the *Official Gazette*.

SAUDI ARABIA

SAUDI DOMESTIC AND FOREIGN CORPORATE LAWS

LEGAL FRAMEWORK: Saudi law is based on Islamic Law, or Sharia. In Islamic law, there are four main schools of jurisprudence: Hanbali. Hanafi. Shafai and Maliki. The Saudi courts and judicial committees generally apply the Hanbali school. The Saudi government, from time to time, issues rules and regulations to supplement Islamic law when the need arises. In the event of a conflict between Islamic law and government rules and regulations, Islamic law will generally prevail.

GENERAL PRINCIPLES OF ISLAMIC LAW: According to Islamic law, the payment or receipt of sums in the nature of interest is not enforceable. Contracting parties must maintain principles of fairness and equity in their dealings. Contracts where one party gains unjustly at the expense of another could be considered void especially if the party gaining unjustly has a monopoly or market dominance in the subject matter of the contract. In each contract. the commercial substance of the transaction must be analysed to evaluate whether or not the party's actions would amount to unjust enrichment under Islamic law.

Contracting parties are free to negotiate the terms of their contracts unless those terms are prohibited and/or relate to activities that are prohibited under Islamic law. There should be no element of deception or uncertainty in contracts. Where there is uncertainty as to the fundamental terms of a contract, such as the subject matter or price, such contracts could be considered as void. Contracts that involve speculation are not permissible and are therefore considered void. The speculation prohibited under Islamic law is not general business speculation, but speculation akin to gambling, particularly gaining something by chance rather than by productive effort.

Saudi courts and judicial committees may not award damages representing loss of profits, indirect losses or other forms of consequential loss. Neither will they enforce a foreign judgement awarding such damages. Any contract provision for liquidated damages should be considered in this context. If challenged by the party responsible for the payment of liquidated damages, a Saudi court or judicial committee is unlikely to enforce a contract provision for the payment of liquidated damages where the agreed liquidated damages are very excessive, notwithstanding the fact that the parties agreed to such a provision.

One of the features of Islamic law is that the owner of an item bears the risk of loss or damage in relation to that particular item. Accordingly, it should be noted that risk of loss or damage cannot pass unless ownership passes. That said, risk could actually pass without ownership passing where either (i) a person is in the business of looking after/protecting/maintaining the asset left in his care; or (ii) the asset is lost or damaged by a negligent/wrongful act.

JUDICIARY: In Saudi Arabia there is no concept of judicial precedent, which means that the decisions of a court or a judicial committee have no binding authority with respect to another case. In general, there is also no system of court reporting in the Kingdom. So, it is not always possible to reach a conclusion on how a Saudi court or judicial committee would view a particular case. There are a number of courts and judicial committees in Saudi Arabia that have jurisdiction in relation to certain types of claims. Documents submitted to Saudi courts need to be in Arabic. Otherwise, they are inadmissible. An action in the courts or judicial committees of the Kingdom may be brought on a document executed in a language other than Arabic if an Arabic translation thereof, certified by an authorised translator, is submitted to the court or committee.

Recently the Saudi Arabian government enacted a new judiciary law that aims to reform the judiciary system and provide for an improved two-level appeals process (adding one level to the existing regime). This is being implemented in stages during the next few years.

GENERAL COURTS: Criminal and civil cases that are not specifically assigned to any other court or judicial committee and disputes relating to land and personal property are generally heard before general courts.

Appeals against decisions of the circuit level of the general courts may be made to the appellate court. Where a sentence of capital punishment is issued, this is automatically referred to the Supreme Judicial

Council for review. Under the recently approved regime, general courts would have jurisdiction over commercial and labour disputes in addition to the current jurisdiction, and special circuits would be designated for commercial, criminal, labour and other types of disputes. Under the new regime, the appellate court would also be a trial court and its judgements/awards are appealed before the new high court.

SAMA COMMITTEE: Disputes of a banking nature involving Saudi or foreign banks or between banks and their customers that are of a banking nature are usually resolved before the Banking Disputes Settlement Committee of the Saudi Arabian Monetary Agency (SAMA). The government is currently reviewing the jurisdiction of the SAMA Committee.

FOREIGN DISPUTES: The courts and judicial committees of Saudi Arabia may not respect provisions related to (i) the choice of non-Saudi law as the governing law of a contract and (ii) the submission by contracting parties to non-Saudi jurisdiction.

A judgment obtained in a foreign country that is a signatory to the Arab League Treaty for the reciprocal enforcement of judgments, or the Agreement on Enforcement of Judgments, Delegations and Judicial Summonses in the member states of the Gulf Cooperation Council (GCC), may be submitted to the Board of Grievances. The board will enforce all or part of such a judgment, provided that the judgment is not inconsistent with Islamic law and/or the laws and regulations of Saudi Arabia as well as certain other procedural conditions have been satisfied.

A foreign judgment in a country that is not a member of either the treaty or the agreement may be submitted to the Board of Grievances for enforcement. The grievances board may enforce all or part of such a judgment provided that (i) the judgment is not inconsistent with Islamic law and/or the laws and regulations of Saudi Arabia and (ii) the judgment creditor can demonstrate to the Board of Grievances that the courts of the jurisdiction granting the judgment will reciprocally enforce the judgments of the Saudi courts in such foreign jurisdiction.

Reciprocity may be demonstrated by way of the existence of a treaty or protocol between Saudi Arabia and the foreign jurisdiction or by requesting the parties seeking to enforce the judgment to provide either a previous Saudi judgment that has been enforced by the court issuing the judgment to be enforced or a letter from a competent authority such as the Ministry of Justice of the originating country of the judgment which is sought to be enforced, confirming that they would enforce a Saudi judgment.

The Board of Grievances may refuse to enforce a foreign judgment if a final judgment had been rendered by a Saudi court or judicial committee in proceedings between the same litigants over the same subject matter or if an action was commenced before a Saudi Arabian court or other judicial committee between the same litigants and involving the same subject matter prior to the commencement of the proceeding in the country where the foreign judgement was issued and the decision of the Saudi Arabian court or other judicial committee is still pending. Saudi Arabia has acceded to the UN Convention on the Recognition and Enforcement of Foreign Arbitral Awards. However. it invoked a "reciprocity reservation" in order to limit its recognition of awards made in foreign jurisdictions. A foreign arbitral award may be submitted to the grievances board, which will enforce all of such an arbitral award, or a part thereof, provided that the award is not inconsistent with Saudi laws and regulations.

ARBITRATIONS: Any agreement to arbitrate must be filed with the authority originally competent to decide on the dispute (the competent court of law or judicial committee, for instance). The parties are bound by the arbitration agreement and cannot avoid it by resorting to the originally competent court or judicial committee without the consent of all parties. The arbitrators must fix a date for the hearing within five days of the date of approval of the arbitration agreement by the competent authority. The competent authority must approve the arbitration agreement and notify the panel within 15 days of the arbitration agreement being submitted to it. Additionally, all documentation must be in Arabic. The secretary of the panel must provide a written copy of the minutes of the hearing. In Saudi arbitration, there may be any number of arbitrators, provided that the number is an odd number. The arbitrator(s) must be Saudi nationals or expatriate Muslim(s) or, with approval, employee(s) of the Saudi government. The parties may represent themselves or be represented by a lawyer. If represented by a lawyer. the lawyer needs a notarised power of attorney evidencing his appointment. This requirement applies to all forms of litigation and instances where a non-Saudi national is involved. The power of attorney will need to be legalised by the relevant foreign office of the non Saudi's home country and certified by the Saudi embassy in that country and then attested by the Saudi Ministry of Foreign Affairs and the Saudi Ministry of Justice.

WTO ACCESSION: Saudi Arabia became the 149th member of the WTO on December 11, 2005. It made certain commitments with regard to a variety of economic activities. Some of Saudi Arabia's WTO commitments simply reflect existing provisions of Saudi law while others represent changes to existing Saudi laws.

The Saudi Arabian Foreign Investment Law stipulates that the Saudi Arabian General Investment Authority (SAGIA) must license all foreign investment in Saudi Arabia. Foreign capital is allowed in all investment activities, except those areas expressly excluded by the list issued by the Supreme Economic Council pursuant to its authority in accordance with Article 3 of the Saudi Arabian Foreign Investment Law. This "negative list" is updated regularly. It should be noted that as a result of Saudi Arabia's accession to the WTO. new fields of business activity have been opened up to foreign investment. SAGIA has the jurisdiction to license foreign investment in Saudi Arabia, unless the licensing of a particular type of foreign investment is entrusted to another state agency. Minimum investment thresholds for Saudis and non-Saudis are identical. except for the minimum investment thresholds as preconditions to obtaining foreign investment licences in the following sectors: (i) SR25m ($6.75m) for agricultural projects and (ii) SR30m ($8.1m) for real estate projects.

LOCAL BRANCHES: Foreign investors can open local branches of a foreign parent company. As a matter of practice, a branch is a common business structure for foreign entities with business in Saudi Arabia relating to a contract with the Saudi government. A branch of a foreign firm would need a foreign investment licence from SAGIA and it would not be a separate legal entity from the entity it represents. Only a limited number of business activities in Saudi Arabia would require the foreign investor to establish a legal entity in Saudi Arabia. This in particular applies to securities businesses.

SCIENTIFIC AND SUPPORT OFFICES: Foreign investors who have products in Saudi markets and who have registered Saudi commercial agents or distributors can establish a scientific office in Saudi Arabia without any capital requirements or local equity participation. The purpose of the scientific office has to be to support the foreign company's agent(s) or distributor(s) and to assist the end users of the products. Therefore, the scientific office cannot operate as a profit centre.

SUBSIDIARY COMPANIES: The Saudi Foreign Investment Law permits registration of 100% foreign-owned companies. For various practical reasons, the limited liability company (LLC) is generally considered the most appropriate corporate form available to foreign companies under the Saudi Arabian Companies Law. Other available vehicles include the joint-stock company (JSC). Although Saudi law recognises sole proprietorships and general partnerships as business vehicles, due to the liability risks associated with them, they are generally not the entities of choice for foreign investors.

LIMITED LIABILITY COMPANIES: LLCs are commonly referred to as limited liability partnerships, which should not be confused with genuine partnerships. These types of companies cannot offer their shares to the public and are generally not permitted to undertake business activities in commercial banking or insurance. An LLC must not have less than two or more than 50 shareholders, and the liability of each shareholder in the LLC is generally limited to their capital contributions in the company. The shares of an LLC are of equal value and must each be fully paid up in cash or kind.

Article 180 of the companies law provides that if a limited liability company incurs losses amounting to 50% or more of its share capital, the shareholders must resolve, within 30 days of such losses reaching the 50% threshold, either to continue the company on the basis that they will be responsible for its debts or liquidate the company, otherwise the protection afforded by limited liability status will be lost.

Each shareholder will be fully responsible (limited only by the extent of that shareholder's private assets) for the company's debts. Article 8 of the companies law provides that dividends may not be distributed to shareholders except from net profits. Furthermore, if any distributions are made to shareholders other than from net profits, the creditors of the company may claim from such shareholders the amount by which distribution exceeded net profits. This applies even though the shareholders may have received the distribution in good faith.

The ability of a limited liability company to distribute profits to shareholders is limited by Article 176 of the companies law, which states that such a company must transfer at least 10% of its annual net profits into a reserve fund until the amount is equal to and not less than 50%. of the company's share capital.

JOINT STOCK COMPANIES: Unlike an LLC, a JSC can offer its shares to the public and can raise debt from the public. A JSC allows foreign investors to limit their liability to their equity contribution. By contrast, investors of an LLC do not enjoy this protection under certain circumstances as in the aforementioned Article 180.

COMMERCIAL AGENCY: Foreign nationals may now participate in wholesale or retail business activities in Saudi Arabia. SAGIA's position is that Saudi Arabia's WTO entry commitments must be met, which include the following:

- Foreign equity is limited to 51% upon Saudi Arabia's accession to the WTO and to 75% after three years from the date of accession;
- Minimum foreign investment of SR20m ($5.4m);
- Minimum of 15% Saudi employees to be trained each year; and

• Minimum size of outlet may be prescribed by SAGIA. Non-Saudi producers of goods are also allowed to appoint local Saudi agents as their representatives to sell their products and/or services in Saudi Arabia. Whether they act as distributors, sales agencies, or otherwise, the Saudi Arabian Commercial Agencies Law governs the arrangement. An appointment of a Saudi commercial agent often enables the foreign business to penetrate Saudi Arabia's market without establishing a direct presence in Saudi Arabia. The Saudi Arabian Commercial Agencies Law establishes a comprehensive framework for the protection of the Saudi agent that is complementary to the agreement between the producer and the Saudi agent. Registration of commercial agency agreements generally gives the parties protections of the Saudi Arabian Commercial Agency Law.

PROPERTY LAW: The Basic Law protects the freedom to hold private property and provides that no one may be deprived of their property by the government unless it serves the public interest and with fair compensation. The law governing ownership and investment in real estate by non-Saudis sets out the principles of foreign ownership of real estate. Foreign individuals who are legal residents of Saudi Arabia may own real estate for use as a residence (subject to obtaining a permit from the Ministry of Interior). Foreign companies licensed to conduct business in Saudi Arabia may own real estate for the purpose of their business and for housing employees. Foreign companies licensed to purchase and develop real estate may do so in accordance with their licence, provided the minimum investment is SR30m ($8.1m) per project and development occurs within five years of the acquisition of real estate. Foreign diplomatic missions may own their land for official purposes and employee housing (provided there is reciprocity), and international and regional organisations may own their premises subject to their agreements and with the approval of the Ministry of Foreign Affairs. Special rules apply with respect to the ownership of land in the Two Holy Cities of Mecca and Medina. Non-Saudi Muslims may lease real estate in the holy cities for a period of up to two years (renewable). Non-Muslims may not obtain title, easement or use of such land, other than rights or property obtained through a transfer upon inheritance.

LABOUR LAW AND SAUDIISATION: The maximum number of working hours for employees is generally eight hours per day. or 48 hours per week, with the exception of the holy month of Ramadan, when actual working hours for Muslim employees may not exceed six hours a day or 36 hours a week. The number of working hours may be raised to nine hours a day in respect of certain categories of employees or in certain industries and operations. The number of daily working hours may be reduced to seven hours for certain categories of employees or in certain industries or operations that are of a hazardous or harmful nature. Hours of work must be arranged so that no employee works more than five consecutive hours without an interval of rest, prayer and meals. Which shall not be less than 30 minutes each time. The employee cannot be required to remain in the place of work for more than 11 hours per day and in their first five years of employment, employees are entitled to an annual leave of at least 21 days. After the first five consecutive years, this period increases to 30 days. When an employee's employment ends, the employer must pay an end-of-service payment to the employee. Saudiisation regulations require that all private sector entities employ Saudi nationals. Certain positions are restricted solely to nationals, such as: receptionists. treasurers and civil security guards, However, Saudiisation is not rigorously enforced.

PATENT LAW: A new Saudi patent law, enacted by royal decree in 2005, is overseen by the King Abdulaziz City for Science and Technology. The law provides protection within the Kingdom for industrial designs, inventions, layout designs of integrated circuits and plant varieties. A Saudi patent is valid for a total of 20 years. The law specifies the annual fees required to maintain validity of a patent. Violating the patent law results in fines of up to SR50,000 ($13,500), with an additional SR50,000 for every repeated violation. As a signatory to several international conventions, the Kingdom extends patent protections to foreigners from any World Intellectual Property Organisation member state.

COPYRIGHTS: The 2003 Saudi copyright law protects original literary, artistic and scientific works as well as computer programmes, designer clothing, books, audio recordings and derivative works, such as translations and encyclopaedias. Unprotected items include judicial decisions and daily reports carried out by the print media and radio. Visual, audio and photographic works, along with movies and computer programmes, are protected for 50 years from the date of first production, while protection for other creative works lasts for the creators lifetime plus 50 years. The copyright law stipulates severe penalties for violators including (but not limited to) six months in jail, a maximum fine of SR250,000 ($67,500) and business shut down. To strengthen copyright protection, the Kingdom has become a signatory to the Berne Convention for the Protection of Literary and Artistic Works and the Universal Copyright Convention.

TRADEMARK: Under Saudi Arabia's 2002 trademark law, protected trademarks include names of distinct shapes, signatures, words, letters, numbers, drawings, Symbols, stamps and protruding inscriptions. Items that may not be registered as trademarks include (but are not limited to) public emblems, flags, misleading geographic names, signs without any specific distinction, signs or drawings violating Islamic law or those that are inconsistent with public morality. Trademark protection in the Kingdom lasts for 10 years and may be renewed. The Ministry of Commerce and Industry is responsible for supervising this law. If the ministry denies a trademark application, the applicant has the right to appeal to the Board of Grievances. The Saudi Trademark law provides for punishments with imprisonment for up to one year and fines of up to SR1m ($270,000) for violations.

SOLVENT LIQUIDATION: The legislative treatment of the liquidation of a corporation is contained in the companies law. The provisions of the companies law relating to liquidation are brief and do not address many of the issues that might arise. They do not apply to insolvent companies until either the company reaches a composition with its creditors, or the Board of Grievances declares the company to be bankrupt and appoints a liquidator. The companies law provides that a solvent company may be liquidated, inter alia, by an agreement of all the partners or shareholders or by an order of the grievances board on the application of any creditor/interested person and for "serious reasons that justify such a step". It is within the power of the Board of Grievances to invite the shareholders to enter into voluntary or compulsory liquidation.

CORPORATE INSOLVENCY: The commercial court law (CCL), enacted by royal decree in 1931, codifies Islamic law principles and appears to cover personal rather than corporate insolvency. It is therefore unclear as to what extent the CCL bankruptcy provisions will be applied for corporate insolvency. In bankruptcy proceedings, the courts seem to rely on Islamic legal principles of fairness. Saudi law recognises preferential debts, such as employee wages, social contributions, and certain Customs duties and expenses incurred in the bankruptcy process. Secured debts are to be paid from the sale of the secured assets of the party or parties in question. Any surplus left over after the sale of the assets should be added to the bankrupt party's estate.

FOREIGN INVESTMENT

The total volume of foreign investment in Saudi Arabia reached US$ 22.5 billion in 1995, and the greatest number of investments came from the United States, Japan, France, Britain, South Korea, Taiwan, the Arabian Gulf countries, Syria and Lebanon. Most of the investments were made in the petrochemical, maintenance, airport services, electrical and electronic manufacturing, and the food and beverage industries.

Saudi Arabia is the world's seventh most popular country for foreign investment. By the end of 1995, there was a total of 1,306 joint-venture projects between Saudi and foreign firms in the Kingdom. The share capital of the projects totaled US$ 34.4 billion with US$ 14.93 billion coming from foreign firms. A total of 621 of these projects were in the industrial sector and represented a total share capital of US$ 31.46 billion.

The United States is the largest foreign investor in Saudi Arabia. American companies have invested US$ 11.94 billion in 229 joint projects, seventy-nine of which were in the industrsector and the remaining 150 in non-industrial projects.

The average flow of foreign investment has picked up steadily in recent years. Foreign investments rose 34 percent in 1995 from the preceding year and have averaged US$ 106 million per month.

In 1995 alone there was a total of 408 new joint-venture projects representing US$ 5.12 billion in share capital. Of these, 302 projects were in the industrial sand the remaining 106 in non-industrial projects, including services. After the US, Britain and Germany had the greatest amount of investments in joint-venture projects in the Kingdom.

PRIVATIZATION

As the Saudis have traditionally resisted privatization, they prefer to refer to this project as "private sector participation." Private finance mechanisms being considered include BOT and BOOT.

The recent US$ 700 million loan syndication raised for Saudi Petrochemical Company (Sadaf), the subsidiary of the majority government-owned Saudi Basic Industries Corporation (Sabot), was a milestone among corporate finance deals in the region. Also in the market is a US$ 500 million loan to finance Saudi Arabia's Ghuzlan Power Station expansion.

SAUDIIZATION

The Sixth Saudi Five Year Development Plan (1996-2000) aims to gain control over the Kingdom's heavy external debt and growing budget deficit by enhancing the private sector's role in the economy. The plan will accomplish this through two complementary strategies, "Saudiization" and privatization.

At the beginning of 1996, there were 6.25 million expatriates from 190 different nations in the Kingdom. These workers are concentrated in the construction trades, and as cashiers, accountants, purchase managers and warehouse officers.

Saudi Arabia's rapid development over the past two decades has been the main justification in allocating such a large number of jobs to non-Saudis. Huge infrastructure projects required extensive labor, but local work ethics made imported workers more desirable.

Traditionally, the Saudi private sector has been unwilling to pay Saudis the salaries they demand, preferring instead to hire expatriate labor. Even now, salary levels provide little or no incentive for Saudis to work in positions typically held by expatriates, a trend which is expected to continue.

The Saudi private sector employment constitutes only 16 percent of the total work force. The rate of Saudi employment in the industrial sector stands at 4 percent and in the services sector at 12 percent. In contrast, their share in the public sector stands at 79.2 percent.

To increase Saudi presence in the private sector, the Saudi authorities are considering establishing a minimum Saudi wage, limiting the work day to eight hours and creating social insurance and pension plans similar to those available in the public sector.

The al-Saud ruling family's push for "Saudiization" is motivated by a desire to eliminate possible threats from the Saudi middle class, a reality which has preoccupied the royal family in recent years. In the past, the Saudi middle class received public sector jobs and benefits and in return backed the al-Saud ruling family's monopoly over the Kingdom's economy, finances and politics. But over the last two years, budgetary constraints have left government ministries and agencies unable to provide the same level of jobs and benefits. It is estimated that 20 to 30 percent of Saudi Arabia's 1995 university graduates are unemployed. Bearing in mind that the middle class is the main target of opposition Islamic movements, the urgent need of the government to find employment alternatives for its traditional supporters is obvious.

This latest plan calls for the absorption of 659,900 Saudis into the private sector. 340,000 new jobs will be created and 319,000 expatriates will be replaced. Of these, about 178,000 expatriates will be replaced within the service sector; 115,700 in clerical jobs, 35,000 in sales, 15,900 in the construction industry and 11,800 in managerial posts.

Although the Sixth Plan is more forceful than previous plans in providing both incentives and mandatory measures to encourage "Saudiization," it seems that it will be impossible for the private sector to achieve all of the government's targets on its own. In spite of the early successes, especially in the banking, oil and petrochemicals sectors, the Kingdom has a long way to go. The greatest challenge may lie in the work ethic of young Saudis and their refusal to accept low wages or to become involved in intensive labor.

STOCK EXCHANGE

The Saudi securities market is not highly developed. Under the Banking Control Law, trading in shares is conducted through a department in the Saudi Arabian Monetary Agency (SAMA). Joint stock companies are the vehicle permitting ownership by a large number of public shareholders, and the formation of such companies has been encouraged by the government through its privatization policy. Trading on the exchange is restricted to wholly-owned or majority-owned Saudi companies. In general, only Saudi nationals may own or deal in shares, but under certain circumstances GCC nationals may also deal in or own shares. Further development of the stock exchange is under review by SAMA, and it is expected that Saudi banks will be given a broader role as coordinators and supervisors of the market.

INVESTMENT INCENTIVES

The Foreign Capital Investment Regulations provide for a number of investment incentives to foreign companies and individuals wishing to conduct business in Saudi Arabia.

The Saudi Industrial Development Fund makes interest-free loans to industrial companies of up to 50 percent of the total cost of the project. Project costs includes agreed pre-operating costs, investment in fixed assets and working capital. A 50 percent loan requires Saudi participation which is not less than 50 percent. If Saudi participation is lower, the loan is reduced proportionally. Soft loans are repayable in five to ten years after a one or two year grace period from the date of production. Although the loans are interest-free, an administrative fee of 2.5 percent is normally charged.

All commodities entering the Kingdom for industrial production are exempt from import duty, including spare parts and all plant and equipment required to set up companies.

In addition, industrial facilities are allowed to rent at low to nominal rental fees. They also pay reduced rates for water and electricity.

The following five categories of development qualify for foreign investment:

- Industrial development including raw material into manufactured or semi-manufactured products, transferring semi-manufactured products into fully manufactured products and packaging fully manufactured products;
- Agricultural development including the cultivation of fruits, vegetables, nurseries, greenhouses, animal resources and fisheries;
- Health development including building, maintenance, operation and management of hospitals, clinics and health centers;

- Services relating to industries such as tourism, training, technology, environment protection, shipping and information systems; and
- Contracting.

OTHER INCENTIVES

Saudi Arabia imposes no exchange control regulations on the entry and repatriation of funds, profits and salpaid to foreigners employed in the Kingdom. Saudi law prescribes no specific debt-to-equity ratios as a prerequisite to doing business in Saudi Arabia, but certain investment incentives may require specified debt-to equity ratios to be satisfied.

TRADE AGREEMENTS

Saudi Arabia is a member of the GCC, and as such, is subject to the GCC agreements regarding trade. These agreements are described in the section on Trade Agreements in thechapter on Bahrain.

IMPORTS AND EXPORTS

Customs

Many items are free of customs-duties, including food, heavy machinery and raw materials. The basic duty is 12 percent, although certain protected industries, favored under the Regulations for the Protection and Encouragement of National Industries, enjoy a 20 percent protective tariff against competing imports.

In accordance with the Unified Economic Agreement among the GCC states, products manufactured in any one of the member states will be exempt from customs duties when exported to any of the GCC states provided that 51 percent of the factory equity is owned by a GCC national.

IMPORTS

Only Saudi nationals and 100 percent Saudi-owned companies may import goods. Importers must be licensed by the Ministry of Commerce and must consult the appropriate ministry about the goods or materials to be imported.
Standard measurements, packaging, ingredients and safety standards should comply with the rules established by the Saudi Arabian Standards Organization. In order to enter the country, imports must have certificates of origin. Any product deemed contrary to Islamic law, e.g., pork products and alcoholic beverages, may not be imported.

EXPORTS

Other than antiques, Arabian horses, livestock or subsidized goods and materials which are in short supply, most goods can be exported from Saudi Arabia. Exporters may need an industrial or an agricultural license.

PROTECTIVE TARIFFS AND NON-TARIFF TRADE BARRIERS

Saudi tariff protections are moderate, but have been increased over the years. A number of Saudi "infant industries" now enjoy 20 percent tariff protection as compared to the general rate of 12 percent. Non-tariff barriers are also increasing and include preferences for national and GCC products in government procurements. Presently, 30 percent of major government procurement contracts are set-aside for local contractors. Foreign contractors obtain imported goods and services exclusively through Saudi agents. Furthermore, an economic offset requirement has been invoked which mandates reinvestment of a portion of the government contract value in indigenous industries for certain high value government procurement contracts.

TRADE BARRIERS

Import licenses are not required for virtually all goods. Foreign exchange for imports is readily available and no restrictions on financial transfers or exchange controls exist.

INVESTING IN SAUDI ARABIA PRACTICAL INFORMATION

Foreigners wishing to conduct business in Saudi Arabia may do so in one of the following ways:

- By establishing an incorporated entity
- By entering into a partnership
- By establishing a branch office
- By establishing a representative office
- By engaging a service agent

FOREIGN INVESTMENT IN SAUDI ARABIA

In 2000, Saudi Arabia implemented the Foreign Investment Act (the "Act"), which liberalizes the foreign investment laws in the Kingdom. The Saudi Arabian General Investment Authority was created under the Act, which has responsibility for licensing all new foreign investment in Saudi Arabia. Under the new Act, foreign persons and entities are permitted to invest in all industries and services except for those which are specifically excluded from foreign investment. The exempted industries include those related to the manufacture of military materials, equipment and explosives; oil exploration and production; services related to security, insurance and real estate brokerage; wholesale distribution and retail services; telecommunications services; and land, air, and space transport, among others.

Foreign investors may wholly own approved foreign investments, or a foreign investor and a Saudi national may jointly own them. Licensed businesses are now permitted to own the real estate necessary for the project and to house necessary staff (with the exception of Mecca and Medinah). Foreign investors may also obtain more than one license so as to enable them to participate in more than one business venture. The minimum capital requirements for projects licensed under the Act are SR 25 million (US$6.7 million) for agricultural projects, SR 5 million (US$1.3 million) for industrial projects and SR 2 million (US$ 533,000) for all other categories of projects. A project licensed under the Act enjoys the same privileges, incentives and guarantees as a national project, with the exception of taxation. Subsidized loans from the Saudi Industrial Development Fund (SIDF) are available to both foreign and Saudi owned enterprises. Additionally, sponsorship of the foreign investor and its non-Saudi employees is undertaken by the licensed entity and not a local person/entity.

III. FORMS OF DOING BUSINESS

Foreigners wishing to conduct business in Saudi Arabia may do so by establishing a permanent presence in Saudi Arabia or by entering into an agency relationship for the distribution and sale of their products. Below is a summary of the business forms available under Saudi law:

A. Limited Liability Company (LLC)

This is the most common form for entering into joint ventures with Saudi partners; however, a Saudi partner is not required since there are no legal limitations on the percentage of foreign ownership.

The minimum capital investment required to establish an LLC is SR 500,000. An LLC must have between 2 and 50 shareholders and is managed and represented by one or more managers. There is no Board of Directors, although shareholders often provide for a Board and other management arrangements in the Memorandum of Association. The LLC must also have an auditor and, where it has more that twenty (20) partners, it must establish a Board of Controllers.

B. Partnerships

Foreign companies seeking to do business in the Kingdom may enter into a limited partnership. The limited partnership, or "sharikat tawsiya baseetah", is a separate business entity comprised of several individuals or companies, including general (at least one) and limited partners. The general partners are liable for partnership debts to the full extent of their personal assets while the limited partners are liable only to the extent of their capital contributions.

C. Joint Stock Corporation

A Joint Stock Corporation ("JSC") is an entity with at least five shareholders holding transferable shares. The minimum capital requirements are SR 2 million for a private JSC and SR 10 million for a public JSC. Liability of shareholders is limited to the par value of each shareholder's share capital. The JSC must be approved by license or Royal Decree published in the Saudi Official Gazette. Additionally, it must be registered with the MOC Companies Department and the MOC Commercial Registry.

D. Branch Offices

Foreign companies may register a wholly foreign-owned Saudi branch office, provided that they obtain the requisite license. The branch office may engage in any government contract or private sector work within the scope of its license. Branch offices are subject to the requirements of the Government Tenders Regulations, where applicable. Branch office registration follows the same general procedure as for the registration of an LLC.

E. Sponsorship and Temporary Commercial Registration
As an alternative to forming one of the above entities, foreign contractors have in the past performed isolated private sector projects under the sponsorship of their Saudi customer and, in contracts with the Saudi government, the foreign contractor may perform its obligation under a temporary commercial registration (TCR).

With respect to sponsorships, they can be in two forms. The first is where the foreign contractor obtains a business visa, sponsored by the Saudi customer. The second form of sponsorship is where the foreign contractor 'seconds' its employees to the employment and sponsorship of the Saudi customer.
If a foreign contractor is awarded a project with the Saudi government and it does not have a registered presence in Saudi in one of the above-discussed forms, it must obtain a TCR (Commerce Ministry Resolution No. 680 dated 10 October 1978). An application for TCR must be filed within 30 days of obtaining the contract, along with a copy of the contract. Additionally, a 'service agent' must be identified pursuant to the Saudi Service Agent Regulations. TCRs are limited in scope and duration to the substance and term of the government contract for which they are issued.

G. Commercial Agencies
Agencies and distributorships are governed by the Commercial Agencies Regulations and the related Implementing Rules (Royal Decree No. M/11, as amended by Royal decree No. M/32; Ministry of Commerce Decision No. 1897). The rules and regulations reserve a monopoly for Saudi nationals and wholly owned Saudi entities on 'trading' activities. Trading activities include the import and local purchase of goods for resale.

Therefore, foreign companies engaging in such activities must use Saudi commercial agents and distributors, who must register their Agency Agreements with the MOC Agency Register. The agent must hold a valid Saudi commercial registration permitting him to act as an agent or distributor and the directors and authorized representatives of the agent must be Saudi nationals. The Commercial Agency Regulations bar appointment of shell agents indirectly owned or controlled by the foreign principal, therefore, the Saudi agent must be independent from the foreign principal.
Agencies do not have to be exclusive, although MOC will not normally register more than one agreement for the same principal.

The Regulations do specify requirements for compensation of a terminated agent. The MOC Model agency contract provides for "reasonable compensation" of the agent upon termination for "activities that may have resulted in the apparent success of the business". Shari'a law, which is applied by both the arbitration and the Grievance Board, excludes indirect or consequential damages.

MOC will not register a new agency agreement with the same foreign principal before the old one has been deregistered. This normally requires a letter of consent by the old agent or administrative cancellation by MOC upon the expiry of the contract.

INDUSTRIAL PROJECTS

All industrial projects, whether Saudi or foreign, and joint ventures whose fixed capital exceeds SR 1million (US $267,000), excluding the value of land and buildings, must be licensed. Licenses are granted pursuant to either the National Industries Protection and Encouragement Act, which applies to projects by Saudi citizens with full Saudi capital, or the New Foreign Investment Law, which applies to projects with full foreign capital or mixed Saudi/foreign capital (see discussion above).

Industrial establishments are entitled to the following incentives and exemptions under Saudi law:

- Certain tariff exemptions;
- Subsidized industrial land, housing and utilities;

- Subsidies for training Saudi employees and other forms of assistance for partially foreign owned Saudi businesses;
- Export assistance for locally manufactured products; and
- Public procurement preference for majority Saudi owned joint venture companies.

QATAR

LAW NO. (13) OF THE YEAR 2000 ON ORGANIZATION OF FOREIGN CAPITAL INVESTMENT IN THE ECONOMIC ACTIVITY.

LAW NO: (13) OF THE YEAR 2000 ON ORGANIZATION OF FOREIGN CAPITAL INVESTMENT IN THE ECONOMIC ACTIVITY.

We, Jassim Bin Hamad Al-Thani, Deputy Emir of the State of Qatar,

Having due regard to the Amended Interim Provisional Constitution, particularly, Articles No. (22), (23), (34), and (51) there of, and

Commercial Companies Law promulgated by Law No. (11) of the year 1981, amended by Law No.(9) of the year 1998, and, Customs Law promulgated by Law No. (5) of the year 1988 and Laws amending that, and,

Law Decree No.(25) of the year 1990 on organization of non-Qatari Capital Investment in the economic activity, amended by Law No.(9) of the year 1995, and Law Decree No.(11) of the year 1993 concerning Income tax, and

Law Decree No.(22) of the year 1993 on organization of Ministry of Economy and Commerce and prescription of its mandates, and the proposal submitted by Minister of Finance, Economy and Commerce, the draft Law submitted by the Cabinet, and having consulted the Advisory Council, have decided the following Law:

CHAPTER ONE Definitions

ARTICLE (1)

In application of this Law, the following terms and expressions shall have the meaning shown opposite to each unless the text requires otherwise

Ministry : Ministry of Finance, Economy, and Commerce Minister : Minister of Finance, Economy, and Commerce

Foreign Investors : Non-Qatari's whether they are natural or judicial who invest their money in any of the projects in which direct investment is permitted by the State in accordance with provisions of this Law.

FOREIGN INVESTED CAPITAL:

Cash, in kind money or rights in rem foreign Investors Invest in the State of Qatar including :

1. Funds transferred to the State (Qatar) through Licensed banks and Financial companies.
2. It is prohibited for Foreign investment mention in items (1) and (2) above, to invest in banks and insurance companies as well as commercial agency rights and trading in real estate.
3. Corporeal assets imported for Investment purposes in accordance with provisions of this Law.
4. Profits, revenues and reserves generated from Foreign capital Investment in a project where by project capital has been increased or if invest in any of the permitted projects in accordance with provisions of this Law.
5. Rights in rem such Licenses, patent right and trade marks registered in the State (Qatar).

CHAPTER TWO Foreign Capital Investment

ARTICLE (2)

1-Subject to provisions of item "3" of this article Foreign Investors may invest in all sectors of national economy provided that they shall have Qatari partner(s) whose share in the capital shall not be less than 51 % and the company is Legally established in accordance with provisions of law.

2-Nevertheless, Foreign investors may, upon Minister's decision, increase their share in project capital from 49% up to 100 % in the fields of agriculture, industry, health, education, tourism, development and exploitation of natural resources, energy or mining provided that such projects match with Development plan of the State (Qatar) and due preference shall be given to projects that would achieve the optimal utilization of domestic raw materials, export industries, or project that would present a new product or in which modern technology is used, in addition to projects that seek to locate worldwide leading industry or develop and qualify national cadre.

3-It is prohibited for Foreign investment mention in items (1) and (2) above, to invest in banks and insurance companies as well as commercial agency rights and trading in real estate.

ARTICLE (3)

The Minister may, after consultation with concerned authority, license Foreign companies engaged in work contracts in the State to implement their contracts if that facilitates delivery of a certain service or for the public interest.

ARTICLE (4)

Unless otherwise specifically stated in this Law, foreign investor desiring to obtain license stipulated for practicing any of the activities in which investment is permitted, such license. Shall be given in accordance with provisions of laws in force in the State in respect to intended business.

CHAPTER THREE Investment Incentives

ARTICLE (5)_

A piece of land may be allotted to the foreign investor to set up his investment project on a long term lease contract for a period not exceeding 50 years renewable.

ARTICLE (6)

Foreign investor has the right to import whatever he needs for the establishment, operation or expansion of his project in accordance with laws applicable in the state.

ARTICLE (7)

The Ministry may :

1-Exempt the foreign capital invested in the fields stated in Article (2) here of, from the Income Tax for a period not exceeding ten years effective from Investment project commissioning date.

2-Exempt Foreign investment projects from custom's taxes in respect to machinery and equipment imported for projects set-up .

3-Grant foreign investment industrial projects, customs exemption on imported rows materials and half-manufactured materials, not available in local markets, necessary for production purposes.

ARTICLE(8)

1-Foreign investment shall in either directly nor indirectly, be subject to expropriation or any other similar procedures unless such measures are for public welfare and implements in a non-discriminating way, against a prompt and reasonable compensation in accordance with legal procedures and general principles stated in item 2of this Article.

2- Compensation shall be equal to actual economic value expropriated investment at time of expropriation or announcement of the same. Compensation shall be estimated in accordance with a normal economic situation or precedent to any notification on expropriation of investment. Compensation shall be paid with immediate effect and shall be transferable at any time. Upto settlement of compensation, an interest shall be calculated for the same in accordance with interest rate prevailing in the state.

ARTICLE (9)

1-Foreign Investors shall have the right to bank for all amounts relevant to their investment from 1 to any external destination without any delay. Transfers shall include

a-Investment revenues.

b-Amounts generated from partial or entire sale or liquidation of investment.

c-Amounts resulting from settlement of investment disputes.

d-Compensation stated in Article (8) hereof.

2-Money transfers can be executed in any exchangeable currency at the exchange rate prevailing on the date of transfer

ARTICLE (10)

Foreign investor shall have the right to transfer his investment ownership to any other foreign or natural investor or to assign ownership to his local partner in case of partnership provided such arraignment or transfer shall be effected in accordance with applicable laws and regulations.

In these cases, treatment of investment shall continue in accordance with provisions of this law provided that the new investor shall have to keep the project running and shall replace the former investor in respect to liabilities and obligations.

ARTICLE (11)

It may be agreed to solve any dispute arising between the investor and any other party through Local or international arbitration commission.

CHAPTER FOUR General provisions

ARTICLE (12)

Provisions of this law shall not be applicable to

1-Companies and individuals assigned by the state to mine, exploit, or manage the natural resources under special lien or agreement insomuch as this shall not be in contradiction with stipulations of provisions of Lien contract or the special agreement.

2-Companies founded by or shared by government and other public institutions and authorities in association with foreign investors , in accordance with Article (90) of above referenced Commercial Companies Law.

ARTICLE (13)

Foreign Investor shall keep the environment safe against pollution and shall adhere to laws, regulations and instructions relevant to security and public health. He is also required not to engage in any acts affecting State's public Order and morals in general.

ARTICLE(14)

Provisions of this law shall not prejudice any customs privileges and exemptions or any other warranties or incentives given to any companies and institutions existing when this law comes into force. These companies and institutions shall keep enjoying such privileges, exemptions, warranties, and incentives in accordance with the regulations, agreements, and contracts they emanate from.

CHAPTER FIVE Penalties and Closing Provisions

ARTICLE (15)

Ministry shall notify the foreign investor in the event that he breaches any of the provisions hereof, who, in turn, shall have to rectify the breach within a period not exceeding 3 months effective from date of notice.

ARTICLE (16)

Without prejudice to any other severer penalty stipulated by any other law, any foreign investor carrying out an economic activity that is in breach of this law, shall be subject to a fine not less than

Q.R. 50,000 / - and not exceeding Q.R. 100,000 / - Any citizen who engages with the foreigner in such illegal activity shall be subject to the same penalty.

ARTICLE (17)

Ministry technical staff designated by minister shall have the capacity of judicial police in seizing and proving crimes committed in violation of provisions of this law and its respective executive decisions. To achieve that end, Ministry shall have access to shops and institutions subjected to this law in order to inspect and review their documents and records .

ARTICLE (18)

Law Decree No.(25) of the year 1990 is hereby revoked in addition to any other provision contradicting provisions of this law.

ARTICLE (19)

Minister shall issue by laws and decisions needed for the implementation of provisions of this Law including determination of relevant fees.

ARTICLE (20)

All competent parties, each within its competence shall execute this law which shall come into force on the date on which it is published in the official Gazette.

JASIM BIN HAMAD AL – THANI DEPUTY EMIR OF THE STATE OF QATAR

Issued at Emir Divan on 19 /7 /1421 A.H Corresponding to 16 / 10 /2000. A.D

FOREIGN INVESTMENTS INVCENTIVES

The Law Regulating the Investment of Non-Qatari Capital in Economic Activities No. 25 of 1990 governs the area of foreign investment in Qatar. Under this law, non-Qataris are allowed to engage in trade, industry, agriculture and services under the condition that the non-Qatari investor must have one or more Qatari partners whose share in the business capital is at least 51 percent and that the business relationship with the Qatari partner must be carried on through a commercial company incorporated according to the Companies Law No.11 of 1986 (see section on Business Forms and Structures). The law does not permit non-Qataris to own shares in a joint stock company unless the shareholder is a national of an Arab country which has reciprocal agreements with Qatar or if there is a need for foreign capital or experience, and a license to that effect is obtained from the Minister of Finance, Economy and Commerce.

Non-Qataris meeting the above requirements may also carry on contracting business upon the fulfillment of additional conditions. A special license from the Minister of Finance, Economy and Commerce must be issued following consultation with relevant government authorities. This requires an application to be made to the Minister supported by all relevant documents. If thirty days elapse without a reply from the Minister, the application is presumed to have been rejected. Applicants whose applications were rejected may appeal to the Minister within thirty days. The decision in the appeal is final.

In determining applications, one of the factors considered is the demand for the type of business for which an application is made. Businesses engaging in fields for which there is a high demand in Qatar include businesses with high technology expertise.

In 1997, Qatar finalized legislation to abolish the requirement of 51 percent Qatari ownership. This step is aimed at attracting foreign investment in small and medium scale businesses. The new legislation will come into force pending the Emir's approval.

TRADE AGREEMENTS

Qatar became a member of the General Agreement on Tariffs and Trade (GATT) in 1996. Prior to that time, it participated in GATT as an observer. As a member of the Gulf Cooperation Council (GCC), Qatar participates in the GCC's free trade arrangements. Qatar also became a member of the World Trade Organization (WTO) in 1995.

Qatar has been engaged through the GCC in trade and investment negotiations with the United States, the European Community and Japan. The dialogue initiated among them is on-going. In addition to the GCC Economic Agreement (1983) signed among member states of the GCC, Qatar has signed economic/commercial agreements with Egypt and Tunisia in recent years.

IMPORT AND EXPORT RESTRICTIONS

Imports

Goods and commodities imported into Qatar are subject to customs tariffs as follows:

Item	Tariff
General goods and commodities	4%
Reinforced Iron Bars, Steel and Cement (similar to local manufacture or equivalent)	20%

Ammonia (similar to local manufacture or equivalent)	30%
Cigarettes and Tobacco Products	50%
Essentials and Personal Items (such as foodstuffs, machinery and raw materials for industrial projects)	Exempt

Imports into Qatar require an import license, which may be issued only to Qatari citizens. Agents and agency agreements are subject to the Law Concerning the Regulation of Activities of Local Commercial Agencies and Their Foreign Principals 4/1986, as discussed in the above section on Commercial Agencies.

In accordance with Islamic tradition, the importation of pork and pork products is prohibited. Also prohibited are firearms, ammunition, immodest prints and pictures, narcotics and artificial pearls. Alcohol and alcohol products are discouraged by the imposition of heavy customs duties.

Goods from other Gulf Cooperation Council countries are given preferential tariff rates. According to a reciprocity agreement among the GCC states, products of GCC origin are exempted from customs duties. Except for steel, along with tobacco and cigarettes, all general merchandise is subject to 4 percent customs duties. The current rate of customs duty for steel is 20 percent, 10 percent for hi-fi equipment and 50 percent for tobacco and cigarettes.

EXPORTS

There are no export charges on goods or commodities exported from Qatar.

The Government of Qatar encourages foreign investment, particularly in joint ventures with Qatari partners. Wholly foreign-owned firms are permitted to operate in Qatar, provided they have a local agent or a sponsor. Foreign-owned firms and the foreign-owned portions of joint ventures are subject to corporate income tax, ranging from 5 percent to 35 percent of net profits. Qatari and GCC nationals and business concerns are exempted from the income tax provisions.

Foreign investors are not allowed to expand their investment beyond limits set forth in the law. An Emiri decree, however, can allow the expansion of a foreign investment in Qatar. Transfer of technology, management and marketing, as was the case in establishing steel, fertilizers and petrochemical industries in the 1970s, were taken as part of the foreign equity (20 or 25 percent).

PRIVATIZATION

Qatar, along with the other countries of the Gulf Cooperation Council has adopted a privatization policy, however, full realization of these policies will require additional revisions to the laws relating to foreign investment in business associations in Qatar. The establishment of the stock exchange is expected to facilitate privatization.

STOCK EXCHANGE

Law No. 4/1995 established the Doha Stock Exchange (DSE), and governs transactions in securities, including bonds and shares of Qatari shareholding companies, government or quasi-government, including government companies, bonds and negotiable instruments and other securities which are authorized for trading. The QCB and all licensed commercial banks in Qatar are members of the Doha Stock Exchange. Several trading activities are limited to brokers, and there are licensing rules applicable to brokers.

The formal stock exchange began operations in the first quarter of 1997. An international consultant was appointed in November 1996 to assist in drawing up its regulatory framework. The firm will also make recommendations to the DSM steering committee on whether the exchange should use electronic or floor-based trading. Initially, trading will be confined to Qatari nationals, although GCC nationals and foreigners may be allowed to participate at a later date. The DSE will be autonomous but indirectly overseen by the Finance, Economy and Trade Ministry.

PRINCIPAL GROWTH SECTORS

Over the past few years, the relative importance of the non-oil sector in the country's GDP ranged from 63 to 69 percent. A review of the performance of the non-oil sector and sub-sectors indicate that agriculture and fishing, electricity and water, building and construction, and communications have all increased their share of GDP while manufacturing industries and services have decreased their share.

Foreign business involvement in the Qatari market since the early 1960s consisted principally of providing a wide range of products, including automotive and spare parts, as well as oil field supplies. In recent years, however, American technology, products and services were imported by various sectors of the Qatari market, including those which were previously dominated by European suppliers. Such sectors are electricity and water, oil and natural gas development and enhancement of recovery of these resources.

BEST INVESTMENT PROSPECTS

Rank	Sector
1	Machinery and Transport Equipment
2	Manufactured Goods Classified Chiefly by Materials
3	Miscellaneous Manufactured Goods
4	Food and Live Animals
5	Chemicals and Related Products
6	Beverages and Tobacco
7	Inedible Crude Materials, Except Fuel
8	Mineral Fuels, Lubricants and Related Materials
9	Animal and Vegetable Oils; Fat and Waxes
10	Others

SYRIA

ENCOURAGEMENT OF INVESTMENT LAW

The Encouragement of Investment Law, No. 10 of May 1991, was enacted to encourage investments in economic and social development projects, approved by the Supreme Council of Investment, which is composed of various government ministers. Applications for approval of projects must be filed with the relevant ministry which will forward them to the Council for approval.

Approved projects may import all equipment and supplies needed, without limitation, in order establish, develop or enlarge the project. Such importation is exempt from taxes, customs and any other duties. Nonetheless, taxes and duties are levied on all imported equipment that is used to operate the project on a continuing basis.

Depending on the type of project, certain tax exemptions are granted for periods ranging from five to seven years. Furthermore, all projects covered under Law No. 10 are exempt from Syrian foreign exchange control. After five years, the portion of foreign investment equal to the amount of shares held in such a project may be repatriated to the foreign investor, based on the actual value of the project. The amount transferred may not exceed the initial currency investment. Should circumstances that are beyond the control of the investors arise, repatriation may begin within the first six months of the project. Annual profits and interest earned, through the use of foreign capital, may be transferred abroad.

The Investment Law's main provisions are as follows:

- The project must correspond to the government's aim for the relevant sector;
- Import of production inputs such as machinery, equipment and vehicles is free of customs duty;
- Mixed-sector companies in which the Syrian government's stake is at least 25 percent or companies that export 50 percent of their products receive a seven year tax holiday;
- Private-sector companies receive tax incentives five years;
- Foreign exchange capital can be repatriated after five years, and, if the project fails through circumstances out of the investor's control, such capital can be repatriated after six months;
- Profits can be transferred freely;
- 50 percent of expatriate salaries and 100 percent of expatriate severance pay can be repatriated.

A 1996 decision by Syria's Supreme Council for Investment states that the expansion, modernization and development of projects under the 1991 Investment Law No. 10 will not receive any new tax benefits.

INCENTIVES FOR THE TOURISM INDUSTRY

Several laws provide incentives for the tourism industry and certain other industries. These incentives, under Decision 186, include a seven year exemption from all taxes on the operation of tourist establishments, an exemption from paying income tax on up to 50 percent of the profits, certain import and customs exemptions, and some exemptions allowing bank accounts to be maintained in foreign currency.
According to Decrees 46 and 162 and Law No. 36, investments in hotels, restaurants and approved tourism projects enjoy certain benefits which may include an exemption from tax for between five to seven years, for example, hotels, restaurants and entertainment areas having a deluxe or first class rating.
Imported building materials, furniture and installations for these tourism businesses are also exempt from customs duties if such imports are used in order to enable a hotel or restaurant to maintain its deluxe or first rate rating.

TRADE REGULATIONS

Before 1990, Syrian policy was geared to substituting imports with domestically produced goods. The government, however, has eased regulations to the point that advance deposits for imports of food and industrial inputs have been abolished. The most significant change has been in financial transactions. According to statistics by the Syrian government, 95 percent of exported and imported goods are priced at the neighboring countries' rate, which has gradually replaced the alternative rates for different goods. Furthermore, exporters do not have to exchange their foreign exchange earnings with the Commercial Bank of Syria if they then want to finance imports. The 25 to 30 percent share in foreign export proceeds that must be exchanged at the commercial banks are now also subject to the neighboring exchange rate.

All documentary transactions for imports must be by a letter of credit opened at the Commercial Bank of Syria. Typically, the bank requires the importer to cover 100 percent of the transaction from his own resources offshore or from funds generated by exports. Syrian importers often use free-of-payment or 180-day-credit facilities clauses. In this case, the importer pays through his offshore bank either cash in advance or via L/C, and the bill of lading is then sent to the Commercial Bank of Syria. Alternatively, an importer may use foreign exchange earned from exports and deposited in the Central Bank of Syria.

FREE TRADE ZONES

Free trade zones have been established in Damascus, Aleppo, Tartus, Lataquia, the Damascus international airport and in Adra. Article 6 of Decree 84 of 1972 encourages certain kinds of investments in free trade zones, authorizes the importation of foreign goods to these zones, and permits re-exportation that is not subject to the laws on foreign trade, customs duties or taxes. The Ministry of Economy and Foreign Trade may authorize the establishment of warehouses in a free trade zone. Up to 20 percent of imports to such warehouses may be granted an exemption from the usual limitations imposed on imports into the Syrian market, provided they do not compete with local industries or with a state-run monopoly. Priority in establishing an operation in a free trade zone is given to industries that use components or raw materials produced in Syria, complement existing industries in Syria, satisfy a local demand or employ a large number of Syrian workers.

TRADE AGREEMENTS

A cooperation agreement has existed between Syria and the EU since 1977 that sets preferential tariffs for a wide range of agricultural produce as well as import ceilings for crude oil, petroleum products and cotton fabrics. These ceilings are above normal customs duties applicable to third countries. Syria is also included in the EU plan which allows industrial products to enter the EU market duty free. There are special regulations to the agreement, regarding technical and financial cooperation, which were renewed in 1991 and are now focused on supporting Syrian economic reform measures, especially in private sector development in agriculture, manufacturing, science and technology, as well as external trade.

Syria entered an agreement for Economic and Social Cooperation and Coordination with Lebanon in September 1993, which regulates the general framework of bilateral relations between the two countries in such areas as trade, movement of people and capital, residence, employment and transport. The sale of agricultural products in both countries is conducted by a joint Syrian-Lebanese marketing company. Other later concluded bilateral accords regulate water sharing in the Orontes river, labor relations (addressing the legalization of an estimated 500,000 or more Syrian workers in Lebanon), tourism and cultural relations.

Trade agreements with other countries, especially Arab countries specify products which can be traded in both directions under preferential terms. Such trade is often limited to specific transactions, such as the importation of equipment under a particular contract or tender. No formal trade relations exist with Israel, although illegal trade has become more prominent since the peace process began.

While the political sector is characteristically hesitant and reserved, the existing illegal trade indicates that the private sector seems interested in entering into trade and general business relations with Israel as soon as the political barriers will be removed.

CUSTOMS

Customs duties can range from 1 percent to over 100 percent on certain items. Law No. 1 of 1980 created a Unified Tax on Imports which ranges from 6 percent for goods exempt from customs, and from 35 percent for goods subject to customs tariff, to more than 100 percent. Machinery and materials imported for new industrial investment, under certain circumstances, may, upon application to and approval from the government, be exempt from import duties.

The customs procedures require that goods imported be accompanied by invoices that list the producer of the goods and their country of origin in Arabic. The invoice must also include an Israeli boycott clause and, in some cases, a health declaration.

PRIVATE SECTOR INVESTMENT

Until the 1990s, private sector involvement in induwas limited by a number of regulations. In the past decade, the relaxation of certain restrictions allowed the private sector to import parts, equipment and other industrial inputs. Currently, private sector involvement is significant in the textile, food, leather, paper, and chemicals sectors, while heavy industry remains state-dominated. The Syrian government, however, has started to open up these industries to private-sector investment as the public sector cannot meet rising demand. There are plans to open the country's first privately-run sugar factory, and a private Saudi-Syrian joint venture has plans to open a cement factory.

In agriculture, the private sector dominates approximately two-thirds of cultivable land, with state-farms and cooperatives accounting for the remainder.

BEST PROSPECTS FOR INVESTMENTS

INDUSTRY

Syrian manufacturing industries began to grow substantially in the 1960s. The government encouraged industrialization by raising tariffs on imported consumer goods and by providing tax exemptions and credit for domestic industries.

Textiles constitute the largest manufacturing industry in Syria. Other industries include petrochemicals, fertilizers, cement, soap, glass, food processing, sugar processing, tobacco, iron and steel, tanning and vegetable oil.

AGRICULTURE

Despite climatic handicaps, Syria produces a wide variety of crops, some in sufficient quantity for export. The major crops are cereals, primarily wheat and barley, cotton, tobacco, grapes, olives, citrus fruits and vegetables. Agricultural land is privately owned for the most part.

TOURISM

The tourism sector in Syria has developed slowly, partly because of ambivalence on the part of the government, which is hesitant about permitting a massive influx of foreign visitors, and partly because Syria's image abroad has deterred would-be tourists. Since 1992, receipts from tourism jumped sharply to US$ 60 million. In 1995, the number of tourists visiting Syria was about two million, most of them from Arab countries. By the year 2000, the Syrian government anticipates an increase in the number of tourists to six million, but this is not realistic without a peace agreement with Israel.

FRANCHISING

The concept of franchising, especially the prospects for opening the first major American fast food restaurant, has captured the imagination of many Syrians. Many capable and well-capitalized Syrian businessmen have applied for major American fast food franchises, but have been refused. Fashion giant Benetton, on the other hand, has an expanding chain of franchise stores in the country.

Rank	Sector
1	Cotton, Leather and Textiles
2	Mineral Fuels and Oils
3	Crude Petroleum
4	Meat (frozen/canned)
5	Fruits and Vegetables
6	Suger
7	Coal
8	Machinery and Spare Parts
9	Base Metals

10	Pharmaceutical Products
11	Chemical Petroleum
12	Transport Equipment
13	Paper and Paper Products
14	Rubber, Resins and Artifical Rubber

TUNISIA

INVESTMENT LAW

Article One . - This Code sets the rules for creating projects and incentives for investments in Tunisia by Tunisian and foreign developers, residents or nonresidents, or partnership in accordance with the strategy of including the acceleration of growth and job creation activities in the following sectors:

- agriculture and fisheries;
- manufacturing;
- public works;
- tourism;
- crafts;
- transportation;
- education and teaching;
- vocational training;
- production and cultural industries;
- entertainment for young and supervision of children;
- health;
- protecting the environment;
- property development;
- other activities and nonfinancial services.

The list of activities in the areas listed above is fixed by decree .

Art. 2 . - Investment in activities under the Article I of this Code are made subject to satisfying the conditions of those activities in accordance with the laws and regulations.

Investment projects are subject to a declaration filed with the departments concerned by the activity. These services are required to issue a certificate of deposit of the declaration.Relevant services and content of the statement required will be specified by the decreementioned in Article I of this Code.

Investments in certain activities, as well as those made in other activities determined bydecree shall remain subject to prior approval of relevant departments in accordance with the conditions and regulations set by the specific laws governing them.

Art. 3 . - The resident and nonresident aliens are free to invest in projects under this Code.

However, the participation of foreigners in certain service activities other than totally exporting a list of which is fixed by decree remains subject to approval by the Higher Commission for Investment under the Article 52 of this Code where such participation exceeds 50% stake in the company.

Foreigners can invest in the agricultural sector as part of the operation by leasing agricultural land. However, these investments may in no case lead to the foreign ownership of agricultural land.

Art. 4 . - The incentives provided by this code are given in the form of common incentives and specific incentives.

Art. 5 . - The provisions of this Code apply to investments relating to:

- creation,
- extension,
- renewal,
- redevelopment
- or processing activity.

Art. 6 . - With the exception of investments in wholly export activities, the benefit of incentives provided by this Code requires the completion of a financing scheme involving the investment rate minimum capital set by decree .

Considering Law No. 93-120 of 27 December 1993 promulgating the Investment Incentives Code and in particular Article 6 ,

Considering Decree No. 78-578 of 9 June 1978 relating to the re-regulation of the promotion and industrial decentralization, as amended and supplemented by subsequent legislation and in particular Articles 5 and 9

Having consulted the State Minister, Minister of the Interior, the Ministers of National Economy, Planning and Regional Development, agriculture, tourism and crafts, education and Science, Youth and Children, culture, vocational training and employment, health, environment and land use and transportation

Considering the opinion of the tribunal, Decrees:

Article I - (new). Note - With the exception of companies engaged in export activities completely, the benefit from the advantages provided by the code of investment incentives is subject to fulfillment by the enterprise of a financing scheme involving capital representing at least:

30% of the cost of investment:

for industrial projects,agricultural projects and fishing in category "C"tourism projects, projects by developers of new industrial activities or performing services under Article 2 of Decree No. 94-538 of 10 March 1994 referred to above,projects in other sectors.

Note 25% of the cost of investment for new projects by developers engaged in activities other than those whose minimum rate is 30% or 10%,

25% of the cost of investment for new projects by developers engaged in activities other than those whose minimum rate is set at 30% and 10% including acquisitions of modern production units of small pelagic within a total investment not exceeding I.000.000 dinars.

10% of the cost of investment for agricultural and fisheries projects in the categories "A" and "B" including those by new promoters.

Own funds are advanced by way of contribution in cash or in kind.

Art. 2. (New). Note - For new developers, equity holdings include refundable or equity investments.

Art. 3. - are repealed all provisions contrary to those of this Decree and in particular Articles 5 and 9 of Decree No. 78-578 of 9 June 1978 referred to above.

Art. 4. - Minister of State Minister of the Interior, the Ministers of Finance, National Economy, Planning and Regional Development, Agriculture, Environment and Spatial Planning, the transport, tourism and crafts, education and science, culture, public health, vocational training and employment and youth and children are responsible, each this is concerned, the execution of this decree will be published in the Official Gazette of the Republic of Tunisia,

INVESTMENT INCENTIVES

Tunisia has enacted several laws to encourage foreign investment in the industrial, agricultural and tourism sectors. Legislation promoting foreign investment in the service sector has been drafted and may be adopted by the Government.

Foreign investors wishing to invest in these sectors under the enabling legislation may do so through the form of a partnership (Association of Person) or as either a public or private company (Association of Capital).

In order to promote economic growth, narrow existing trade imbalances and increase exports, Tunisia offers extensive investment incentives. These incentives have been available since the 1970s. The Investment Incentives Code, which became effective in January 1994, promotes these goals. The Investment Incentives Code offers two types of incentives. The first kind of investment incentives is applied to all investment projects, except projects relating to mining, energy and finance. The second kind of investment incentives is reserved for projects engaged in specified fields or projects of a special nature.

All investment projects, except projects relating to mining, energy and finance are entitled to the following investment incentives:

1. A deduction from taxable income, of up to 35 percent of net income or profits, for income or profits reinvested in share capital or invested in capital increase;
2. A suspension of VAT and sales tax on locally produced equipment;
3. A reduction of 10 percent from customs duties and the suspension of VAT and sales taxes on imported equipment for which there is no Tunisian manufactured substitute;
4. An option to apply an installment method of depreciation for production plants and equipment, excluding offequipment, having a life expectancy of more than seven years.

The second kind of investment incentives is available to investment projects in the field of exporting (whether in whole or in part), regional development projects, or projects engaged in agriculture, environmental protection, research and development and new small enterprises. The investment incentives are substantial and vary depending on the field in which the enterprise engages and the industry concerned. A brief overview of some of the incentives available follows:

5. A full deduction of income or profits from taxable income or corporate taxable income for a period of ten years, and a reduction of up to 50 percent beginning in the eleventh year;
6. A full tax allowance in respect of profits reinvested in share capital or in the increase of the company's registered share capital;
7. A full tax allowance in respect of profits reinvested in the company;
8. Financial support for amounts paid for social security levies;
9. Investment bonuses equal to 8 percent of the cost of the investment made;
10. The option to elect a flat-tax rate of 20 percent of gross earnings.

In addition to the incentives available under the Investment Incentives Code, non-residents enjoy the tax-free transfer of capital invested in the investment project and the profits arising as a result thereof. Also, non-residents may freely repatriate their profits and capital upon the sale of their holdings in such investment projects.
The High Commission for Investments is authorized to grant further incentives to investment projects deemed to be of special or significant importance. Such benefits may take the form of exemptions from income tax or corporate tax for a period up to five years, state funded contributions to the costs of infrastructure development, an investment bonus of up to 5 percent of the total investment in the project or the suspension of tariffs and taxes levied on equipment.

TRADE AGREEMENTS

Tunisia prides itself on maintaining preferential trading-partner relations with African, Arab and Mediterranean nations. Tunisia has entered into trade agreements with forty-one developed and developing countries, which granted Tunisia most-favored-nation status. Tunisia has entered into bilateral and regional trade preference agreements with the European Union and the Arab Maghreb Union as well as certain agreements under the framework of the Inter-Arab Cooperation, the Inter-African Cooperation and the Organization of the Islamic Conference. Furthermore, Tunisia is a member of the world trade organization (WTO) and is a signatory to the Global System on Trade Preferences.
In 1995, the Tunisian government and the European Union negotiated a major economic agreement on free trade. The pact establishes the framework for free trade between Tunisia and the European Union. The agreement, which came into effect in 1997, has a twelve year phase-in period.

FREE TRADE ZONES

Over 130 companies have submitted requests to invest in Tunisia's two free trade zones. Sixty companies, of which fifty are foreign, made requests to operate in the Bizerte Harbor Free Trade Zone, located sixty kilometers north of Tunis. Most of these companies are French, but requests have also come from American, German, British, Danish, Belgian, Japanese, Indonesian and Egyptian companies. These foreign companies are seeking to invest in the electronics, metals, pharmaceuticals and food industries.

The second free trade zone, in Zarzis Harbor, is 450 kilometers south of Tunis, near the Libyan border. Over seventy foreign companies have already submitted requests to invest in this zone, most of them French. The Zarzis zone spans over 380,000 square meters. Twenty million dollars have been invested to establish this zone, part of which will be utilized to expand the harbor facilities at Zarzis. The harbor is currently used to import oil from Libya, among other activities.

CUSTOMS

Since March 1994 and the enactment of Law No. 94-41, which embodies the policy of the free trade principle adopted in other liberalization measures, Tunisia has allowed the free importation and exportation of goods, with the exception of restrictions relating to national security, public order, health and hygiene and the protection of flora, fauna and natural heritage.

Tunisia's basic tariff rate ranges from 10 percent to 43 percent. In addition, several years ago Tunisia imposed a temporary supplemental duty on certain imports that compete with locally produced goods. This duty was originally scheduled to be phased out at the end of 1994, but remains in effect.

PRIVATIZATION

Tunisia has launched a program to privatize non-strategic state-owned companies, particularly companies operating in competitive sectors. In addition to the privatization measures described above, Tunisia recently launched international tenders to sell assets in two state-owned textile firms and a state-controlled mineral water firm. Furthermore, Tunisia has launched an international tender to sell part of the state-owned Sahara Palace Hotel. Among the companies that were undergoing full or partial privatization in 1995 and 1996 are TunisAir, the ferry company, CTN, and the Coca Cola and beer bottler, SBFT.

Legal and regulatory framework

The legal and regulatory framework that regulates the privatization programme is composed primarily of the following texts:

Laws

Law N° 89-9 of February 1st, 1989 relative to public sector participations, enterprises and establishments modified and completed by the law N° 94-102 of August 1st, 1994, the law N° 96-74 of July 29, 1996, the law N° 2001-33 of March 29, 2001, and the law N°36-2006 of June 12, 2006.

The Law N° 85-109 of December 31, 1985 bearing the Law for finances for the year 1986 relative to the creation of the special treasury fund (fund for the restructuring of the capital of public enterprises) modified by the Law n°89-115 of December 30, 1989 relative to the Law for finances for the year 1990.

Decrees

Decree N° 96-270 of February 14, 1996 fixing the attributions of the Ministry of Economic Development that is modified by the Decree N° 96-1225 of July 1st, 1996.

Decree N° 96-271 of February 14, 1996 relative to the organisation of the Ministry of Development that is modified and completed by the Decree N° 96-1226 of July 1st, 1996.

Decree N° 97-410 of February 21, 1997 fixing the composition of CAREPP as well as the composition and the attributions of CTP modified and completed by the Decree N° 98-1440 of July 13, 1998.

Decree N°2000-2280 of October 10, 2000, relative to the methods of naming and the conditions of remuneration of liquidators of public sector establishments and enterprises and the methods and procedures for approval of the liquidation programme.

Decree N° 2002-2130 of September 30,2002 relative to the attachment of the structure (relevant previously to the ex-Ministry of Economic Development) to the Prime Ministry.

Circulars

Circular N° 33 of June 21, 1989 relative to management, guardianship, restructuring and list of public enterprises.

Circular N° 21 of April 21, 1990 relative to the ceding of shares or assets and the taking in of new participation by the participants or public enterprises.

Circular N° 3 of January 29, 1992 relative to the methods of the sales of assets of the enterprises that have public sector participation.

Circular N° 55 of August 11, 1993 relative to the attribution and procedure to follow for privatisation operations.

Circular N° 15 of March 30, 1995 relative to the attribution and procedure to follow for privatization operations.

Circular N° 19 of June 02, 1998 relative to the participation of banks in the capital of enterprises with public participation.

STOCK EXCHANGE

The Tunis Stock Exchange was established in 1969, and as of 1995, had over twenty companies listed with a total market capitalization of $2.5 billion. Tunisian companies on the stock exchange are required to publish semi-annual corporate reports audited by a certified public accountant. Due to a decree issued in 1995, it is easier today for foreigners to purchase shares in Tunisian companies. Foreigners can buy up to 10 percent of a company's shares on the Tunis Stock Exchange and up to 30 percent of a private company without central bank approval.

The Tunisian stock exchange is also playing a role in the country's search for development capital, though up until now foreign interest has been minimal, largely because of small trading volumes and related fears of insider manipulation. Still, news that the well respected chief executive of the Banque de Developement Economique de Tunisie, Tijani Chelli, has now been appointed the stock exchange's chief could encourage wider local activity and, in the longer run, lead to greater foreign involvement. Foreign & Colonial Emerging Markets, for example, is now considering greater involvement there.

PRICE CONTROLS AND COMPETITION POLICY

Until the mid-1980s, Tunisia maintained stringent price controls. In conjunction with trade liberalization policies in the 1980s, domestic price controls were liberalized in 1986. The Competition Law, enacted in 1991, declared free competition with regard to prices as the primary rule for the domestic market, with some exceptions for goods and services deemed to be necessities, such as food, public utilities, petrol, and medicines. Sectors where free market prices do not apply are subject to special rules regarding anti-competitive practices, including the abuse of dominant market positions, the violation of which are punishable by fine and imprisonment.

INVESTMENT PROSPECTS

Rank	Sector
1	Telecommunications Equipment
2	Construction and Engineering Services
3	Electrical Power Systems
4	Medical Equipment and Services
5	Computer Equipment and Services
6	Pollution Control Equipment and Services

UNITED ARAB EMIRATES

INVESTMENT

Foreign investment in capital, technology or expertise is more than welcome in the UAE. Generally, any locally incorporated company must be at least 51 percent owned by UAE nationals, but the apportionment and distribution of profits is not similarly constrained.

FREE TRADE ZONES

Dubai, which has far less oil wealth than Abu-Dhabi, has undertaken a major promotion campaign to attract more foreign investment and tourism. Its vast Jebel Ali Free Trade Zone now houses more than 950 international operations, most of which engage in the distribution or light to medium manufacturing of products for domestic consumption and export. The Zone is built around the Dubai Port Authority's Jebel Ali Terminal and enables customers to take full advantage of the port's ISO-certified container and general cargo operations. A Free Zone Authority is assisting in administrative proceedings.

The principal advantage of free trade zones in the UAE, and especially Jebel Ali, is that companies locating in a free zone may be 100 percent foreign owned. Registration procedures tend to be relatively simple. Furthermore, since the nominal customs duty is only 4 percent and as much as 3 percent of it is often rebated, the entire country is a virtual Free Trade Zone.

Dubai Law No. 2 of April 3, 1993, is designed to treat equally goods manufactured by firms which are at least 51 percent owned by UAE or GCC nationals and which are licensed by the Ministry of Finance as UAE products, regardless of whether manufactured inside or outside free trade zones. The net effect of the law will be to exempt products produced in free trade zones from UAE customs duty. Over the long term, it is hoped that all GCC countries will cease to levy import duties on free zone products.

Under Dubai law No. 9 of 1992, a company may set up a separate legal entity, referred to as a free zone establishment (FZE). Theentity needs only one shareholder, whose liability may be limited to the amount of share capital paid in to the FZE (minimum share capital DH 1 million). No memorandum or articles of incorporation will be necessary. The Jebel Ali Free Zone Authority will provide to every applicant upon request the implementation regulations for foreign investors in the zone. The Zone Authority also maintains a FZE register.

The Jebel Ali Free Zone provides an opportunity to businesses to base their manufacturing, warehousing and trading operations in the Free Zone without the normal requirements attendant to the conduct of business in the Arab Gulf States. Businesses in Jebel Ali are exempted from the requirement of local ownership, payment of taxes and duties and are guarantied the freedom to transfer capital, profits and salaries. The Jebel Ali Free Zone Authority allows foreign companies to establish branch operations in Jebel Ali without any requirements of local sponsorship or agency. It is now also possible to incorporate wholly-owned subsidiaries in the Jebel Ali Free Zone. Gulf nationals may also establish operations which are not incorporated.

Recently, new Free Trade Zones similar in structure to the Jebel Ali Zone were opened at Dubai International Airport and in Sharjah International Airport.

TRADE AGREEMENTS

The UAE is a member of the GCC, and as such, is subject to the GCC agreements regarding trade. These agreements are described in the section on Trade Agreements in the chapter on Bahrain.

The UAE is a signatory to the General Agreement on Tariffs and Trade (GATT).

CUSTOMS

Tariffs reflect the cost of the imported goods as indicated on the supplier's or manufacturer's invoice. In accordance with GCC initiatives, new customs duties were announced August 1, 1994, which provide a consistent duty of 4 percent on the CIF value of imports throughout the UAE.

It is expected that many items imported by the government, including personal effects, goods in transit, foodstuffs and medicines will be duty-free.

REAL ESTATE INVESTMENT

Until recently, in foreign ownership of land was not restricted in practice throughout the UAE with the exception of Abu-Dhabi and Dubai, where even transfers between Abu-Dhabi citizens are subject to government approval. A proposed federal real estate law, however, would prohibit foreigners and foreign companies (except those from other GCC states) to hold property, granting a transitional period to those who already own property. Enforcement, however, will likely take into consideration individual cases. Since land is available at nominal rents under the Organization of Industrial Affairs Act, the proposed law is generally believed to have hardly any adverse effect on foreign investment.

Building permits are granted only to construction engineers, and any construction without the appropriate permit from the local municipality will be illegal.

One of the most obvious ways to exploit land is to grant leases, particularly in the UAE, where the majority of the residents are expatriates, and, therefore, are obliged to rent. Until 1994, Sharjah was the only Emirate to have enacted a landlord and tenant law of general applicability. Sharjah's Landlord and Tenant Law of 1977, as amended in 1986, applies to almost all kind of leases. It requires leases to be registered with the municipal authorities.

Legislation regarding renting of real property in Abu-Dhabi, which was enacted in 1994, is more comprehensive than the Sharjah law, and covers all lease contracts. It requires that leases be registered with the relevant municipality. It further requires that lease agreements be in writing. Nonetheless the law also provides that the terms of a lease, though in writing may be established by all means of proof including oral or other extrinsic evidence not incorporated in the written lease.

COLLATERIZATION OF LOANS

Governed by the Federal Commercial Transactions Law, No.18 of 1993, various types of securities are available to secure loans and facilities granted by banks and financial institutions. These include a mortgage on land, a pledge on movable assets, a pledge on shares in a joint stock or limited liability company as well as a pledge on the commercial business on the whole (comprising material and intangible assets for the practice of commercial business). The latter two, which are particularly attractive to foreign investors not owning land, do not bar those pledging from managing their pledged business in the ordinary course of business.

PRIVATIZATION

All six members of GCC currently have privatization plans of some form as a means to reduce government expenditures and to turn around unprofitable state-owned businesses. The UAE especially has been testing plans for privatization on small agricultural enterprises and now hopes to open strategic sectors of its economy, such as the petrochemical industries, to private investors. Further, Abu Dhabi's Crown Prince, Sheik Khalifa bin Zayed, has ordered, in May 1997, the formation of a special committee to oversee the privatization of the power and water sectors in Abu Dhabi. The Committee, headed by the Crown Prince himself, has the authority to draft legislation and regulations governing the execution of the privatization process and the implementation of privatization plans.

As part of the UAE's ongoing commitment to the privatization process, in 1996 Abu Dhabi sold shares by public subscription in Food Co., a food products retailer and floated majority stake in the joint-stock company Abu Dhabi Shipbuilding Co. In 1997, shares were publically sold for al-Kanza Insurance Company and Oasis International Leasing Company. The General Industrial Corporation, a diversified Abu Dhabi-owned company, is also slated for sale, although the Emirate would prefer local citizens to be the major purchasers.

Unlikely to ever be sold are government holdings in the oil sector. Foreign companies Nestle and Statoil have formed a joint venture with Abu Dhabi National Oil Company in the Ruwais project. Giat Industries has proposed buying the Taweelah power and desalinization complex as part of its offset obligations.

STOCK EXCHANGE

Although public stock companies may be registered in the UAE, there is no official stock exchange at the present time. Trade is conducted informally by phone. Shares of public companies are bought and sold through private investment agencies, and share price information is based on the latest transactions.

After several delays and previous announcements, the UAE is expected to open a formal stock exchange in 1999. A proposed law is expected to provide the regulatory framework for the exchange. The UAE stock market is believed to currently have a market capitalization of more than DH 67 billion, and the primary market is also expected to become very active in the future. The Emirates Bank group has currently established the Emirates Equity Index (Emnex), a composite of thirty-one actively traded UAE stocks. There are also sub-indices for the three main market segments-banking, services and insurance. Yet to be resolved is the issue of whether to allow foreign investment in the proposed exchange. Official reports state that the UAE is keen on setting up an exchange to absorb planned privatization of service sector companies and shares in new commercial joint ventures, to be set up to offset foreign military sales to the UAE.

YEMEN

INVESTMENT LAW

In the name of the people, President of the Republic, after reviewing the constitution of the Republic of Yemen, and after the approval of the Council of Parliament

Hereby decree as follows: -

SECTION I PRELIMINARY PROVISIONS

ARTICLE 1

This law is designed to promote and regulate the investment of Yemeni, Arab and foreign capitals, subject to the provisions of this Law within the context of the state general policy, goals and priorities of the national economic and social development plan, and not in contradiction with the Islamic jurisdiction, in all of the sectors except the following:

1. **Exploration and extraction of oil**, gas and minerals that are governed by special agreements.
2. Weapons industry and explosive materials.
3. Industries that harm the environment and health.
4. Banks and exchange bureaus
5. Financial trade, importing, wholesale and retail trade.

ARTICLE 2

For the purposes of executing the provisions of this Law and unless the content shall otherwise imply, the terms and expressions appearing in this Law, shall have the meaning shown against each, as follows:

1. Republic

Republic of Yemen.

2. GOVERNMENT

The Government of the Republic of Yemen

3. MINISTER

The competent Minister.

4. Authority

The General Investment Authority established pursuant to this Law.

5. BOARD OF DIRECTORS

Board of Directors of the Authority.

6. CHAIRMAN OF BOARD

Chairman of the Board of Directors of the Authority.

7. Executive Administration

The Executive Administration of the Authority.

8. Authority President

President of the Authority Executive Administration.

9. General Manager

General Manager of the Authority

10. Competent Body

The government agency concerned, or the executive in-charge of the sector in which a project is operating or to be established or for any matters relating to a project.

11. Regulation

The executive regulations issued by the council of ministers comprising procedural provisions, directives and rules required for the execution of this Law.

12. Project

Every activity, whatever its legal status, included in the areas of investment referred to in Article (1), and authorized pursuant to the rules and procedures provided for in this Law and the decrees issued in execution thereof.

13. Registration

Registration at the Authority to establish, expand or rehabilitate or undertake project amendments including issuance of lists of exempted requirements and other certificate issued or amended by the authority.

14. Investor

Every Yemeni, Arab or foreign natural person or juridical entity desirous of investing, owning or participating in a project pursuant to the provisions of this Law.

15. Investment Company

A Company established by investor or investors to establish investment project or projects.

16. Fixed Assets

Machinery, instrument, equipment, supplies, and spare parts needed to establish, expand or rehabilitate a project including buses especially designed to transport tourists, vessels for maritime transport and fishing and furniture and furnishings for hotels and hospitals whether imported, or locally manufactured or procured.

17. Invested Capital

In application of this Law, invested capital shall mean the estimated value of foreign or local capital invested in a project and shall be determined as follows:

I. Foreign Capital

a. Freely negotiable foreign currency for investment in establishment, expansion or rehabilitating of projects, as well as freely convertible financial securities transferred to the Republic by an Arab or foreign person or persons for investment in a project.

b. Fixed assets imported from abroad for investment in a project.

c. Arab or foreign incorporeal rights such as licenses, patents and trade marks invested in a project and registered in the Republic which are protected under an international or bilateral agreement to which the Republic is a party.

d. Profits and gains earned by investment of foreign funds in the Republic and converted to capital by reinvestment in a project.

e. Land and buildings investment cost related to a project.

II.Local Capital:

a. Local currency paid in Yemeni Rials by a Yemeni natural person or a juridical entity the majority of equity holders of which is Yemeni.

b. Local incorporeal rights and assets furnished for use in establishing, expanding or rehabilitating a project.

c. Profits and gains by investment of local funds in the Republic and which are converted to capital by reinvestment in a project.

d. Evaluation of investment capital in part I (b) and (c) and in part II

(b) shall be in accordance with the rules and procedures specified in the executive regulations.

18. Service Fees

Fees charged for a service or a benefit such as port fees, storage fees and the like.

19. Expansion

Addition of new fixed assets serving to increase a project's production capacity of goods and services, or manufacture of goods previously imported, or for the purpose of producing and supplying new goods and services provided such an addition is within the scope of activity carried out by the licensed project in conformity with the rules and procedures provided for in the Law and the decrees issued in execution thereof.

20. Rehabilitating

Full or partial replacement or exchange of the fixed assets of a project by installing other new or more sophisticated assets or updating existing fixed assets by adding new assets or parts thereof to improve the efficiency of operation and improve or rehabilitate the type of goods or services produced, or make them more advanced, as the case may be.

21. Production Inputs

All materials needed to operate a project such as raw materials, intermediate commodities, spare parts and maintenance requirements appropriate to the nature of the project's activity.

22. Transfer of Technology

a. Licensing, transfer, sale, use of patents, expertise, trade marks and other incorporeal rights.

b. Furnishing expertise, technical know-how or other engineering services in any manner or form.

c. Management and marketing services and the like.

23. a. Authorized Capital

Total capital agreed upon by the founders in the company's articles of association under which they are authorized to establish the company.

b. Paid in Capital

That portion of the capital to be paid any time during the company's duration.

c. Issued Capital

That portion of the capital purposely issued to be put up for public or private subscription whether paid in at the time of subscription or over a given number of years.

24. THE LAW

The Investment Law No. 22 of 2002.

25. DAY

The official working day.

26. Recruitment Regulation

Authority recruitment regulation issued by a prime minister decree as proposed by the President of the Authority with the approval of the Board of Directors.

ARTICLE 3

a. The provisions of this Law shall be applicable to all projects registered under its provisions.

b. Yemeni, Arab or foreign capital may invest solely or in partnership in any project pursuant to the provisions of Article (1) of this law.

SECTION II GUARANTEES AND BENEFITS ACCORDED TO PROJECTS

ARTICLE 4

The State shall guarantee Yemen, Arab and foreign investor's freedom to invest in investment projects in accordance with the provisions of this Law.

ARTICLE 5

Arab and foreign capital and Arab and foreign investors shall be on a par with Yemeni capital and Yemeni investors without discrimination with respect to the rights, obligations, rules and procedures set forth in this Law and the decrees and regulations enacted in the execution thereof.

ARTICLE 6

Projects registered in accordance with the provisions of this Law, whatever their legal status, shall be deemed to be private sector projects whatever the legal nature of the contributed capitals may be.

ARTICLE 7

Investment projects and companies and Arab and foreign investors shall be entitled to purchase or lease land and buildings owned by the private sector or the State to be used for the purposes for which the project is registered under this Law; all rights and dispositions devolving on lands and buildings shall be recorded in accordance with the rules indicated by the executive regulations of this Law.

Article 8

Industrial and agricultural projects may open commercial stores, either solely or in collaboration with other projects, from which to sell their products, subject to the business of such stores being restricted to marketing such products regardless of the nationality of those participating in the capital or management of such projects.

Article 9

When making procurement for government or public establishments, a (15%) fifteen percent maximum preference in the price of the production of local agricultural and industrial projects shall be accorded over comparable imports, subject to quality being consistent with that of imported products.

Article 10

Investors shall be entitled to manage their projects in the light of their appraisal of economic conditions and the status of their businesses.

Articlc 11

No additional financial or other burdens or obligations shall be imposed resulting in violation of the principal of parity amongst private, public, cooperative and mixed sector projects carrying out the same type of activity which are established under this Law or any other Law.

Article 12

All project products shall be exempted from compulsory price regulation and profit limiting, provided project not creating or indulging in monopolistic practices or trying to fix prices in overt or implicit agreement with other producers or vendors of similar products and services.

ARTICLE 13

a. Projects may not be nationalized or seized.

b. Funds may not be blocked, frozen, or sequestered by other decision than the courts of Law.

c. 1- All or part of project real estate may not be expropriated save for the public interest according to the Law and a final court judgment and against fair compensation on the basis of such market price on the issuance date of court judgment.

2-Compensation shall be paid not later than three months from the date of the court final decision.

3-In the event of a delay in payment beyond this period, the investor is entitled to request the revaluation of the compensation on the basis of the then prevailing price of that time and place.

4-The juridical verdict execution shall be concurrent with payment of the compensation defined in the juridical verdict.

5-In cases where the invested funds, subject of such action mentioned in the pervious paragraphs are foreign funds, such compensations may be freely transferred abroad and all the procedures and restrictions concerning the regulating and banning of funds transfers outside Yemen shall not be applied.

d. Consistent with the provisions of article (71) of this Law, project registration, and any right or exemption issued and accorded under this Law may not be nullified or withdrawn except upon a final juridical verdict.

ARTICLE 14

With out prejudice to the project's rights to benefit from any monetary facilities being made available by the competent authorities in this regards, the government is under no obligation to provide any foreign currencies needed to carry out the project or to cover its authorized foreign currencies transactions or fund its foreign currencies bank accounts the project shall be entitled to obtain the foreign currencies it requires at any time from its foreign currencies accounts.

ARTICLE 15

1-An investor shall be entitled to transfer abroad his foreign currency funds and net profit earned by investment or any of its accrued returns to any transferable currency.

2-The foreign investors shall have the right to retransfer abroad their invested capital upon liquidation or disposal, and not in contradiction with the procedures provided for in Article (19) of this Law, and in case of assignment the new owner shall replace the former owner in the rights and claims and in accordance with provisions of this Law.

ARTICLE 16

Projects may import directly or through some other party, their requirements to establish, expand, rehabilitate or operate the project including fixed assets, means of transportation and production inputs appropriate to the nature of their activity. The Authority shall be the competent body to approve project exempted imported requirements. Customs authorities shall release such exempted imports on arrival promptly upon presentation of the project lists of requirements issued by the Authority without the need for any other documentation or procedures.

ARTICLE 17

a. Project shall recruit and train the maximum number of Yemenis possible, and shall present replacement plan of Yemeni cadres substituting the foreign cadres within appropriate period of time and according to the nature of project, and project may recruit non-Yemenis in accordance with the requirements stated in its requirements list and are entitled to obtain work permits and residence visa for such personnel for three-year period renewable upon a recommendation of the authority. The executive regulations shall indicate all matters relating to advertising posts available, the issue and renewal of work and residence permits for foreigners, the procedures and timing to be observed in this regard, renewal fees and fines for delays as well as cases where exemption may be made to them.

b. Projects shall be at liberty to recruit, discipline and temporary layoff personnel as may be deemed fit by project management, subject to adhering to the terms of the contract of employment and to the provisions of labor Law and the fulfillment of all rights provided for in favor of the staff member.

SECTION III CUSTOMS DUTY AND TAX EXEMPTIONS ACCORDED TO PROJECTS, PROMOTING OF LOCAL PRODUCTION AND INCRESING EXPORTS

CHAPTER I CUSTOMS DUTY &TAX EXEMPTIONS

Article 18

a. Fixed assets imported to establish, expand or rehabilitate a project shall be exempted from all types of customs duties and taxes, save for the service fees specified in Article (2) paragraph (18) of this Law subject to their being imported during the period specified in the project requirement list.

b. It shall suffice to present the project requirement lists and its list of duty free imported fixed assets and nonexempt production input requirements issued by the Authority to obtain exemption at the Customs posts and entries without the need for an approval or a declaration from any other agency.

c. The exemption provided for in paragraph (a) shall not be refused or limited in any of the following cases:
1- Should the exempted fixed assets that arrived to the port is less than its value specified in the project requirement lists certificate.

2- Should the total value of the exempted assets not exceed by more than (10%) ten percent the delivered to port (CIF) value specified in the registration certificate denominated in foreign currency.

3- Should the arrival date is delayed by less than (6) six months after the date specified.

4- Should there be minor differences in the items or types indicated in the project requirement lists according to the controls and standards indicated in the executive regulations.

d.Should there be differences in the value, timing, items or types that exceed the limits specified in paragraph (c) of this article or should the project need new fixed assets, the Authority shall be responsible for issuing amended project requirements lists and prerequisites, or changing them as it may deem appropriate in the light of convincing justifications presented to it.

e.The cost of spare parts and maintenance requirements exempted under paragraph (a) shall not exceed (10%) ten percent of the total value of the imported fixed assets to be exempted, during the permissible exemption period.

f.When deciding on exemptions for imported fixed assets, the Authority shall take into consideration preference for local production, should such production satisfy the requirements of the project with respect to specifications and prices.

g. Fisheries, livestock and agricultural production inputs shall be exempted from Customs duty throughout the execution of activity by the project, and production inputs of other projects shall be exempted (50%) fifty percent of all the customs duty throughout the execution of activity by the project including the established, licensed and registered projects

h. It shall be stipulated that in order to exempt furniture, furnishing and fixtures for hotels, hospitals and educational projects imported for the purpose of replacement and rehabilitating, that furniture, furnishings and fixtures intended to be replaced have already served a project for a period of not less than five years pursuant to the standards and basis described in the executive regulations.

ARTICLE 19

a. The projects lists of requirements and Customs exemptions provided for in Articles (16), (18) and (19) of this Law, shall be deemed to be relating to projects registered by the Authority.

b.Imported fixed assets exempted from Customs duty and taxes in accordance with Article (18) may not be disposed of , unless the project or the investor:

1. Notifies the Authority of the required disposition and the authority should not refuse the disposition unless the disposition is in contradiction with the effective regulations. Its lack of response within (30) thirty days shall be deemed as approval.
2. Pay all Customs duty and taxes on all exempted fixed assets as determined at the time of sale according to its book value.

c. Should the authority be convinced that the project suffered circumstances beyond its desires that hindered its activities or if this circumstances was the cause of project burdens, the authority may and based on an appeal from the concerned parties exempt the portion that it deemed appropriate of the fixed assets customs duty and taxes, the authority may exempt the project altogether from payment in case of disposal to another project entitled to benefit from the exemption of the same assets.

d. Projects shall maintain formal accounting records in which they shall specify the location and use of goods imported on behalf of the project pursuant to the provisions of this Law.

e. The Authority has the right to inspect the project locations and records during the working hours to verify that the use or disposal of goods and assets has taken place in accordance with the purpose designated and specified by the Authority, the executive regulation shall specify all the rules and provisions related to inspections procedures.

ARTICLE 20

Without prejudice to any more advantageous tax exemption granted, or to be granted, under any other Law, all projects shall enjoy exemption from taxes in the following manner:

    1. Projects shall be exempted from profit tax for (7) seven years and the investment projects extensions issued by the Authority shall be exempted from profit tax for seven years pursuant to this law. Starting from the date on which they commence production or activity, as the case may be. The Authority shall be the body responsible for determining the date of commencement of production or activity. The Council of Ministers, upon a recommendation by the Authority's Board of Directors, may specify certain projects or fields of activity that shall be entitled to
    2. benefit from the exemption provided for above for periods ranging from (7) seven to (10) ten years as the Council may deem fit in accordance with the exigencies of the public interest. To this end, the Authority shall issue periodic lists of projects subject to the provisions of this paragraph.

2. Projects shall be exempted from the real estate tax.
3. Contracts establishing projects, and all project related contracts until implementation is complete, shall be exempted from the notarization fees, the Authority determining which of such contracts are project related as well as the date of completing the implementation.
4. Projects shall be exempted for five years as of the date of commencement of production or activity, as the case may be, from all taxes and fees specified under the provisions of Article (64) of this Law on the proceeds from licensing the use of imported technology utilized in the project.
    1. a. Interest on loans granted by local and foreign banks operating in Yemen to finance establishing or expanding or rehabilitating projects shall be exempted from (50%) fifty percent of taxes levied thereon.
        1. Dividends distributed by projects established under this Law shall be exempted from income tax.

2. The taxation authorities concerned shall implement the foregoing exemptions promptly upon presentation of the project tax exemption certificate.

Article 21

1. The exemption referred to in Paragraph (1) of Article (1) shall be extended for an additional two years for each of the following project conditions which are realized:

a.Should the project be established in investment zone (b) referred to in Article (22) of this Law or should project establish in this zone not less than (50%) fifty percent of the total project component.

b.Should the project be owned by a joint stock company in which public subscription of Yemeni nationals is no less than (25%) twenty five percent of the paid in capital.

c.Should the proportion of the local component of fixed assets exceed (25%) twenty five percent of the total value of the project's total fixed assets, the Authority shall be the competent body to increase such proportion. In all cases the total period of exemption granted in accordance with the provisions of this Article shall not exceed sixteen years starting from the commencement of the project production or activity.

1. Should a project incur losses during profit tax exemption years or any one year thereof, losses accumulated during such year (s) in which they occurred shall be deducted and carried forward for no more than three years, with effect from the first year following the exemption years, subject to submitting tax declaration from certified public accountant approving the accounts for those years.
2. In addition to the provisions of Article (20) and the preceding paragraphs and the provisions of this article, projects upon expansion shall be accorded the same tax exemptions for the same duration according to the value added to the expansion relative to project total capital registered at the authority.

Article 22

a. In order to benefit from the increased exemption provided for in paragraph (a) of the preceding Article, the Republic shall be divided into two investment zones (a) and (b) according to standards specified by the Council of Ministers for each. Zone boundaries shall be delineated by decree of the Council of Ministers. The council of Ministers may amend such boundaries every five years according to the development exigencies and requirements therein.

b.Upon a proposal by the Board of Directors, the Council of Ministers may exclude one or more sectors in any investment zone, or any part thereof and accord such sector, or part thereof, the exemptions granted in the other zone or any sector therein.

Article 23

For projects to benefit from the tax exemptions provided for in Articles (20) paragraph (a) (1) and article (21) of this law, the following conditions shall be met by the projects:

1. With the exclusion of construction, agricultural and small projects --in which a number of employees not less than ten-- the value of fixed assets shall be no less than Y.R. fifty millions, or the equivalent thereof in freely convertible foreign currency. In calculating such value, funds invested in land and buildings shall
2. not be included. The Authority shall be the competent Authority concerned to determine such value.

2. The number of housing units in housing projects shall be no less than (50) fifty units built to the specifications of, and on the terms specified and approved by the Ministry of Works and Urban Planning, and shall be reserved for home ownership or rental to third parties.
3. Tourist establishments shall be rated at no lower than three stars according to the competent authority ratings.

CHAPTER II PROMOTION OF LOCAL PRODUCTION AND INCREASING EXPORTS

Article 24

With a view to protecting local production and upon a recommendation of the Authority, the Customs Tariff Committee should impose or increase Customs duty on the import of made-up goods competing with local production that rely on local material on it's production and subject to the following being taken into consideration:

1. Consumer interest in the specifications of such goods, in particular with respect to quality and price.
2. Protection shall not entail the creation of any form of monopoly or control of the encouraged commodities.

Article 25

a. With the exclusion of service fees, the minimum level of fees and duty charged on imported end production commodities which are comparable to locally-produced commodities shall be no less than the total fees and duty charged on production inputs and on local production during its various stages.

b.In the case of any increase over the fees proportion referred to in the preceding paragraph, the relevant project shall be granted a reduction in the total fees and duty referred to, equal to the increase by means of a Discount Voucher issued by the Authority to the project in accordance with terms and procedures to be indicated in the executive regulations. The Discount Voucher shall indicate the reduction granted and production inputs benefiting there from.

c. It shall suffice to present the Discount Voucher given to the project by the Authority to obtain the reduction at the Customs point and the Tax Authority as the case may be without need for any further approval or procedure.

d. When the increase diminishes or is eliminated as a result of amendments to the tariff schedule or any other factor, the reduction granted to the project shall be reduced by the same rate as the diminishing difference, or shall end when the difference ends, as the case may by, according to a decree to be issued by the Authority to that effect.

Article 26

Any existing project that exports all or part of its production abroad shall be entitled to the following:

1. Exemption from all fees or taxes of any kind levied on exports.
2. Exemption from production and consumption excise or any other taxes levied on goods and services exported abroad which are produced by projects registered under the Law.
3. Exemption of tax payable on profits earned from export revenues after termination of the exemption period accorded to the project, subject to such profit being transferred in foreign currency to the Republic through an authorized bank.
    1. Recovery of all Customs fees and duties of whatever kind paid on imported inputs included in that portion of production exported.
    2. Should it not be possible to make the recovery in cash, the Authority shall issue to the project a Rebate Voucher to the extent of the amount due to it, which the project has the right to use to settle Customs fees and duty payable on future imports. Use of the Rebate Voucher in such case shall be deemed to be a cash payment. The executive regulations shall specify the procedures, timing and rules to be observed to recover customs fees and duty receivable, the issuing of Rebate Vouchers and their use pursuant to the provisions of this article.
4. Export on its own or through an intermediary without license or need for registration in the Exporters Registry.

SECTION IV GENERAL INVESTMENT AUTHORITY

Article 27

a. Establishment of a General Investment Authority as a juridical entity with an autonomous financial status and accountability to the Prime Minister.

b. The Authority's head office shall be in Sana'a and it shall have branches in locations within the Republic designated by the prime Minister, exercising the Authority's functions in the manner to be specified in the decrees establishing them in the light of controls and principles to be set forth in the executive regulations. The Authority may also have offices outside the Republic created by decree of the Chairman of the Board of Directors upon a recommendation by the President of the Authority and with the approval of the Board of Directors.

c. The Authority shall have an Executive Administration composed of specialists and administrators appointed in accordance with the terms and conditions Stated in the Authority recruitment policy.

d. Appointment of the President and General Manager of the Authority shall be by Republican Decree.

e. Offices shall be set up in the Authority representing :

1. Ministry of Industry and Trade.
2. Ministry of Works and Urban Planning .
3. Ministry of Public Health and Population.
4. Ministry of Social Affairs and Labor.
5. Passports Authority.
6. Customs Authority. 7.Taxation Authority .

8. General Tourism Authority. and other specialized agencies that the council of Ministers decides shall have offices representing them in the Authority. These offices shall have direct authority to issue all permits and approvals required of such agencies for the purpose of establishing or operating projects by virtue of the provisions of this Law. The offices shall be administratively responsible to the Authority and subject to its direct orientation and oversight as may be specified in this connection by the Authority's bylaws in this regard.

Article 28

a.The Authority shall execute the provisions of this Law and to this end may:

1. Receive applications made by investors or projects and register them in accordance with the rules, procedures and conditions specified by virtue of the provisions of this Law.
2. Issue exempted project requirement lists related to carrying out, expanding, rehabilitating or operating projects, and to the rights, exemptions and benefits accorded to them pursuant to the provisions of this Law.
3. Obtain, on behalf of projects sponsors, all approvals needed to carry out and operate their projects.
4. Assist projects in dealing with agencies concerned to overcome any impediments or obstacles facing project implementation and operation.
5. Allot lands needed to establish projects and sign the relevant contracts on behalf of the agencies concerned. Such agencies are obliged to furnish the Authority with all maps and information concerning land available for such purposes, including rules and conditions of contracting therefore.
6. Study the Laws, regulations and decrees relating to investment in the Republic, as well as regional and international agreements dealing with investment matters and make appropriate proposals in that regard.
7. Make necessary appraisals of troubled projects in coordination with the competent agencies concerned, and make appropriate proposals to remedy any impediments or obstacles encountered.

8. Conduct research relating to investment and the problems and obstacles hampering effective promotion and orientation of investment to serve development purposes and make appropriate proposals in this regard.
9. Identify investment opportunities and viable projects available for investment in the Republic, and promote them in the likely prospective investors mediums in the Republic and abroad.
10. Prepare and publish lists of feasible investment opportunities and projects to which Yemeni, Arab and foreign capital could be invited to invest pursuant to the provisions of this Law.
    1. Collect and publish information and statements needed to familiarize investors with the investment climate in the Republic
    2. and facilitating the acquisition of studies, information and data needed for project establishment by potential investors.
11. Keep a record of invested capital in the units of currency in which received, if cash, valued in kind subscriptions, and review the valuation of invested capital upon disposal or liquidation for re-export or transfer abroad.
12. Approve the transfer of net profits and retransfer of capital abroad after examining the documents concerning a project's financial position and verifying, in particular, that reserves and allocations provided for in Law and in recognized technical and accounting practices have been set aside, and that taxes have been paid upon completion of the exemption period provided for in this Law.
13. Carry out other duties and functions assigned to the Authority in matters relating to investment or project transactions and related issues.

b.The Authority may sue in its own name, and defend itself in suits against it, in all matters relating to its business and duties concerning execution of the provisions of this Law.

c. The Authority shall have the competence to own and dispose of any moveable or non-moveable property in accordance with the Expropriation Law, as well as to sign contracts and transactions needed for it to carry out its duties.

d.The Authority shall have the competence to purchase or lease lands for the purpose of establishing projects, industrial area's or complexes and investment zones that may be set up in accordance with the provisions of this Law. It may also, with the approval of the council of Ministers upon a recommendation by the Authority President, reserve and expropriate lands that it deems necessary to achieve this end in conformity with the Expropriation Law and against fair compensation to its owners on the basis of the price for that time and place. The Authority may re-grant interested projects and investors the ownership or leasing of such lands according to the principles and conditions approved by the Board of Directors ensuring that prices, rents and terms of ownership or lease are encouraging.

e. The Authority, by resolution of the President of the Authority upon the request of the parties concerned, may assist in all or part of the cost of studies and research relating to exploring investment opportunities and project feasibility or investment conditions and issues in the Republic which the President of the Authority considers to be beneficial in facilitating the Authority's business and achieving its objectives in execution of policy endorsed by the Board in this regard.

Article 29

The Authority shall have a Board of Directors composed as follows:

1. Prime Minister Chairman
2. Senior Vice-Premier Vice-Chairman
3. Foreign Minister member
4. Minister of Industry and trade. member
5. Minister of Petroleum and Mineral Resources member
6. Minister of Planning and Development member
7. Minister of Finance member

Article 30

The Board of Directors shall be deemed to be the supreme authority overseeing the affairs of the Authority, disposing of its business and formulating the policies it pursues. It may take such decisions as it deems necessary to achieve the purposes for which it was established. In addition to the powers and competence provided for in this Law, the Board shall, in particular, carry out the following:

1. Formulate Policies relating to the Authority's competencies in the context of overall State policy.
2. Approve plans and programs for the Authority activity in the context of State general plan.
    1. Act to develop the Authority's activity on basis of modern technical and administrative systems including the standards, methods and rules of project appraisal in accordance with the provisions of this Law, and keeping pace with the various
    2. developments that have impact on the reality of the national economy and requirements of State general policy.
3. Consider the periodic reports presented by the President of the Authority on progress of work in the Authority and matters relating to the investment conditions, climate and issues in the Republic and take whatever action is required when needed.
4. Consider the financial position of the Authority and approve its draft annual budget and closing Statement of accounts.
5. Approve the contracting of loans and credit facilities offered to the Authority under government, bank or specialized financial institution guarantees in accordance with established rules and regulations, subject to the purposes thereof being restricted to financing the Authority's activities to the extent of the competence provided for under the provisions of Article (28).
6. Perform the tasks assigned to it by the Government in investment related matters.
7. Consider matters presented by the Chairman of the Board relating to investment issues that are within the competence of the Authority, so that decisions needed in this regard may be taken when necessary.
8. Determine fees for the services provided by the Authority to projects and investors.

Article 31

a. The Authority's Executive Administration shall execute the policies and resolutions of the Board of Directors and conduct of all the Authority's duties provided for in Article (28). It shall also exercise all competence vested in the Authority by virtue of the provisions of this Law, save those wholly retained by the Board of Directors, in conformity with all the rules, procedures and provisions provided for in this Law and the regulations and resolutions enacted in execution thereof.

b. Authority personnel designated by decree of the Minister of Justice in agreement with the President of the Authority shall be vested with the powers of judicial enforcement to the extent of their competence.

Article 32

a. The Board of Directors shall meet at least once every three months at the invitation of the chairman, or in the event of his absence, the Vice-chairman. The invitation shall be addressed to Board members no less than three days before the date of a meeting. In urgent cases such period need not be adhered to. The Board may also meet at the request of one third of members should this be necessary. A quorum shall be constituted by the attendance of a majority of members. Resolutions shall be adopted by a majority of the members present. In case of a tie, the session's Chairman shall cast the deciding vote. The executive regulations shall determine the internal rules and procedures for the conduct of Board of Directors business.

b. The Board of Directors may constitute one or more committees composed of its members to which it may delegate some of its competencies or assign to perform certain tasks within its purview.

Article 33

The President of the Authority shall oversee the execution of the general policy formulated by the Board of Directors and shall, in particular, perform the following functions:

a.Oversee the management of the Authority, and control and develop work processes to ensure achievement of its objectives.

b. Arrange and prepare for meetings of the Board of Directors and monitor execution of Board resolutions.

c. Appoint staff according to the provisions of the Law and the Authority recruitment policy.

d. Form internal committees to perform certain tasks to assist in achieving authority objectives.

e. Oversee the preparation of draft plans and programs relating to Authority activities for presentation to the Board of Directors.

f.Represent the Authority in litigation and in relations with third parties.

g. Oversee preparation of the Authority's proposed budget and closing Statement of accounts.

h. Oversee Authority offices located within the Republic and abroad.

I.Exercise all other authorities vested in him in accordance with the provisions of this Law and as may be assigned to him by the Chairman of the Board of Directors.

Article 34

a. The General Manager shall act as Vice President of the Authority and shall assume responsibility in case of the President's absence.

b.The General Manager shall be responsible before the president of the authority for managing the Authority's Executive administration and disposing of its business and executing the President of the authority directives according to the policies approved by the Board of Directors and shall exercise the following authorities:

1. Oversee all Authority departments, divisions and units and coordinate their activities.
2. Conduct Authority business administratively, technically and financially and develop working processes to achieve the Authority's objectives.
3. Enter into contracts on behalf of the Authority to the extent prescribed in the Authority's bylaws, within the limits of his authority, or as may be vested in him by the Board of Directors or the president of the Authority.
4. Assist the President of the Authority to execute the resolutions of the Board of Directors.
5. Exercise all the authorities vested in him by the Chairman of the Board, the Board of Directors or the President of the Authority.
6. Prepare periodic reports on Authority activity and level of performance and make the necessary proposals for improvement.
7. Prepare draft plans and programs relating to Authority activities for presenting such to the President of the Authority.

Article 35

a.The Authority shall have an autonomous annual budget drawn up and executed according to rules specified in the authority executive regulations without being restricted to provisions relating to the budgets of public organizations and authorities.

b.Authority funds shall be deemed public property, and may not become the property of third parties by prescription and shall be disposed of as indicated in the Authority bylaws.

Article 36

The resources of the Authority shall be made up of the following:

a.Revenues earned in consideration for services rendered or fees collected in the course of the Authority's activity in accordance with the terms and conditions provided for under the provisions of this Law.

b. Loans and credit facilities contracted for by the Authority and permissible by Islamic Sharia and pursuant to the procedures and conditions provided for in Article 30 (6) of this Law.

c.Grants and donations approved by the Board of Directors.

d.Allocations earmarked by the government in the Authority's budget.

Article 37

The Authority's bylaws shall be enacted by a decree of the prime Minister and shall include a definition of the Authority's administrative divisions and the functions of each, as well as all

SECTION V PROJECT REGISTRATION AND EXEMPTION PROCEDURES

Article 38

a. No Investment project may be established, expanded or rehabilitated under the provisions of this Law only after registration at the Authority on the basis of an application submitted to it in writing on the form devised for that purpose at the authority. The Authority shall decide acceptance or rejection of the application within (15) days following the date on which the application was presented complete with all documents and information required. The Authority may extend such period for not more than (10) additional days in the case of applications relating to the construction of large- scale projects.

b. Agencies concerned shall take their decisions approving, rejecting or requiring amendments within a period not exceeding (15) days following referral of the request to them by the Authority. The Authority may take a decision on an application for a registration without referring to the agency concerned and without requiring its approval in any of the cases indicated in the executive regulations.

c. Lack of a reply within the periods specified in the preceding paragraph (a) and (b) shall be considered approval. In case of rejection, the decision shall be substantiated. The party concerned may appeal the decision in accordance with the provisions of Section VII of this Law.

d. The executive regulations shall indicate the application form and papers and documents that must be presented for a decision to be taken in accordance with the provisions of this Article.

Article 39

1. The tax exemptions provided for in Articles 20 (a) (1,2,4) and article (21) of this Law shall be granted according to the following procedures:

a.The Authority shall be notified when the installation of fixed assets in the projects is completed and the date of commencement of production or pursuit of activity before any products are put on the market or services made available to the public, as the case may be.

b. An application, with all substantiating evidence of entitlement to the exemption in accordance with the provisions of this Law, shall be presented to the Authority within 90 days following commencement of production or pursuit of project activity.

c.The Authority may examine the project and its records and assets to verify the conditions needed for Tax Exemption requested.

d. The Authority shall issue, within (60) days following receipt of all documents needed, the Tax Exemption Certificates granted to the project.

1. The taxation authorities concerned shall execute the exemption promptly upon presentation of the certificate mentioned in Paragraph (1-d) of this Article.
2. The executive regulations shall determine the exemption application form and the supporting documents issued by the Authority in this respect.

Article 40

Any project may be expanded or rehabilitated according to the following procedures:

a. The application submitted to the Authority to register a project may provide that the project will be executed in phases, subject to the application including all information needed, as the case may be. In such case the project registration certificate may indicate that registration certificate cover all phases needed.

b. Project shall register at the Authority in case of undertaking any project expansion or rehabilitating. Decisions on application for expansion and rehabilitating shall be governed by the same rules and procedures needed for applications to establish projects.

c. Projects expansion and rehabilitating shall enjoy the guaranties, rights and exemptions provided for in this law.

ARTICLE 41

a. A register of investment projects governed by the provisions of this Law shall be established in the Authority to record all basic data and information relating to registered projects and all modifications thereto. The executive regulations shall specify procedure and fees for registration, modification, deletion, and issue to those concerned or publish of formal extracts of the official record or publish them.

b. Investors shall notify the Authority of any major modification taking place to registered projects. A major modification shall be any change affecting how it is treated according to the provisions of this Law. In the event of any major modification occurring in a registered project prior to its implementation; investors shall be required to suspend such modifications pending completion of formalities relating to a decision on the modification. Major modifications in registered projects shall be governed by the same procedures as those governing the project registrations upon establishment specified in this Law and the executive regulations thereto.

SECTION VI INVESTMENT COMPANIES

ARTICLE 42

Without prejudice to the provisions of Article (43) of this Law, the establishment of an investment company and the amendment of its articles of association shall be upon a decree issued by the Authority President pursuant to the provisions contained in this section.

When established, investment companies shall take any of the legal forms provided for in the Companies Law and the civil Law, subject to joint stock companies that put up their shares for public subscription or limited stock partnership companies satisfying the following conditions:

Founders shall number no less than two and the founders' subscription to capital shall be no less than 20%.

Non-Yemeni subscription to capital shall not exceed (45%) forty five percent of paid in capital. That proportion may, by decree of the council of Ministers, be increased according to exigencies of the public interest upon a proposal by the Board of Directors.

Article 43

The founding of a joint stock company putting up its shares for public subscription, or amendment of its statutes, shall be by resolution of the Board of Directors of the Authority as presented by the Authority's Executive body in accordance with the provisions of this Law.

Article 44

Joint stock companies that do not put up their shares for public subscription companies may be founded, or may amend their statutes, by a decision of the president of the Authority in accordance with the provisions of this Law.

Article 45

The resolution licensing the foundation of a company or amending its statutes or articles of incorporation shall be issued within (15) days following the date of submission of a completed application which shall meet all the conditions Stated in Article (42) of this Law within

(45) days for companies Stated in Article (43) of the Law. Should such period elapse without issuance of a resolution thereon the company shall be deemed to have been legally founded and the amendment approved and publishable in the official gazette. It shall be required that registration formalities pursuant to regulations in force be completed without objection.

Article 46

Paid-in capital of joint stock companies that put their shares up for public subscription shall be no less than (20 %) twenty percent of capital.

Article 47

Capital of an investment company may be paid wholly in foreign, local currency or in both, as may be agreed upon by the investors. The company's statutes, articles of incorporation, books and records shall show each investor's subscription to company capital in the currency invested. A company may also issue shares, stock in either or both foreign and local currency.

Article 48

a.A joint stock company's shares shall be nominal or to bearer, but shall remain nominal until the full value is paid in. A nominal share holder upon full payment of the value may request that the shares be converted to bearer bonds unless otherwise provided for in company statutes.

b.No share's nominal value may exceed Y.R. 50.000 or the equivalent thereof in freely convertible foreign currency.

Article 49

A joint stock company may issue, stocks and shares at a premium subject to such fact being recorded in the company's establishment instruments at the Authority.

Article 50

A joint stock company shall be managed by a Board of Directors, company statutes determining members number which shall be no less than three. A member of board of directors may appoint someone other than himself as his representative in the membership of the Board regardless of the subscription in the company or nationality of such proxy. Furthermore there shall be nothing to prevent a person being a member of the Board of more than one public joint stock company.

Article 51

Representation of shareholders on a company's Board of Directors shall be proportional to the number of shares held, regardless of any provision providing otherwise in other Laws and regulations.

Article 52

A joint stock company's statutes may provide for the following:

a.Authorized capital upon foundation may amount to three multiples the issued capital.

b. Issued capital may be increased by issuing new shares, pursuant to a resolution by the company's Board of Directors, to the extent of the authorized capital subject to all previous issues being subscribed to.

Article 53

Without prejudice to the provisions of Articles (3) and (42) of this Law, Yemeni and non-Yemeni subscriptions shall not be governed by any specific proportion in investment companies regardless of any provisions providing otherwise in any other Law.

Article 54

Investment company shares and founders' shares may not be circulated during the first two years of a company's duration save with the approval of the Authority's Board of Directors.

Article 55

Projects that take the form of joint stock investment companies may invest part of their capital in subsidiary projects outside the scope of this Law, as may be decided by the Authority's Board of Directors. Guarantees, benefits and exemptions provided for in this Law shall not apply to such subsidiary projects or invested funds, without prejudice to the rights of such project to benefit from any guarantees, benefits or exemptions provided for under other Laws.

Article 56

Without prejudice to the companies law and commercial register, all investment companies shall indicate the following information in all their documents, correspondence and any literature they distribute to the public:

a.Company name.

b.Legal status.

c.Address of company Head office.

d. Commercial Registry number.

Article 57

All matters not regulated by an expressed provision in this Section shall conform to the provisions of the Companies Law and the authority shall replace the ministry in executing the indicated law provisions upon the investment companies.

SECTION VII ADMINISTRATIVE APPEALS AND SETTLEMENT OF INVESTMENT DISPUTES

Article 58

The Authority and all other parties concerned shall settle all problems or obstacles encountered by investors or investment projects and shall seek to solve them by all expeditious and appropriate means. The executive regulations of this Law shall indicate all rules and procedures regulating such action.

Article 59

Investors and projects may appeal decisions by the authorities concerned infringing on their interests in accordance with the provisions of this Law, by applying in writing to the decision making authority or to the President of the Authority within thirty days following notification of the decision. The party appealed to shall decide on the appeal within twenty days of its submission. Elapse of such time without reply shall be deemed an acceptance of the appeal and in such case the party appealed to should rectify its decision in consistency with the appeal submitted by the investor. If appeal was rejected, the appellant shall be entitled to submit his appeal to the Prime Minister who shall take a decision thereon in ten days or refer it to the Council of Ministers to take such decision as may be appropriate within no more than thirty days.

Article 60

An appeal regarding decision provided for in the preceding Article may be filed directly with the competent court after exhausting the appeal before the president of the authority or the prime minister, and may be referred to an arbitration tribunal to be agreed upon without the need for continuing with the administrative appeal.

Article 61

Without prejudice to the right to resort to Yemeni courts, investment disputes relating to the execution of the provisions of this Law arising between the Government and a project may be settled by arbitration resorting to any of the following procedures as may be selected by the investor or the project:

1. The Standardized Agreement for Arab Capital Investment in Arab Countries.
2. The International Convention for the Settlement of Investment Disputes between the State and the nationals of another State.
3. Any international or bilateral agreement to which the Republic is a party.
4. Commercial arbitration rules and procedures of the United Nations' Commission on International Trade Law at the nearest regional center for international commercial arbitration using such rules.
5. Rules and procedures of arbitration within the Republic of Yemen.

Article 62

a. Settlement of disputes arising between investors in a project or between a project and other projects shall be through the medium of either Yemeni courts of Law or arbitration on the basis of a written agreement between the parties concerned executed in advance or at any other time. It may also be part of any other written agreement including the documents establishing a company. The arbitration tribunal shall be composed of a member selected by each of the two parties to the dispute and a third member agreed upon by the two parties concerned, who shall preside over the tribunal. Should they fail to agree on his selection or fail to delegate some other person, party or organization to make such selection, the president of the Authority shall make a selection.

b.With the exception of that which is explicitly provided for in the provisions of this Law and the executive regulations thereto, or as may be explicitly agreed upon by the parties concerned or as may be decided by the majority vote of the arbitrators, arbitration may be conducted according to the rules for conducting commercial arbitration of the United Nations commission on International Trade Law prevailing at that date.

c. Disputes relating to agreements on the transfer of technology shall be applicable to the parties concerned before the courts of Law in the Republic and all parties involved shall be entitled to settle disputes by arbitration in accordance with the provisions of this Article.

Article 63

Decisions reached by arbitrators issued in accordance with the rules set forth in this Section shall have the same power and effectiveness of the rulings of Yemeni courts and the courts of competence in the Republic shall order that they be enforced promptly upon receipt of a request in writing to this effect from the party concerned.

SECTION VIII OBLIGATION OF INVESTORS AND PROJECT SPONSORS: VIOLATIONS AND SUBSEQUENT PENALTIES

Article 64

a.At the end of the exemption period provided for in Article 20 (4), projects licensed to use foreign technology in production or in the pursuit of their activity against regular royalties paid to the foreign licensers shall deduct and pay to the competent taxation authorities 10 percent of such royalties for the following:

1. Rights to benefit from trade mark licenses.
2. Rights to benefit from patent licenses.
3. Rights to benefit from technical know-how.
4. Rights to benefit from management know-how and other services rendered in the Republic.

b. The tax percentage specified in paragraph (a) shall be in effect except where otherwise provided for in any international or bilateral agreement in the field of transfer and use of technology to which the government of the Republic is a party with the country of the foreign licenser for the technology used in the project.

Article 65

Without prejudice to the obligations provided for in other Articles of this Law, investors and project sponsors shall:

a.Maintain regular accounts according to project requirements and of production or services rendered.

b. Maintain separate accounts when expanding projects or merging with other projects if either or any of them benefits from entitlements or exemptions granted in accordance with Law.

c. Furnish any lists, data or documents relating to project execution and operation requested by the Authority within the time limit specified in the request.

d.Refrain from disposing of lands owned or leased to the project by the Authority for purposes other than those for which licensed without the prior written consent of the Authority. In case of violation, the contract signed with the investor or project in this regard shall be deemed to be void and all relevant rights shall revert to the Authority and be registered in its name.

e. Allow an Authority employee, duly authorized in writing, the opportunity to enter the project during normal working hours of business to examine project records, books, fixed assets and inventory of production inputs and the like. The project shall furnish any clarifications requested to verify that obligations are being met in accordance with this Law.

Article 66

1. The Authority shall accord the registered project therein specified period to execute the project and shall state in the registration certificate the designated date of the commencement of the project or the production.
2. Should an investor fail to begin carrying out the relevant project within the period specified by the authority, the Authority shall notify the investor of the expiry of such period and Notice shall specify a further period of time for the investor to begin implementing the project.
3. Should the additional grace time provided for in the preceding paragraph elapse and the investor fails to begin implementing the project, the Authority shall warn the investor of registration cancellation within the period specified in the warning if the investor fail to begin project implementation during this period.
4. Should the project not be implemented within the period specified in the registration certificate and upon presenting convincing reasons , the Authority may grant a further period of time not exceeding two years if applied for at least two months prior to the deadline of the start of implementation.
5. Should the registered project be unable to conduct its activities in the date specified in the registration certificate and failed to present convincing reasons to the Authority of this delay, the delayed time shall be deducted from the original exemption period granted to the project pursuant to Articles of this law except projects with a cost of no less than one billion Y.R which their exception shall be extended to five years if they pay half of the annual fees for every extended years.
6. Should an investor have begun carrying out the project, the Authority may institute proceedings to cancel the project registration, or wholly or partially withdraw the rights or exemptions accorded after due warning and notice to the investor or project in the following cases:

a. Should the registration or rights and exemptions were granted to the project on the basis of false information which has considerably influenced the decision of it's registration and granting those rights

b.Should the project use any right or exemption granted to it under the provisions of this Law for other than the purposes specified therefore in violation of the provisions of Article 19 (a) of this Law.

c.Should the project or investor, as the case may be, fail to fulfill any of the conditions listed in the registration certificate, as may be decided by the Law and its regulation.

d.Should the project deliberately violate, or deal leniently with a substantial violation of, any provision of this Law, as may be decided by the Law and its executive regulation.

e.Should the project suspend activity for longer than one year without justification acceptable to the Authority.

1. An investor or project whose registration has been canceled or whose rights and exemptions have been withdrawn may apply for a new registration or restoration of withdrawn rights one year after the cancellation decision is taken.
2. When convincing reasons are present, the Authority may accord a project an operations testing period not exceeding four months at the end of which, for the purposes of this Law, operations will immediately be deemed to have actually begun.

The executive regulations shall specify the rules needed to determine the date of commencement of operations of a project if several production lines for various goods are included.

Article 67

a. Without prejudice to any more stringent penalty provided for in any other Law, a person who deliberately furnishes false, misleading or forged information and data to the Authority, and to the agency concerned with the project, or who acts leniently in such regard, for the purpose of obtaining a registration, rights or exemptions pursuant to this Law shall be punished a fine of no less than Y.R. 50.000 and no more than Y.R. 500.000 and shall refund all fees and taxes from which the relevant project was exempted. The same penalty shall apply in the event of failure to report any modification in the project with the intent to mislead in violation of the provisions of Article 41 (b) of this Law, provided the violations are terminated. Further more a person who uses the exemption certificates granted under the provisions of this Law for other than the purposes specified therefore in violation of the provisions of Article 19 (a) shall be liable to the same penalty.

b. (1) A person who violates any of the provision of Articles (65,54,19) of this law shall be punished with a fine of no less than Y.R. 50.000 and no more than Y.R. 500.000, with due consideration of such violation.

(2) A person who violates any of the provision of Articles (39,56) of this law shall be punished with a fine no less than Y.R. 20,000 and no more than Y.R. 100,000, with due consideration of the violation.

c. Disposal of exempted, imported fixed assets in violation of the provisions of paragraph (b) Article (19) shall entail payment of double the fees and taxes payable on their importation at the time of such disposal.

d.In any of the violations previously listed, any project or company manager or official aware thereof without notifying the authorities concerned, shall be subject to the same penalty as provided for each type of violation.

e. No public proceedings shall be instituted in respect of any of the preceding violations save at the request, or with the approval in writing, of the president of the Authority. The President of the Authority or whomever he may delegate may arrange a reconciliation in such public proceedings against payment of the maximum amount of the fine provided for if the violation is proved.

f.All amounts ruled for violations of the provisions of this Law, or which the violator may pay by a way of reconciliation, shall revert to the Authority.

Article 68

a. All Authority and competent agency personnel shall perform their duties in such a way as shall facilitate completion of all dealings relating to projects and their implementation and operation. Anyone causing harm to a project or delaying or impeding its transactions, implementation or operation without clear justification shall be disciplined according to the disciplinary code in the public Law including termination of service.

b. Authority and competent agency personnel authorized to review project business shall maintain the confidentiality of information and documents available to them by reason of their duties and shall use such information solely in application of the provisions of this Law. Anyone violating this provision shall be punished in accordance with Laws in force, including termination of service. The executive regulations shall specify the nature of information and data to be considered confidential for the purposes of this paragraph.

SECTION IX TRANSITIONAL PROVISIONS

Article 69

Operating projects not accorded the exemptions and benefits provisioned in this Law or Laws repealed there under shall be entitled to obtain investment registration for their expansion or rehabilitating; and for project expansion and rehabilitating the same obligations and benefits contained in this Law relating to expansion and rehabilitating of register projects shall be applicable.

Article 70

All agencies concerned shall establish in their structures investment sub-departments or liaison units to coordinate with the Authority in respect of investment transactions and execution of related procedures devolving upon them by virtue of the provisions of this Law and the regulations and decrees enacted in execution thereof.

SECTION X GENERAL PROVISIONS

ARTICLE 71

a. At least the following provisions shall be amended by decree of the Council of Ministers upon presentation by the Board of Directors in accordance with considerations required by the public interest every (5) years :

1. The amounts and terms provided for in Articles (21 and 23).
2. The amounts, terms and standards provided for in Articles (42, 46, and 48 (b)).
3. Non-Yemeni capital subscription provided for in Article 42 (b).

b.Amendment of these lists provided for in Article 3 (b) and 20 (a & b), will be by a decree of the Council of Ministers upon presentation by the Board of Directors for considerations required by the public interest and according to the conditions and rules set by the Authority's Board of Directors.

c.Any of the amendments provided for in the preceding paragraphs

(a) and (b) shall not involve:

1. Infringement of the guarantees, exemptions and rights accorded in accordance with the provisions of this Law.
2. Retroactive withdrawal of any guarantees, rights or exemptions granted to the project registered according to provisions of this Law, before the amendment becomes effective.

Article 72

All notices and correspondence shall be in writing, the executive regulations specifying the timing and manner of receipt.

Article 73

All projects shall pay to the Authority in return for its administrative and technical services the following:

a. Fees at a rate of (three quarters of one per thousand) of the value of exempted fixed assets and exempted production inputs upon registration issuance.

b.Annual fees at a rate of (three quarters of one per thousand) of the value of exempted fixed assets intended to be used for the establishment, expansion or rehabilitating of a project which shall be valid throughout the period of tax exemption starting from the date on which a project commence production or a activity.

c. Government shall cover investment promotion expenses locally and at the international levels.

Article 74

The executive regulations to this decree of Law shall be enacted by prime minister decree based on presentation from the Broad of Directors within a period not exceeding (90) days following enactment of this decree of Law.

Article 75

a. Any provision conflicting with the provisions of this Law shall be repealed. The provisions of this Law shall prevail should they conflict with provisions of other Laws, bylaws and regulations.

b.Investment Law and organization No. (18) of 1975 enacted in Sana'a and Investment Law No. (5) of 1990 enacted in Aden and Investment law No. (22) of 1991 and its amendments by the republican decree No. (14) of 1995 and Law No. (29) of 1997 enacted in Sana'a shall be repealed with effect from date of entry into force of this Law.

Article 76

This law shall come into force since its date of issue and shall be published in the official Gazette. Issued at the Presidency of the Republic - Sana'a

SUPPLEMENTS

PRINCIPAL ISLAMIC BANKS

Albania
Arab Albanian Islamic Bank, Tirana
Algeria
Banque Albaraka D'Algerie, Algiers
Australia
MCCA (Muslim Community Co-operative, Australia) MCCU (Muslim Community Credit Union)
Bahamas
Akida Islamic Bank International Ltd Bank Al Taqwa Ltd Dar al Mal al Islami Trust, Nassau Islamic Investment Company of the Gulf Ltd, Nassau. Istishara Consulting Trust, Bahamas Massraf Faysal Islamic Bank & Trust, Bahamas Ltd.
Bahrain
ABC Investment & Services Co EC Al Amin Co. for Securities and Investment Funds Albaraka Islamic Investment Bank Arab Islamic Bank E.C Bahrain Islamic Bank Bsc. Bahrain Islamic Investment Co. Bsc. Closed Bahrain Institute of Banking & Finance Bank Melli Iran Chase Manhattan Bank N.A. Citi Islamic Investment Bank (Citicorp) Dallah Albaraka (Europe) Ltd Dallah Albarakah (Ireland) Ltd Faysal Investment Bank of Bahrain Faysal Islamic Bank of Bahrain (Massraf Faisal Al Islami) Gulf International Bank BSC Islamic Investment Company of the Gulf Islamic Trading Company ABC Islamic Bank ABN Amro Bank Deutsche Bank Rep office Investors Bank TAIB Bank of Bahrain Turk Gulf Merchant Bank Bahrain Monetary Agency Shamil Bank Khaleej Investment Company First Islamic Investment Bank
Bangladesh
Albaraka Bangladesh Ltd (Dallah Al Baraka Group), Dhaka Islami Bank Bangladesh Ltd, Dhaka Faisal Islamic Bank
British Virgin Islands

Ibn Khaldoun International Equity Fund Ltd
Brunei
Islamic Bank of Brunei Berhad Islamic Development Bank of Brunei Berhad Tabung Amanah Islam Brunei
Canada
Islamic Co-operative Housing Corporation Ltd, Toronto
Cayman Islands
Ibn Majid Emerging Marketing Fund (International Investor Group) Al Tawfeek Co. for Investment Funds Ltd. Subsidiary of Albarka Group "DBG"
Denmark
Faisal Finance (Denmark) A/S
Djibouti
Banque Albaraka Djibouti
Egypt
Alwatany Bank of Egypt, Cairo Egyptian Company for Business and Trade S.A.E Egyptian Saudi Finance Bank (Dallah Al Baraka), Cairo Gulf Company for Financial Investment Faisal Islamic Bank of Egypt, Cairo Islamic Bank International for Investment and Development, Cairo Islamic Investment and Development Co., Cairo National Bank for Development, Cairo
France
Algerian Saudi Leasing Holding Co. (Dallah Al Baraka Group) Societe General Capital Guidance BNP Paribas
Gambia
Arab Gambian Islamic Bank
Germany
Bank Sepah, Iran Commerz Bank Deutsche Bank
Guinea
Massraf Faisal al Islami of Guinea, Conakry Banque Islamique de Guinee
India
Al Ameen Islamic Financial & Investment Corp. (India) Ltd., Karnatka Bank Muscat International (SOAG) Al-Falah Investment Ltd
Indonesia
Al Barakah Islamic Investment Bank Bank Muamalat Indonesia, Jakarta Dar Al-Maal Al-Islami Trust PT Danareksa Fund Management, Jakarta

Iran
Bank Keshavarzi (Agricultural Bank), Tehran Bank Maskan Iran (Housing Bank), Tehran Bank Mellat, Tehran Bank Melli Iran, Tehran Bank Saderat Iran, Tehran Bank Sanat Va Maadan (Bank of Industry and Mines), Tehran Bank Sepah, Tehran Bank Tejarat, Tehran
Iraq
Iraqi Islamic bank for Investment and Development
Italy
Bank Sepah, Iran
Ivory Coast
International Trading Co. of Africa
Jordan
Jordan Islamic Bank (Subsidiary of Dallah Al Barka Group) Jordan Islamic Bank for Finance and Investment, Amman
Kuwait
Gulf Investment Corporation The International Investment Group The International Investor, Safat Kuwait Finance House, Safat Kuwait Investment Co - Dar Al-IsethmarSecurities House
Lebanon
Gulf International Bank, Bahrain Al Barakah Bank Bank of Beirut
Luxembourg
Faisal Finance (Luxembourg) S.A Faisal Holding, Luxembourg Takafol S.A Islamic Finance House Universal Holding S.A
Malaysia
Adil Islamic Growth Fund (Innosabah Securities Sdn Bhd), Labuan Arab Malaysian Merchant Bank Berhad, Kuala Lumpur Bank Bumiputra Malaysia Berhad, Kuala Lumpur Bank Islam Malaysia Berhad, Kuala Lumpur Bank Kerjasama Rakyat Malaysia Berhad, Kuala Lumpur Dallah Al Baraka (Malaysia) Holding Sdn Bhd Lembaga Urusan Dan Tabung Haji (Fund), Kuala Lumpur Malayan Banking Berhad (Maybank), Kuala Lumpur Multi-Purpose Bank Berhad, Kuala Lumpur United Malayan Banking Corp. Berhad, Kuala Lumpur Bank Muamalat Berhad, Malaysia Securities Commission Labuan Offshore Financial Services Authority (LOFSA) Islamic banking & Takaful Dept, Bank Negara Malaysia
Malaysian banks with Islamic windows

Commercial Banks:
Affin Bank Berhad
Alliance Bank Berhad
Arab-Malaysian Bank Berhad
Bank Utama (Malaysia) Berhad
Citibank Berhad
EON Bank Berhad
Hong Leong Bank Berhad
HSBC Bank (M) Berhad
Malayan Banking Berhad
OCBC Bank (Malaysia) Berhad
Public Bank Berhad
RHB Bank Berhad
Southern Bank Berhad
Standard Chartered Bank Malaysia Berhad
Finance Companies:
Alliance Finance Berhad
Arab-Malaysian Finance Berhad
Asia Commercial Finance Berhad
EON Finance Berhad
Hong Leong Finance Berhad
Kewangan Bersatu Berhad
Mayban Finance Berhad
MBf Finance Berhad
Public Finance Berhad
United Merchant Finance Berhad
Merchant Banks:
Alliance Merchant Finance Berhad
Arab-Malaysian Merchant Bank Berhad
Aseambankers Malaysia Berhad
Malaysian International Merchant Bank Berhad
Affin Merchant Bank Berhad
Discount Houses:
Abrar Discounts Berhad
Affin Discount Berhad
Amanah Short Deposits Berhad
BBMB Discount House Berhad
KAF Discounts Berhad
Malaysia Discount Berhad
Mayban Discount Berhad

	Mauritania
	Banque Alabaraka Mauritaninne Islamique (Dallah Al Baraka Group), Mauritania
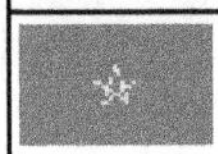	Morocco
	Faisal Finance Maroc S.A The Netherlands Faisal Finance (Netherlands) B.V Faisal Finance (Netherlands Antilles) N.V
	Niger
	Banque Islamique Du Niger, Niamey
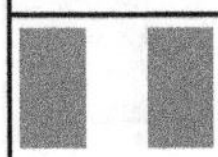	Nigeria
	Habib Nigeria Bank Ltd Ahmed Zakari & Co

	Oman
	Bank Muscat International Bank Saderat Iran, Muscat Oman Arab Bank
	Pakistan
	Al Faysal Investment Bank Ltd, Islamabad Al Towfeek Investment Bank Ltd (Dallah Al Baraka Group), Lahore Faysal Bank Ltd, Pakistan National Investment Trust Ltd., Karachi Shamil Bank Meezan Bank Limited
	Palestine
	Arab Islamic Bank Arab Islamic International Bank (AIIB) Plc Cairo Amman Bank Palestine International Bank The Palestine Islamic Bank
	Qatar
	Islamic Investment Company of the Gulf Ltd, Sharjah Qatar International Islamic Bank, Doha Qatar Islamic Bank SAQ, Doha
	Russia
	BADR Bank
	Saudi Arabia
	Albaraka Investment and Development Co., Jeddah Al Rajhi Banking and Investment Corp., Riyadh Arab Leasing International Finance (ALIF) Ltd Faysal Islamic Bank of Bahrain E.C., Dammam Islamic Development Bank, Jeddah. National Commercial Bank Ltd, Jeddah Riyad Bank Saudi American Bank, Jeddah Saudi Holland Bank Bank Al Jazira
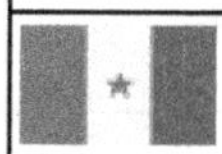	Senegal
	Banque Islamique Du Senegal
	South Africa
	Albaraka Bank Ltd, Durban (Dallah Al Baraka Group)
	Srilanka
	Amana Islamic Bank Amana Takaful Limited
	Sudan

	**Sudan**
	Al Baraka Al Sudani, Khartoum. (Dallah Al Baraka Group) Al Shamal Islamic Bank Al Tadamon Islamic Bank, Khartoum Animal Resources Bank El Gharb Islamic Bank (Islamic Bank for Western Sudan) Faisal Islamic Bank of Sudan, Khartoum Islamic Bank of Western Sudan, Khartoum Islamic Co-operative Development Bank, Khartoum Sudanese Islamic Bank
	**Switzerland**
	Cupola Asset Management SA, Geneva Dar Al Maal Al Islami Trust, Geneva Faisal Finance (Switzerland) SA, Geneva Pan Islamic Consultancy Services Istishara SA, Geneva Pictet & Cie
	**Tunisia**
	Beit Ettamwil al Tunisi al Saudi, Tunis (Dallah Al Baraka Group) B.E.S.T. Re-Insurance (Dallah Al Baraka Group)
	**Turkey**
	Albarakah Turkish Finance House Istanbul Emin Sigorts A.S Faisal Finance Institution, Istanbul. Faisal Islamic Bank of Kibris Ltd, Turkey Ihlas Finance House Kuwait-Turket Evkaf Finance House Asya Finans Kurumu A.S
	**United Arab Emirates**
	Abu Dhabi Islamic Bank Bank Muscat International (SOAG) Dubai Islamic Bank, Dubai Gulf International Bank, Bahrain Islamic Investment Company of the Gulf Ltd, Abu Dhabi. Islamic Investment Company of the Gulf Ltd, Sharjah Subsidiary of Dar Al Maal Islami Trust National Bank of Sharjah HSBC, Dubai National Bank of Dubai
	**United Kingdom**
	Albaraka International Ltd, London Albaraka Investment Co. Ltd, London Al Rajhi Investment Corporation, London Al Safa Investment Fund Bank Sepah, Iran Dallah Al Baraka (UK) Ltd., London Takafol (UK) Ltd, London Barclays Capital HSBC Amanah Finance ABCIB Islamic Asset Management, Arab Banking Corp
	United Kingdom banks with Islamic windows

United Kingdom banks with Islamic windows

ABC International Bank, London
ANZ International Merchant Banking, London
Arab Bank Plc, London
Riyadh Bank, London
Citibank International Plc, London
Cedel International, London
Dawnay Day Global Investment Ltd
Global Islamic Finance, HSBC Investment Bank Plc
Gulf International Bank Bsc, Bahrain
The Halal Mutual Investment Company Plc
IBJ International, London (Subsidiary of Industrial Bank of Japan)
J. Aron & Co. (Goldman Sachs International Finance) Ltd., London
Islamic Investment Banking Unit (IIBU), United Bank of Kuwait, London

Ireland

Al Meezan Commodity Fund Plc, Dublin
Jersey, UK (+534)
The Islamic Investment Company, St Helier.
MFAI (Jersey) Limited (formerly - Massraf Faysal Al-Islami Ltd, Jersey)

United States of America

Abrar Investments, Inc., Stamford CT
Al-Baraka Bancorp Inc, Chicago
Al-Madina Realty, Inc., Englewood NJ
Al-Manzil Islamic Financial Services
Amana Mutual Funds Trust, State St, Bellingham WA
Ameen Housing Co-operative, San Francisco
American Finance House
Bank Sepah, Iran
BMI Finance & Investment Group, New Jersey
Dow Jones Islamic Index Fund of the Allied Asset Advisors Funds
Failaka Investments, Inc., Chicago IL
Fuloos Incorporated, Toledo OH
Hudson Investors Fund, Inc., Clifton NJ
MSI Finance Corporation, Inc., Houston TX
Samad Group, Inc., Dayton OH
Shared Equities Homes, Indianapolis IN
HSBC, USA
MEF Money, USA
Islamic Credit Union of Minnesota, (ICUM)
United Mortgage

Yemen

Islamic Bank of Yemen for Finance and Investment, Sana
Saba Islamic Bank, Sana
Faisal Islamic Bank
Yemen Islamic Bank, Sana
Yemen National Investment Co., Sana

ISLAMIC EQUITY FUNDS

	Fund Name	Fund Manager(s)	Fund Promoter(s)	Inception Date	Min. Invst
Global Equity Funds					
1	Al Baraka Global Equity	Mercury Asset Management	Al Baraka Investment Bank	Dec-97	$25,000
2	Al Rajhi Global	UBS Asset Management	Al Rajhi Banking &	Jul-96	50 Shares

	Equity		Investment		
3	Al-Ahli Global Trading Equity	Wellington Management Co. LLP	National Commercial Bank (NCB)	Jan-95	$2,000
4	Al-Bait Global Equity	Fremont Investment Advisors Inc.	Securities House	Apr-00	$50,000
5	Al-Bukhari Global Equity	Wafra Investment Advisory Group	Wafra Investment Advisory Group	Aug-98	$100,000
6	Al-Dar World Equities	Pictet & Cie	The International Investor/Pictet & Cie	Feb-98	$100,000
7	Alfanar Investment Holdings	Worms & Cie/SEDCO	Permal Asset Management	Dec-97	$5,000
8	Al-Firas Global Equity	Arab Bank Plc	Arab Bank Plc	Oct-00	$10,000
9	Al-Kawthar Fund	Wellington/Al-Ahli Global Trading Eq.	National Bank of Kuwait	Jan-95	$10,000
10	Al-Khair Global Equity Fund	Pictet & Cie	Bank Al-Jazira	Sep-98	$5,000
11	Al-Safwa International Equity	Roll & Ross Asset Management	Al-Tawfeek Co. for Investment Funds	May-96	$10,000
12	Arab Investor Crescent Fund	Schroder Investment Mgmt Int'l	Arab National Bank	Apr-99	$5,000
13	Arzaq Investment Fund	Global Alliance/Securities House	Securities House	Mar-98	$50,000
14	Bank Kanz Global Islamic Equity	Bank Kanz	Bank Kanz	N/A	$100,000
15	Barclays Global Equity	Wellington Management Co. LLP	Barclays Private Bank	Feb-00	$1,000,000
16	Caravan Fund	Wellington Management Co. LLP	Commerical Bank of Qatar/BNP	Dec-99	$10,000
17	Citi Global Portfolios	SSB Citi Asset Management	Citi Islamic Investment Bank	Oct-97	$10,000
18	Dow Jones Islamic Index Fund	Brown Brothers Harriman & Co.	Wafra Invest. Advisory / AlTawfeeq	Jul-99	$10,000
19	Global Equity 2000 Sub-Fund	Alliance Capital Management LP	First Investment Co	Mar-00	$10,000
20	Hegira Global Equity	Wellington Management Co. LLP	Wellington Management Co. LLP	Sep-96	$5,000,000
21	HSBC Amanah Global Equity	HSBC Investment Funds (Lux.) SA	HSBC Amanah Finance	May-00	$5,000
22	Islamic Global Equity *	N/A	HSBC Bank USA	Late 2001	$2,500
23	Miraj Global Equity	Royal Bank of Canada	Miraj International Investment Ltd.	Aug-98	$10,000
24	Musharaka Equity Fund	N/A	Riyad Bank	Jun 97	$10,000
25	Parsoli Global Equity	Parosoli Capital & Finance Ltd.	Parosoli Capital & Finance Ltd.	Jun-01	£1,000
26	QIB Global Equities	Global Asset Management	Qatar Islamic Bank	N/A	

		(GAM)			
27	SAMBA Global Equity	SAMBA Capital Management	SAMBA Capital Management	Dec-99	$2,000
28	SUT Ethical Growth Fund	Singapore Unit Trust Ltd.	Malayan Banking & Daiwa Securities	Aug-01	S$1,000
29	SUT Ethical Value Fund	Singapore Unit Trust Ltd.	Malayan Banking & Daiwa Securities	Aug-01	S$1,000
30	TAIB Crescent Global Fund	Wright Investors' Service	TAIB Bank of Bahrain	Mar-00	$100,00
31	UBS Islamic Fund Global Equities	UBS, AG & UBS Brinson	UBS Islamic Fund Mgmt Co	May-00	$100,000
North American Equity Funds					
32	Al-Ahli US Trading Equity	INVESCO Capital Mgmt Inc.	National Commercial Bank (NCB)	Dec-92	$2,000
33	Alfanar US Capital Growth	Worms & Cie/SEDCO	Permal Asset Management	Jun-99	$5,000
34	Alfanar US Capital Value	Worms & Cie/SEDCO	Permal Asset Management	May-99	$5,000
35	Amana Growth *	Saturna Capital	Saturna Capital	Feb-94	$100
36	Amana Income *	Saturna Capital	Saturna Capital	Jun-86	$100
37	Azzad DJIM Index Fund *	Azzad Asset Management	Azzad Asset Management	Dec-00	1,000
38	Azzad Growth Fund LP	Azzad Asset Management	Azzad Asset Management	Feb-98	$50,000
39	Azzad Income Fund	Azzad Asset Management	Azzad Asset Management	Sep-01	$1,000
41	Dow Jones Islamic Index (US) Fund *	Allied Asset Advisors Funds	Allied Asset Advisors Funds	Jun-00	$500
42	SAMI Navigator	Nova Bancorp Group	Nova Bancorp Group	Jul-99	C$500
European Equity Funds					
43	Al-Ahli Europe Trading Equity	Gulf Int'l Bank (UK) Ltd.	National Commercial Bank (NCB)	Nov-94	$2,000
44	Al-Dar Europe Equities	Pictet & Cie	The International Investor/Pictet & Cie	Feb-98	$100,000
45	Alfanar Europe	Worms & Cie/SEDCO	Permal Asset Management	Jan-99	$5,000
46	Al-Sukoor European Equity	Commerz Int'l Cap Mgmt/Al-Tawfeeq Co.	Commerz Bank/Burgan Bank	Mar-00	1 Share
47	Al-Thoraiya European Equity	Lomard Odier & Cie	Bank Al-Jazira	Sep-99	$5,000
Small Cap & Technology Equity Funds					
48	Al Rajhi Small Companies	Franklin Mgmt & Lord Abbott	Al Rajhi Banking & Investment	Jun-99	200 Shares
49	Al-Ahli Small-Cap Trading Equity	Wellington Management Co. LLP	National Commercial Bank (NCB)	Aug-98	$2,000
50	Alfanar Essex Technology	Worms & Cie/SEDCO	Permal Asset Management	Jun-99	$5,000
51	Orbitex Islamic	Orbitex Management Ltd.	Orbitex Management	Dec-99	$50,000

	Comm. & IT Fund		Ltd.		
52	TII Small Cap Equity (European)	Pictet & Cie	The International Investor	Dec-96	$100,000
Balanced, Secured & Other Equity Funds					
53	Al Hilal Fund	Mercury Asset Management	Abu Dhabi Islamic Bank (ADIB)	Apr-00	$10,000
54	Al Kawthar Global Equity Secured	National Commercial Bank (NCB)	National Bank of Kuwait	Sep-99	$10,000
55	Al Rajhi Balanced Fund I	Al Rajhi Banking & Investment	Al Rajhi Banking & Investment	Nov-98	$5,000
56	Al Rajhi Balanced Fund II	Al Rajhi Banking & Investment	Al Rajhi Banking & Investment	Dec-98	$5,000
57	Al-Ahli Global Equity Secured (Series B)	Wellington Management Co. LLP	National Commercial Bank (NCB)	Nov-99	$25,000
58	Al-Ahli International Equity Secured	Deutche Bank	National Commercial Bank (NCB)	Feb-00	$25,000
59	Al-Ahli US Equity Secured	Deutche Bank	National Commercial Bank (NCB)	Oct-99	$25,000
60	Alkhawarizmi Fund	AXA Rosenberg	The International Investor	Jul-97	$100,000
61	BHLB Pacific Dana Al Mizan (Balanced)	BHLB Pacific Trust	BHLB Pacific Trust	Mar-01	RM 1,000
62	Faysal Shield Fund	Banque National de Paris	Faysal Islamic Bank of Bahrain	Nov-99	$100,000
63	Mutajarah Fund (Balanced)	Swiss Alternative Investment Strategies Group (SAIS)	Towry Law International	Oct-01	$100,000
64	Profit Sharing Fund (Aman-1) (secured)	Al Rajhi Banking & Investment	Al Rajhi Banking & Investment	N/A	$2,000
Emerging Market & Country Equity Funds					
65	Al Arabi Saudi Co. Shares	Arab National Bank	Arab National Bank	May-93	SR 10,000
66	Al Rajhi Egypt Equity	EFG Hermes	Al Rajhi Banking & Investment	Jun-97	200 Shares
67	Al Rajhi Local Share Fund	Al Rajhi Banking & Investment	Al Rajhi Banking & Investment	Jul-92	1 Share
68	Al Rajhi Middle East Equity	Bakheet Financial Advisors	Al Rajhi Banking & Investment	May-98	200 Shares
69	Al-Ahli Saudi Trading Equity	Bakheet Financial Advisors	National Commercial Bank (NCB)	Jun-98	SR 5,000
70	Al-Dar Eastern Europe Equities	Pictet & Cie	The International Investor/Pictet & Cie	Feb-98	$100,000
71	Al-Taiyibat Fund (local share)	Bank Al-Jazira Invesmtent Services	Bank Al-Jazira	Sep-98	SR 10,000
72	First Arabian Equity 2000	N/A	First Investment Company	N/A	
73	Ibn Majid Emerging	UBS Brinson	The International	Nov-95	$100,000

	Markets		Investor		
74	Khaled Ibn el-Waleed Fund	PrimeCorp. Investment Management	Al-Mal Islamic Company	N/A	
75	Oasis Crescent Fund	Oasis Asset Management Ltd.	Oasis Asset Management Ltd.	Jan-99	
76	Parsoli Islamic Equity	Parosoli Capital & Finance Ltd.	Parosoli Capital & Finance Ltd.	1996	
77	Pure Specialist Fund	Futuregrowth Unit Trust Management	Futuregrowth Unit Trust Management	Jun-92	R 200
78	Riyad Equity Fund 2 (Saudi Shares)	Riyad Bank	Riyad Bank	Nov-96	SR 10,000
Asian Equity Funds					
79	Al-Ahli Asia Pacific Trading Equity	Gulf Int'l Bank (UK) Ltd.	National Commercial Bank (NCB)	May-00	$2,000
80	Al-Mashariq Japanese Equity	Julius Baer Asset Management	Bank Al-Jazira	Apr-00	$5,000
81	Al-Nukhba Asian Equity	Nomura Investment Bank	Al-Tawfeek Co. for Investment Funds	Jul-98	$10,000
82	Mendaki Global Fund	DBS Asset Mgmt	Mendaki Holding Pte. Ltd	Sep-97	S$1,000
83	Mendaki Global Fund	DBS Asset Mgmt	Mendaki Holding Pte. Ltd	May-91	S$500
Malaysian Equity Funds					
84	Abrar Investment Fund	Abrar Unit Trust Managers	Abrar Unit Trust Managers	1996	
85	Amanah Saham Bank Islam	BIMB Unit Trust Mgmt Bhd.	Bank Islam Malaysia Bhd	Jun-94	500 Shares
86	Amanah Saham Darul Iman	PTB Amanah Saham Darul Iman	PTB Amanah Saham Darul Iman	Oct-94	
87	Amanah Saham Wanita	Hijrah Unit Trust Management Bhd	Hijrah Managers Bhd	May-98	RM 100
88	BBMB Dana Putra	BBMB Unit Trust Management	BBMB Unit Trust Management	Jun-96	
89	BHLB Dana Al-Ihsan	BHLB Pacific Trust	BHLB Pacific Trust	May-98	RM 500
90	Dana Al-Aiman	Mara Unit Trust	Mara Unit Trust	May-68	RM 100
91	Kuala Lumpur Ittikal Fund	Kuala Lumpur Mutual Funds	Kuala Lumpur Mutual Funds	May-97	RM 1,000
92	Mayban Dana Yakin	Mayban Mgt Berhad	Mayban Mgt Berhad	Nov	RM 1,000
93	Pacific Dana Amana	Pacific Mutual Fund Trust	Pacific Mutual Fund Trust	Apr-98	RM 1,000
94	RHB Mudarabah Fund	RHB Unit Trust Management	RHB Unit Trust Management	May-96	500 Shares
95	Tabung Amanah Bakti	Asia Unit Trust Berhad	Tabung Amanah Bakti	May-71	RM 500
96	Tabung Ittikal Arab-Malaysian	Arab-Malaysian Unit Trusts Bhd	Arab-Malaysian Unit Trusts Bhd	Jan-93	500 Shares

Islamic Bonds (Sukuk) Funds					
97	RHB Islamic Bond	RHB Unit Trust Mgt	RHB Unit Trust Mgt	Jun-00	RM 1,000
98	Kuala Lumper Islamic Bond Fund	Kuala Lumper Mutual Funds	Kuala Lumper Mutual Funds	Aug-01	RM 1,000
99	Dahlia Syariah Income Fund	Mayban Life Assurance Bhd.	Mayban Life Assurance Bhd.	Aug-01	RM 1,000

OPIC FUNDS

Fund	Fund Manager	Stage	Geographic Focus	Size of Fund $M	Short Description
Africa Growth Fund	Equator Overseas Services Limited	Fully Invested	Sub-Saharan Africa	25	Equity investments in mining, manufactoring and financial services.
Africa Millennium Fund	Savage Holdings LLC	Raising Capital	Sub-Saharan Africa	350	Equity or quasi-equity securities of companies that work in the Infrastructure Sector and that operate in countries eligible for investment in sub-Saharan Africa.
Agribusiness Partners International	Agribusiness Management Company, LLC	Fully Invested	NIS/Baltics	95	Equity investments in agriculture, food firms, infastructure projects, privatizations, food storage and distribution facilities.
AIG Brunswick Millennium Fund	American International Group/Brunswick Capital Mgm	Fully Invested	Russia, NIS and Baltics	288.5	Equity investments in large infrastructure projects. Including power, transportation, natural resource development and related industries.
Allied Small Business Fund	Allied Capital Corp.	Fully Invested	All OPIC eligible countries	20	Equity investments in basic manufacturing and service industries sponsored by qualifying U.S. small business.
Aqua International Partners Fund	Texas Pacific Group	Investing	All OPIC eligible countries	237.75	Equity investments in operating and special purpose companies involved in the treatment, bulk supply and distribution of water in emerging market countries.
Asia Development Partners	Olympus Capital Holdings (Asia)	Investing	Bangledesh, India, Indonesia, Korea, Laos, Philippines, Sri Lanka, Thailand and Vietnam	150	Telecommunications, consumer products, and financial services
Asia Pacific Growth Fund	Hambrecht &Quist Asia Pacific	Fully Invested	Indonesia, Malaysia, the Phillipines, Thailand, Taiwan, Singapore	75.25	Equity investments in light manufactoring, financial, construction, high tech, and telecom services.

Fund	Fund Manager	Stage	Geographic Focus	Size of Fund $M	Short Description
Bancroft Eastern Europe Fund	Bancroft UK, Ltd.	Fully Invested	Central Europe/Baltic republics: Albania, Bulgaria, Croatia, the Czech Republic, Estonia, Hungary, Latvia, Lithuania, Poland, Romania, Slovakia, Slovenia	90.85253	Equity investments in distribution networks, basic manufactoring, consumer goods and related service networks.
Caucasus Fund	Caucasus Advisors, LLC	Closed	Azerbaijan, Armenia, Georgia	92	Equity investments in telecommunications projects.
Draper International India Fund	Draper International	Fully Repaid	India	41.09589	Equity investments in information technology, telecommunications and consumer goods.
Emerging Europe Fund	TDA Capital Partners, Inc.	Fully Invested	Central and Eastern Europe:Poland, Czech Republic, Slovakia, Romania, Bulgaria, Hungary, Slovenia; capped at 40% of commitments in any single country	60	Equity investments in sustainable development industries.
First NIS Regional Fund	Baring Asset Mgmt.	Repaid	Nis/Baltic Republics	200	Equity investments in natural resource -related companies, telecommunications, light manufacturing and consumer products and services.
Global Environment Emerging Markets Fund I	GEF Management	Fully Invested	All OPIC eligible countries	66.7	Equity investments in environment-oriented sectors relating to the developing, financing, operating or supplying of infastructure relating to clean energy and water.
Global Environment Emerging Markets Fund II	GEF Management	Fully Invested	All OPIC eligible countries	120	Equity investments in environment-oriented sectors relating to the developing, financing, operating or supplying of infastructure relating to clean energy and water.
India Private Equity Fund	Indocean Capital Advisors	Fully Invested	India	140	Equity investments in consumer goods, basic manufacturing, banking, computer, and related industries.
Inter-Arab Investment Fund	InterArab Management, Inc.	Investing	Jordan, West Bank/Gaza, Oman	45	Equity investments in basic industries that create intra- and inter-regional synergies.
Israel Growth Fund	Apax-Leumi Partners, Inc.	Fully Repaid	Israel	40	Equity investments in technology.

Fund	Fund Manager	Stage	Geographic Focus	Size of Fund $M	Short Description
					telecommunications, consumer retailing and consumer products.
Modern Africa Growth And Investment Fund	Modern Africa Fund Managers LLC	Investing	Sub-Saharan Africa (excluding S. Africa)	117	Equity investments in all sub-Saharan countries excluding South Africa with focus on manufacturing, telecommunications and natural resources.
New Century Capital Partners	NCH Advisors	Fully Invested	Ukraine, Russia, Kazakstan, Armenia, Belarus, Georgia, Romania, Bulgaria, Moldova, Estonia, Lithuania, and Latvia (no more than 25% in Baltics, 20% in Russia)	250	Equity investments in diversified manufacturing, consumer products, financial and service industries.
Newbridge Andean Partners	ACON Investments, LLC	Investing	Bolivia, Columbia, Ecuador, Peru, Venezuala, Argentina, Belize, Brazil, Chile, Costa Rica, El Salvador, Guatemala, Honduras, Nicaragua, Panama, Paraguay and Uruguay	160	Equity investments in diversified manufacturing, financial and service industries.
PBO Fund		Closed		240	
Poland Partners	Landon Butler & Company	Fully Investing	Poland	63.5	Equity investments in manufacturing, consumer goods, distribution networks, merchandising and related service networks.
Russia Partners A	Sigular Guff & Co.	Fully Invested	Russia Fund 'A' may invest up to 25% in other OPIC-covered NIS states	105	Equity investments in natural resource-related companies, telecommunications, light manufacturing and consumer products and services.
Russia Partners B	Sigular Guff & Co.	Fully Invested	Russia	50	Equity investments in natural resource-related companies, telecommunications, light manufacturing and consumer products and services.
Soros Investment Capital Ltd.	Soros Private Funds Management LLC	Investing	Albania, Bosnia & Herzegovina, Bulgaria, Croatia, FYR Macedonia, Montenegro, Romania. Slovenia.	200	Fund was established to provide equity capital to Southeast Europe as part of the international recovery effort.

Fund	Fund Manager	Stage	Geographic Focus	Size of Fund $M	Short Description
			Turkey, and, should they become eligible, Serbia and Kosovo.		
South America Private Equity Growth	Baring Latin America Partners LLC	Fully Invested	South America, with focus on Argentina, Brazil, Chile, and Peru	180	Equity investments in diversified manufacturing, financial and service industries.
The Great Circle Fund, L.P.	Great Circle Capital, LLC	Investing	All OPIC- Eligible countries	200	Equity and quasi-equity investments in companies operating in the maritime transportation, logistics and services industries that are new, expanding, or in the process of being restructured or privatized.
West Bank / Gaza & Jordan Fund	International Capital Advisors	Closed	West Bank/Gaza and Jordan at least 60% in West Bank/Gaza	60	Equity investments in basic service and manufacturing companies.
ZM Africa Investment Fund	Zephyr Management LP	Fully Inveested	South Africa and regional SADC countries	120	Equity investments in diversified manufacturing, financial and service industries.

SELECTED INVESTMENT AND BUSINESS CONTACTS

BAHRAIN

BAHRAINI GOVERNMENT AGENCIES

The following websites provide the most comprehensive information and links for the government of Bahrain:

www.bahrain.gov.bh
www.arab.net/bahrain

Ministry of Finance and National Economy
H.E. Abdulla Saif, Minister
P.O. Box 333
Manama, Bahrain
Tel: (973) 530-800
Fax: (973) 532-853
Home page: www.mofne.gov.bh

Bahrain Monetary Agency
P.O. Box 27
Manama, Bahrain
Tel: (973) 535-535
Fax: (973) 530-399
Home page: www.bma.gov.bh
E-mail: bmalbr@BATELCO.com.bh

Shaikh Ahmed M. H. A. Al Khalifa
Governor
Tel: 547-777
Fax: 530-399

Economic Development Board
Mr. Jamal Ali Al Hazeem,
Chief Eexecutive Officer
P.O. Box 11299
Manama, Bahrain
Tel: (973) 229-946
Fax: (973) 217-456

Bankers Society of Bahrain
Mrs. Wendy Toorani
P.O. Box 2851
Manama, Bahrain
Tel: (973) 728-003
Fax: (973) 729-802

Bahrain Stock Exchange
P.O. Box 3203
Manama, Bahrain
Tel: (973) 261-260
Fax: (973) 276-181
E-mail: bseceo@batelco.com.bh

Mr. Shaker Al Shater, Director of Operations

P.O. Box 3203
Manama, Bahrain
Tel: (973) 273-381
Fax: (973) 212-979

Ministry of Oil
H.E. Shaikh Isa Bin Ali Al Khalifa, Minister
P.O. Box 1435
Manama, Bahrain
Switchboard: (973) 291-511
Fax: (973) 293-007

Small and Medium Enterprise Unit
Dr. Haitham Al Qahtani, Director
Tel: (973) 525-559
Fax: (973) 290-302

Ministry of Labor and Social Affairs
H.E. Abdul Nabi Al Shoa'la, Minister
Mr. Saeed Al Sayed Ahmed, Advisor for Manpower Development
P.O. Box 32333
Manama, Bahrain
Tel: (973) 682-557
Fax: (973) 687-907
Home page: www.bah-molsa.com

Ministry of Transportation
(note: includes Telecommunications)
H.E. Ali bin Khalifa Sulman Al Khalifa, Minister
P.O. Box 10325
Manama, Bahrain
Tel: (973) 535-200
Fax: (973) 537-537

Civil Aviation Affairs
Mr. Ibrahim Abdulla Al Hamer
Undersecretary for Civil Aviation Affairs
P.O. Box 586
Manama, Bahrain
Tel: (973) 321-000
Fax: (973) 325-757

Hesham bin Abdul Aziz Al Khalifa
Airport Director
Tel: (973) 321-150
Fax: (973) 324-096

Bahrain Telecommunications Company (BATELCO)
Andrew B. Hearn, Chief Executive
P.O. Box 14
Manama Bahrain
Tel: (973) 881-881
Fax: (973) 611-441
E-mail: batelco@btc.com.bh
Home page: www.batelco.com.bh

Ministry of Cabinet Affairs
H.E. Mohammed Al Mutawa, Minister
Tel: (973) 214-889
Fax: (973) 277-730

Ministry of Information
H.E. Mr. Nabeel Yacoub Al Hamar, Minister
(includes Tourism)
P.O. Box 253
Manama, Bahrain
Tel: (973) 781-888
Fax: (973) 682-777

Dr. Kadhim Rajab, Assistant Undersecretary for Tourism
Tel: (973) 223-366
Fax: (973) 210-969
Home page: www.bahraintourism.com.bh

Mr. Jamal Dawood
Director, Directorate of Publications and Press
Tel: (973) 717-525
Fax: (973) 717-515

Ministry of Works
H.E. Fahmi Ali Al Jawder, Minister
P.O. Box 5
Manama, Bahrain
Tel: (973) 524-600
Fax: (973) 533-974

Committee for Organizing Engineering Professional Practice (CFOEPP)
Dr. Hassan Abdulla Fakhro, Chairman
P.O. Box 167
Manama, Bahrain
Tel: (973) 534-747
Fax: (973) 536-371

Ministry of Electricity and Water
Shaikh Daij Al Khalifa, Minister
P.O. Box 2
Manama, Bahrain
Tel: (973) 522-002
Fax: (973) 537-151

Mr. Nabeel Al Maskati
Assistant Undersecretary, Planning and Studies
Tel: (973) 522-120
Fax: (973) 532-786

Ministry of Commerce and Industry
H.E. Ali Saleh Al Saleh, Minister
P.O. Box 5479
Manama, Bahrain
Tel: (973) 532-121
Fax: (973) 530-469

Abdul Razak Zainalabedin
Director of Foreign Trade Relations
Tel: (973) 555-633
Fax: (973) 555-779

Mohammed Dharar Al Sha-er

Director of Agencies and Industrial Property
Tel: (973) 530-335
Fax: (973) 536-479

Mr. Mohammed Ali Ajoor
Acting Director of Standards and Metrology
Tel: (973) 530-100
Fax: (973) 530-730

Ministry of Education
H.E. Dr. Mohammed Jassim Al Ghattam, Minister
P.O. Box 43, Manama, Bahrain
Tel: (973) 680-071
Fax: (973) 680-161
Home page: www.education.gov.bh

Ministry of Health
H.E. Dr. Faisal Al Mousawi, Minister
P.O. Box 12
Manama, Bahrain
Tel: (973) 270-443
Fax: (973) 252-569
Home page: www.batelco.com.bh/mhealth

Bahrain Chamber of Commerce and Industry
Mr. A. Rahim Naqi
Deputy Secretary General
P.O. Box 248
Manama, Bahrain
Tel: (973) 229-555
Fax: (973) 212-937
E-mail: bahcci@batelco.com.bh
Home page: www.bahchamber.com

Market Research Firms in Bahrain

Fortune PromoSeven
Mr. Tariq Al Saffar, Managing Director, Bahrain
P.O. Box 5989
Manama, Bahrain
Tel: (973) 225-148
Fax: (973) 224-375

Arthur Andersen & Co.
Mr. Mounir Al Borno, Partner
P.O. Box 20323
Manama, Bahrain
Tel: (973) 530-400
Fax: (973) 530-321

Middle East Research and Consultancy (MERAC)
Mrs. Loren Irwin, Country Manager, Bahrain
P.O. Box 26018
Manama, Bahrain
Tel: (973) 742-024
Fax: (973) 742-061

Ernst & Young
Mr. Ismail Amin, Chairman
P.O. Box 140
Manama, Bahrain
Tel: (973) 535-455
Fax: (973) 535-405

PriceWaterhouse Coopers
Mr. Jawad Habib Jawad, Senior Partner
P.O. Box 26403
Manama, Bahrain
Tel: (973) 530-077
Fax: (973) 226-966

Principal Commercial Banks

Citibank, N.A.
P.O. Box 548
Manama, Bahrain
Tel: (973) 223-344
Fax: (973) 210-000

National Bank of Bahrain B.S.C.
P.O. Box 106
Manama, Bahrain
Tel: (973) 228-800
Fax: (973) 228-998
Home page: www.nbbonline.com

Bank of Bahrain and Kuwait B.S.C.
P.O. Box 597
Manama, Bahrain
Tel: (973) 223-388
Fax: (973) 229-822
Home page: www.bbkonline.com

U.S. Embassy Trade Personnel

Alfred Fonteneau, Chief, Political and Economic Officer
Tracy L. Hailey, Economic and Commercial Officer
Madeleine Khouri, Commercial Assistant
Lucy Fahim, Commercial Assistant

U.S. Mail: U.S. Embassy
PSC 451
FPO AE 09834-5100

Intl. Mail: U.S. Embassy
P.O. Box 26431
Manama, Bahrain

Tel: (973) 273300 ext 2072
Fax: (973) 273011
Home page: www.usembassy.com.bh
E-mail: usmanama@batelco.com.bh

Agricultural Trade Office
P.O. Box 9343
Dubai, U.A.E.
Tel: 971-4-331-4063
Fax: 971-4-331-4998
E-mail: atodubai@emirates.net.ae

Home page:
www.usembabu.gov.ae/atodubai.htm
Contact: Ron Verdonk, Regional Director
(Covers: Bahrain, Kuwait, Oman, Qatar and U.A.E)

Washington-based U.S. Government Contacts

David L. Guglielmi, Country Officer
U.S. Department of Commerce
IEP/ANESA/ONE
Room 2029B, HCHB
Washington, DC 20230
Tel: (202) 482-1860
Fax: (202) 482-0878
E-mail: David_Guglielmi@ita.doc.gov
home page: www.ita.doc/gov/mena/econof.html

Michelle Hopkins, Desk Officer
U.S. Department of State
NEA/ARP
Room 4224, Main State
2201 C Street, NW
Washington, DC 20520
Tel: (202) 647-6571
Fax: (202) 736-4459
E-mail: hopkinsmm@state.gov

TPCC Trade Information Center, Washington
1-800-USA-TRADE

Trade Assistance and Promotion Office (TAPO)
Foreign Agricultural Service (FAS)
U.S. Department of Agriculture
Ag Box 1052
Washington, D.C. 20250-1052
Tel: (202) 720-7420
Fax: (202) 690-4374

EGYPT

U.S. CONTACTS IN EGYPT:

American Mideast Educational & Training Services, Inc. (AMIDEAST)
Mrs. Elizabeth B. Khalifa/Country Director
23 Mossadak St., Dokki, Giza
Tel: 337-8265, Fax: 795-2946

American Research Center in Egypt (ARCE)
Mr. Bob Springbord/Director
2 Kasr El Doubara Sq., Garden City, Cairo
Tel: 794-8239, 795-8683, Fax: 795-3052

American University in Cairo (AUC)
Mr. John Gerhart, President
113 Kasr El Aini St., Cairo
Tel: 794-2964 (9 lines), Fax: 795-7565

Community Services Association (CSA)
Ms. Stephanie Frasher, Executive Director
4 Road 21, Maadi
Tel: 798-0764, Fax: 376-8319

Ford Foundation
Dr. Humphrey Davies/Regional Rep. for Middle East & North Africa
1 Osiris St., Garden City, Cairo
Tel: 795-2121, 794-4450, 794-9635, Fax: 795-4018

Fulbright Commission
Ms. Ann B. Radwan/Executive Director
1081 Corniche El Nil St., Belmont Bldg., Cairo
Tel: 794-4799, 794-8679, Fax: 795-7893

Int'l Executive Service Corps. (IESC)
Mr. Spencer King/Chief of Party
Al Boustan Commercial Center, Suite 1, 10th Fl.
Al Boustan St., Bab El Louk, Cairo
Tel: 390-3232, Fax: 390-2929

Project Hope
Dr. Hoda Zaki/Program Director
86 Mohi El Din Aboul Ezz St., Mohandessin, Cairo
Tel: 348-0915, 360-6295, Fax: 360-6295

Small Business Administration (SBA)
Mr. Kamel Nasser, Deputy Director
1 Latin America St., Garden City
Tel: 794-8669/795-8886, Fax: 794-0344

Women's Association
21 Boulos Hanna St., Dokki, Cairo
Tel: 760-3457

EGYPTIAN GOVERNMENT CABINET:

Prime Minister
H.E. Dr. Atef Mohamed Ebeid
Magles El Shaab St., Kasr El Aini St., Cairo
Tel: 795-8025/36/39/795-7370/6/8
Fax: 795-8016/2048

Ministry of Agriculture, Animals & Fish Wealth & Land Reclamation Affairs
H.E. Dr. Youssef Amin Wally
Deputy Prime Minister & Minister
Nadi El Seid St., Dokki, Cairo
Tel: 337-2566/3388
Fax: 749-8128

Ministry of Defense & Military Production
H.E. Field Marshal Mohamed Hussein Tantawy, Minister
Khalifa Al Ma'amoun, Heliopolis
Tel: 263-5681/260-2566/2466
Fax: 291-6227

Ministry of Information

H.E. Mr. Safwat El-Sherif, Minister
Maspero, Corniche El Nil, Cairo
Tel: 574-8984/8986
Fax: 575-8781

Ministry of Foreign Affairs
H.E. Mr. Ahmed Maher El Sayed, Minister
Maspero, Corniche El Nil, Cairo
Tel: 574-9816/7/574-9820
Fax: 574-9533/8822

Ministry of Justice
H.E. Counselor Farouq Seif El Nasr, Minister
Lazoughly Sq., Justice & Finance Bldg., Cairo
Tel: 795-1176/8103/5700
Fax: 795-8103

Ministry of Culture
H.E. Mr. Farouk Hosny, Minister
2 Shagaret El Dor St., Zamalek, Cairo
Tel: 738-0761/2
Fax: 735-6449

Ministry of Education
H.E. Dr. Hussein Kamel Baha' El Din, Minister
4 Ibrahim Naguib St., Garden City, Cairo
Tel: 578-7644/7643
Fax: 796-2952

Ministry of Economy and Foreign Trade
H.E. Dr. Youssef Boutros Ghali, Minister
8 Adly St., Cairo
Tel: 391-9661
Fax: 390-3029/395-9015

People's Assembly & Shura Council Affairs
H.E. Mr. Kamal El-Shazli, Minister of State
Magles El Shaab St., Cairo
Tel: 794-3855/7750
Fax: 795-7681

Ministry of Tourism
H.E. Dr. Mamdouh El-Beltagui, Minister
Abbassia Square, Borg Misr Travel, Cairo
Tel: 282-8439/284-1707
Fax: 685-9551

Ministry of Administrative Development
H.E. Dr. Mohamed Zaki Abou Amer, Minister of State
Leadership Development Center, Next to Central Auditing Agency, Salah Salem Road, Heliopolis, Cairo
Tel: 402-4152/4167
Fax: 261-4126

Ministry of Housing, Utilities & New Communities
H.E. Dr. Mohamed Ibrahim Sulaiman, Minister
1 Ismail Abaza St., off Kasr El Aini St., Cairo
Tel: 792-1384/1385/1403/1405
Fax: 792-1387

Ministry of Manpower & Immigration
H.E. Mr. Ahmed Ahmed Al Ammawy, Minister
3 Youssef Abbas St., Nasr City, Cairo
Tel: 404-2910/1/2
Fax: 260-9891

Ministry of Awqaf (Religious Trusts)
H.E. Dr. Mahmoud Hamdi Zaqzouq, Minister
Sabry Abou Alam St., Bab El Louk, Cairo
Tel: 392-9403/393-3011
Fax: 393-6335

Ministry of Health & Population
H.E. Dr. Ismail Sallam, Minister
Magles El Shaab St., Cairo
Tel: 794-1507/3462/0526
Fax: 795-3966

Ministry of Higher Education & Scientific Research Affairs
H.E. Dr. Mufeed Shehab, Minister and Minister of State for Scientific Research Affairs
4 Ibrahim Naguib St., Garden City, Cairo
Tel: 795-6962/2155
Fax: 796-2952/794-2163

Ministry of Public Works and Water Resources
H.E. Dr. Mahmoud Abu Zeid, Minister
El Nil St., Embaba, Cairo
Tel: 312-3309/3315
Fax: 312-3257

Ministry of Environmental Affairs
H.E. Nadia Riyad Makram Ebeid, Minister of State
30 Misr-Helwan Agricultural Road, Behind Sofitel Hotel, Maadi, Cairo
Tel: 525-6465/85/70/72
Fax: 525-6461

Ministry of Interior
H.E. Gen. Habib Al Adly, Minister
El Sheikh Rihan St., Bab El Louk, Cairo
Tel: 795-7500/2300/7286
Fax: 795-8068

Ministry of Local Development
H.E. Gen. Mustafa Abdel Qader
Minister of State
4 Shooting Club St., Dokki, Cairo
Tel: 749-7470/7656
Fax: 749-7788

Ministry of Social Affairs and Insurance
H.E. Dr. Amina Al Guindy, Minister
19 El Maraghy St., Agouza
Tel: 337-5404/0039
Fax: 591-7799

Ministry of Industry & Technological Development
H.E. Dr. Mustafa Al Refa'ei, Minister
2 Latin America St., Garden City, Cairo
Tel: 792-1168/1170
Fax: 795-5025

Ministry of Electricity and Energy
H.E. Dr. Ali Al Sei'dy, Minister
Abbassia, Nasr City, Cairo
Tel: 261-6514/6317
Fax: 260-2888

Ministry of Military Production
H.E. Dr. Sayed Meshaal, Minister of State
5 Ismail Abaza St., Cairo
Tel: 795-2428/3822
Fax: 794-8739

Ministry of Transportation
H.E. Dr. Ibrahim El Demeiry, Minister
105 Kasr El Aini St., Cairo
Tel: 795-5562/3
Fax: 795-5564

Ministry of Youth
H.E. Dr. Aley El Din Hilal Dessouki, Minister
Supreme Council of Youth, 26th July St., Sphinx Square, Mohandessin, Cairo
Tel: 346-1113/8859
Fax: 346-9025

Ministry of Supply & Domestic Trade
H.E. Dr. Hassan Ali Khedr, Minister
99 Kasr El Aini St., Cairo
Tel: 795-7606/7598/7613
Fax: 795-6387

Ministry of Planning & International Cooperation
H.E. Dr. Ahmed Mahrous El Darsh, Minister of State for International Cooperation
Salah Salem Road, Nasr City, Cairo
Tel: 401-4719/4516
Fax: 401-4733

Ministry of Public Business Sector
H.E. Dr. Mokhtar Abdel Moneim Khattab, Minister
Magles El Shaab St., Cairo
Tel: 795-8026/0164
Fax: 795-5882

Ministry of Finance
H.E. Dr. Medhat Hassanein, Minister
Lazoughly Square, Justice & Finance Bldg., Cairo
Tel: 795-7027/7176/794-1055
Fax: 795-1537

Ministry of Communication and Data
H.E. Dr. Ahmed Nazeef, Minister
Ramsis Exchange Bldg., Ramsis St., Cairo
Tel: 576-2640/577-0222
Fax: 574-4215

Ministry of Petroleum
H.E. Eng. Sameh Fahmi, Minister
El Mokhayyam El Da'em St., Nasr City, Cairo
Tel: 263-1000/2000
Fax: 263-6060

Cairo Governorate
H.E. Dr. Abdel Rehem Shehata, Governor of Cairo
Abdin, Cairo
Tel: 390-7754/63
Fax: 390-4620

Alexandria Governorate
H.E. Mr. Abdel Salam Mahgoub, Governor of Alexandria
60 El-Horreya Rd., Alexandria
Tel: (20-3) 484-8345

EGYPTIAN GOVERNMENT AGENCIES

Arab Organization for Industrialization (AOI)
Ret. Marshal Salah Halaby, Chairman
2D Midan El Abbassia, Cairo
Tel: 482-3377/3394
Fax: 482-6010

Capital Market Authority
Mr. Abdel Hamid Ibrahim, Chairman
20 Emad El Din St., Cairo
Tel: 574-1000/3111
Fax: 575-5339/5749-4156/574-5598

Central Agency for Public Mobilization & Statistics (CAPMAS)
Mr. Ahab Elwy, President
Salah Salem St., Nasr City, Cairo
Tel: 402-0574
Fax: 402-4099

Central Bank of Egypt
Dr. Ismail Hassan Mohamed, Governor
31 Kasr El Nil St., Cairo
Tel: 392-6211/6108
Fax: 392-5045/6361

Commercial Representation Office
Mr. El Said Kassem, First Undersecretary of State and Head
96 Ahmed Orabi St., Mohandessin, Cairo
Tel: 347-1892/3/4/5/6
Fax: 345-1840

Customs Authority
Mr. Mohamed Sheishaa, Director General
4 El Tayaran St., Nasr City, Cairo

Tel: 402-4344
Fax: 403-5557

EgyptAir
Eng. Mohamed Fahim Rayyan, Chairman
Cairo Int'l Airport, Cairo
Tel: 267-4500/7001/7002
Fax: 418-3715

Egyptian Environmental Affairs Agency (EEAA)
Dr. Ibrahim Abdel Gelil, Chairman
30 Misr-Helwan Agricultural Road, behind Sofitel Hotel, Maadi, Cairo
Tel: 525-6442/52
Fax: 525-6454/90

Egyptian Export Promotion Center (EEPC)
Mr. Hamdi Salem, Executive Director
106 Gameat El Dowal El Arabia St., 5th Fl., Mohandessin, Giza
Tel: 749-3919/20/21/22
Fax: 748-4142/4056

Egyptian General Petroleum Corp. (EGPC)
Eng. Mohamed Tawela, Chairman
Palestine St., 4th Sector, New Maadi, Cairo
Tel: 518-4960
Fax: 518-4963

Egyptian Radio & TV Union (ERTU)
Mr. Abdel Rahman Hafez, President
TV Bldg., Corniche El Nil, Cairo
Tel: 579-8494/5
Fax: 574-6989

Egyptian Tourist Authority (ETA)
Mr. Adel Abdel Aziz, Chairman
Misr Travel Bldg., Abbassia, Cairo
Tel: 683-9968/685-4509
Fax: 685-4363/4658

General Authority for Export & Import Control (GOEIC)
Mr. Fakhr Eldin Aboul Ezz, Chairman
1 El Sheikh Maarouf St. (Corner of Ramses St.) Down Town, Cairo
Tel: 579-2314/2330/2393/2433
Fax: 575-0749/8195

General Organization for Int'l Exhibitions & Fairs (GOIEF)
Mr. Mohamed Said Saleh, Chairman
Fair Grounds, Nasr City, Cairo
Tel: 260-7810/1/5
Fax: 260-4548/4521

General Authority for Investment & Free Zones (GAFI)
Dr. Mohamed El Ghamrawy Dawoud, Executive Director
8 Adly St., Cairo
Tel: 390-4611/6163/3776/391-5627
Fax: 390-7315

General Authority for Supply Commodities
Mr. Mohamed Abdel Razek Abdel Rahman, Vice Chairman
99 Kasr El Aini St., Cairo
Tel: 796-0766/0677
Fax: 796-1255

General Organization for Industrialization (GOFI)
Eng. Imam Abdel Moneim Mohamed, Vice Chairman
6 Khalil Agha St., Garden City, Cairo
Tel: 794-4640/795-7005
Fax: 794-4984

Immigration & Egyptians Abroad Administration
Mr. Sohail Mohamed Lashin
96 Ahmed Orabi St., Mohandessin
Tel: 303-4439/4441/6431
Fax: 303-5332

Information & Decision Support Center (IDSC)
Dr. Raafat Radwan, Chairman
Cabinet Bldg., Magles El Shaab St., Cairo
Tel: 795-1551/6077
Fax: 795-1716

New Community Authority
Eng. Hussein Hosny
Housing Bldg., 1 Ismail Abaza St., Cairo
Tel: 792-1409
Fax: 792-1406

Public Enterprise Office (PEO)
Mr. Fouad Abdul Wahab, Director
2 Latin America St., Garden City, Cairo
Tel: 795-9288/81
Fax: 795-9233

Sales Tax Authority
Mr. Mahmoud Mohamed Ali
4 El Tayaran St., Nasr City, Cairo
Tel: 401-2692/21/22/23/24
Fax: 401-6681

Social Fund for Development (SFD)
Mr. Hussein El Gammal, President
Hussein Hegazy St., & Kasr El Nil St., Cairo
Tel: 794-8339
Fax: 795-0628/796-1660

Cairo Alexandria Stock Exchange
Mr. Sameh El Torgoman, Director
4A El Sherifien St., Downtown, Cairo
Tel: 392-1402/47
Fax: 392-4214

Suez Canal Authority
Marshall Ahmed Ali Fadel, Chairman
6 Lazoghly St., Garden City, Cairo
Tel: 794-0746/7/8/9
Fax: 795-1592

Taxation Authority
Mr. Talaat Hammam, Chairman
5 Hussein Hegazi St., Cairo
Tel: 792-0767/0768/795-2128
Fax: 792-0757

Telecom Egypt
Eng. Akil Hamed Beshir, Chairman
Ministry of Transport, Communications & Civil Aviation, Ramses St., Cairo
Tel: 577-7551/578-1414
Fax: 579-3444

EGYPTIAN TRADE ASSOCIATIONS/ CHAMBERS OF COMMERCE

I. EGYPTIAN TRADE ASSOCIATIONS

Alexandria Business Association (ABA)
Mr. Mohamed Ragab, President
C/o Ragab Export. & Import Company
52 Avenue El Horria St., Alexandria
Tel: (20-3) 487-2206
Fax: (20-3) 487-2411

Assiut Business Association (ASBA)
Dr. Mohamed Gamal El Din Abdel Mettal
Chairman
Al Shark Insurance Tower, El Geish St., Assiut
Tel: (20-88) 341-766
Fax: (20-88) 341-755

Borg El Arab Business Association
Eng. Mohamed Farag Amer
First Industrial Zone, Borg El Arab, Alexandria
Tel: (20-3) 459-2079/3650/3075
Fax: (20-3) 459-2044

Egyptian American Friendship Association
Dr. Ibrahim Fawzi
83 Ramses St., 2nd Floor, Cairo
Tel: 575-2211

Egyptian Businessmen's Association (EBA)
Mr. Mohamed Youssef, Secretary General
21 Giza St., Nile Tower, Giza, Cairo
Tel: 573-6030/572-3855
Fax: 573-7258

Egyptian Federation for Consumer Protection Associations (EFCA)
Prof. Hassan Gemei, Secretary General
Faculty of Law, Cairo University
14 Nagi Farid St., off Mohy El Din Aboulezz, Mohandessin, Cairo
Tel/Fax: 760-1558/336-8442

Egyptian Junior Businessmen Group
Mr. Hassan Abdalla or Mr. Hatem Khater
2 Sherif St., El Lewa Bldg., 5th Fl., Apt. 58, Cairo
Tel: 393-2203
Fax: 392-4089

Egyptian Small Enterprise Development
Mr. Hussein Enan, Chairman
13 Salem Salem St., El Agouza, Giza, Cairo
Tel: 336-3980/1/2/4/5
Fax: 336-3983

Egypt's International Economic Forum
Ms. Nadia M. Lamloum, Manager
Mr. Shafik Gabr, Chairman
Semiramis InterContinental Hotel, Suite 405, Corniche El Nil, Garden City, Cairo
Tel: 797-1761
Fax: 797-1757

Sadat City Business Association
Mr. Ahmed Ezz, President
8 El Sad El Aali St., Dokki, Cairo
Tel: 760-0150/4/(20-49) 601-614
Fax: 760-0154/(20-49) 601-468

Sharkeya Business Association (SBA)
Mr. Hamdy El Koronfoly, Chairman
1 Salma St. (Corner Talaat Harb St.,) Zagazig
Tel: (20-55) 326-407/408/311-821/3
Fax: (20-55) 328-308

Sixth of October Investors Association
Mr. Saleh Gheith, Chairman
6th of October, Quarter 5, Central Avenue, Villa # 64
Tel: (20-11) 338-326/7
Fax: (20-11) 335-687

Small Enterprise Development Association (SEDA)
Eng. Ali Ali Soliman, Chairman
El Bareed Bldg., El Geish & Mohamed Mahmoud St., Port Said
Tel: (20-66) 336-452
Fax: (20-66) 336-454

Tenth of Ramadan Business Association
Mr. Mahmoud Soliman, Chairman
10th of Ramadan City, Banks District, Kafrawy Garden, P.O. Box 73
Tel: (20-15) 363-654/372-750/1/2
Fax: (20-15) 363-413

The Egyptian Exporters Association (EXPOLINK)

Mr. Sherif El Maghraby, Executive Director
23 El Esraa St., Mohandessin, Cairo
Tel: 304-6886
Fax: 304-6889

II. EGYPTIAN CHAMBERS OF COMMERCE (Affiliated with the Federation of Egyptian Chambers of Commerce)

Federation of Egyptian Chambers of Commerce
Mr. Khaled Abou Ismail, President
4 Falaky Square, Cairo
Tel: 395-8367/8/9
Fax: 395-8371

Alexandria Chamber of Commerce
Mr. Mostafa Yakout EL Naggar, President
31 Chamber of Commerce St., Alexandria
Tel: (20-3) 480-8779
Fax: (20-3) 480-8993

Assiut Chamber of Commerce
Mr. Ibrahim Abou El Eyoun, President
23rd July St., Assiut
Tel: (20-88) 332-082
Fax: (20-88) 346-044

Aswan Chamber of Commerce
Mr. Mostafa Abdel Kerim Mohamed, President
Cornish El Nil St., Aswan
Tel & Fax: (20-97) 301-177

Beni Suef Chamber of Commerce
Mr. Ragy Abdel Fattah Abdel Reheem, President
Mamdouh Fissal St., Mokebel District, Beni Suef
Tel: (20-82) 322-094/319-047
Fax: (20-82) 322-094

Cairo Chamber of Commerce
Mr. Abdel Halim Nawara, President
4 Midan El Falaki St., Cairo
Tel: 795-8261/2
Fax: 796-3603

Dakahleya Chamber of Commerce
Mr. Hamd El Touhamey Hassanien, President
El Bahr St., Midan Saleh Ayoub, El Mansoura
Tel: (20-50) 322-720/312-720
Fax: (20-50) 320-670/310-670

Damietta Chamber of Commerce
Mr. Mostafa Kamal Arafi, President
Saad Zaghloul St., Damietta
Tel: (20-57) 322-799/323-177
Fax: (20-57) 320-632

El Arish Chamber of Commerce
Mr. Mohamed Hamdy Gouda, President
El Saha El Shabiya St., El Arish, Sinai
Tel: (20-68) 340-327

El Beheira Chamber of Commerce
Mr. Fouad Ahmed Ellakkani, President
Midan El Seah, El Gomhouria St., Damanhour
Tel: (20-45) 322-207
Fax: (20-45) 317-531

El Fayoum Chamber of Commerce
Mr. Mohamed Abdel Rehman El Gahed, President
El Sad El Aley St., El Fayoum
Tel: (20-84) 322-148

El Giza Chamber of Commerce
Dr. Ahmed Bahgat, President
6 El Ghorfa El Tegarya St., Giza, Cairo
Tel: 572-1761
Fax: 568-3971

El Kaliobia Chamber of Commerce
El Moderia St., Midan Saad Zaghloul, Banha
Tel: (20-13) 222-177
Fax: (20-13) 232-477

El Menia Chamber of Commerce
Mr. Ahmed Shehata Ahmed, President
El Tegara St., El Menia
Tel: (20-86) 363-232
Fax: (20-86) 323-232

Menofia Chamber of Commerce
Mr. Adel El Ebiarey, President
Ibn El Fared St., Shebeen El Koum
Tel & Fax: (20-48) 221-511

El Wadi El Gedid Chamber of Commerce
Eng. Gad Mohamed Hamedallah, President
Port Said St., El Khargah
Tel: (20-92) 921-548
Fax: (20-92) 921-528

Gharbeya Chamber of Commerce
Eng. Aly Mohamed Ahmed, President
7 El Geish St., Tanta
Tel: (20-40) 330-4090
Fax: (20-40) 330-3793

Ismalia Chamber of Commerce
Mr. Abdel Rehman El Faramawy, President
163 Saad Zaghloul St., Ismailia
Tel: (20-64) 321-663/325-974
Fax: (20-64) 325-974

Kafr El Sheikh Chamber of Commerce
Mr. Abdel Shafie El Bahrawey, President
El Zawy Bldg., Kafr El Sheikh
Tel: (20-47) 234-191
Fax: (20-47) 232-916

Kena Chamber of Commerce
Mr. Ismail Youssef Weshahy, President

El Goumhouria St., Kena
Tel & Fax: (20-96) 332-690

Matrouh Chamber of Commerce
Mr. Kassem Taher Eissa, President
Marsa Matrouh
Tel: (20-46) 935-864
Fax: (20-46) 930-985

Port Said Chamber of Commerce
Mr. Mohamed Abdel Fattah Elmasri, President
Chamber of Commerce Building, Mohamed Ali St., Port Said
Tel: (20-66) 222-733/236-141/344-841
Fax: (20-66) 236-141/345-542

Sharkia Chamber of Commerce
Mr. Reda Alla Helmy, President
18 Gala St., El Zagazig
Tel: (20-55) 349-744

Sohag Chamber of Commerce
Mr. Ahmed Khalil Badawi, President
El Kesaria El Sharki St., Sohag
Tel & Fax: (20-93) 323-036

Suez Chamber of Commerce
Mr. Samer Farouk Ismail, President
47 Salah Eldin Elayoubi St., Suez
Tel: (20-62) 331-351, 227-783
Fax: (20-62) 223-456

The Red Sea Chamber of Commerce
Mr. Sidi Ahmed Ibrahim, President
Old City Council Bldg., Hurghada
Tel: (20-65) 549-298
Fax: (20-65) 548-494

South Sinai Chamber of Commerce
Mr. Gamal Abdel Wahab Omer
El Tour City
Tel: (20-62) 773-331

III. OTHER CHAMBERS OF COMMERCE IN EGYPT

American Chamber of Commerce in Egypt (Alexandria Office)
Ms. Sherine El Kharadly, Administrative Manager
36 Bani Abbas, Alexandria
Tel: (20-3) 484-4415
Fax: (20-3) 484-4413

American Chamber of Commerce in Egypt
Mr. Mohamed Mansour, President
33 Soliman Abaza St., Zamalek, Cairo
Tel: 338-1050
Fax: 338-1060

German-Arab Chamber of Commerce in Egypt
3 Abul Feda St., Zamalek, Cairo
Tel: 736-3664/2
Fax: 736-3663

Greek-Arab Chamber of Commerce in Egypt
17 Soliman El Halabi St., Cairo
Tel: 574-1190
Fax: 575-4970

Italian-Arab Chamber of Commerce in Egypt
33 Abdel Khalek Tharwat St., Cairo
Tel: 392-2275
Fax: 391-2503

Japanese Foreign Trade Organization
World Trade Center, 1191 Cornish El-Nil, Boulaq, Cairo
Tel: 574-1111
Fax: 756-966

IV. EGYPTIAN CHAMBERS OF INDUSTRIES (Members of the Federation of Egyptian Industries)

Federation of Egyptian Industries
Dr. Abdel Moneim Seoudi, Chairman
26A Cornish El Nil, 2nd floor, near WTC
Tel: 579-6590/1/2
Fax: 579-6593/4

Chamber of Building Materials Industries
Mr. Samir Allam, President
23 Sherif St., Cairo
Tel & Fax: 392-8820

Chamber of Grains & Related Products
Mr. Mahmoud Ghanem Diab, President
65 El Horria Avenue, Alexandria
Tel & Fax: (20-3) 391-6121

Chamber of Chemical Industries
Dr. Mahmoud Fouad Mahmoud, President
26A Sherif St., Immobilia Bldg., Cairo
Tel: 393-5436
Fax: 390-0063

Chamber of Cinema Industry
Mr. Monib Mahmoud Shafei, President
33 Orabi St., Downtown, Cairo
Tel: 574-1677/1638
Fax: 575-1583

Chamber of Engineering Industries
Eng. Aly Fahmy El Sawah, President
13 Sherif St., 5th Floor, Cairo
Tel: 392-1238
Fax: 391-8099

Chamber of Food Industries
Eng. Ismail Baligh Sabry, President
26A Sherif St., Immobilia Bldg., Cairo
Tel: 392-5767, 392-6170

Fax: 392-6170

Chamber of Leather Industry
Eng. Salama Mostafa Hamza, President
26A Sherif St., Immobilia Bldg., Cairo
Tel: 393-8294/392-8140
Fax: 390-8016

Chamber of Metallurgical Industries
Eng. Mohamed Abdel Aziz Khattab, President
13 Sherif St., 5th Floor, Cairo
Tel: 392-1238
Fax: 391-8099

Chamber of Petroleum & Mining
Dr. Eng. Hamed Hassanein Amer, President
8 Batel Ahmed Abdel Aziz St., off Fatma Rushdi St., Abdin, Cairo
Tel: 392-6462
Fax & Tel: 393-0098

Chamber of Printing, Binding and Paper Products
Mr. Ahmed Atef Abdel Rahman, President
19 Mariet St., Abdel Moneim Riad Sq., El Tahrir, Cairo
Tel: 574-4343
Fax & Tel: 578-6709

Chamber of Pharmaceutical, Cosmetics and Medical Appliances Industries
Dr. Mohamed Galal Ghorab, President
26A Sherif St., Immobilia Bldg., Cairo
Tel: 393-7270
Fax: 393-7260

Chamber of Tanning, Leather & Fur Industries
Mr. Mamdouh Thabet Mekki, President
26A Sherif St., Immobilia Bldg., Cairo
Tel: 395-9143/393-0872
Fax: 393-4098

Egyptian Textile Manufacturers Federation "ETMF"
Mr. El Motaz Bellah Abdel Maksoud, President
43 Sherif St., Down Town, Cairo
Tel: 392-6932/395-2239
Fax & Tel: 390-0005

Chamber of Woodworking Industries
Mr. Redalla Mohamed Helmy, President
23 Sherif St., 3rd Floor, Cairo
Tel & Fax: 393-5920

EGYPTIAN MARKET RESEARCH FIRMS:

Rada Research & Public Relations Co.
Mrs. Loula Zaklama, President
1 Mostafa El Wakil Street, Heliopolis, Cairo
Tel: 291-7956, 291-5437, Fax: 291-7563

Transcentury
Mr. Anis Aclimandos, President
20 Adly Street, Kodak Passage, Cairo
Tel: 393-6425, Fax: 393-6425

Shortcuts Institutional Business Development
Mrs. Lamia Hamdy, Managing Director
42 Eden St., Mohandessin, Cairo
Tel: 336-4297, 012-210-4368, Fax: 336-0560

B2LS
Mr. Bethoven Abdel Wanis, President
14 Roshdi St., Abdin, Cairo
Tel/Fax: 395-2134, 012/325-1501

ProMark Corp. Ltd.
Mr. Medhat El Madany, Managing Director
41 El Horreya St., Heliopolis, 6th Fl., Cairo
Tel: 418-7793, 414-3136/7, Fax: 418-6357

Intermarkets Advertising
Mr. Galal Zaki, President
42 Abdel Moneim Riad Street, Dokki, Cairo
Tel: 360-3017/8, Fax: 360-3019

Research & Advertising Consultants
Dr. Sami Abdel Aziz, President
30 Gameat Al Dowal Al Arabia St., Mohandessin, Cairo
Tel: 360-8439, Fax: 360-4815

The Economic Studies and Consultancy Department (ESCD)
5 El Borsa El Gedida St.
Tel: 795-9785, 392-3245, Fax: 795-9782
Ms. Sanaa El Shinnawi

International Business Associates (IBA)
Mrs. Ann Marie Harrison, Chairman
1079 Corniche El Nil, Garden City, Cairo
Tel: 797-1312, 797-1372, 797-1300, Fax: 797-1317, 797-1318

Marketeers
52 Youssef Abbas St., Nasr City, Cairo
Tel: 262-2810, Fax: 262-2810

Middle East Marketing Research Bureau
21 Dr. Mohamed Gomaa St., Heliopolis, Cairo
Tel: 240-1799, Fax: 639-7099

Fiani & Partners
Mrs. Josse Dorra Fiani
143 Tahrir Street, Dokki, Cairo
Tel: 748-7353/54/55/56, Fax: 748-5204

Wafai and Associates
El Forsan Bldg., behind Sheraton Heliopolis, Bldg. A, Heliopolis, Cairo
Tel: 267-6681/2, Fax: 266-9263

COMMERCIAL BANKS:

See complete list of banks under Chapter 8.

U.S. EMBASSY TRADE PERSONNEL:

The Commercial Service – American Embassy Cairo
Bobette Orr, Counselor for Commercial Affairs
Edward Yagi, Commercial Attaché
5 Latin America Street, Garden City, Cairo
Tel: 797-2330, 797-2426, Fax: 795-8368
www.usembassy.egnet.net .

The Commercial Service – American Center Alexandria
John Abdelnour, Sr. Commercial Specialist
Heba Abdel Aziz, Commercial Specialist
3 El Pharaana Avenue, American Center Bldg., Alexandria
Tel: (03) 482-5607, 487-6330, Fax: (03) 482-9199

USDA/Foreign Agricultural Service (FAS)
Thomas Pomeroy, Counselor for Agricultural Affairs
Ali Abdi, Agricultural Attaché
8 Kamal El Din Salah St., Garden City, Cairo
Tel: 797-2388/9, Fax: 796-3989

U.S. Information Service
David Ballard, Press Attaché
5 Latin America St., Garden City, Cairo
Tel: 797-3473/4, Fax: 797-3740

U.S. Agency for International Development (USAID)
Willard J. Pearson, Jr., Director
Anne Aarnes, Deputy Director
Roberta Mahoney, Associate Director
Economic Growth Directorate
Plot 1/A off El Laselki Street
New Maadi, Cairo
Tel.: 522-7000 Fax 516-4652

U.S. Department of State
Eugene Cretc, Minister-Counselor for Political & Economic Affairs
Richard Albright, Counselor for Political and Economic Affairs
8 Kamal El Din Salah St., Garden City, Cairo
Tel: 797-2251, Fax: 797-2181

Office of Economic & Commercial Affairs
Embassy of the Arab Republic of Egypt
Alaa El Din Shalaby, Minister-Counselor for Economic & Commercial Affairs
2232 Massachusetts Ave., NW
Washington, D.C. 20008
Tel: 202-265-9111, Fax: 202-328-4517

WASHINGTON-BASED USG CONTACTS

U.S. Department of Commerce
Tom Sams, Egypt Desk Officer
MAC/ONE, Room 2029B
Washington, D.C. 20230
Tel: 202-482-1860, Fax: 202-482-0878

U.S. Department of Commerce
The Commercial Service
Kevin Brennan, Regional Director - ANESA
HCH Bldg., Room 1223
Washington, D.C. 20230
Tel: 202-482-4836, Fax: 202-482-5179

U.S. Department of Agriculture
AgExport Services Division
Charles T. Alexander, Director
Room 4939-S, 14th Independence Ave., SW
Washington, D.C. 20250
Tel: 202-720-6343, Fax: 202-690-4374

U.S. Department of State
Christopher Henzel, Deputy Director
Office of Egyptian and North African Affairs
NEA/ENA, Room 5250
Washington, D.C. 20520
Tel: 202-647-7449, Fax: 202-736-4458

U.S. Export-Import Bank (EXIM Bank)
811 Vermont Avenue NW
Washington, D.C. 20571
Tel: 202-566-8990, 202-566-2117, Fax: 202-566-7524

U.S.-Arab Chamber of Commerce (Pacific) Inc.
PO Box 422218
San Francisco, CA 94142
Tel: 415-398-9200, Fax: 415-398-7111

U.S. International Trade Commission (USITC)
500 E Street, SW
Washington, D.C. 20436
Tel: 202-252-1000, Fax: 202-252-1798

U.S. Small Business Administration (SBA)
409 3rd St., SW
Washington, D.C. 20416
Tel: 202-205-6531, Fax: 202-205-6928

U.S. Trade and Development Agency (USTDA)
John Richter, Regional Director for Africa & Middle East
SA-16, Room 309
Washington, D.C. 20523-1602
Tel: 703-875-4357, Fax: 703-875-4009

OTHER U.S. AND EGYPTIAN ORGANIZATIONS AND ENTITIES:

American Chamber of Commerce Egypt/U.S.
Graham Wisner, Executive Director
815 Connecticut Ave. NW
Washington, DC 20006-4078
Tel: 202-496-9299, Fax: 202-833-6919

American Egyptian Cooperation Foundation (AECF)
330 East 39th Street, Suite 32L
New York, NY 10016
Tel: 212-867-2323, Fax: 212-697-0465

Arab-American Business & Professional Association
P.O. Box 700
746 Walker Road
Great Falls, VA 33066-0700
Tel: 703-759-2235, Fax: 703-759-9300

Consulate General of Egypt
1110 Second Ave., Rm. 201
New York, NY 10022
Tel: 212-759-7120, Fax: 212-308-7643

Consulate General of Egypt
3001 Pacific Ave.
San Francisco, CA 94115
Tel: 415-346-9700, Fax: 415-346-9480

Consulate General of Egypt
1990 Post Oak Blvd., Suite 2180
Houston, TX 77056
Tel: 713-961-4915, Fax: 713-961-3868

Consulate General of Egypt
500 N. Michigan Ave., Suite 1900
Chicago, IL 60611
Tel: 312-828-9162, Fax: 312-828-9167

Egyptian American Businessmen's Association (EABA)
50 Broad Street, Suite 1609
New York, NY 10004
Tel: 212-797-3474, Fax: 212-344-1050

Embassy of the Arab Republic of Egypt
3521 International Court, NW
Washington, D.C. 20008
Tel: 202-895-5400, Fax: 202-244-4319

National U.S.-Arab Chamber of Commerce
1100 New York Avenue, NW
East Tower, Suite 550
Washington, D.C. 20005
Tel: 202-289-5920, Fax: 202-289-5938

Overseas Private Investment Corporation (OPIC)
1615 M street, NW
Washington, D.C. 20527
Tel: 800-424-OPIC or 202-457-7010, Fax: 202-223-3514

Permanent Mission of Egypt to the United Nations
36 East 67 Street
New York, NY 10021
Tel & Fax: 212-879-6300

JORDAN

U.S. Embassy, Amman, Economic/Commercial Section Personnel

Tom Goldberger, Economic Counselor
Ian Campbell, Economic/Commercial Officer
Rick Ortiz, Commercial Officer
Greg Garramone, Economic/Commercial Officer
Scott Wright, Economic/Commercial Officer
Gabi Afram, Economic/Commercial Specialist
Muna Farkouh, Commercial Specialist
Rana Safadi, Environmental Specialist
Georgina Abu Manneh, Commercial Assistant
Hala Khoury, Agricultural Specialist

International mailing address:
Economic/Commercial Section
U.S. Embassy Amman
P.O. Box 354
Amman 11118, Jordan

U.S. domestic mail address:
U.S. Embassy Amman,
Economic/Commercial Section
APO, AE 09892-0200

Telephone: (962) (6) 592-0101, ext. 2558 or 2632
Fax: (962) (6) 592-7653 / 592-0146

U.S. Embassy Amman, U.S. Agency for International Development

International mailing address:
USAID/Jordan Economic Opportunities Office
U.S. Embassy Amman
P.O. Box 354
Amman 11118, Jordan

U.S. domestic mail address:
U.S. Embassy Amman, USAID
APO, AE 09892-0200

Toni-Christiansen-Wagner, Director
Telephone: (962) (6) 592-0101, ext. 2614/2615
Fax: (962) (6) 592-0143
E-mail: ToniC@dosnet.usaid.gov

Jordan-United States Business Partnership (JUSBP)
Suite 500, Qammou Building
30 Prince Shaker Bin Zaid Street

Shmeisani, Amman, Jordan
Mr. Lewis Reade, CEO
Telephone: (962) (6) 568-4308/56843081/5684250
Fax: (962) (6) 568-4266
E-mail: jusbpoff@globalone.com.jo

AMIR Program
66, Abdul Hameed Badees Street, Shmeisani
P.O. Box 940503 Amman 11194, Jordan
Telephone: (962) (6) 566-1831/2
Fax: (962) (6) 560-3599
E-mail: info@amir-jordan.org
www.amir-jordan.org

U.S. Department of State, Office of Business Affairs
2201 C Street NW, RM 2318
Washington, D.C. 20520
Telephone: (202) 746-1625
Fax: (202) 647-3953

U.S. Department of Commerce
14th Street and Constitution Avenue, NW
Washington, D.C. 20230
Telephone: (202) 482-1209
Fax: (202) 482-5179

Relevant Jordanian Government Departments

Ministry of Industry and Trade
Mr. Wasef Azer, Minister
P.O. Box 2019, Amman, Jordan
Telephone: (962) (6) 560-7191/5663774
Fax: (962) (6) 560-3721 / 568-4692
www.mit.gov.jo

Jordan Investment Board
Ms. Reem M. Badran, Director General
P.O. Box 893, Amman 11821, Jordan
Telephone: (962) (6) 553-1081/2/3
Fax: (962) (6) 552-1084
E-mail: info@jip.com.jo
www.jordaninvestment.com

Jordan Export Development and Commercial Centers Corporation (JEDCO)
Mr. Farouk Hadidi, Director General
P.O. Box 7704, Amman 11118, Jordan
Telephone: (962) (6) 560-3507
Fax: (962) (6) 568-4568
E-mail: jedco@jedco.gov.jo
www.jedco.gov.jo

Jordan Industrial Estates Corporation
Mr. Amer Majali, Director General
P.O. Box 950278, Amman 11195, Jordan
P.O. Box 17, Sahab Industrial Estate, Amman, Jordan
Telephone: (962) (6) 402-2101/3
Fax: (962) (6) 402-1194
E-mail: info@jiec.com.jo
www.jiec.com

Free Zones Corporation
Mr. Ali Madadha, Director General
P.O. Box 20036, Amman, Jordan
Telephone: (962) (5) 382-6429
Fax: (962) (5) 382-6430
www.free-zones.gov.jo

Central Bank of Jordan
Dr. Umayya Toukan, Governor
P.O. Box 37, Amman 11118, Jordan
Telephone: (962) (6) 463-0301/9
Fax: (962) (6) 463-8889/463-9730
www.cbj.gov.jo

General Sales Tax Department
Mr. Iyad Al-Qudah
Telephone: (962) (6) 582-3441/5823392
Fax: (962) (6) 582-3395

Aqaba Special Economic Zone Authority
Mr. Imad Fakhoury, Commissioner for Investment & Economic Development
P. O. Box 2565, Aqaba 77110, Jordan
Telephone: (962) (3) 203-5757
Fax: (962) (3) 203-0912
E-Mail: aseza-inv@nic.net.jo
www.aqabazone.com

Chambers of Commerce and Trade Associations

Jordanian American Business Association (JABA)
American Chamber of Commerce
Mr. Fawaz Shalan, President
P.O. Box 941865, Amman 11194, Jordan
Telephone: (962) (6) 565-1860/1
Fax: (962) (6) 565-1862
E-mail: mail@jaba.org.jo
www.jaba.org.jo

Federation of Jordanian Chambers of Commerce and
Amman Chamber of Commerce (ACC)
Mr. Haidar Murad, Chairman
P.O. Box 287, Amman, Jordan
Telephone: (962) (6) 566-5492/566-6151
Fax: (962) (6) 568-5997/566-6155
www.fjcc.com
www.ammanchamber.org

Amman Chamber of Industry
Mr. Othman Bdeir, Chairman
P.O. Box 1800, Amman, Jordan
Telephone: (962) (6) 464-4569/464-3001
Fax: (962) (6) 464-7852
E-mail: aci@aci.org.jo

www.aci.org.jo

Jordan Trade Association
Dr. Samih Darwazeh, Chairman
P.O. Box 830432, Amman, Jordan
Telephone: (962) (6) 568-5603/4
Fax: (962) (6) 568-5605
E-mail: jta@go.com.jo
www.jta-jordan.com

Jordanian Businessmen Association (JBA)
Mr. Hamdi Tabba'a, Chairman
P.O. Box 926182, Amman, Jordan
Telephone: (962) (6) 568-0855/5604424
Fax: (962) (6) 568-0663
E-mail: jba@nets.com.jo
www.jba.com.jo

Amman World Trade Center
Mr. Mohammed Asfour, Chairman
Mr. Yaser Toukan, General Manager
P.O. Box 962140, Amman, Jordan
Telephone: (962) (6) 560-5791/2
Fax: (962) (6) 560-5793
E-mail: lsarhni@awcc.com
www.awcc.com

Information Technology Association of Jordan (INTAJ)
Mr. Raed Bilbeisi, Executive Director
P.O. Box 2383
Amman 11953, Jordan
Telephone: (962) (6) 515-2322
Fax: (962) (6) 515-2344
E-mail: info@intaj.net
www.intaj.net

Business and Proffessional Women's Association (BPWA)
Mr. Ala'a M. Kurdi, Director
Telephone: (962) (6) 551-1647/8
www.bpwa.org.jo

Jordan Society of Tourist & Travel Agents (JSTA)
Mr. Marwan Khoury, Managing Director
Telephone: (962) (6) 463-8599
Fax: (962) (6) 567-8295
E-mail: jtb@nets.com.jo
www.jsta.gor

Licensed Banks & The Stock Exchange

Citibank
Ms. Suhair Al-Ali, General Manager
P.O. Box 5055, Amman 11183, Jordan
Telephone: (962) (6) 464-4065/2276
Fax: (962) (6) 465-8693/464-1923
www.citibank.com/jordan

HSBC
Mr. Robert Bray, General Manager
P.O. Box 925286, Amman 11110, Jordan
Telephone: (962) (6) 560-7471
Fax: (962) (6) 568-2047
E-mail: hsbc-jo@nets.com.jo
www.hsbc.com

ANZ Grindlays Bank
Mr. Hiofrances John Verjeson, General Manager
P.O. Box 9997, Amman 11191, Jordan
Telephone: (962) (6) 560-7201
Fax: (962) (6) 567-9115
E-mail: zahranm@anz.com
www.anz.com

Arab Bank Limited
Mr. Abdulmajeed Shoman, Chairman/General Manager
P.O. Box 950545, Amman 11195, Jordan
Telephone: (962) (6) 560-7231
Fax: (962) (6) 560-6793
E-mail: international@arabbank.com.jo
www.arabbank.com

The Housing Bank
Mr. Zuhair Khouri, Chairman
Mr. Abd-Al-Qader Dweik, General Manager
P.O. Box 7693, Amman 11118, Jordan
Telephone: (962) (6) 560-7315
Fax: (962) (6) 567-8121
E-mail: hbho@go.com.jo
www.iskanbank.com.jo

Cairo-Amman Bank
Mr. Yazid Mufti, General Manager
P.O. Box 950661, Amman 11195, Jordan
Telephone: (962) (6) 461-6910
Fax: (962) (6) 464-2890
E-mail: info@ca_bank.com.jo
www.ca_bank.com

Arab Banking Corporation/Jordan
Mr. Mohammad Al-Mana'i, Chairman
Mr. Amer Al-Salti, General Manager
P.O. Box 926691, Amman 11110, Jordan
Telephone: (962) (6) 566-4183
Fax: (962) (6) 568-6291
E-mail: info@abc.com.jo
www.abc.com.jo

Jordan National Bank
Mr. Rajai Muasher, Chairman, General Manager
P.O. Box 3103, Amman 11181, Jordan
Telephone: (962) (6) 562-2282
Fax: (962) (6) 562-2281
E-mail: jnb@go.com.jo
www.ahli.com

Bank of Jordan

Mr. Tawfiq Fakhoury, Chairman
Mr. Mohammed Jomah, acting General Manager
P.O. Box 2140, Amman 11181, Jordan
Telephone: (962) (6) 569-6277
Fax: (962) (6) 569-6291
E-mail: boj@go.com.jo
www.boj.com.jo

Jordan Gulf Bank
Mr. Nabil Barakat, Chairman
Mr. Fayez Abu Elenin, General Manager
P.O. Box 9989, Amman 11191, Jordan
Telephone: (962) (6) 560-3931
Fax: (962) (6) 566-4110
E-mail: r&d-jgb@firstnit.com.jo

Jordan Kuwait Bank
Mr. Abd Al-Kareem Al-Kabarity, Chairman
Mr. M. Suheil Tahboub, Deputy Chairman
Mr. M. Yasser Al-Asmar, General Manager
P.O. Box 9776, Amman 11191, Jordan
Telephone: (962) (6) 568-8814
Fax: (962) (6) 569-5604
E-mail: webmaster@jkbank.com.jo
www.jordan-kuwait-bank.com

Union Bank for Savings and Investment
Mr. Isam Salfiti, Chairman/General Manager
P.O. Box 35104, Amman 11180, Jordan
Telephone: (962) (6) 560-7011
Fax: (962) (6) 566-6149
E-mail: info@unionbankjo.com
www.unionbankjo.com

Jordan Investment and Finance Bank
Mr. Nizar Jardaneh, Chairman
Mr. Basil Jardaneh, General Manager
P.O. Box 950601, Amman 11195, Jordan
Telephone: (962) (6) 566-5145
Fax: (962) (6) 568-1410
E-mail: jifbank@index.com.jo
www.jifbank.com

Arab Jordan Investment Bank
Mr. Abdel Kader Al-Qadi, Chairman
Mr. Hani Al-Qadi, General Manager
P.O. Box 8797, Amman 11121, Jordan
Telephone: (962) (6) 560-7126
Fax: (962) (6) 568-1482
E-mail: suhail54@firstnet.com.jo
www.ajib.com

Philadelphia Bank
Mr. Issa Musbah Al-Kathemi, Chairman
Mr. Nimer Wadlied Al-Shakn'a, General Manager
P.O.Box 925993, Amman 11110, Jordan
Telephone: (962) (6) 566-3141
Fax: (962) (6) 568-3247
E-mail: piblrs@jo.com.jo
www.philibank.com

Middle East Investment Bank
Acting Manager
P.O.Box 560, Amman 11118, Jordan
Telephone: (962) (6) 569-5470
Fax: (962) (6) 569-3410

Export and Finance Bank
Mr. Mohammed Ali/Khaldoun Al-Hosary, Chairman
Mr. Hagop Banayan, Acting General Manager
P.O.Box 941283, Amman 11194, Jordan
Telephone: (962) (6) 569-4250
Fax: (962) (6) 569-2062
E-mail: info@efbank.com.jo
www.efbank.com.jo

Industrial Development Bank
Mr. Saad Tal, Chairman
Mr. Tayseer Wahbeh, General Manager
P.O. Box 1982, Amman, Jordan
Telephone: (962) (6) 464-2216
Fax: (962) (6) 464-7821

Jordan Islamic Bank
Mr. Mahmoud Hassoubah, Chairman
Mr. Moussa Shehadeh, General Manager
P.O. Box 926225, Amman 11110, Jordan
Telephone: (962) (6) 566-6326
Fax: (962) (6) 566-6326
E-mail: jib@islamicbank.com
www.jordanislamic.com.jo

Amman Stock Exchange
Mr. Jalil Tarif, Director General
P.O. Box 212466, Amman 11121, Jordan
Telephone: (962) (6) 566-4109/566-4081
Fax: (962) (6) 566-4071
E-mail: exchange@go.com.jo
www.ammanstockex.com

Jordan Securities Commission (JSC)
Mr. Bassam Al-Saket, Executive Chairman
P.O. Box 8802, Amman, Jordan
Telephone: (962) (6) 560-7171
Fax: (962) (6) 568-6830
www.jsc.gov.jo

Securities Depository Center (SDC)
Mr. Samir Jaradat, Director
P.O. Box 212465, Amman 11121, Jordan
Telephone: (962) (6) 567-2788
www.sdc.com.jo

Institute of Banking Studies
Mr. Adib Haddad, Dean
P.O. Box 1378, Amman 11953, Jordan
Telephone: (962) (6) 553-6395
Fax: (962) (6) 553-2199
E-mail: generaldirector@ibs.edu.jo
www.ibs.edu.jo

Arab Credit and Commercial Information
Ms. Rasha Baalbaki, Commercial Department
Amman, Jordan
Telephone: (962) (6) 568-3798/9
Fax: (962) (6) 568-3791
E-mail: info@acs.com.jo

Washington-based U.S. Government Contacts

TPCC Trade Information Center / Washington
Telephone: 1-800-USA-TRADE

Doug Bell
Desk Officers for Jordan, Syria and Lebanon
NEA/ARN, Department of State
Washington, DC 20520
Telephone: (202) 647-1058
Fax: (202) 647-0989

Paul Thanos
Jordan Desk Officer
Office of the Near East
Department of Commerce
Washington, DC
Telephone: (202) 377-1870
Fax: (202) 377-0878

Paul Hoffman
Area Officer
Department of Agriculture
Washington, DC
Telephone: (202) 720-7053
Fax: (202) 720-6063

Overseas Private Investment Corporation (OPIC)
1100 New York Avenue, N.W.
Washington, D.C. 20527
Telephone: (202) 336-8799
Fax: (202) 408-9859
www.opic.gov

Export-Import Bank (Exim-Bank)
811 Vermont Avenue, N.W.
Washington DC 20571
Telephone: (800) 565-3946 or (202) 565-3946
Fax: (202) 565-3380
www.exim.gov

U.S. Trade & Development Agency (TDA)
1621 North Kent Street, Suite 300
Arlington, VA 22209
Telephone: (703) 875-4357
Fax: (703) 875-4009
www.tda.gov

Other Relevant Contacts

Jordanian Embassy, WASHINGTON
Mr. Samir Mansour (JEDCO)
3504 International Drive, N.W.
Washington DC 20008
Telephone: (202) 966-2664
Fax: (202) 244-0239
E-mail: jordanctr@aol.com
www.jordanembassyus.org

National U.S. Arab Chamber of Commerce
1100 New York Avenue, N.W.
East Tower, Suite 550
Washington, DC 20005
Telephone: (202) 289-5920
Fax: (202) 289-5938
www.nusacc.org

Other Relevant Web-Sites:

U.S. Government

U.S. Embassy, Amman, Jordan
www.usembassy-amman.org.jo

American Business Center web-site:
www.usembassy-amman.org.jo/wwwhcom.html

U.S. State Department
www.state.gov

U.S. Customs Department
www.customs.ustreas.gov

U.S. trade and development agency
www.tda.gov

U.S. foreign agricultural service
www.fas.usda.gov

Jordanian Government

National Information Center, Amman, Jordan
www.nic.gov.jo

Royal Scientific Society
www.rss.gov.jo

Ministry of Tourism & Antiquities
www.mota.gov.jo

Jordan Customs Department
www.customs.gov.jo

Petra (Jordanian government news agency)
www.petra.gov.jo

Jordan Telecommunications Company
www.jtc.com.jo

Telecommunications Regulatory Commission
www.trc.gov.jo

Ministry of Post & Communications
www.mopc.gov.jo

Jordan Department of Statistics
www.dos.gov.jo

Jordan Civil Aviation Authority
www.jcaa.gov.jo

Links to other Jordanian government ministries
www.nic.gov.jo

Jordanian Organizations and Businesses

Amman Financial Market (stock exchange)
www.access2arabia.com/afm

Jordanian Association of Manufacturers of Pharmaceuticals and Medical Appliances (JAPM)
www.japm.com

Jordan Exporters and Producers Association for Fruit and Vegetables
www.access2arabia.com/jepafv

Arab Potash Company
www.nic.gov.jo/industry/apc

The Jordan Times
www.access2arabia.com/jordantimes

The Star
www.star.arabia.com

Jordan University of Science and Technology
www.just.edu.jo

Yarmouk University
www.yu.edu.jo

University of Jordan
www.ju.edu.jo

Interarab Investment Fund
www.interarab.com.jo

JTMS-Fastlink (mobile phones)
www.jmts-fastlink.com

Kawar Group
www.kawar.com

The Unified Company for Organizing Land Transport
www.unified.com.jo

Nabresco (land transport)
www.nabresco.com.jo

Miscellaneous

His Majesty The Late King Hussein's Web Page
www.kinghussein.gov.jo

Her Majesty Queen Noor's Web Page
www.noor.gov.jo

His Majesty King Abdullah
www.kingabdullah.jo

His Royal Highness Prince Hassan
www.princehassan.gov.jo

Ministry of Health
www.health.gov.jo

Baladna (general interest site)
www.baladna.com.jo

Jordan's Yellow Net
www.mideastweb.com/yellow

Accessme (general interest)
www.accessme.com.jo

Primus/CNS (general interest)
www.cns.com.jo

Arabia Online
www.arabia.com

Trade Point Development Center Association
www.iebb.com

LEBANON

U.S. AND COUNTRY CONTACTS

Investment Development Authority of Lebanon (IDAL)
Kamal Hayek, Chairman
Nijmeh Square, Hussein Al-Ahdab Street, Bldg No 1145
Tel: 961-1-983306/9
Fax: 961-1-983302/3
Email: invest@idal.com.lb
Home Page: www. idal.com.lb

Council for Development and Reconstruction (CDR)
Mahmoud Osman, President
Tallet Al Serail, Beirut
Tel: 961-1-981431/2; 961-1-980099
Fax: 961-1-981381
Home Page: www.cdr.gov.lb

Trade Information Center
Rafif Berro, Office Director

Ministry of Economy and Trade
Rue Artois, Beirut
Tel: 961-1-345250; 961-1-345255
Fax: 961-1-349459
E-Mail: tic@economy.gov.lb
Home Page: www.economy.gov.lb

Beirut Chamber of Commerce, Industry and Agriculture
Adnan Kassar, President
Beirut Chamber of Commerce, Industry and Agriculture Bldg.
Justinien St., Sanayeh
P.O. Box: 11-1801 Beirut
Tel: 961-1-744160/2, 961-1-745287/8, 961-1-341328
Fax: 961-1-745288, 961-1-602050
Email: akassar-president@ccib.org.lb
Home Page: www.ccib.org.lb

American Lebanese Chamber of Commerce
Salim Zeenni, President
Venice Bldg., 1153 Foch St., Beirut Central District
Tel/Fax: 961-1-985330/1
Email: amchamlb@cyberia.net .lb

Lebanese Bankers Association
H.E. Farid Raphael, President
Dora Highway, Moucarry Center, 4th Floor
Tel: 961-1-970500
Fax: 961-1- 970501
Email: abl@abl.org.lb

Lebanese Industrialists' Association
Jacques Sarraf, President
Beirut Chamber of Commerce, Industry and Agriculture Bldg.
Justinien St., Sanayeh
P.O.Box: 11-1502 Beirut
Tel: 961-1-350280/2
Fax: 961-1-351167, 961-1-350282
Email: ali@sodetel.net.lb; ali@ali.orglb.
Home Page: www.ali.org.lb

Beirut Merchants' Association
Nadim Assi, President
Beirut Chamber of Commerce, Industry and Agriculture Bldg.
Justinien St., Sanayeh
Tel/Fax: 961-1-345735, 961-1-347997
Fax: 961-1-747887

Masri Etudes et Expertises
Habib Khalil Masri, General Manager
Jisr El-Bacha, Bacha Gardens Bloc A
Tel: 961-1-513666
Fax: 961-1-511109
URL: www.masri.com.lb

Consultant and Research Institute (CRI)
Dr. Kamal Hamdan
Carlton Bldg, Raouche
POBox 13-5216 Beirut
Tel: 961-1-867605; 961-1-801108
Fax: 961-1-792058
Email: cri@dm.net.lb

Etudes et Consultations Economiques (ECE)
Dr. Samir Nasr, Director
Tour St Nicolas, St Nicolas Str.
Ashrafieh
P.O.Box: 16-5048 Beirut
Tel: 961-1-217232/3
Fax: 961-1-325200
Email: snasr@inco.com.lb

Centre de Recherches et d'Etudes Agricoles
Dr. Riad Saadeh, Director
New Jdeidet St.
Jdeidet Al-Metn
Tel/Fax: 961-1-899433, 961-1-601574

American Task Force For Lebanon (ATFL)
Dr. George Cody, Executive Director
Washington, DC
Tel: 202-223-9333
Fax: 202-223-1399

Trade Information Center Number in Washington: 1-800-USA-TRADE

US Department Of State
Office of Business Affairs
Tel: 202-647-1625
Fax: 202-647-3953
Home Page: www.state.gov

U.S. Department Of State
Lebanon Desk (Economics)
Doug Bell
Tel: 202-647-1058
Fax:202-647-0989
E-mail: Belldm@state.gov

U.S. Trade and Development Agency
Cybill Sigler
Middle East and North Africa Country Manager
Tel: 703-875-4357
Fax: 703-875-4009
E-mail: info@tda.gov
Home Page: www.tda.gov

U.S. Department of Commerce
Foreign Commercial Service
Tom Sams, Lebanon Desk
Tel: 202-482-1860
Fax: 202-482-0878
E-mail: tom_sams@ita.doc.gov
Home Page: www.ita.doc.gov

US Department Of Agriculture

Foreign Agricultural Service
Trade Assistance and Promotion Office
Tel: 202-720-7420
Home Page: www.usda.gov

Overseas Private Investment Corporation
Abed Tarbush
Tel: 202-336-8799
Home Page: www.opic.gov

U.S. Export Import Bank
Ms. Veronique Cavaillier, Business Development
Tel: 202-565-Exim
Home Page: www.exim.gov

MAURITANIA

US MISSION IN MAURITANIA

American Embassy
2430 Nouakchott Place
Washington, DC 20521-2430
Tel: (222) 25-26-60; 25-26-63
Fax: (222) 25-15-92

Ambassador:
Timberlake Foster

Deputy Chief Of Mission
Carol Colloton

Consular, Economic, And Commercial Officer
Katherine Metres until February 2001
metreskm@state.gov
[Peter Chisholm from February 2001]
USEFUL STATESIDE CONTACTS

- US Department of Commerce
International Trade Administration
Office of Africa, Mauritania Desk
Tel: (202) 377-4388

- The Mauritanian Embassy
2129 Leroy Place, N.W.
Washington, D.C. 20008
Tel: (202) 232-5700

For additional information or assistance, please contact the US Department of Commerce Export Assistance Center nearest you.

MAURITANIAN GOVERNMENT AGENCIES

Investment Promotion Office (Guichet Unique des Investissements)
Ministère des Affaires Economiques et Développement
Boite Postale (B.P.) 238
Nouakchott, Mauritanie
Tel: [222] 29-04-35
Fax: [222] 29- 04-35
email: UCP@OPT.mr
Mr. Kelly Oumar Sada, Director

Mauritanian Chamber of Commerce
B.P. 215
Nouakchott, Mauritanie
Tel: [222] 25-22-14
Fax: [222] 25-38-95
Mr. Mahmoud Ould Ahmedou, President
Mr. Habib Ould Ely, Director

Customs Office
Direction Generale des Douanes
Ministère des Finances
B.P. 198
Nouakchott, Mauritanie
Tel: [222] 25-14-04 or 25-63-02
Fax: [222] 25-63-04
Colonel N'Diaga Dieng, Director

National Statistics Office
B.P. 240
Nouakchott, Mauritanie
Tel: [222] 25-30-70, 25-39-26, or 25-51-70
Mr. Sidina Ould N'Dah, Director

Centre d'Information Mauritanien pour le Developpement Economique et Technique (CIMDET)
Ministere du Commerce, de l'Artisanat et du Tourisme
B.P. 2119
Nouakchott, Mauritanie
Tel: [222] 25-87-38
Fax: [222] 25-86-48
Email: cimdet@pactec.org
Mr. Cheibani Ould Mohamed Abdoullah, Director

MAURITANIAN PRIVATE AGENCIES

Mauritanian Employers Federation
B.P. 383
Nouakchott, Mauritanie
Tel: [222] 25-21-60 or 25-33-01
Mr. Mohamed Ould Bouamatou, President
Mr. Cheikh El Moctar El Hassen, Secretary General

Mining and Industry Federation
B.P. 3475
Nouakchott, Mauritanie
Tel: [222] 25-39-74
Mr. Lafdal Ould Bettah, President

Fishing National Federation
B.P. 43
Nouadhibou, Mauritanie
Tel: [222] 74-50-89
Fax: [222] 74-54-30
Mr. Mohamed Mahmoud Sidina Sadegh, Secretary General

Banque Mauritanienne pour le Commerce

International (BMCI)
B.P. 622
Nouakchott, Mauritanie
Tel: [222] 25-43-49, 25-43-50, or 25-43-51
Fax: [222] 25-20-45
Mr. Moulaye Abass, President

Banque Nationale de Mauritanie (BNM)
B.P. 614
Nouakchott, Mauritanie
Tel: [222] 25-26-02 or 25-27-07
Fax: [222] 25-33-97
Mr. Mohamed Ould Noueigued, President

Banque Al Baraka Mauritanienne Islamique (BAMIS)
B.P. 650
Nouakchott, Mauritanie
Tel: [222] 25-14-24 or 25-22-66
Fax: [222] 25-16-21
Mr. Abdallahi El Moctar, General Manager

Generale de Banque de Mauritanie (G.B.M.)
B.P. 5558
Nouakchott, Mauritanie
Tel: [222] 25-36-36
Fax: [222] 25-46-47
Mr. Mohamed Ould Bouamatou, President

Banque pour le Commerce et l'Industrie (B.C.I.)
Avenue Gamal Abdel Nasser, no.120
Nouakchott, Mauritanie
Tel: [222] 29-28-76
Fax: [222] 29-28-77
Mr. Isselmou Ould Tagidine, President

AMERICAN COMPANIES AND TRADEMARKS REPRESENTED IN MAURITANIA

Caterpillar
Tel: [222] 25-74-56
Fax: [222] 25-74-55
Mr. Bechir El Hassen, SDPA, Representative

Dell, Echostar, Hewlett-Packard, Lanier, 3M
Tel: [222] 25-57-94
Fax: [222] 25-57-95
Mr. Echbih Ould Ahmed Saleck, Top Technology, Representative

Delta Airlines
Code share with Air France flights to/from Mauritania

DHL
Tel: [222] 25-47-06
Mr. Redwane Ouelladj, Representative

Harris Corporation
Tel: [222] 25-19-46
Fax: [222] 25-54-94
Mr. Chighali Ould Amara, Representative

Hayes Mondial Corporation
Tel: [222] 25-86-37; 25-76-85; 25-11-92
Fax: [222] 25-13-84
Mr. Sidi Ould Maham, MAURAL, Joint Venture Partner

IBM
Tel: [222] 25-29-24
Fax: [222] 25-18-31
Mr. Elimane Kane, Representative

Louis Berger
Tel/Fax:[222] 25-00-54
Mr. Hadrami Ould Maham, Representative

MEDISCO Healthcare Pharmacy
Tel: [222] 25-72-89
Mr. Mohamed Mahmoud Ould Cheikh Abderrahmane, Manager

Mining Services International
Tel: [222] 25-75-31
Fax: [222] 25-75-31
Mr. Noureddine Ould Allaf, Representative

Mobil Oil
Tel: [222] 25-21-26
Fax: [222] 25-23-35
Mr. Taher El Kateb, Representative
Mr. Abderrahmane Ould Deddah, Deputy Representative

Philip Morris
Tel: [222] 25-39-60
Fax: [222] 25-11-59
Mr. Mohamed Ould Bouamatou, Representative

Phyto-Riker Pharmaceuticals
Tel: [222] 25-50-19
Dr. Cheikh Brahim Ould Taki, Representative

UNISYS
Tel: [222] 25-94-34
Fax: [222] 25-90-25
Mr. Abdallahi El Moctar, Representative

UPS
Tel: [222] 25-29-28-89
Fax: [222] 25- 56-57
Mr. Ahmed Baba Ould Azizi, TRANSAC, Representative

WANG
Tel: [222] 25-13-63
Fax: [222] 25-13-64
Mr. Saleh Ould Oubeid, Representative

MOROCCO

U.S. Embassy Trade Related Contacts

AMERICAN CONSULATE GENERAL CASABLANCA
Kathleen Kriger, Commercial Counselor
The U.S. Commercial Service
8, Bd. Moulay Youssef
Casablanca, Morocco
Tel: (212) (22) 26-45-50
Fax: (212) (22) 22-02-59
Email: Kathy.Kriger@mail.doc.gov

AMERICAN EMBASSY RABAT
Richard Johnson, Economic Counselor
Peter Haas, Economic Officer
Merritt Chesley, Agricultural Attaché
James Bednar, Director USAID
Address: 2, Avenue de Marrakech
Rabat, Morocco
Tel: (212) (37) 76-22-65
Fax: (212) (37) 76-56-61

American Chamber and/or Bilateral Business Councils

AMERICAN CHAMBER OF COMMERCE
Contact: Simon O'Rourke, Executive Director
Hyatt Regency Hotel
Place Mohammed V
Casablanca, Morocco
Tel: (212) (22) 29-30-28
Fax: (212) (22) 48-15-97
simono@amcham-morocco.com

U.S.- MOROCCO COUNCIL ON TRADE & INVESTMENT
Contact: Julianne Furman, Director
5 Bd. Abdellatif Benkadour, 4eme etage
Casablanca, Morocco
Tel: (212) (22) 39-04-12
Fax: (212) (22) 39-04-06
council@council.org.ma

U.S.-MOROCCO COUNCIL ON TRADE & INVESTMENT
Azedine Assassi, Managing Director
10 Rockefeller Plaza, Suite 800,8th floor
New York, N.Y. 10020
Tel: (212) 218-5750
Fax: (212) 218-5751
aassassi@muscfi.org

Country Government Offices Relating to Key Sectors

Ministere des Affaires Generales du Government
(Ministry of Government Affairs)
Contact: Youssef Tazi Mezalek
Chef du Cabinet du Ministre
Palais Royal
Rabat, Morocco
Tel: 212 037 77 17 16
Fax: 212 037 77 47 76

Ministere Du Tourisme
(Ministry of Tourism)
Contact: Jawad Ziyat
Directeur des Amenagements et des Investissements Touristiques
Quartier Administratif
Rabat, Morocco
Tel: 212 037 77 06 35
Fax: 212 037 77 06 26

Direction Des Douanes et Impots Indirects
(Customs Office)
Contact: Abderrazak El Mossadaq, Director
Avenue Hassan II (ex rue Essafi)
Rabat, Morocco
Tel: (212) (37) 57 90 00
Fax: (212) (37) 73-09-85
E-mail: adii@douane.msie.gov.ma

Agence du Nord
(Government Agency in charge of the North Region)
Contact: Hassan Amrani
Managing Director
22, Av. Omar Ibn El Khattab Agdal
Rabat, Morocco
Tel: 212 037 77 60 13
Fax: 212 037 77 60 46

Direction De Statistique
(Department of Statistics)
Rue Mohamed Bel Hassan El Ouazzani
Haut Agdal-Rabat, Morocco
Tel: (212) (37) 77-36-06
Fax: (212) (37) 77-32-17
E-mail: webmaster@statistic.gov.ma

Ministere de L'economie et des Finances
(Ministry of Economy and Finance)
Contact: Fath Allah Oualalou, Minister
Contact: Mohamed Chafiki, Chief de Cabinet
(Tel:037 76 11 13/Fax:037 76 50 68)
Ancien Quartier Administratif
Rabat, Morocco
Tel: (212) (37) 76-06-61
Fax: (212) (37) 76-40-81

Direction des Investissements Exterieurs
(Foreign Investment Office)
Contact: Hassan Bernoussi, Director
32 Rue Honain, Angle rue Michlifen
Agdal-Rabat, Morocco
Tel: (212) (37) 67-33-75
Fax: (212) (37) 67-34-17/42

E-mail: info@invest-in-morocco.gov.ma

Ministere de L'industrie, du Commerce et de l'Energie et des Mines
(Ministry of Industry, Trade and Handicraft)
Contact: Mohamed Mansouri, Minister
Quartier des Ministeres
Avenue Mohamed V
Rabat-Chellah, Morocco
Tel: (212) (37) 76-18-78
Fax: (212) (37) 76-62-65
Web: www.mcinet.gov.ma

Direction du Commerce Exterieur
(Foreign Trade Office)
Contact: Jamal El Jamali, Director
63 Avenue Moulay Youssef
Rabat, Morocco
Tel: (212) (37) 70-33-63
Fax: (212) (37) 73-51-43
Email: sayehk@ncnet.gov.ma

Office National de l'Electricite (ONE)
(National Office of Electricity)
Contact: Driss Benhima, General Manager
65 Rue Othman Ben Affane
Casablanca, Morocco
Tel: (212) (22) 66-80-80
Fax: (212) (22) 22-00-38

Agence Nationale de Reglementation des Telecommunications (ANRT)
(National Regulatory Agency for Telecommunications)
Contact: Mustafa Terrab, General Manager
Centre d'affaires B.P 2939
Aile Nord
Hay Riad, Rabat
Tel: (212-37) 71-84-00 / 71-73-12
Fax: (212-37) 71-64-89
Web: www.anrt.net.ma

Maroc Telecom (IAM)
(National Telephone Company)
Contact: Abdeslam Ahizoune, President General Manager
Avenue Annakhil, Hay-Riad
Rabat, Morocco
Tel: (212) (37) 71-41-41
Fax: (212) (37) 71-48-61
E-Mail: alam@iamdg.net.ma

Office National de l'Eau Potable (ONEP)
(National Office of Potable Water)
Contact: Ali Fassi Fihri, General Manager
6 Bis Rue Patrice Lumumba
Rabat-Chellah, Morocco
Tel: (212) (37) 72-65-15
Fax: (212) (37) 72-67-07

Office Cherifien des Phosphates (OCP)
(National Office of Phosphates)
Contact: Mohamed Berrada, General Manager
Bd. de la Grande Ceinture
Route d'El Jadida
Casablanca, Morocco
Tel: (212) (22) 23-06-35
Fax: (212) (22) 25-09-99

Office d'Exploitation des Ports (ODEP)
(Moroccan Ports Authority)
Contact: Mustapha Barroug, General Manager
175 Bd. Mohamed Zerktouni
Casablanca, Morocco
Tel: (212) (22) 23-23-24
Fax: (212) (22) 25-81-58

Royal Air Maroc
(National Airline Company)
Contact: Mohamed Hassad, President
Aeroport d'Anfa
Casablanca, Morocco
Tel: (212) (22) 91-20-21/91-20-22
Fax: (212) (22) 91-20-95

Office National de Recherches et d'Exploitations Pétrolières (ONAREP)
(Bureau of Mining and oil Exploration Research)
Contact: Amina Benkhadra, Managing Director
34 avenue Al Fadila B.P. 8030
Rabat, Morocco
Tel: 212 037 28 16 16
Fax: 212 037 28 16 34
Email: benkhadra@onarep.com

Country Trade Associations

Confederation Generale des Entreprises du Maroc (CGEM)
(Moroccan Employers Association)
Contact: Hassan Chami, President
Angle Avenue des FAR et rue Mohamed Errachid
Casablanca, Morocco
Tel: (212) (22) 25-26-96
Fax: (212) (22) 25-38-39
E-mail: cgem@mail.cbi.net.ma

A.F.A.C.
(Feed Millers Association)
Contact: Ibrahim Assimi; President
123 Bd Imile Zola
Casablanca, Morocco
Tel: (212) (22) 31-12-49/44-22-76
Fax: (212) (22) 44-22-76

APEBI
(Telecommunications and Computers Association)
Contact: Khalid El Hariryi, President

17, rue Najib Mahfoud. Quartier Gauthier.
Casablanca, Morocco
Tel: (212) (22) 27-47-57
Fax: (212) (22) 27-47-28

Federation de l'Industrie Miniere
(Mining Industry Association)
Contact: Abdelaziz Abarro, President
1 Place de l'Istiqlal
Casablanca, Morocco
Tel: (212) (22) 30-68-98
Fax: (212) (22) 31-99-96

Association des Marchands et Importateurs de Materiel Agricole
(Association of Moroccan Importers of Agricultural Equipment)
Contact: Abdellatif Ouazzani, President
C/o Comicom
9 Bd. d'Oujda
Casablanca, Morocco
Tel: (212) (22) 30-22-11
Fax: (212) (22) 30-60-82

Association Marocaine du Conseil et de l'Ingenierie
(Engineering Association)
Contact: Rachid Balafrej, President
10 Avenue Alaouine, Imm. ONEP
Rabat, Morocco
Tel: (212) (37) 70-42-24
Fax: (212) (37) 20-03-47
E-mail: fmciass@maghrebnet.net.ma

Office des Foires et Expositions de Casablanca
(Trade shows and Exhibitions Office)
Contact: Ahmed Ouzzani, General Manager
11, Rue Boukraa (ex Jules Mauran)
Casablanca, Morocco
Tel: (212) (22) 27-15-45 / 27-16-64 / 27-15-32
Fax: (212) (22) 26-49-49
Email: foire@ofec.co.ma
Web: http://www.ofec.co.ma

Specialized Agricultural Trade Associations

Federation Interprofessionnelle du Secteur Avicole (FISA)
(Poultry Feed, Poultry, and Eggs Federation)
Moulay Youssef Alaoui; President
123, Boulevard Emile Zola
Casablanca, Morocco
Phone: (212-22) 31-12-49
Fax: (212-22) 44-22-76

7) Association des Fabricants d'Aliments Composes(AFAC)
(Feed Manufacturters Association)
M. ASSIMI, Brahim; President
123 Boulevard Emile Zola
Casablanca
Phone: (212-2)231-1249/244-2276
Fax:(212-2)231-1249/244-2276

8) Office des Foires et des Expositions de Casablanca (OFEC)
M. OUAZZANI, Ahmed; CEO
11, Rue Boukraa (ex Jules Mauran)
Casablanca
Phone: (212-2)229-3071/227-1664/227-1545
Fax:(212-2)222-5823/226-4949
Email: Web:

9) Lesieur
(oilseed crusher, refiner)
M. TRAKI, Driss; CEO
1, Rue Caporal Corbi, Ain Sebaa
Casablanca (05)
Phone: (212-2)235-4636/235-4327/235-8740
Fax:(212-2)226-8957/235-4097

10) Association des Negociants en Cereales et Legumineuses(ANCL)
(Grains and Pulses Importers and Traders Association)
M. EL HADDAJ, Bouchaib; CEO
193, Avenue Hassan II
Casablanca
Phone: (212-2)247-6438/247-6468
Fax:(212-2)247-4207

11) Federation Nationale de la Minoterie(FNM)
(Wheat Millers Federation)
M. BOUAIDA, Ahmed; President
Angle Ibn Majid Bahar & Brihmi El Idrissi (Ex Girardot/Havre)
Casablanca
Phone: (212-2)230-1801/230-1158
Fax:(212-2)230-6551/230-5913

12) Association Nationale des Eleveurs de Bovins de Races Pures(ANEB)
Purebred Dairy Cattle Association)
M. BATTAR, Mokhtar; Directeur
5, Rue Mohamed Triki, Residence Tissir, Im. B. Apt. 2
Rabat 10050
Phone: (212-3)723-0244
Fax:(212-3)723-0262

Country Market Research Firms

SEMMA
Contact: Mr. Pierrick Gautier, Director
18, Rue Ibn Sina
Casablanca, Morocco
Tel: (212-22) 39-60-30
Fax: (212-22) 39-60-33

AMER
Contact: Mme Fatiha Batal, Manager
Immeuble El Ouahda, Entrée A No.126
Bd. Lahcen ou Idder
Casablanca, Morocco
Tel: (212-22) 44-92-53/54
Fax: (212-22) 44-19-17

CREARGIE
Contact: Ms. Dominique Schwartz, General Manager
34 Rue de la Convention
Residence El Alami, quartier Racine
Casablanca, Morocco
Tel: (212-22) 94-98-42/46
Fax: (212-22) 94-98-41

Country Commercial Banks

Banque Centrale Populaire
Contact: Daoudi Houcine, Director Int'l Affairs
101 Bd. Mohammed Zerktouni
Casablanca, Morocco
Tel: (212) (22) 46-91-67
Fax: (212) (22) 29-34-54

Banque Commerciale du Maroc
Contact: Mohamed Cherkani, Head of Int'l Department
2 Bd. Moulay Youssef
Casablanca, Morocco
Tel: (212) (22) 47-64-39
Fax: (212) (22) 29-41-23

Banque Marocaine du Commerce Exterieur
Contact: Mohamed Bennani, Head of Int'l Department
140 Avenue Hassan II
Casablanca, Morocco
Tel: (212) (22) 20-04-20
Fax: (212) (22) 22-05-23
E-mail: mohamedbennani1@hotmail.com

Banque Marocaine pour le Commerce et l'Industrie
Contact: Mustapha Faris, President
26 Place Nations Unies
Casablanca, Morocco
Tel: (212) (22) 46-11-59
Fax: (212) (22) 22-46-04

Citibank-Maghreb
Contact: Eric Stoclet, Managing Director
52 Avenue Hassan II
Casablanca, Morocco
Tel: (212) (22) 22-41-68
Fax: (212) (22) 20-57-23
E-mail: eric.stoclet@citicorp.com

Credit Agricole (CNCA)
Daoudi, Tahar; Head of International Division
28, Rue Abou Farris El Marini
Rabat, Morocco
Phone: (212-37) 208231/208220/208221
Fax: (212-37) 208267

Credit du Maroc
Contact: Jamal Lemridi, Director Int'l Affairs
48-58 Bd. Mohammed V
Casablanca, Morocco
Tel: (212) (22) 47-78-00
Fax: (212) (22) 47-78-07/01

Societe Generale Marocaine de Banques
Contact: Omar Skalli, General Manager
55 Bd. Abdelmoumen
Casablanca, Morocco
Tel: (212) (22) 20-02-83
Fax: (212) (22) 20-09-61

WAFABANK
Contact: Ahmed Layine, Head of Int'l Department
163 Avenue Hassan II
Casablanca, Morocco
Tel: (212) (22) 54-54-54
Fax: (212) (22) 47-03-98

ABN-AMRO BANK
Contact: Mohamed Haitami, Senior VP
47, Rue Allal Ben Abdallah, 4th floor
Casablanca, Morocco
Tel: (212) (22) 49-73-05
Fax: (212) (22) 20-91-45

Casablanca Finance Group
Contact: Adil Douiri, CEO
5/7 Rue Ibnou Toufail (Angle Bd. Zerktouni)
Casablanca, Morocco
Tel: (212) (22) 25 50 50
Fax: (212) (22) 98 39 89
Email: a.douiri@cfgmorocco.com

Casablanca Stock Exchange
Contact
Avenue de l'Armee Royale
Casablanca, Morocco
Tel: 212 22 45 26 26
Fax: 212 22 45 26 25
Email:

Upline Securities
Contact : Hassan Ait Ali
41-43 boulevard d'Anfa
Casablanca, Morocco
Tel: 212 22 47 51 24
Fax : 212 22 47 46 14

Multilateral Development Bank Offices in Country and Trade Assistance Offices in the U.S.

World Bank Representation
Contact: Olivier Godron, Representative

7, Rue Larbi Benabdellah
Rabat, Morocco
Tel: (212) (37) 63-60-50
Fax: (212) (37) 63-60-51

IFC
Contact: Joumana Cobein
At World Bank
Tel: 212 37 63 60 49

Washington-Based USG Country Contacts

U.S. Department Of Commerce
Kevin Brennan, Regional Director
OIO/ANESA, US&FCS
U.S. Department of Commerce, Washington, D.C.
Tel: (202) 482-4836; Fax: (202) 482-5179

Cherie Loustaunau, Morocco Desk Officer
U.S. Department of Commerce, Washington, D.C.
Tel: (202) 482-1860; Fax: (202) 482-0878

Multilateral Development Banks Office
U.S. Department of Commerce
Tel: (202) 482-3399; Fax: (202) 482-5179

TPCC Trade Information Center in Washington
Tel: 1-800-USA-TRADE

U.S. Department Of State
Morocco Desk Officer: Julie Fisher, NEA/ENA
Washington, D.C.
Tel: (202) 647-4675; Fax: (202) 736-4458

Office of the Coordinator for Business Affairs
Tel: 202-746-1625; Fax: 202-647-3953

U.S. Department of Agriculture, Foreign Agriculture Service
Trade Assistance and Promotion Office:
Director Grain & Feed Division, Robert Riemenshneider, Washington, D.C.
Tel: (202) 720-6219; Fax: (202) 720-0340

U.S. Export Import Bank (Ex-Im)
North Africa Desk Officer, Talaat Rahman
Tel: (202) 565-3911; Fax: (202) 565-3931

Overseas Private Investment Corporation (OPIC)
North Africa Desk Office, Abed Tarbush
Tel/(Info Line): (202) 336-8799
Tel/(Facts Line): (202) 336-8700
Fax: (202) 408-9859
WEB: http://www.opic.gov
Email: info@opic.gov

U.S. Trade Development Agency
Henry Steingass, Regional Director Africa/Middle East
Cybill Sigler, Country Director
Tel: (703) 875-4357; Fax: (703) 875-4009

Moroccan Embassy in Washington
1601 21 Street, NW
Washington, D.C. 20009-1002
Tel: (202) 462-7979
Fax: (202) 265-0161
Contact: Ambassador Abdallah El Maaroufi

OMAN

American Business Council of Oman (ABCO)
P.O. Box 121 - Barka.
Postal Code: 320
Sultanate of Oman
Phone: (968) 597-730 Fax : (968) 597-730
President: William Ali Mills
Office Director: Cynthia Albano
(Office is closed in July and August.)

Major trade-related Omani government agencies, with the commercial organizations and then Ministries listed first (in alphabetical order) followed by petroleum-sector mixed enterprises:

Oman Center for Investment Promotion and Export Development (OCIPED)
Salim bin Nasser Al-Ismaili, Executive President
P.O. Box 25 - Wadi al-Kabir
Postal Code: 117
Sultanate of Oman
Phone: (968) 771-2344; Fax: 771-0890
Email: info@ociped.com

Oman Chamber of Commerce and Industry
Sheikh Abdulla bin Salim bin Amer Al-Rawas, President
P.O. Box 1400 Ruwi
Postal Code 112
Sultanate of Oman
TEL: (968) 707-674/84/94, FAX: (968) 708-497
E-mail: info@omanchamber.org
(The O.C.C.I. is the only authorized commercial/industrial association and reports to the Minister of Commerce and Industry. It has branches in Salalah, Nizwa, Ibri, Buraimi, and Sur and Sohar. It can be very helpful to foreign businesspersons seeking contact with Omani firms. Its Arabic and English bi-monthly Al Ghorfa (The Chamber) reaches all Omani firms).

Ministry of Commerce and Industry
P.O. Box 550 Muscat
Postal Code 113
Sultanate of Oman
TEL: (968) 774-240, FAX (968) 794-239/771-7239

Ministry of Housing, Electricity and Water
P.O. Box 1491 - Ruwi
Postal Code 112
Sultanate of Oman
TEL: (968) 603-800/603-906, FAX: (968) 699-180/699-185

Ministry of National Economy and Ministry of Finance
P.O. Box 506 - Muscat
Postal Code 113
Sultanate of Oman
TEL: (968) 738-201 thru 210/739-764 thru -772, FAX: (968) 737-068

Ministry of Health
P.O. Box 393 - Muscat
Postal Code 113
Sultanate of Oman
TEL: (968) 602-177, FAX: (968) 602-162/601-430

Ministry of Oil and Gas
P.O. Box 551 - Muscat
Postal Code 113
Sultanate of Oman
TEL: (968) 603-333/341/563, FAX: (968) 696-972

Ministry of Regional Municipalities, Environment and Water Resources
P.O. Box 461 - Muscat
Postal Code 113
Sultanate of Oman
TEL: (968) 692-550/696-444, FAX: (968) 693-995/693-858

Ministry of Transport and Telecommunications
P.O. Box 338 Ruwi
Postal Code: 112
Sultanate of Oman
TEL: (968) 697-888/698-931, FAX: (968) 696-817/696-670
(Note: Omantel, the national telecommunications authority, reports to this ministry.)

Central Bank of Oman
P.O. Box 1161 - Ruwi
Postal Code 112
Sultanate of Oman
TEL: (968) 702-222, FAX: (968) 707-913, 702-253

Public Establishment for Industrial Estates
P.O. Box 2 - Rusayl
Postal Code 124
Sultanate of Oman
TEL: (968) 626-080/626-094, FAX (968) 626-053
(The Public Establishment promotes industrial development by making available industrial park settings for light industrial purposes, complete with utilities and, if desired, plant shells.)

Capital Market Authority / Muscat Securities Market
P.O. Box 3265 - Ruwi
Postal Code 112
Sultanate of Oman
TEL: (968) 771-2607, FAX: (968) 771-2609

Oman LNG LLC
PO Box 560
Postal Code 116
Sultanate of Oman
TEL: (968) 707-807, FAX: 707-656.

Oman Refinery Co. (LLC)
PO Box 3568 - Ruwi
Postal Code 112
Sultanate of Oman
TEL: (968) 561-200, FAX (968) 561-384

Petroleum Development Oman LLC
P.O. Box 81 - Muscat
Postal Code 113, Oman
TEL: (968) 678-111, FAX: (968) 677-106

GOVERNMENTAL DEVELOPMENT BANKS:

Oman Development Bank
P.O. Box 309 - Muscat
Postal Code 113
Sultanate of Oman
General Manager, Murtada M. Fadhil
TEL: (968) 738-021 thru 4, FAX: (968) 738-026

Oman Housing Bank
P.O. Box 2555 - Ruwi
Postal Code 112
Sultanate of Oman
Acting Gen. Manager, Mahmud Muhammad bin Umar Bahram
TEL: (968) 704-444, FAX: (968) 704-071

COUNTRY COMMERCIAL BANKS (NATIONAL STATUS):

Bank Dhofar Al Omani Al Fransi (SAOG)
P.O. Box 1507 - Ruwi
Postal Code 112
Sultanate of Oman
General Manager, Ahmed Ali al-Shanfari
TEL: (968) 790-466/8, Fax: (968) 797-246

Bank Muscat
P.O. Box 134 - Ruwi
Postal Code 112
Sultanate of Oman
Chief Executive Officer, Abdulrazzaq Ali Issa
TEL: (968) 703-044, FAX: (968) 793-536

National Bank of Oman (SAOG)

P.O. Box 751 - Ruwi
Postal Code 112
Sultanate of Oman
General Manager, Aubyn R. Hill
TEL: (968) 708-894; FAX: (968) 704-522/707-781

Oman Arab Bank
P.O. Box 2010 - Ruwi
Postal Code 112
Sultanate of Oman
Managing Director, Abd al-Kader Askalan
TEL: (968) 700-161 thru 3, FAX: (968) 797-736
(Majority control rests with the same Jordanian parent as the Arab Bank of New York.)

Oman International Bank (SAOG)
P.O. Box 1727 - CPO Seeb
Postal Code 111
Sultanate of Oman
Chief Executive, James T.M. McNie
TEL: (968) 682-500, FAX (968) 682-800

Majan International Bank (SAOC)
P. O. Box 2717 - Ruwi
Postal Code 112
Sultanate of Oman
General Manger, Salam Shaksi
Tel: (968) 780388
Fax: (968) 703613

COUNTRY BANKS (FOREIGN):

Bank Melli Iran
P.O. Box 2643 - Ruwi
Postal Code 112
Sultanate of Oman
General Manager, Ali Jaffari Lafti
TEL: (968) 708-125/701-579, FAX (968) 793-017

Bank of Baroda
P.O. Box 231 - Mutrah
Postal Code 114
Sultanate of Oman
Chief Manager, N. Ramani
TEL: (968) 714-549/714-559, FAX: (968) 714-560

Bank Saderat Iran
P.O. Box 1269 - Ruwi
Postal Code 112
Sultanate of Oman
Manager, Seyed Mohammed Sefidari
TEL: (968) 793-923/787-189, FAX: (968) 796-478

Banque Banorabe
P.O. Box 1608 - Ruwi
Postal Code 112
Sultanate of Oman
Manager, Peter Carvalho
TEL: (968) 704-274/703-850, FAX: (968) 707-782

HSBC
P.O. Box 240 - Ruwi
Postal Code 112
Sultanate of Oman
Chief Executive Officer, Richard Inglis
TEL: (968) 799-920/700-020, FAX: (968) 704-241
(U.S. HSBC affiliate is the Marine Midland Bank, New York)

Citibank N.A.
P.O. Box 1994 - Mutrah
Postal Code 114
Sultanate of Oman
Country Corporate Officer, Ravi Bhatia
TEL: (968) 795-705, FAX: (968) 795-724

Habib Bank Ltd.
P.O. Box 1326 - Ruwi
Postal Code 112
Sultanate of Oman
Senior VP & General Manager, Waiz-ur Rehman
TEL: (968) 705-276/795-282, FAX: (968) 795-283

National Bank of Abu Dhabi
P.O. Box 303 - Muscat
Postal Code 113
Sultanate of Oman
Manager, Saeed S. Al-Mubarak
TEL: (968) 798-842, FAX: (968) 794-386

Standard Chartered Bank
P.O. Box 2353 - Ruwi
Postal Code 112
Sultanate of Oman
Manager, Murtadha M. Ali
TEL: (968) 703-999, FAX: (968) 796-864

U.S. EMBASSY TRADE PERSONNEL

Economic/Commercial Section
P.O. Box 202, P.C. 115
Madinat al-Sultan Qaboos
Sultanate of Oman
Economic/Commercial Officer: Craig White
Commercial Assistants: Shereen Uzaizi, V.S. Chandran
TEL: (968) 699-094, or 698-989, x463 FAX: (968) 604-316, 694-355
E-mail: aemcteco@omantel.net.om

Office of Military Cooperation
P.O. Box 202, P.C. 115
Madinat Al-Sultan Qaboos
Sultanate of Oman
Col. Rodger Oetjen
TEL: (968) 698-989, FAX: (968) 604-327

QATAR

U.S. Embassy trade related contacts:

Embassy of the United States of America
Ambassador: Maureen Quinn
Deputy Chief of Mission: Adam Ereli
Economic Commercial Officer: Susannah Cooper
Economic Commercial Advisor: Jiryis H. Khoury
Commercial Clerk: Sima Carri
P.O. Box 2399
Doha, State of Qatar
Phone: (Comm): (974) 488-4165 or (Embassy): (974) 488-4101
Fax: (Comm): (974) 488-4163 or (Embassy): (974) 488-4298
E-mail: bfif97@qatar.net.qa

Agricultural Trade Office
U.S. Agricultural Trade Office
U.S. Consulate General
P.O.Box 9343
Dubai, U.A.E.
Phone: (971-4) 331-4063, Fax: (971-4) 331-4998
E-mail: atodubai@emirates.net.ae
Home page: http://www.usembabu.gov.ae/atodubai.htm
Contact: Ron Verdonk, Regional Director; Hovig Kizirian, Assistant
(Covers: Bahrain, Kuwait, Oman, Qatar and U.A.E.)

Amcham and/or Bilateral Business Councils:

U.S. Qatar Business Council
Ambassador Patrick N. Theros, President
5335 Wisconsin Ave., Suite 440
Washington, DC 20015-2034
U.S.A.
Phone: (202) 895-1712
Fax: (202) 244-8257
E-mail: qatarbiz@erols.com

National U.S. -Arab Chamber of Commerce
1100 New York Ave., N.W., East Tower, Suite 500
Washington, DC 20005
U.S.A.
Phone: (202) 289-5920
Fax: (202) 289-5938
Internet: http://www.nusacc.org

Affiliate Office:
U.S. Arab Chamber of Commerce (Pacific), Inc.
P.O. Box 422218
San Francisco, CA 94141-2218
U.S.A.
Phone: (415) 398-9200
Fax: (415) 398-7111

American Business Council
President: Dr. Richard Stallard
Contact: Ms. Stephanie Carvel, Secretary
P.O. Box 10861, Doha, State of Qatar

Country Trade or Industry Associations in Key Sectors:

Qatar Chamber of Commerce and Industry:
H.E. Sheikh Hamad bin Jassim bin Mohammed Al-Thani, President
Mr. Saleh Mubarak Al-Khuleifi, Vice President
P.O. Box 402, Doha, State of Qatar
Phone: (974) 462-1491
Fax: (974) 462-1131

Management:
Dr. Majid Al-Malki, Director-General
Mr. Nasser Al-Fayhanni, Office Director
Mr. Nasser Al-Dulaimi, Public Relations Manager
[Phone: (974) 442-3677]

Country Government Offices Relating to Key Sectors and/or Significant Trade Related Activities:

Office of H.H. the Emir:
H.H. Sheikh Hamad bin Khalifa Al-Thani, Emir of the State of Qatar
H.E. Abdullah bin Mohammed bin Saud Al-Thani, Head of the Emiri Diwan and Office Director
H.H. Sheikh Jassim bin Hamad bin Khalifa Al-Thani, Heir Apparent
P.O. Box 923, Doha, State of Qatar
Phone: (974) 442-3939; (974) 441-6664; (974) 446-2262
Fax: (974) 443-7660

Economic Studies Department:
Dr. Nasser Abdulghani
Phone: (974) 446-2320
Phone: (974) 441-2942; (974) 441-6964; (974) 442-7370

Legal Affairs Department:
Mr. Adel Ahmed Al-Sharbini, Legal Advisor
Phone: (974) 446-2328; (974) 441-2849
Fax: (974) 446-2172

Emiri Protocol Department:
Sheikh Mohammed bin Fahd bin Mohammed Al-Thani, Director
Sheikh Abdulrahman bin Saud Al-Thani, Deputy Director
Mr. Ibrahim Ahmed Al-Malki, Assistant Director
Mr. Abdul Aziz Mohammed Khaled Al-Rabban, Assistant Director
Phone: (974) 442-2322; (974) 441-5299; (974) 436-1639
Fax: (974) 443-7660

Ministry of Energy and Industry:

Office of the Minister:
H.E. Abdullah bin Hamad Al-Attiyah, Minister
Mr. Abdulaziz Al-Malki, Office Director
Mr. Sabri Kazim, Technical Advisor [Phone: (974) 449-1381, Fax: (974) 483-6994]
P.O. Box 3212, Doha, State of Qatar
Phone: (974) 449-1491; (974) 449-1444
Fax: (974) 483-6999

Department of Industrial Affairs:
Mr. Saleh Ali Al-Mannai, Director
Mr. Abdulwahid Al-Mashadi, Deputy Director
P.O. Box 2599, Doha, State of Qatar
Phone: (974) 483-2121/2/3/4
Fax: (974) 483-2024

Ministry of Communications and Transport (to be dissolved late 2001):
Minister's Office:
H.E. Sheikh Ahmed bin Nasser Al-Thani, Minister
Mr. Tariq bin Ahmed Al-Sulaiti, Office Director
P.O. Box 22228, Doha, State of Qatar
Phone: (974) 483-5353; (974) 483-5522
Fax: (974) 488-5101

Office of the Undersecretary:
Mr. Salem Butti Al-Noaimy, Undersecretary
Phone: (974) 483-5500
Fax: (974) 483-5888

Department of Post (to become a public corporation late 2001):
Mr. Mohammed Ali, Director
P.O. Box 713, Doha, State of Qatar
Phone: (974) 483-5555
Fax: (974) 483-7777

Department of Ports (to become a public corporation late 2001):
Mr. Ghulam Abdullah Genkeer, Director
Phone: (974) 441-4763
Fax: (974) 441-3563

Department of Civil Aviation (to become a public corporation late 2001):
Mr. Abdulaziz Al-Noaimi, Director
P.O. Box 3000, Doha, State of Qatar
Phone: (974) 442-6262
Fax: (974) 442-9070

Ministry of Municipal Affairs and Agriculture:
P.O. Box 2727, Doha, State of Qatar
Phone: (974) 433-6336
Fax: (974) 441-4868; (974) 443-7630

Minister's Office:
H.E. Ali Al-Khater, Minister
Mr. Jaber Hajaj Al-Shahwani, Office Director [Phone: (974) 441-3580, Fax: (974) 441-3395]

Mr. Mohammed Fahad Al-Faihani, Assistant Undersecretary for Agricultural Affairs [Phone: (974) 433-6336]
Mr. Abdulrahman Al-Buainain, Assistant Undersecretary for Municipal Affairs [Phone: (974) 441-4352]
Mr. Ahmed Al-Dosari, Assistant Undersecretary for Town Planning [Phone: (974) 433-6336]
Mr. Issa Abdullah Al-Kubaisi, Assistant Undersecretary for Engineering Affairs [Phone: (974) 433-6336]

Civil Engineering Department:
Sheikh Ali bin Nasser Al-Thani, Director
Mr. Nasser Al-Nasr, Office Director
P.O. Box 22188, Doha, State of Qatar
Phone: (974) 433-7337
Fax: (974) 443-9104

Building Engineering Department:
Mr. Abdulla BuHumid,Director
P.O. Box 22306, Doha, State of Qatar
Phone: (974) 442-7140
Fax: (974) 441-8620; (974) 443-0475

Mechanical Equipment Department:
Mr. Hassan Sultan Al-Kawari, Director
Mr. Atif Al-Batal [Phone: (974) 444-4633; (974) 444-4634]
P.O. Box 39, Doha, State of Qatar
Phone: (974) 432-8241
Fax: (974) 436-5937

Environmental Affairs Department:
Mr. Khalid Al-Ghanim, Director
P.O. Box 7634, Doha, State of Qatar
Phone: (974) 432-0825
Fax: (974) 441-5246

Agricultural Development Department:
Mr. Ali Al-Kubeisi
Director
(Live plants and pesticide import regulations)
P.O. Box 1966, Doha, State of Qatar
Phone: (974) 449-2666
Fax: (974) 432-2002

Dr. Majid R. Al-Kuwari
Asst. Director for Animal Health Affairs
(Live animal and pet import control)
P.O. Box 1966
Doha, State of Qatar
Phone: (974) 465-3083
Fax: (974) 466-3163

Ministry of Finance, Economy and Commerce:
P.O. Box 1968, Doha, State of Qatar
Phone: (974) 446-1444
Fax: (974) 441-3617

Minister's Office:
H.E. Yousuf Kamal, Minister

Mr. Abdulrahman Al-Dashti, Office Director
Phone: (974) 441-3366; (974) 441-4914

Department of Economic Affairs:
Mr. Ali Al-Khalaf, Director
Mr. Saud Al-Jufairi, Assistant [Phone: (974) 441-3566, Fax: (974) 441-3682]
P.O. Box 1968, Doha, State of Qatar
Phone: (974) 441-6234
Fax: (974) 441-5731

Department of Commercial Affairs:
Mr. Abdulaziz Al-Khulaifi, Director
Mr. Abdulrazzak Al-Kawari, Office Manager
P.O. Box 22355, Doha, State of Qatar
Phone: (974) 443-2103
Fax: (974) 443-1412

Commercial Registration:
Mr. Mohammed Al-Saadi, Manager
Phone: (974) 443-0772

Commercial Agencies:
Mr. Abdullah Sultan Al-Asiri, Manager
Phone: (974) 441-6884

Trademark:
Mr. Ahmed Al-Jufairi, Manager
Phone: (974) 443-4281

Intellectual Property Rights Department:
P.O. Box 5147, Doha, State of Qatar
Mr. Abdullah Qayid, Director
Phone: (974) 443-4323
Fax: (974) 443-1412

Exhibitions Department:
Mr. Ali Ibrahim, Director
Mr. Yousuf Al-Zaini, Head of International Affairs
P.O. Box 1968, Doha, State of Qatar
Phone: (974) 483-4450
Fax: (974) 483-4480

Central Tenders Committee:
Mr. Khalifa Al-Hitmi, Director
P.O. Box 1968, Doha, State of Qatar
Phone: (974) 441-3089

Standards, Measurements & Consumer Protection:
H.E. Sheikh Abdullah bin Saud Al-Thani, Director
(Food safety and other standards)
P.O. Box 1968, Doha, State of Qatar
Phone: (974) 440-8500
Fax: (974) 447-8849

Customs Department:
Sheikh Abdullah bin Jassim bin Fahd Al-Thani, Director
Mr. Miqbil Al-Hitmi, Assistant Director
Mr. Hijji Al-Malki, Office Director
P.O. Box 81, Doha, State of Qatar
Phone: (974) 441-4333
Fax: (974) 441-4959

Ministry of Public Health:
P.O. Box 42, Doha, State of Qatar
Phone: (974) 444-0146; (974) 441-4777
Fax: (974) 442-9786

Office of the Minister:
Dr. Hajar Ahmed Hajar [Also Chairman of Hamad Medical Corporation (HMC)]
Mr. Hitmi Mubarak Al-Hitmi, Office Manager
Phone: (974) 435-5370
Fax: (974) 435-0012

Mr. Turki Al-Khater, Undersecretary

Dr. Khalifa Al-Jaber, Assistant Undersecretary/Technical
Phone: (974) 441-7022
Fax: (974) 444-2722

Pharmaceuticals and Medicines Control Department:
Dr. Mohammed Ibrahim Al-Hail, Director
Dr. Aisha Al-Malki, Drug Registration [Phone: (974) 449-3187]
P.O. Box 1919, Doha, State of Qatar
Phone: (974) 444-7828
Fax: (974) 442-5399

Mr. Jassim Al-Jaidah
Director of Central Laboratories
(Inspection and analysis of imported food products)
P.O. Box 9374, Doha, Qatar
Phone: (974) 441-7676
Fax: (974) 435-3769

Dr. Ahmad Kamal Naji
Deputy Director of Preventive Medicine
(Food import regulations)
P.O. Box 9374, Doha, Qatar
Phone: (974) 442-5005
Fax: (974) 442-9786

Ministry of Interior:
P.O. Box 2433, Doha, State of Qatar
Phone: (974) 433-0000
Fax: (974) 444-3750

Logistics Department:
Captain Omair Mohammed Al-Ramzani, Director
P.O. Box 4020, Doha, State of Qatar
Phone: (974) 442-6633
Fax: (974) 444-9228

Ministry of Defense:
Qatar Armed Forces
Procurement Department, General Headquarters

Col. Saleh Al-Rumaihi, Director
P.O. Box 37
Doha, State of Qatar
Phone: (974) 440-4270; (974) 443-6920
Fax: (974) 4433-464

Government/Quasi-Government Organizations:

Qatar General Petroleum Corporation:
H.E. Abdullah bin Hamad Al-Attiyah (Minister of Electricity and Water/Energy and Industry), Chairman and Managing Director
P.O. Box 3212, Doha, State of Qatar
Phone: (974) 449-1491
Fax: (974) 483-6999

Public Relations Department:
Mr. Khalifa Al-Sowaidi, Director
P.O. Box 3212, Doha, State of Qatar
Phone: (974) 449-1320
Fax: (974) 483-1995

Marketing Department:
Mr. Jassim Naame, Director, Crude Oil/Natural Gas
Sheikh Mohammed bin Ahmed Al-Thani, Manager, Refined Products
P.O. Box 3212, Doha, State of Qatar
Phone: (974) 449-1348

Exploration and Development of New Ventures Department:
P.O. Box 3212, Doha, State of Qatar
Phone: (974) 449-1288; (974) 483-3091
Fax: (974) 483-1850
Mr. Nasser K. Jaidah, Director
Mr. Rashid Ahmed Al-Sulaiti, Manager, Exploration and Joint Ventures [Phone: (974) 483-1286]
Mr. Ismail Nasralla, Manager, Downstream Joint Ventures [Phone: (974) 449-1448]

Corporate Planning Department:
Mr. Issa Al-Ghanim, Director
P.O. Box 3212, Doha, State of Qatar
Phone: (974) 449-1390
Fax: (974) 483-1257

Operations Department:
Mr. Saied Al-Mohannadi, Director
P.O. Box 47, Doha, State of Qatar
Phone: (974) 440-2400
Fax: (974) 440-2900

Legal Affairs and Contracts Department:
Mr. Mohammed Nasser Al-Fuhaid, Acting Director
Dr. Hassan Omar, Advisor
P.O. Box 3212, Doha, State of Qatar
Phone: (974) 430-8266
Fax: (974) 447-8175

Information and Computer Services Department:
Mr. Abdullah Talib, Director
P.O. Box 47, Doha, State of Qatar
Phone: (974) 440-2240
Fax: (974) 441-3629

Production Department:

A. Offshore Production:
Mr. Eid Al-Mohannadi, Director
P.O. Box 47, Doha, State of Qatar
Phone: (974) 440-2655
Fax: (974) 440-2752

B. Onshore Production:
Mr. Ali Salem Al-Marri, Director
P.O. Box 71, Doha, State of Qatar
Phone: (974) 471-6339
Fax: (974) 471-1790

Materials Department:
Mr. Ghanim Al-Kubaisi, Director
P.O. Box 47, Doha, State of Qatar
Phone: (974) 433-2222
Fax: (974) 442-2498

Technical Department:
Dr. Mohammed Al-Saada, Director
P.O. Box 47, Doha, State of Qatar
Phone: (974) 440-2697
Fax: (974) 440-2897

Umm Said Operation Department:
Mr. Hamad Al-Tamimi, Director
P.O. Box 50070, Umm Said, State of Qatar
Phone: (974) 477-4300
Fax: (974) 477-2020

Gas Processing and Distribution Department:
Mr. Abdulrahman Al-Sowaidi, Director
P.O. Box 50070, Umm Said, State of Qatar
Phone: (974) 477-4237
Fax: (974) 477-0420

Qatar General Electricity and Water Corporation (Kahrama)
Note: This state-owned corporation replaced the former Ministry of Electricity and Water in July 2000.
P.O. Box 41, Doha, State of Qatar
Phone: (974) 484-5555
H.E. Abdullah bin Hamad Al-Attiyah (Minister of Electricity and Water/Energy and Industry), Chairman; Mr. Hamza Al-Kuwari, Vice-Chairman

Public Relations Department:
Mr. Hamad Al-Kuwari
Phone: (974) 484-5454
Fax: (974) 484-5496

Procurement Department:
Mr. Tarek Al-Yousuf
Phone: (974) 484-5125/6/7
Fax: (974) 484-5193/4

Financial Administration:
Mr. Abdulaziz Al-Sayed
Phone: (974) 484-5444; (974) 484-5400
Fax: (974) 484-5492

Materials Department:
Mr. Mansour Al-Yami
Phone: (974) 484-5150
Fax: (974) 484-5192

Qatar Telecom (Q-Tel):
Mr. Hamad Al-Attiyah, General Manager
P.O. Box 217, Doha, State of Qatar
Phone: (974) 440-0445
Fax: (974) 483-0008
Mr. Rashid Al-Bader, Office Director

Public Relations Department:
Mr. Abdulwahid Fakhroo, Director
Phone: (974) 440-0638
Fax: (974) 441-4514

Finance Department:
Mr. Aubrey Cloke, Finance Manager
Phone: (974) 440-0640
Fax: (974) 483-0641

Procurement Section:
Mr. Ibrahim Al-Obaidly, Manager
Phone: (974) 440-0363
Fax: (974) 483-0850

Hamad Medical Corporation (HMC):
Hamad General Hospital (HGH):
H.E. Dr. Hajar A. Hajar, Chairman (Minister of Public Health)
Dr. Saad Rashid Al-Kaabi, Medical Director
Dr. Abdul Wahab Al-Musleh, Deputy Medical Director
P.O. Box 3050, Doha, State of Qatar
Phone: (974) 439-2222
Fax: (974) 444-3099

Public Relations Department:
Mr. Salem Al-Mohannadi, Director
Phone: (974) 439-2012
Fax: (974) 439-2263

Materials Management Department:
Mr. Mahmoud Al-Mahmoud, Director
Phone: (974) 439-2262, Fax: (974) 442-3399

Country Commercial Banks:

Central Bank of Qatar
H.E. Abdullah Bin Khalid Al-Attiyah, Governor
P.O. Box 1234, Doha, State of Qatar
Phone: (974) 445--6456
Fax: (974) 441-5587

Al-Ahli Bank of Qatar
Mr. Kassim Al-Kassim, General Manager
P. O. Box 2309, Doha, State of Qatar
Phone: (974) 432-6611
Fax: (974) 444-4652

Arab Bank Ltd.
Mr. Ghassan Ahmed Bundakji, Senior Manager
P. O. Box 172, Doha, State of Qatar
Phone: (974) 443-7979
Fax: (974) 441-0774

Bank Saderat Iran
Mr. Mohammed Zamani, Manager
P. O. Box 2256, Doha, State of Qatar
Phone: (974) 441-4646
Fax: (974) 443-0121

BNP Paribas
Mr. Jacques Poirier, General Manager
P. O. Box 2636, Doha, State of Qatar
Phone: (974) 443-3844/7
Fax: (974) 441-0861

HSBC Bank Middle East
Mr. Matthew Smith, Chief Executive Officer
P. O. Box 57, Doha, State of Qatar
Phone: (974) 438-2222
Fax: (974) 441-6353; (974) 438-2247 (CEO)

Commercial Bank of Qatar Ltd.
Mr. Andrew Stevens, General Manager
P. O. Box 3232, Doha, State of Qatar
Phone: (974) 449-0222
Fax: (974) 444-3807; (974) 432-0716 (GM)

Doha Bank Ltd.
Mr. Salah Al-Jaidah, General Manager
P. O. Box 3818, Doha, State of Qatar
Phone: (974) 445-6600; (974) 445-6611 (GM)
Fax: (974) 441-6631; (974) 435-5288 (GM)

Grindlays Bank Plc
Mr. John Fleming Murray, General Manager
P. O. Box 2001, Doha, State of Qatar
Phone: (974) 447-3700
Fax: (974) 447-3710

Mashreq Bank Psc
Mr. Adel Al-Mannai, General Manager
P. O. Box 173, Doha, State of Qatar
Phone: (974) 441-3213/7
Fax: (974) 441-3880

Qatar Industrial Development Bank
Dr. Sheikh Hamad bin Nasser Al-Thani, General Manager

P. O. Box 22789, Doha, State of Qatar
Phone: (974) 442-1600
Fax: (974) 435-0433

Qatar International Islamic Bank
Mr. Abdulbasit Al-Sheibi, General Manager
P. O. Box 664, Doha, State of Qatar
Phone: (974) 433-2600
Fax: (974) 444-4101

Qatar Islamic Bank
Mr. Maher Dewaik, Acting General Manager
P. O. Box 559, Doha, State of Qatar
Phone: (974) 443-8000; (974) 443-9498
Fax: (974) 441-2700

Qatar National Bank
Mr. Saeed Abdulla Al-Misnad, General Manager
P. O. Box 1002, Doha, State of Qatar
Phone: (974) 440-7407
Fax: (974) 441-3753

Standard Chartered Bank Plc
Mr. Aris Mansoor, General Manager
P. O. Box 29, Doha, State of Qatar
Phone: (974) 441-4251
Fax: (974) 441-3739

United Bank Ltd.
Mr. Mohammed Abdul Raouf, General Manager
P. O. Box 242, Doha, State of Qatar
Phone: (974) 443-8666
Fax: (974) 442-4600

Multilateral Development Bank Offices in Country: Not available

TPCC Trade Information Center in Washington:
Phone: 1-800-USA-TRAD(E)
Fax: (202) 482-4473.

U.S. Department of State Office of Business Affairs:
Phone: (202) 746-1625
Fax: (202) 647-3953

U.S. Department of Commerce Country Desk Officer:
(For market access and regulatory problems only)
Mr. D. Guglielmi
Office of the Near East, Room 2039
U.S. Department of Commerce
14th St. & Constitution Ave. N.W.
Washington, DC 20230
Phone: (202) 482-1860
Fax: (202) 482-0878

Country Desk Officer: State Department:
Mr. Atul Keshap
NEA/ARP, Room 4224
Department of State
Washington, DC 20520-6258
Phone: (202) 647-6579
Fax: (202) 736-4459

U.S. Department of Agriculture, Foreign Agricultural Service, Trade Assistance and Promotion Office:

Trade Assistance and Promotion Office (TAPO)
Foreign Agricultural Service (FAS)
U.S. Department of Agriculture
Ag Box 1052
Washington, D.C. 20250-1052
Phone: (202) 720-7420
Fax: (202) 690-4374

The FAS Home Page address on the Internet is:
http://www.fas.usda.gov

Overseas Private Investment Corporation (OPIC):
Phone: (202) 336-8799

Leading Qatari Firms:

Al-Fardan Group
Mr. Fahad Al-Fardan, Managing Director
P.O. Box 63, Doha, State of Qatar
Phone: (974) 440-8408
Fax: (974) 435-1885

Al-Jabor Group Holdings
H.E. Sheikh Salman bin Jabor, Managing Director
P.O. Box 295 (4694 pob directors), Doha, State of Qatar
Phone: (974) 432-8500
Fax: (974) 444-5543; (974) 444-9411

Almana Group
Mr. Omar Hamad Almana, Chairman; Mr. Badr Almana, Managing Director; Mr. Saud Almana, Executive Director
P.O. Box 491, Doha, State of Qatar
Phone: (974) 462-1222
Fax: (974) 462-2420

Al-Muftah Group
Mr. Abdulrahman Muftah Al-Muftah, Chairman;
Mr. Ibrahim Muftah al-Muftah, Managing Director;
Mr. P.A. Abu Bakker, General Manager
Mr. Said Gul, Head of Projects Development
P.O. Box 875, Doha, State of Qatar
Phone: (974) 444-6868
Fax: (974) 444-1415

Al-Mukhtar Trading & Contracting Co.
Mr. Abdulrahman Abdullah Abdulghani, Managing Director; Mohammad Abdulla

Abdulghani, General Manager
P.O. Box 5536, Doha, State of Qatar
Phone: (974) 447-8454
Fax: (974) 447-8226

Arabian Construction Engineering Co. (ACEC)
H.E. Sheikh Hamad bin Jassim Al-Thani, Chairman; Mr. Ghalib Shoush'a, Managing Director
P.O. Box 1277, Doha, State of Qatar
Phone: (974) 441-7521; (974) 441-7522
Fax: (974) 443-0112

Faisal bin Jassim Group
Sheikh Faisal bin Jassim Al-Thani, Chairman; Mr. Ibrahim Naameh, General Manager
P.O. Box 3288, Doha, State of Qatar
Phone: (974) 441-9555
Fax: (974) 444-7189

GEMCO (Gulf Electrical Materials Co.)
Mr. Ahmed Saleh Al-Obaidley, Owner
P.O. Box 157, Doha, State of Qatar
Phone: (974) 432-9480; (974) 432-1753
Fax: (974) 432-1752

Ghanim Al-Thani Holdings
Sheikh Ghanim bin Ali Al-Thani, Owner
P.O. Box 5319, Doha, State of Qatar
Phone: (974) 442-8201
Fax: (974) 444-5248

Hamad bin Khalid (HBK)
Mr. Amal Azzi, General Manager
P.O. Box 1362, Doha, State of Qatar
Phone: (974) 443-3644
Fax: (974) 443-8729

Hassan Ali Bin Ali Establishment (HABA)
Mr. Hassan Ali Bin Ali, Chairman
P.O. Box 3331, Doha, State of Qatar
Phone: (974) 441-8181
Fax: (974) 442-3484

Hassan Ali bin Ali Group
Mr. Adel Ali bin Ali, Chairman; Mr. Nabil Ali bin Ali, Managing Director
P.O. Box 3331, Doha, State of Qatar
Phone: (974) 442-1915; (974) 442-6201
Fax: (974) 443-3778

International Project Development Company
Mr. Ahmed Hussain Khalaf, Managing Director
P.O. Box 19613, Doha, State of Qatar
Phone: (974) 436-3840
Fax: (974) 436-1925

Jaidah Motors & Trading Co.
Mr. Jassim Jaidah, Managing Director
P.O. Box 150, Doha, State of Qatar
Phone: (974) 442-6161
Fax: (974) 441-4100; (974) 441-5400

KABAS
Mr. Mahmoud Abu Errub, Managing Director
P.O. Box 1760, Doha, State of Qatar
Phone: (974) 468-3203
Fax: (974) 468-4033

Kassem Darwish Fakhroo & Sons (KDS)
P.O. Box 350, Doha, State of Qatar
Mr. Hassan Darwish, Managing Director
Phone: (974) 442-3463
Fax: (974) 442-6378

Mannai Corporation
Mr. Ahmed Mannai, Managing Director
P.O. Box 76, Doha, State of Qatar
Phone: (974) 441-2555; (974) 441-2800
Fax: (974) 441-1982

Nabina Trading Establishment
Mr. Ibrahim Nabina, General Manager
P.O. Box 130, Doha, State of Qatar
Phone: (974) 465-2345
Fax: (974) 465-2386

Nasir bin Abdullah and Sons Trading Co.
Sheikh Abdullah bin Nasser Al-Thani, General Manager
P.O. Box 329, Doha, State of Qatar
Phone: (974) 441-7575
Fax: (974) 444-0203

Nasser bin Khalid (NBK) Group
Sheikh Nawaf bin Nasser bin Khalid Al-Thani, Owner
P.O. Box 82, Doha, State of Qatar
Phone: (974) 444-3838
Fax: (974) 442-5181; (974) 432-8412 (Owner)

Salam Group
Mr. Issa Abu Issa, Chairman; Mr. Bassem Abu Issa, General Manager
P.O. Box 121, Doha, State of Qatar
Phone: (974) 483-2050
Fax: (974) 483-2103

Saud Bin Khalid Co. (SBK)
Mr. Inqaz Al-Jasser, General Manager
P.O. Box 22147, Doha, State of Qatar
Phone: 974-321-297; 974-321-298
Fax: 974-322-181

Teyseer Trading & Contracting Co.
Mr. Abdulrahman Mannai, General Manager
P.O. Box 1556, Doha, State of Qatar
Phone: (974) 462-2226
Fax: (974) 462-2225

SAUDI ARABIA

US Embassy Personnel

1) US Embassy
Commercial Service (CS) - Riyadh
Contacts: Charles Kestenbaum, Senior Commercial Officer
Thomas Moore, Deputy Senior Commercial Officer
Robert Peaslee, Commercial Officer
Unit 61307
APO AE 09803-1307
Phone: (966 1) 488-3800, Fax: (966 1) 488-3237
E-mail: riyadh.office.box@mail.doc.gov

2) US Consulate General
CS - Jeddah
Contact: David H. Rundell, Principal Commercial Officer
Unit 62112
APO AE 09811-2112
Phone: (966 2) 606-2479, Fax: (966 2) 606-2567
E-mail: jeddah.office.box@mail.doc.gov

3) US Consulate General
Commercial Service (CS) - Dhahran
Contact: Nasir Abbasi, Principal Commercial Officer
Unit 66803
APO AE 09858-6803
Phone: (966 3) 330-3200, Fax: (966 3) 330-2190
E-mail: dhahran.office.box@mail.doc.gov

4) US Embassy Riyadh
Agricultural Trade Office
Contact: Quintin Grey, Agricultural Trade Officer
Phone: (966 1) 488-3800, Fax: (966 1) 482-4364
E-mail: fasriyadh@hotmail.com

5) US Embassy Riyadh
Economic Section
Contact: Alice Dress, Counselor for Economic Affairs
Phone: (966 1) 488-3800, Fax: (966 1) 488-3278

- Saudi Embassy and Consulates in the US

1) Royal Embassy of Saudi Arabia
601 New Hampshire Ave, NW
Washington, DC 20037
Phone: (202) 333-2740, Fax: (202) 944-3140

2) Saudi Consulate General in New York
866 United Nations Plaza, Suite 480
New York, NY 10017
Phone: (212) 752-2740, Fax: (212) 688-2719

3) Saudi Consulate General in Houston
One Westheimer Plaza
5718 Westheimer, Suite 1500
Houston, TX 77057
Phone: (713) 785-5577, Fax: (713) 785-1163

4) Saudi Consulate General in Los Angeles
Sawtelle Courtyard Building
2045 Sawtelle Blvd
Los Angeles, CA 90025
Phone: (310) 479-6000/914-9011, Fax: (310) 479-2752

- US-Based Multipliers Relevant for Country

1) US-Saudi Arabian Business Council
1401 New York Ave, NW, Suite 720
Washington, DC 20005
Phone: (202) 638-1212, Fax: (202) 638-2894

2) National US-Arab Chamber of Commerce
1100 New York Ave, NW
East Tower, Suite 550
Washington, DC 20005
Phone: (202) 289-5920, Fax: (202) 289-5938

3) American Business Council of the Gulf Countries (ABCGC)
c/o Intercom International Consultants
1101 30th Street, NW, Suite 500
Washington, DC 20007
Phone: (202) 887-1887, Fax: (202) 887-1888

4) ARAMCO
1667 K Street, NW
Washington, DC 20006
Phone: (202) 223-7750, Fax: (202) 223-7756

5) ARAMCO Services Company
PO Box 4534
Houston, TX 77210-4534
Phone: (713) 432-4000, Fax: (713) 432-8566

6) Saudi Petroleum International
527 Madison Ave
22 & 23 Floors
New York, NY 10002
Phone: (212) 832-4044, Fax: (212) 446-9200

7) SABIC Americas, Inc.
2500 City West Blvd,
Suite 650
Houston, TX 77042
Phone: (713) 532-4999, Fax: (713) 532-4994

8) Riyadh Bank
700 Louisiana
Suite 4770
Houston, TX 77002
Phone: (713) 224-8071, Fax: (713) 224-8072

9) Saudi International Bank
520 Madison Ave
New York, NY 10022

Phone: (212) 355-6530, Fax: (212) 758-5360

- Saudi Arabian Trade Associations/Chambers of Commerce

1) Council of Saudi Chambers of Commerce and Industry
Contact: Eng. Usama M. Kurdi, Secretary General
PO Box 16683 Riyadh 11474, Saudi Arabia
Phone: (966 1) 405-3200, Fax: (966 1) 402-4747

2) Riyadh Chamber of Commerce and Industry
Contact: Hussein Al-Athel, Secretary General
PO Box 596 Riyadh 11421, Saudi Arabia
Phone: (966 1) 404-0044, Fax: (966 1) 402-1103

3) Jeddah Chamber of Commerce and Industry
Contact: Dr. Majid A Al-Qusabi, Secretary General
PO Box 1264 Jeddah 21431, Saudi Arabia
Phone: (966 2) 651-5111, Fax: (966 2) 651-7373

4) Chamber of Commerce and Industry for the Eastern Province
Contact: Dr. Ibrahim Abdullah Al-Mutref, Secretary General, Ext 4555
PO Box 719 Dammam 31421, Saudi Arabia
Phone: (966 3) 857-1111, Fax: (966 3) 857-0607

5) Federation of GCC Chambers
Contact: Mohammad Abdullah Al-Mulla, Secretary General
PO Box 2198 Dammam 31451, Saudi Arabia
Phone: (966 3) 826-5943/3792, Fax: (966 3) 826-6794
E-mail: fgccc@Zajilnet

6) American Businessmen's Group of Riyadh
PO Box 8273 Riyadh 11482, Saudi Arabia
Phone: (966 1) 478-2738/1652, Fax: (966 1) 476-4363

7) American Businessmen of Jeddah
PO Box 8483 Jeddah 21482, Saudi Arabia
Phone: (966 2) 665-6359/652-1234, Fax: (966 2) 660-0389

8) American Business Association - Eastern Province
PO Box 88 Dhahran Airport 31932, Saudi Arabia
Phone: (966 3) 874-2886, Fax: (966 3) 873-8883/857-8130

- Saudi Arabian Government and Quasi-Government Agencies

1) Arab Satellite Communication Organization
Contact: Eng. Saad Al-Badana, Director General
PO Box 1038 Riyadh 11431, Saudi Arabia
Phone: (966 1) 464-6666, Fax: (966 1) 465-6983

2) Board of Grievances
Contact: HE Sheikh Mansour Al-Malek, President
Riyadh 11138, Saudi Arabia
Phone: (966 1) 402-1724, Fax: (966 1) 403-4296

3) Central Department of Statistics
Contact: Abdullah Al-Othaim, Director General
PO Box 3735 Riyadh 11118, Saudi Arabia
Phone: (966 1) 405-9638, Fax: (966 1) 405-9493

4) Civil Defense
Contact: Major General Fahad Al-Tuwaijri, Director General
Riyadh 11174
Phone: (966 1) 479-2828, Fax: (966 1) 477-6579

5) Directorate General for Mineral Resources
Contact: Ibrahim Khaberi, Deputy Minister for Minerals
PO Box 2880 Jeddah 21461, Saudi Arabia
Phone: (966 2) 667-4800, Fax: (966 2) 667-2265

6) Directorate General of Zakat and Income Tax
Contact: Saad Hamdan Al-Hamdan Acting Director General
Riyadh 11187
Phone: (966 1) 401-0182/404-1537, Fax: (966 1) 404-1495

7) Economic Offset Secretariat
Contact: Major General Hamad Al-Sugair, Secretary to the Offset Committee
PO Box 27040 Riyadh 11417, Saudi Arabia
Phone: (966 1) 478-4330, Fax: (966 1) 478-4123

8) General Electricity Corporation
Contact: Fehaid Fahd Al-Shareef, Acting Governor
PO Box 1185 Riyadh 11431, Saudi Arabia
Phone: (966 1) 477-6666, Fax: (966 1) 477-5322

9) General Organization for Grain Silos and Flour Mills
Contact: HE Saleh Mohammad Al-Suleiman, Director General
PO Box 3402 Riyadh 11471, Saudi Arabia
Phone: (966 1) 464-3500, Fax: (966 1) 463-1943

10) General Organization for Social Insurance
Contact: HE Suliman Saad Al-Humaid, Governor
PO Box 878 Riyadh 11421, Saudi Arabia
Phone: (966 1) 478-5721, Fax: (966 1) 477-9958

11) General Organization for Technical Education and Vocational Training
Contact: HE Ali Nasser Al-Ghafis, Governor
PO Box 6041 Riyadh 11442, Saudi Arabia
Phone: (966 1) 405-2770, Fax: (966 1) 406-5876

12) General Presidency for Youth Welfare

Organization
Contact: HRH Prince Sultan Bin Fahd Bin Abdulaziz Al-Saud, President
PO Box 965 Riyadh 11421, Saudi Arabia
Phone: (966 1) 401-4576, Fax: (966 1) 401-0376

13) Institute of Public Administration
Contact: HE Mohammad Al-Shigawi, Director General
PO Box 205 Riyadh 11411, Saudi Arabia
Phone: (966 1) 476-8888, Fax: (966 1) 479-2136

14) King Abdul Aziz City for Science and Technology
Contact: HE Dr. Saleh Abdel Rahman Al-Athel, President
PO Box 6086 Riyadh 11442, Saudi Arabia
Phone: (966 1) 488-3555, Fax: (966 1) 488-3756

15) King Faisal Foundation
Contact: HRH Prince Khalid Al-Faisal, Managing Director
PO Box 352 Riyadh 11411, Saudi Arabia
Phone: (966 1) 465-2255, Fax: (966 1) 465-6524

16) Meteorology and Environmental Protection Agency (MEPA)
Contact: Dr. Nizar Tawfiq, President
PO Box 1358 Jeddah 21431, Saudi Arabia
Phone: (966 2) 651-8887, Fax: (966 2) 651-1424

17) Naif Arab Academy for Security Sciences and Training
Contact: Dr. Abdul Aziz Sagr Al-Ghamdi, President
PO Box 6830 Riyadh 11452, Saudi Arabia
Phone: (966 1) 246-3444, Fax: (966 1) 246-4713

18) National Shipping Company of Saudi Arabia
Contact: Ahmad Banaja, Chairman
PO Box 8931 Riyadh 11492, Saudi Arabia
Phone: (966 1) 478-5454, Fax: (966 1) 477-8036

19) Presidency of Civil Aviation
Contact: HE Dr. Ali Bin Abdulrahman Al-Khalaf, President
PO Box 887 Jeddah 21421, Saudi Arabia
Phone: (966 2) 667-9000, Fax: (966 2) 671-7376

20) Public Investment Fund
Contact: HE Mansour Saleh Al-Maiman, Secretary General
PO Box 6847 Riyadh 11452, Saudi Arabia
Phone: (966 1) 478-3580, Fax: (966 1) 474-2693

21) Royal Commission for Jubail and Yanbu
Contact: HE Saud Bin Thunayyan Al-Saud, Acting President
PO Box 5864 Riyadh 11432, Saudi Arabia
Phone: (966 1) 479-4445, Fax: (966 1) 477-5404

22) Saline Water Conversion Corporation (SWCC)
Contact: HE Eng. Abdullah Al-Hussayen, Governor
PO Box 5968 Riyadh 11432, Saudi Arabia
Phone: (966 1) 463-1111/0503, Fax: (966 1) 463-1952

23) Saudi Arabian Agricultural Bank
Contact: Abdullah S. Al-Shoaibi, Director General
PO Box 1811 Riyadh 11126, Saudi Arabia
Phone: (966 1) 402-3911, Fax: (966 1) 402-2359

24) Saudi Arabian Airlines
Contact: Dr. Khaled A Al-Bakr, Director General
PO Box 620 Jeddah 21421, Saudi Arabia
Phone: (966 2) 686-0000, Fax: (966 2) 686-4552

25) Saudi Arabian Department of Customs
Contact: HE Saleh Al-Barrak, Director General
PO Box 3483 Riyadh 11471, Saudi Arabia
Phone: (966 1) 401-3334, Fax: (966 1) 404-3412

26) Saudi Arabian General Investment Authority
Contact: HH Abdallah Bin Faisal Bin Turki Al-Saud, Governor
PO Box 5927 Riyadh 11432, Saudi Arabia
Phone: (966 1) 263-5010, Fax: (966 1) 263-5020

27) Saudi Arabian Mining Company
Contact: Dr. Abdallah E. Al-Dabbagh, President & CEO
PO Box 68861 Riyadh 11537, Saudi Arabia
Phone: (966 1) 472-1222, Fax: (966 1) 472-1333

28) Saudi Arabian Monetary Agency
Contact: HE Hamad Saud Al-Sayyari, Governor
PO Box 2992 Riyadh 11461, Saudi Arabia
Phone: (966 1) 463-3000, Fax: (966 1) 463-4262

29) Saudi Arabian National Guard
Contact: HRH Prince Badr Bin Abdul Aziz Al-Saud, Vice President
Riyadh 11173, Saudi Arabia
Phone: (966 1) 491-2222, Fax: (966 1) 491-4429

30) Saudi Arabian Oil Company (Saudi Aramco)
Contact: HE Abdallah Saleh Jumaa, President & CEO
PO Box 5000 Dhahran Airport 31311, Saudi Arabia
Phone: (966 3) 876-5229, Fax: (966 3) 876-6520

31) Saudi Arabian Public Transport Company
Contact: Dr. Abdul Aziz Al-Ohali, Director General
PO Box 10667 Riyadh 11443, Saudi Arabia
Phone: (966 1) 454-5000, Fax: (966 1) 454-2100

32) Saudi Arabian Railway Organization
Contact: HE Naser Mohammed Al-Ajami,

President
PO Box 36 Dammam 31241, Saudi Arabia
Phone: (966 3) 871-5151/3001, Fax: (966 3) 871-5154

33) Saudi Arabian Standards Organization
Contact: Dr. Khaled Youssef Al-Khalaf, Director General
PO Box 3437 Riyadh 11471, Saudi Arabia
Phone: (966 1) 452-0000, Fax: (966 1) 452-0086

34) Saudi Basic Industries Corporation (SABIC)
Contact: Eng. Mohammad Al-Madi, Vice Chairman & CEO
PO Box 5101 Riyadh 11422, Saudi Arabia
Phone: (966 1) 401-2033, Fax: (966 1) 401-3831

35) Saudi Electric Company, Central Province Branch
Contact: Eng. Abdul Aziz Abdul Wahed, President
PO Box 57 Riyadh 11411, Saudi Arabia
Phone: (966 1) 403-1033, Fax: (966 1) 405-1191

36) Saudi Electric Company, Eastern Province Branch
Contact: Fehaid Fahd Al-Shareef, Chairman
PO Box 5190 Dammam 31422, Saudi Arabia
Phone: (966 3) 857-2300, Fax: (966 3) 858-6060

37) Saudi Electric Company, Southern Province Branch
Contact: Eng. Abdulrahman Al-Tuwaijri, Chairman
PO Box 616, Abha, Saudi Arabia
Phone: (966 7) 227-1111, Fax: (966 7) 227-1627

38) Saudi Electric Company, Western Province Branch
Contact: Eng. Mahmmoud Abdullah Taiba, Chairman
PO Box 9299 Jeddah 21413, Saudi Arabia
Phone: (966 2) 651-1008, Fax: (966 2) 653-4139

39) Saudi Fund for Development
Contact: HE Mohammad Al-Soghair, Director General
PO Box 50483 Riyadh 11523, Saudi Arabia
Phone: (966 1) 464-0292, Fax: (966 1) 464-7450

40) Saudi Industrial Development Fund
Contact: Saleh Al-Noaim, Director General
PO Box 4143 Riyadh 11491, Saudi Arabia
Phone: (966 1) 477-4002, Fax: (966 1) 479-0165

41) Saudi Ports Authority
Contact: HE Abdul Aziz Al-Manie, Minister of State, President
PO Box 5162 Riyadh 11188, Saudi Arabia
Phone: (966 1) 405-0005, Fax: (966 1) 405-3508

42) Saudi Red Crescent Society
Contact: HE Dr. Abdulrahman Abdulaziz Al-Suwailem, President
Riyadh 11129, Saudi Arabia
Phone: (966 1) 474-0925/0027, Fax: (966 1) 474-0430

43) Saudi Telecommunications Company
Contact: Khaled Al-Melhem, President
PO Box 87912 Riyadh 11650, Saudi Arabia
Phone: (966 1) 452-5000, Fax: (966 1) 452-5559

- Saudi Arabian Government Ministries

1) Ministry of Agriculture and Water
Contact: HE Dr. Abdullah Abdul Rahman Al-Moaammar, Minister
PO Box 2639 Riyadh 11195, Saudi Arabia
Phone: (966 1) 401-2777/403-0030, Fax: (966 1) 404-4592

2) Ministry of Civil Service
Contact: HE Mohammed Ali Al-Fayiz, Minister
Riyadh 11114
Phone: (966 1) 402-6666, Fax: (966 1) 405-6258

3) Ministry of Commerce
Contact: HE Dr. Oussama Jaafar Faquih, Minister
PO Box 1774 Riyadh 11162, Saudi Arabia
Phone: (966 1) 401-2222, Fax: (966 1) 402-6640

4) Ministry of Communications
Contact: HE Dr. Nasser Al-Salloum, Minister
PO Box 3813 Riyadh 11178, Saudi Arabia
Phone: (966 1) 404-3000/2928, Fax: (966 1) 403-1401

5) Ministry of Defense and Aviation
Contact: HRH Prince Sultan Bin Abdul Aziz Al-Saud, Minister
Riyadh 11165, Saudi Arabia
Phone: (966 1) 478-9000/477-7313, Fax: (966 1) 406-2146

6) Ministry of Education
Contact: HE Dr. Mohammad Bin Ahmad Al-Rasheed, Minister
Riyadh 11148, Saudi Arabia
Phone: (966 1) 404-2888, Fax: (966 1) 403-7229

7) Ministry of Finance and National Economy
Contact: HE Dr. Ibrahim Al-Assaf, Minister
PO Box 6902 Riyadh 11177, Saudi Arabia
Phone: (966 1) 405-0080/0000, Fax: (966 1) 405-9202

8) Ministry of Foreign Affairs
Contact: HRH Prince Saud Al-Faisal, Minister
Riyadh 11124, Saudi Arabia
Phone: (966 1) 406-7777, Fax: (966 1) 402-0100

9) Ministry of Health
Contact: HE Dr. Osama Abdul Majeed Shobokshi, Minister
PO Box 21217 Riyadh 11176, Saudi Arabia
Phone: (966 1) 401-2220, Fax: (966 1) 402-6395

10) Ministry of Higher Education
Contact: HE Dr. Khaled Al-Anqari, Minister
Riyadh 11153, Saudi Arabia
Phone: (966 1) 441-5555, Fax: (966 1) 441-9004

11) Ministry of Industry and Electricity
Contact: HE Dr. Hashim Abdallah Yamani, Minister
PO Box 5729 Riyadh 11127, Saudi Arabia
Phone: (966 1) 477-6666, Fax: (966 1) 477-5488

12) Ministry of Information
Contact: HE Dr. Fuad Abdul Salam Al-Farsi, Minister
PO Box 843 Riyadh 11161, Saudi Arabia
Phone: (966 1) 406-8888, Fax: (966 1) 405-0674

13) Ministry of Interior
Contact: HRH Prince Naif Bin Abdul Aziz Al Saud, Minister
PO Box 3743 Riyadh 11481, Saudi Arabia
Phone: (966 1) 401-1111, Fax: (966 1) 403-3614

14) Ministry of Islamic Affairs, Endowments and Guidance
Contact: HE Saleh Abdul Aziz Mohammad Al-Sheikh, Minister
Riyadh 11137, Saudi Arabia
Phone: (966 1) 473-0401, Fax: (966 1) 477-2938

15) Ministry of Justice
Contact: HE Dr. Abdullah Mohammad Ibrahim Al-Sheikh, Minister
Riyadh 11137, Saudi Arabia
Phone: (966 1) 405-7777, Fax: (966 1) 405-9042

16) Ministry of Labor and Social Affairs
Contact: HE Dr. Ali Al-Namlah, Minister
Riyadh 11157, Saudi Arabia
Phone: (966 1) 477-1480/477-8888, Fax: (966 1) 477-2250

17) Ministry of Municipalities and Rural Affairs
Contact: HE Dr. Muhammad Ibrahim Al-Jarallah, Minister
Riyadh 11136, Saudi Arabia
Phone: (966 1) 456-9999, Fax: (966 1) 456-3196

18) Ministry of Petroleum and Mineral Resources
Contact: HE Eng. Ali Al-Naimi, Minister
PO Box 247 Riyadh 11191, Saudi Arabia
Phone: (966 1) 478-1661/1133/7777, Fax: (966 1) 478-1980

19) Ministry of Pilgrimage
Contact: HE Iyad Amin Madani, Minister
Riyadh 11183, Saudi Arabia
Phone: (966 1) 402-2200, Fax: (966 1) 402-6583

20) Ministry of Planning
Contact: HE Dr. Khaled Al-Gosaibi, Minister
PO Box 358 Riyadh 11183, Saudi Arabia
Phone: (966 1) 401-3333/1444, Fax: (966 1) 401-0385

21) Ministry of Posts, Telephone and Telegraph
Contact: HE Dr. Khaled Al-Gosaibi, Acting Minister
Riyadh 11112, Saudi Arabia
Phone: (966 1) 463-4444, Fax: (966 1) 463-7072

22) Ministry of Public Works and Housing
Contact: HRH Prince Miteb Bin Abdul Aziz Al Saud, Minister
PO Box 56095 Riyadh 11151, Saudi Arabia
Phone: (966 1) 405-8300, Fax: (966 1) 402-2723

- Saudi Arabian Market Research Firms

1) Al-Saif Management and Economic Consultants
Contact: Prof. Khaled A. Al-Saif, Executive Director
PO Box 17212 Riyadh 11484, Saudi Arabia
Phone: (966 1) 465-1982, Fax: (966 1) 464-4668
E-mail: alsaifcons@suhuf.net.sa

2) Business Consultants International Group
Contact: Raed Al-Khaldi, Managing Director
PO Box 91450 Riyadh 11633, Saudi Arabia
Phone: (966 1) 478-6154/4275, Fax: (966 1) 478-3794
E-mail: b.sartawi@bcigcms.com

3) Consultancy & Research Center
Contact: Charles Glover, General Manager
PO Box 7188 Riyadh 11462, Saudi Arabia
Phone: (966 1) 479-3321/2673, Fax: (966 1) 479-4122
E-mail: Cglover@memrbksa.com

4) The Consulting Center for Finance and Investment
Contact: Dr. Abdulaziz M. Al-Dukheil, President
PO Box 2462 Riyadh 11451, Saudi Arabia
Phone: (966 1) 478-2525, Fax: (966 1) 476-8021

5) The Economic Bureau
Contact: Sherif Fathi Hanafi, Administration & Financial Manager
PO Box 86619 Riyadh 11632, Saudi Arabia
Phone: (966 1) 464-3938, Fax: (966 1) 465-4669
E-mail: shanafy@teb.com.sa

6) Arthur D. Little International

Contact: Charles Parry, General Manager
PO Box 3266 Riyadh 11471, Saudi Arabia
Phone: (966 1) 477-0153/0227, Fax: (966 1) 477-0134
E-mail: Parry.charles@adlittle.com

7) Amer/A.C. Nielsen
Contact: Maher Obaid, General Manager
PO Box 222 Riyadh 11382, Saudi Arabia
Phone: (966 1) 403-2887, Fax: (966 1) 403-7491

- Saudi Arabian Commercial Banks

1) Arab National Bank
Contact: Nemeh Sabbagh, Managing Director
PO Box 56921 Riyadh 11564, Saudi Arabia
Phone: (966 1) 402-9000, Fax: (966 1) 403-0052

2) Saudi French Bank
Contact: Bertrand Viriot, Managing Director
PO Box 56006 Riyadh 11554, Saudi Arabia
Phone: (966 1) 404-2222, Fax: (966 1) 404-2155

3) Saudi American Bank
Contact: Mike de Graffenried, Managing Director
PO Box 833 Riyadh 11421, Saudi Arabia
Phone: (966 1) 477-4770, Fax: (966 1) 478-0823

4) Saudi Hollandi Bank
Contact: Hank Mulder, Managing Director
PO Box 1467 Riyadh 11431, Saudi Arabia
Phone: (966 1) 401-0288, Fax: (966 1) 401-0968

5) Saudi British Bank
Contact: David Hodgkinson, Managing Director
PO Box 9084 Riyadh 11413, Saudi Arabia
Phone: (966 1) 405-0677, Fax: (966 1) 405-0069

6) Al-Rajhi Investment and Banking Corporation
Contact: Abdallah Suleiman Al-Rajhi, President
PO Box 28 Riyadh 11411, Saudi Arabia
Phone: (966 1) 460-1000/2015, Fax: (966 1) 460-2040

7) Riyad Bank
Contact: Alan Thompson, President & CEO
PO Box 22622 Riyadh 11416, Saudi Arabia
Phone: (966 1) 401-0908, Fax: (966 1) 403-0010

8) The Saudi Investment Bank
Contact: Saud Al-Saleh, General Manager
PO Box 3533 Riyadh 11481, Saudi Arabia
Phone: (966 1) 477-8433, Fax: (966 1) 478-1557

9) Bank Al-Jazira
Contact: Mishari Ibrahim Al-Mishari, General Manager
PO Box 6277 Jeddah 21442, Saudi Arabia
Phone: (966 2) 651-8070, Fax: (966 2) 653-0923

10) National Commercial Bank
Contact: Abdallah S. Bahamdan, Managing Director
PO Box 3555 Jeddah 21481, Saudi Arabia
Phone: (966 2) 644-6644, Fax: (966 2) 643-9595

- Multilateral Development Bank Offices in Saudi Arabia

Islamic Development Bank
Contact: Dr. Ahmed Mohammad Ali, President
PO Box 5925 Jeddah 21432, Saudi Arabia
Phone: (966 2) 636-1400, Fax: (966 2) 636-6871

The World Bank
Contact: Edgar Saravia, Resident Representative
P.O. Box 5900 Riyadh 11432, Saudi Arabia
Phone: (966 1) 483-4956, Fax: (966 1) 488-5311

- Washington-based USG Country Contacts

1) U.S. Department of Commerce
Contact: Kevin Brennan, Regional Director, US&FCS/ANESA
14th & Constitution Ave, NW
Washington, DC 20230
Phone: (202) 482-4836, Fax: (202) 482-5179

2) U.S. Department of Commerce
Contact: David Guglielmi, Desk Officer, MAC/ANESA/ONE, Room 2029b
14th & Constitution Ave, NW
Washington, DC 20230
Phone: (202) 482-1860, Fax: (202) 482-0878

3) TPCC Trade Information Center
Phone: 1-800-USA-TRADE

4) US Department of Agriculture
Foreign Agricultural Service
Trade Assistance and Promotion Office
Phone: (202) 720-7420, Fax: (202) 690-4374

5) US Department of State
Office of the Coordinator for Business Affairs
Phone: (202) 746-1625, Fax: (202) 647-3953

SYRIA

U.S. EMBASSY TRADE CONTACTS:

telephone: (963-11) 333-1342; fax: (963-11) 224-7938

Daniel Rubinstein: Economic/Commercial Head of Section
Andrew Dickson: Economic/Commercial Officer
Nate Jensen: Economic/Commercial Officer
Christopher Molnar : Economic/Commercial Officer
Benjamin Watson: Economic/Commercial Officer

Thomas Pomeroy
Agricultural Counselor
U.S. Embassy Cairo
telephone: (20-2) 797-2388/9
fax: (20-2) 796-3989

COUNTRY TRADE ASSOCIATIONS/
CHAMBERS OF COMMERCE

The Federation of Syrian Chambers of Commerce: President: Dr. Ratib Shallah, P.O. Box 5909, Damascus, Syria; telephone: 963-11-3311756, 3337344, 3311504; fax: 963-11-3331127

Damascus Chamber of Commerce: President: Dr. Ratib Shallah, P.O. Box 1040, Damascus, Syria; telephone: 963-11-2245475, 2232348, 2211339, 2218339; fax: 963-11-2225874

Damascus Chamber of Industry: President: Dr. Yahya Hindi, P.O. Box 1305, Damascus, Syria; telephone: 963-11-2222205, 2213475, 2215042; fax: 963-11-2245981

Damascus Suburb Chamber of Commerce: President: Mr. Adnan al-Nen, P.O. Box 5859, Damascus, Syria; telephone: 963-11-2315391, 2318828; fax: 963-11-2313798

Aleppo Chamber of Commerce: President: Mr. Mohammed Saleh Al-Mallah, P.O. Box 1261, Aleppo, Syria; telephone: 963-21-2238236, 2269910, 2238237; fax: 963-21-2213493

Aleppo Chamber of Industry: President: Mr. Muhammad Oubari, P.O. Box 1859, Aleppo, Syria; telephone: 963-21-3620600/1/2, 3639700; fax: 963-21-3620040

Homs Chamber of Commerce and Industry: President: Dr. Tarif al-Akhras, P.O. Box 440, Homs, Syria; telephone: 963-31-471000, 469440; fax: 963-31-464247

Hama Chamber of Commerce and Industry: President: Mr. 'Izzat Habbal, P.O. Box 147, Hama, Syria; telephone: 963-33-233304, 517700; fax: 963-33-517701

Latakia Chamber of Commerce and Industry: President: Mr. Kamal Ismail Al-Assad, P.O. Box 124, Latakia, Syria; telephone: 963-41-479530/1; fax: 963-41-478526

Tartus Chamber of Commerce and Industry: President: Mr. Wahib Kamel Mur'i, P.O. Box 403, Tartus, Syria; telephone: 963-43-329851/2; fax: 963-43-329728

Dayr Al-Zur Chamber of Commerce and Industry: President: Mr. Bashir Tu'meh, Dayr Al-Zur, Syria; telephone: 963-51-222091; fax: 963-51-224756

Idlib Chamber of Commerce and Industry: President: Mr. Ahmad al-Hasan, Idlib, Syria; telephone: 963-23-235744, 250644; fax: 963-23-238744

Raqqa Chamber of Commerce and Industry: President: Mr. Omar Humeidi, al-Raqqa, Syria; Telephone: 963-22-234110; fax: 963-22-235218

Hasakah Chamber of Commerce and Industry: President: Mr. Makram Youssef Sabbagh, P.O. Box 243, al-Hasakah, Syria; Telephone: 963-52-321142, 311506; fax: 963-52-313842

Sweida Chamber of Commerce and Industry: President: Mr. Hamad Hammoud Nasr, Mazra'a Square, Sweida, Syria; telephone: 963-16-234585; fax: 963-16-232512

Dar'a Chamber of Commerce and Industry: President: Mr. Abdul Karim al-Khalili, Hanano Street, Dar'a, Syria; telephone: 963-15-231253; fax: 963-15-235452

Quneitra Chamber of Commerce and Industry: President: Mr. Jihad Mohammed Ismail, P.O. Box 25435, Damascus, Syria; telephone: 963-11-2247186; fax: 963-11-2228794

SYRIAN GOVERNMENT CONTACTS

Ministry of Petroleum and Mineral Resources
Minister - Dr. Mohammed Maher Jamal
Address: Adawi, Damascus, Syria
telephone: 963-11-4451624, 4455972, 4453795
fax: 963-11-4463942

Ministry of Irrigation
Minister - Mr. Taha al-Atrash
Fardous, P.O. Box 4451, Damascus, Syria
telephone: 963-11-2225748, 2212741, 2228571, 2221400/1/2/3
fax: 963-11-2246888

Ministry of Agriculture and Agricultural Reform
Minister - Mr. As'ad Mustafa
Hijaz Square, Damascus, Syria
telephone: 963-11-2221513/4, 2213613/4, 2322950/1
fax: 963-11-2244078, 2244023

Ministry of Transport
Minister - Mr. Makram Obeid
Abou Rumaneh, P.O. Box 134, Damascus, Syria

fax: 963-11-3333031

The Syrian Center for Consulting, Research, Training, and Business Administration
Dr. M. Ayman Midani
P.O. Box 7825, Damascus, Syria
telephone: 963-11-3316075
fax: 963-11-3313000

Arab Quality Makers
Mr. Hassan Hamwi
P.O. Box 3304, Damascus, Syria
telephone: 963-11-6112313, 3316522,
fax: 963-11-3316522

Financial & Economic Consulting Office
Dr. Nidal Kouli
P.O. Box 2675, Damascus, Syria
telephone: 963-11-3334145, 3334243
fax: 963-11-3323958, 3314631

COMMERCIAL BANKS

Commercial Bank of Syria
Director General: Mr. Mahmud Mithqal
Yousef Al-Azmah Square
P.O. Box 933, Damascus, Syria
telephone: 963-11-221-4508
fax: 221-6975, 222-8524

WASHINGTON-BASED USG CONTACTS

U.S. Department of State
Office of Business Affairs
telephone: (202) 647-3953

U.S. Department of State
NEA/ARN, Syria Desk
Ms. Jillian Burns
U.S. Department of State
Washington, D.C. 20520
telephone: (202) 647-1131
fax: (202) 647-0989

U.S. Department of Commerce
Office of the Near East
Mr. Thomas A. Sams
Washington, D.C.
telephone: (202) 482-1860
fax: (202) 482-0878
e-mail: tom_sams@ita.doc.gov

Office of Anti-Boycott Compliance
Bureau of Export Administration
U.S. Department of Commerce
HCHB, BXA, Rm 6098
14th St. & Constitution Ave, N.W.
Washington, D.C. 20230
Mr. Robert Diamond
Policy Director
telephone: (202) 482-2381
fax: (202) 482-0913
e-mail: rdiamond@bxa.doc.gov;
www.bxa.doc.gov

Office of Export Licensing/Enforcement Support
Bureau of Export Administration
U.S. Department of Commerce
Mr. Mark D. Menefee
telephone: (202) 482-2252
fax: (202) 482-0964
e-mail: eemm@bxa.doc.gov

Office of Strategic Trade and Foreign Policy Controls
Bureau of Export Administration
U.S. Department of Commerce
telephone: (202) 482-0092
www.bxa.fedword.gov

U.S. Department of Commerce
Bureau of Export Administration
Foreign Policy Controls Division
14th & Pennsylvania Avenue, N.W.
Room 2620, Mail Stop 2705H
Washington, D.C. 20230
Ms. Karen Vogel
telephone: (202) 482-2365
fax: (202) 482-6088
e-mail: kvogel@bxa.doc.gov

U.S. Department of Treasury
Office of Foreign Assets Control
telephone: (202) 622-2000
fax: (202) 622-6415
e-mail: dennis.wood@do.treas.gov
www.treas.gov/ofac

Africa and Middle East Area Officer
Mr. Paul Hoffman
Room 5094-S
U.S. Department of Agriculture
14th & Independence St., S.W. 20250
telephone: (202) 720-7053
fax: (202) 720-5183
e-mail: hoffmanp@fas.usda.gov

TUNISIA

AMERICAN CHAMBER OF COMMERCE

TUNISIAN-AMERICAN CHAMBER OF COMMERCE (TACC)
15 AVE. MOSBAH JARBOU RUE 7116
EL MANAR III 2092
TUNIS
TEL: 216-1-889.780
FAX: 216-1-889.880

GOVERNMENT CONTACTS

MINISTRY OF INTERNATIONAL COOPERATION
AND FOREIGN INVESTMENT
149, AVENUE DE LA LIBERTE
TUNIS
TEL: 216-1-798.522
FAX: 216-1-799.069

MINISTRY OF INDUSTRY
RUE 8010 CITE MONTPLAISIR
IMMUEBLE ENNOUZHA
1002 TUNIS
TEL: 216-1-791.132
FAX: 216-1-782.742

MINISTRY OF COMMERCE
37, AVENUE KHEREDDINE PACHA
TUNIS
TEL: 216-1-890.263
FAX: 216-1-781.324

MINISTRY OF ECONOMIC DEVELOPMENT
PLACE ALI ZOUAOUI
TUNIS
TEL: 216-1-334.022
FAX: 216-1-351.666

MINISTRY OF FINANCE
PLACE DU GOUVERNEMENT
LA KASBAH
TUNIS
TEL: 216-1-566.210
FAX: 216-1-563.959

MINISTRY OF ENVIRONMENT
CENTRE URBAIN NORD
TUNIS
TEL: 216-1-704.000
FAX: 216-1-703.286

MINISTRY OF AGRICULTURE
30 RUE ALAIN SAVARY
TUNIS
TEL: 216-1-681.654
FAX: 216-1-890.391

MINISTRY OF TOURISM AND HANDICRAFTS
AVENUE MOHAMED V
TUNIS
TEL: 216-1-341.077
FAX: 216-1-350.997

MINISTRY OF TRANSPORT
ZONE MONTPLAISIR
AVENUE MOHAMED V
TEL: 216-1-781.824
FAX: 216-1-790.149

FOREIGN INVESTMENT PROMOTION
AGENCY (FIPA)
63 RUE DE SYRIE
TUNIS
TEL: 216-1-792.144
FAX: 216-1-782-971

ENTREPRISE TUNISIENNE DES ACTIVITIES
PETROLIERES (ETAP)
27 BIS AVENUE KHEIREDDINE PACHA
TUNIS
TEL: 216-1-782.288
FAX: 216-1-784.092
(STATE PETROLEUM COMPANY)

AGENCE DE PROMOTION DE L'INDUSTRIE
(API)
RUE DE SYRIE
TUNIS
TEL: 216-1-792.144
FAX: 216-1-782.482

INSTITUT NATIONAL DE LA NORMALISATION
ET DE LA
PROPRIETE INDUSTRIELLE (INNORPI)
CITE EL KHADRA
TUNIS
TEL: 216-1-785.922
FAX: 216-1-781.563
(INDUSTRIAL STANDARDS AND COPYRIGHT
AUTHORITY)

TUNISIAN GAS AND ELECTRICITY COMPANY
(STEG)
38, RUE KAMEL ATATURK
TUNIS
TEL: 216-1-341.311
FAX: 216-1-341.401

OFFICE NATIONAL D'ASSAINISSMENT
32 RUE HEDI NOUIRA
TUNIS
TEL: 216-1-343.200
FAX: 216-1-350.411
(STATE SANITATION AGENCY)

TUNISIE TELECOM
RUE ASDRUBAL
(EN FACE DU GALAXIE 2000)
TUNIS
TEL: 216-1-801.011
FAX: 216-1-800.777
(TELECOMMUNICATIONS PARASTATAL)

TUNISAIR
BOULEVARD DU 7 NOVEMBRE
TUNIS
TEL: 216-1-700.100
FAX: 216-1-700.008
(STATE AIRLINE)

CENTRAL BANK OF TUNISIA
RUE HEDI NOUIRA
TUNIS
TEL: 216-1-340.588
FAX: 216-1-340.615

BUREAU OF CUSTOMS
RUE ICH-BILIA
TUNIS
TEL: 216-1-333.600
FAX: 216-1-353.255

TUNISIAN EMBASSY
1515 MASSACHUSETTS AVE., N.W.
WASHINGTON D.C. 20005
TEL: (202) 862-1850
FAX: (202) 862-1858

MARKET RESEARCH

GTN TUNISIE (GLOBAL TECHNOLOGY NETWORK)
RYM BEDOUI, REPRESENTATIVE
INTERNATIONAL EXECUTIVE SERVICE CORPS
10 AVENUE MOSBAH JARBOU
RUE 7116 EL MANAR III
TUNIS
TEL: 216-1-87-42-44/87-04-54
FAX: 216-1-87-22-79

TACC (SEE ABOVE)

TUNISIAN AMERICAN ASSOCIATION FOR MANAGEMENT STUDIES (TAAMS)
10, RUE MOSBAH JARBOU
EL MANAR III
TUNIS
TEL: 216-1-889.566
FAX: 216-1-872.033

COMMERCIAL BANKS

CITIBANK
55, AVENUE JUGURTHA
TUNIS
TEL: 216-1-790.066
FAX: 216-1-785.556
(ONLY U.S. BANK IN TUNISIA WITH ONSHORE AND OFFSHORE SERVICES)

INTERNATIONAL MAGHREB MERCHANT BANK
IMMEUBLE MAGHREBIA TOUR A
Z.I. CHARGUIA 2035
TEL: 216-1-708-220
FAX: 216-1-708-020

AMEN BANK
13 AVENUE DE FRANCE
TUNIS
TEL: 216-1-340.511
FAX: 216-1-349.909

BANQUE INTERNATIONAL ARABE DE TUNISIE (BIAT)
70-72, AVENUE HABIB BOURGUIBA
TUNIS
TEL: 216-1-340.722
FAX: 216-1-340.680

BANQUE NATIONALE AGRICOLE (BNA)
RUE HEDI NOUIRA
TUNIS
TEL: 216-1-791.200
FAX: 216-1-793.031

U.S. EMBASSY TRADE CONTACTS

AMERICAN EMBASSY TUNIS
144, AVENUE DE LA LIBERTE
1002 TUNIS-BELVEDERE
TEL: 216-1-782-566
FAX: 216-1-789-719

EDWARD V. O'BRIEN, COMMERCIAL ATTACHÉ
CHARLOTTE JOULAK, COMMERCIAL SPECIALIST
MOURAD EL ALMI, ECONOMIC SPECIALIST
NELLY ALI, TRANSLATOR/COMMERCIAL SPECIALIST

COL MICHAEL BLATTI, CHIEF
OFFICE OF DEFENSE COOPERATION

MERRITT CHESLEY, AGRICULTURAL COUNSELOR
OFFICE OF AGRICULTURAL AFFAIRS
(RESIDENT IN RABAT, MOROCCO)

WASHINGTON-BASED U.S. GOVERNMENT COUNTRY CONTACTS

U.S. DEPARTMENT OF COMMERCE
CHERIE LOUSTAUNAU
TUNISIA DESK OFFICER
OFFICE OF THE NEAR EAST
HERBERT HOOVER BUILDING ROOM 2039
WASHINGTON D.C. 20230
TEL: (202) 482-1860
FAX: (202) 482-0878

U.S. DEPARTMENT OF STATE

TUNISIA DESK OFFICER
NEA/ENA
ROOM 5250
WASHINGTON D.C. 20520

TEL: (202) 647-3614
FAX: (202) 736-4458

U.S. DEPARTMENT OF STATE
OFFICE OF THE COORDINATOR FOR BUSINESS AFFAIRS
TEL: (202) 647-1625
FAX: (202) 647-3953
TPCC TRADE INFORMATION CENTER
WASHINGTON, DC
TEL: 1 - 800 - USA - TRADE

U.S. DEPARTMENT OF AGRICULTURE
FOREIGN AGRICULTURAL SERVICE
TRADE ASSISTANCE AND PROMOTION OFFICE
TEL: (202) 720-7420

UNITED ARAB EMIRATES

US Government Trade Related Contacts in the UAE

Senior Commercial Officer: Nancy Charles-Parker
US Embassy, Commercial Section
P.O. Box 4009, Abu Dhabi
Tel: (971-2) 627-3666
Fax: (971-2) 627-1377
E-mail: abudhabi.office.box@mail.doc.gov
Website: www.usembabu.gov.ae/abfcs.htm

Principal Commercial Officer: John Lancia
US Consulate General, Commercial Section
P.O. Box 9343, Dubai
Tel: (971-4) 311-6000
Fax: (971-4) 311-6140
E-mail: dubai.office.box@mail.doc.gov
Website: www.usembabu.gov.ae/fcs.htm

Regional Director: Ronald Verdonk
US Consulate General, Agriculture Trade Office
P.O. Box 9343, Dubai
Tel: (971-4) 311-6183
Fax: (971-4) 311-6189
E-mail: atodubai@emirates.net.ae
Website: www.usembabu.gov.ae/atodubai.htm
Office covers: Bahrain, Kuwait, Oman, Qatar and UAE

US Government Trade Related Contacts in Washington, D.C.

UAE Desk Officer: David Guglielmi
US Department of Commerce
14th St. & Constitution Avenue, N.W.
Washington, D.C. 20230-0001
Tel: (202) 482-5545
Fax: (202) 482-0878; Flash Fax:(202) 482-1064

Regional Director USFCS/ANESA: Kevin Brennan
Deputy Director USFCS/ANESA: JeNelle Matheson
US Department of Commerce
14th St. & Constitution Avenue, N.W.
Washington, D.C. 20230-0001
Tel: (202) 482-4836
Fax: (202) 482-5179

Trade Information Center (TIC)
US Department of Commerce
Washington, D.C. 20230-0001
Tel: 1-800-USA-TRADE

Trade Assistance and Promotion Office (TAPO)
Foreign Agricultural Service (FAS)
US Department of Agriculture
Box 1052
Washington, D.C. 20250-1052
Tel: 202-720-7420
Fax: 202-690-4374
The FAS home page address on the Internet is: www.fas.usda.gov

UAE Embassy in US

Embassy of the United Arab Emirates
3522 International Court, N.W Suite 400
Washington, D.C. 20008
Tel: 202-243-2400,
Fax: 202-243-2432

UAE Consulate General
747the Ave 36th Floor
New York, NY 10017
Tel: 212-371-0419
Fax: 212-577-3888

US Based Multipliers relevant for UAE

National US Arab Chamber of Commerce
1100 New York Ave., N.W.
East Tower, Suite 550
Washington, D.C. 20005
Tel: 202-289-5920
Fax: 202-289-5938
Website: www.awo.net

American Business Council of the Gulf Countries (ABCGC)
C/o Intercom International Consultants
1101 30th Street, N.W., Suite 500
Washington, D.C. 20007
Tel: 202-887-1887
Fax: 202-887-1888

Government of Dubai
Department of Tourism & Commerce Marketing
8 Penn Center
Philadelphia, PA 19103
Tel: 215-751-9750

Fax: 215-751-9551
E-mail: dtcm_usa@dubaitourism.co.ae
(covers North America – East and Central)

901 Wilshire Boulevard
Santa Monica, CA 90401
Tel: 310-752-4488
Fax: 310-752-4444
E-mail: dubaiusa@aol.com
(covers North America - West Coast)

Major UAE Trade Associations/Chambers of Commerce

The American Business Council of Dubai and Northern Emirates
P.O. Box 9281, Dubai, UAE
Tel: 971-4-331-4735; Fax: 971-4-331-4227
Email: amchamdx@emirates.net.ae
Website: www.abcdubai.com
Contact: Mr. T.B. "Mac" McClelland, Jr., President

The American Business Group of Abu Dhabi
P.O. Box 43710, Abu Dhabi, UAE
Tel: 971-2-626-2086; Fax: 971-2-626-2087
Email: abgroup@emirates.net.ae
Website: www.abg-ad.com
Contact: Mr. John Veliquette, President

Federation Chamber of Commerce & Industry
P.O. Box 3014, Abu Dhabi
Tel: 971-2- 621-4144; Fax: 971-2-633-9210
Email: fcciauh@emirates.net.ae
Secretary General: Mr. Abdulla Sultan Abdulla

Abu Dhabi Chamber of Commerce & Industry
P.O. Box 662, Abu Dhabi, UAE
Tel: 971-2-621-4000, Fax: 971-2-621-5867
Email: services@adcci.gov.ae
Website: www.adcci-uae.com
Director General: Mr. Mohammed Omar Abdulla

Dubai Chamber of Commerce & Industry
P.O. Box 1457, Dubai
Tel: 971-4-228-0000; Fax: 971-4-221-1646
Email: info.center@dcci.gov.ae
Website: www.dcci.org
Director General: Abdul Rahman G. Al Mutaiwee

Sharjah Chamber of Commerce & Industry
P.O. Box 580, Sharjah
Tel: 971-6-554-1444; Fax: 971-6-554-1119
Email: scci@sharjah.gov.ae
Website: www.sharjah.gov.ae
Director General: Saeed Obeid Al Jarwan

UAE Federal Ministries

Ministry of Agriculture and Fisheries
P.O. Box 213, Abu Dhabi, UAE
Tel: 971-2-666-2781, Fax: 971-2-665-4787
Minister: H.E. Saeed Mohammed Raqabani

UAE Armed Forces General Headquarters (GHQ)
P.O. Box 3755, Abu Dhabi, UAE
Tel: 971-2-441-4999, Fax: 971-2-441-4082
Chief of Staff: H.H. Sheikh Mohamed Bin Zayed Al Nahyan

UAE Armed Forces Directorate of General Purchasing
GHQ, P.O. Box 2501, Abu Dhabi, UAE
Tel: 971-2-441-5300, Fax: 971-2-441-5687
Director: Colonel Sayed Mohd Al Mansoori

Ministry of Communications
P.O. Box 900, Abu Dhabi, UAE
Tel: 971-2-665-1900, Fax: 971-2-665-1691
Minister: H.E. Ahmed Humaid Al Tayer

Ministry of Economy and Commerce
P.O. Box 901, Abu Dhabi, UAE
Tel: 971-2-626-5000, Fax: 971-2-626-0000
Website: www.economy.gov.ae
Minister: H.E. Shaikh Fahim Bin Sultan Al Qassimi

Ministry of Electricity and Water
P.O. Box 629, Abu Dhabi, UAE
Tel: 971-2-627-4222, Fax: 971-2-626-9738
Minister:H.E. Humaid Bin Nasser Al Owais

Ministry of Health
P.O. Box 848, Abu Dhabi, UAE
Tel: 971-2-633-0000,331000, Fax: 971-2-621-7722
Minister: H.E. Hamad Abdul Rahman Al Midfa

Ministry of Petroleum and Mineral Resources
P.O. Box 59, Abu Dhabi, UAE
Tel: 971-2-667-1999, Fax: 971-2-666-3414
Minister: H.E. Obeid Bin Saeed Saif Al Nasseri

General Secretariat of Municipalities (A)
P.O. Box 5665, Dubai, UAE
Tel: 971-4-223-7785, Fax: 223-6136
General Secretary: Mr. Jassim Darwish

Important Government Authorities in Abu Dhabi

Abu Dhabi Department of Civil Aviation
P.O. Box 20, Abu Dhabi, UAE
Tel: 971-2-575-7500, Fax: 971-2-575-7285
Director General: Mr. Fahd Al Hosni
Chairman: H.H. Sheikh Hamdan Bin Mubarak Al Nahyan

Abu Dhabi Municipality
P.O. Box: 263, Abu Dhabi, UAE

Tel: 971-2-678-8888, Fax: 971-2-677-4919
Chairman: H.E. Shaikh Mohamed Bin Butti

Customs Department
P.O. Box 255
Abu Dhabi, UAE
Tel: 971-2-673-0700, Fax: 971-2-673-1150
Chairman: H.E. Mohd Saleh Bin Badouh

Abu Dhabi Seaport Authority
P.O. Box 422
Abu Dhabi, UAE
Tel: 971-2-6730336, Fax: 971-2-6731023
Website: www.portzayed.gov.ae
Chairman: H.H. Shaikh Saeed Bin Zayed Al Nahyan

Food & Environment Control Center (**A**)
P.O. Box 3111, Abu Dhabi, UAE
Tel: 971-2-672-5008, Fax: 971-2-678-5961
Director: Dr. Amin Yousuf

Important Government Authorities in Dubai

Dubai Civil Aviation Department
P.O. Box 2525, Dubai, UAE
Tel: 971-4-224-5555, Fax: 971-4-224-4074
Wesbite: www.duabiairport.com
President: Sheikh Ahmed Bin Saeed Al Maktoum

The Dubai Department of Economic Development
P.O. Box 13223, Dubai, UAE
Tel: 971-4-222-9922, Fax: 971-4-222-5577
Website: www.dubaided.com
Director General: Mohammed Ali Al Abbar

Port Customs & Freezone Corporation
P.O. Box 63, Dubai, UAE
Tel: 971-4- 345-5555, Fax: 971-4- 345-0450
Website: www.dxbcustoms.gov
Executive Chairman: Sultan Ahmed Bin Sulayem

Dubai Ports Authority
P.O. Box 17000, Dubai, UAE
Tel: 971-4-804-0500, Fax: 971-4-881-6093
Website: www.dpa.co.ae
Managing Director: Jamal Majid Bin Thaniah

Dubai Municipality
P.O. Box 67, Dubai, UAE
Tel: 971-4-221-5555, Fax: 971-4-224-6666
Website: www.dm.gov.ae
Director: Mr. Qassim Sultan

Dubai Municipality - Food Control Section (**A**)
P.O. Box 67, Dubai, UAE
Tel: 971-4-221-5555, Fax: 971-4-223-1905
Section Head: Mr. Khalid Sherif

Dubai Municipality Central Laboratories
P.O. Box 67, Dubai, UAE
Tel: 971-4-221-5555, Fax: 971-4-224-6666
Director: Mr. Rashid bin Fahed

WEST BANK – PALESTINE

U.S. Embassy, U.S. Consulate General, and Trade-related Contacts

Ann Bacher, Senior Commercial Officer
The Commercial Service
U.S. Consulate
Ground Floor
19 Keren Hayesod Street
Jerusalem 94188
Tel: 972-2-625-5201
Fax: 972-2-623-5132
E-mail: ann.bacher@mail.doc.gov

Wajdi Odeh, Commercial Assistant (for aviation, construction, automotive, energy, electronics, and franchising)
The Commercial Service
71 Hayarkon Street
Tel Aviv 63903
Tel: 972-3-519-7586
Fax: 972-3-510-7215
E-mail: wajdi.odeh@mail.doc.gov

Issa Noursi, Commercial Specialist (for medical, environment, telecommunications, and general consumer goods)
Ground Floor
19 Keren Hayesod Street
Jerusalem 94188
Tel: 972-2-625-5201
Fax: 972-2-623-5132
E-mail: issa.noursi@mail.doc.gov

Assad Barsoum, Commercial Assistant (for computers, financial services, tourism, textiles, and food)
Ground Floor
19 Keren Hayesod Street
Jerusalem 94188
Tel: 972-2-625-4742
Fax: 972-2-623-5132
E-mail: assad.barsoum@mail.doc.gov

Deborah R. Schwartz, Economic Counselor
Economic Section
U.S. Embassy
71 Hayarkon Street
Tel Aviv 63903
Tel: 972-3-519-7364
Fax: 972-3-510-1035
E-mail: schwartzdr@state.gov

Mr. Timothy Wilder, Economic Section Chief
Economic Section

Fax: 972-8-286-3926

Ministry of Postal Services & Telecommunications
Jericho, West Bank
Contact: Mr. Imad El-Falouji, Minister
Tel: 972-2-232-2574
Fax: 972-2-232-2233 /232-2499 /232-2574

Ministry of Environment
Ramallah, West Bank
Contact: Dr. Youssef Abu Saffieh, Minister
Tel: 972-2-240-3495/6/7/8
Fax: 972-2-240-3494

Civil Aviation Department
P.O. Box 4043
Gaza
Contact: Mr. Fayez Zaidan, Director General
Tel: 972-8-282-2800
Fax: 972-8-282-1309

Palestinian Energy Authority
P.O. Box 3591
El-Bireh, West Bank
Contact: Dr. Abdul Rahman Hamad, Chairman
Tel: 972-2-298-6190 or 972-2-298-6192
Fax: 972-2-298-6191
Gaza:Tel & Fax:972-8-280-8488/9

Country Market Research Firms

DAI: Market Access Program (MAP)
P.O. Box 54807
Ramallah, West Bank
Contact: Mr. Jim Winkler, Director
Tel: 972-2-298-7187
Fax: 972-2-295-9220
http:// www.dai.com

Ernst & Young International
P.O. Box 1373
Ramallah, West Bank
Contact: Mr. Hanna Quffa, Resident Representative
Tel: 972-2-298-0080

Arthur Andersen
P.O. Box 851
Ramallah, West Bank
Contact: Mr. Hilal Salah, Senior Partner
Tel: 972-2-298-6056/7
Fax: 972-2-298-6058

DATA - Studies & Consultation
P.O. Box 486
Bethlehem, West Bank
Contact: Dr. Samir Hazboun, Director
Tel: 972-2-274-2742
Fax: 972-2-276-4402

Global Management Consulting Group
P.O. Box 2429
Ramallah, West Bank
Contact: Mr. Nael Shabaro, Director
Tel: 972-2-295-8771
Fax: 972-2-295-8772

Bir Zeit University
Continuing Education Department
P.O. Box 14
Bir Zeit, West Bank
Contact: Mrs. Haifa Baramki, Director
Tel: 972-2-295-6229
Fax: 972-2-295-4383

Massar Associates
P.O. Box 2439
Al Bireh, West Bank
Contact: Mr. Bashar Masri, Director
Fax: 972-2-628-2981
Tel: 972-2-298-5624 / 295-2818
Fax: 972-2-295-9110

Mashreq for Research & Studies
P.O. Box 543
Ramallah, West Bank
Contact: Mr. Fawwaz Abboushi, Director
Tel & Fax: 972-2-295-5393

Bethlehem University
Business Development Center
P.O. Box 9
Bethlehem, West Bank
Contact: Mr. Hanna Sahar, Director
Tel & Fax: 972-2-274-5559

Country Commercial Banks

Arab Bank
P.O. Box 1476
Al Harajeh Building
Ramallah, West Bank
Contact: Mr. Shukri Bishara, Regional Director
Tel: 972-2-295-4817/18/19
Fax: 972-2-298-2444

Bank of Jordan
P.O. Box 1829
Ramallah, West Bank
Contact: Mr. Aziz Shaker, Deputy Regional Director
Tel: 972-2-295-2694/5/6/7/8
972-2-295-8686
Fax: 972-2-295-8684

Cairo Amman Bank
P.O. Box 1870
Ramallah, West Bank
Contact: Mr. Mazen Abu Hamdan, Regional Director
Tel: 972-2-298-9435/6

972-2-298-5790/91/92
Fax: 972-2-295-5437

Commercial Bank of Palestine
P.O. Box 1799
Ramallah, West Bank
Contact: Mr. Khaled Al Gabeesh, Director
Tel: 972-2-295-4141
Fax: 972-2-295-3888

Bank of Palestine
P.O. Box 50
Omar El-Mukhtar Street
Gaza
Contact: Mrs. Ismat Elrayes
Tel: 972-8-282-3272/3/4/5/6/7
Fax: 972-8-282-6598

Standard Chartered Bank *(No branches in Gaza)*
Shweitteh Street,
P.O. Box 1
Nablus, West Bank
Contact: Mr. Ahmad Tarifi, Regional Manager
Tel: 972-9-238-4555
Fax: 972-9-238-4563

Jordan-Gulf Bank (No branches in Gaza)
Anabtawi Building
Nablus, West Bank
Contact: Mr. Ibrahim Al Atrash, Regional Manger
Tel: 972-9-238-4402
Fax: 972-9-238-1953

The Housing Bank
Rukab Building
Ramallah, West Bank
Contact: Mr. Anis Alhagah, Regional Manager
Tel: 972-2-298-6270-4
Fax: 972-2-298-6276

Palestine Investment Bank
Omar Mukhtar Street
Gaza
Contact: Mr. Ali Hussein Suleiman
Tel: 972-8-282-5105
Fax: 972-8-282-0544

Union Bank (No branches in Gaza)
Post Office Street
Ramallah, West Bank
Contact: Mr. Musa Shammieh, Director
Tel: 972-2-298-6412
Fax: 972-2-298-6416

Arab Land Bank
El-Bireh, West Bank
Contact: Mr. Fouad Jabr, Regional Manager
Tel: 972-2-295-8421/2/3/4
Fax: 972-2-295-8425

Jordan National Bank (No branches in Gaza)
Ramallah - Al Bireh, West Bank
Contact: Mr. Hanna Ghattas, Regional Manager
Tel: 972-2-298-6370/ 972-2-295-9343
Fax: 972-2-298-6372/ 972-2-295-9341

Jordan Kuwait Bank (No branches in Gaza)
Sufian Street
Nablus, West Bank
Contact: Mr. Muhammed Yasser Al Asmar, General Manager
Tel: 972-9-237-7223
Fax: 972-9-237-7181

Arab Palestinian Investment Bank
P.O. Box 1268 Al Harajeh Building
Ramallah, West Bank
Contact: Dr. Samir Abdullah, General Manager
Tel: 972-2-298-2452
Fax: 972-2-298-2444

Palestine International Bank
P.O. Box 3636
El-Bireh, West Bank
Contact: Mr. Abdel Salam Abu Issa, Chairman
Tel: 972-2-2987467 /972-2-2987197
Fax: 972-2-2987148

HSBC (No branches in Gaza)
P.O. Box 2067
Ramallah, West Bank
Contact: Mr. Albert Noursi, Director
Tel: 972-2-298-7802/3
Fax: 972-2-298-7804

Multilateral Development Bank Offices

IBRD - International Bank for Reconstruction and Development
P.O. Box 54842, Jerusalem
Contact: Mr. Nigel Roberts, Country Director
Tel: 972-2-236-6500
Fax: 972-2-236-6543

Washington-Based USG Personnel

U.S. Department of Commerce
Contact: Mr. Paul J. Thanos
Desk Officer
U.S. Department of Commerce
Room 2029B
14th & Constitution Avenues, NW
Washington DC 20230
Tel: 202-482-1860
Fax: 202-482-087
E-mail: Paul_Thanos@ita.doc.gov

U.S. Department of State
Contact: Ms. Nicole Rothstein
Office of Israel and Arab-Israeli Affairs
U.S. Department of State
2201 C Street, NW Room 624

Washington, DC 20520
Tel: 202-647-2647
Fax: 202-736-4461

U.S. Trade Representative (USTR)
Contact: Mr. Edmond Saums
600 17th St., NW
Washington, DC
Tel: 202-395-3320
Fax: 202-395-3974

U.S. Agency for International Development (USAID)
Contact: Mr. John Wall
Business Advisor
1300 Pennsylvania Ave., N.W.
Suite 4.10-033
Washington DC, 20523-4101
Tel: 202-712-0511
Fax: 202-216-3028

Contact: Ms. Kim Finan
Country Officer
1300 Pennsylvania Ave., N.W.
Suite 4.10-033
Washington D.C. 20523-4101
Tel: 202-712-0316
Fax: 202-216-3028

U.S. Trade & Development Agency
USTDA
North Kent Street, Ste. 200
Arlington 22209-2131
Washington, DC 20523
Tel: 703-875-4357
Fax. 703-875-4009

Export-Import Bank of the United States (EXIM)
Contact: Mr. Talaat Rahman
811 Vermont Ave., NW
Washington, DC 20571
Tel: 202-565-3911
Fax: 202-565-3931

Overseas Private Investment Corporation (OPIC)
Contact: Mr. Abed Tarbush
1100 New York Ave., NW
Washington, DC 20527
Tel: 202-336-8632
Fax: 202-408-9859

US Department of Agriculture, Foreign Agricultural Service, Trade Assistance and Promotion Office

U.S. Department of Agriculture
Foreign Agricultural Service
Washington, DC 20250-1000
Contact: Mr. Paul Hoffman
Area Officer
Africa and the Middle East
Room 5951S
Tel: 202-720-7053
Fax: 202-690-1149
E-mail: hoffmanp@fas.usda.gov

Contact: Mr. Gary Meyer, Team Leader
Eastern Europe, Africa and the Middle East
FAS-International Trade Policy Division
Room 5503S
Tel: 202-720-2258
Fax: 202-690-2079
E-mail: meyerg@fas.usda.gov

Contact: Mr. Dan Berman, Director
Agricultural Export Services Division
Room 4939S
Tel: 202-720-0142
Fax: 202-690-4374
E-mail: berman@fas.usda.gov

U.S.-Based Multiplier Organizations

Eastern U.S. Agricultural and Food Export Council, Inc.
Contact: Ms. Evalina (Vel) D. Vengco, (Acting) Executive Director
1036 Public Ledger Building
214 Senate Ave. Suite 600
150 South Independence Mall,
West Philadelphia, PA 19106-3410
Tel: 215-829-9111
Fax: 215-829-9777
Web: www.foodexportusa.org

Mid-America International Agri-Trade Council (MIATCO)
Contact: Mr. Timothy Hamilton, Executive Director
400 West Erie St., Suite 100
Chicago, IL 60610-4041
Tel: 312-944-3030
Fax: 312-944-1144
Web: www.miatco.org

Southern U.S. Trade Association (SUSTA)
Contact: Mr. Jim Ake
Executive Director
World Trade Center, Suite 1540
2, Canal Street
New Orleans, LA 70130-1408
Tel: 504-568-5986
Fax: 504-568-6010

Western U.S. Agricultural Trade Association (WUSATA)
Contact: Mr. Bruce Prenguber, Executive Director
13101 N.E. Highway 99, Suite 200
Vancouver, WA 98686-2786
Tel: 206-574-2627
Fax: 206-574-7083

Animal and Plant Inspection Service
47000 River Road
Unit 139
Riverdale, MD 20737
Contact: Mr. Jonathan Jones, Senior Export Specialist
Tel: 301-734-3818
Fax: 301-734-5786

Contact: Veterinary Services
Dr. Najam Q. Faizi
Senior Staff, Veterinary/Export
Tel: 301-734-8364
Fax: 301-734-6402

Contact: Nicholas Guttierez
USDA/APHIS/IS From U.S.:
FAS-USEU USDA/APHIS/IS
40 Blvd. Du Regent FAS-ESEU
1000 Brussels PSC 82
Belgium Box 002
Brussels APO AE 09724
Tel: (32) 2-508-2762
Fax: (32) 2-511-0918

Contact: Kenneth Bedat From U.S.:
Officer in Charge USDA/APHIS/IS
USDA/APHIS/IS Postbus 435
Achterweg Zuid 33 2160 AK Lisse
2161 DX Lisse The Netherlands
The Netherlands
Tel: (31) 252-421-555
Fax: (31) 252-417-019

International Organizations

UNSCO - United Nations Office of the Special Coordinator in the Occupied Territories (Office Headquarters in Gaza)
Mailing Address:
P.O. Box 490
Government House
Jerusalem 91004
Contact: Mr. Terje Larson, Undersecretary General
Tel: 972-2-582-9962/3 or 972-8-286-0074
Fax: 972-2-582-9716
UNDP - United Nations Development Program
Sheikh Jarah - Jerusalem
Contact: Mr. Oscar Fernandez Taronco, Deputy Administrator
Tel: 972-2-626-8200
Fax: 972-2-628-0089

UNRWA - United Nations Relief & Works Agency for Palestine
Sheikh Jarah - Jerusalem
Contact: Mr. Peter Hansen, Commissioner General
Gaza Office: Fax: 972-8-677-7699
Jerusalem: Tel: 972-2-589-0401
Fax: 972-2-532-2714
Contact: Mr. Lionel Brisson, Director
UNRWA - Gaza
Tel: 972-8-677-7264
Fax: 972-8-677-7390

US State Offices

American State Office Association
Sherwin Pomerantz, Chairperson
Atid EDI Ltd
Building 2, Har Hotzvim
P O B 45005, 91450 Jerusalem
Tel: 972-2-571-0199
Fax: 972-2-571-0713
Mobile: 972-53-825-641
E-mail: atidedi@netvision.net.il

California
Sherwin Pomerantz, Israel Director
California Trade & Commerce Agency
Atid EDI Ltd
Building 2, Har Hotzvim
P O B 45005, 91450 Jerusalem
Tel: 972-2-571-0199
Fax: 972-2-571-0713
Mobile: 972-53-825-641
E-mail: atidedi@netvision.net.il, jerusalem@commerce.ca.gov
Web: www.atid-edi.com/california.htm

Delaware
Sherwin Pomerantz, Israel Director
Delaware Department of Economic Development
Atid EDI Ltd
Building 2, Har Hotzvim
P O B 45005, 91450 Jerusalem
Tel: 972-2-571-0199,
Fax: 972-2-571-0713
Mobile: 972-53-825-641
E-mail: atidedi@netvision.net.il
Web: www.atid-edi.com/delaware.htm

Indiana
Sherwin Pomerantz, E Mediterreanean Regional Director
Indiana Department of Commerce
Atid EDI Ltd
Building 2, Har Hotzvim
P O B 45005, 91450 Jerusalem
Tel: 972-2-571-0199
Fax: 972-2-571-0713
Mobile: 972-53-825-641
E-mail: sherwin@atid-edi.com
Web: www.atid-edi.com/indiana.htm

Missouri
Sherwin Pomerantz, E Mediterranean Regional Director
Missouri Department of Economic Development
Atid EDI Ltd

Building 2, Har Hotzvim
P O B 45005, 91450 Jerusalem
Tel: 972-2-571-0199
Fax: 972-2-571-0713
Mobile: 972-53-825-641
E-mail: atidedi@netvision.net.il
Web: www.atid-edi.com/missouri.htm

New Mexico
Sherwin Pomerantz, Israel Director
New Mexico Economic Development Depratment
Atid EDI Ltd
Building 2, Har Hotzvim
P O B 45005, 91450 Jerusalem
Tel: 972-2-571-0199
Fax: 972-2-571-0713
Mobile: 972-53-825-641
E-mail: atidedi@netvision.net.il
Web: www.atid-edi.com/nm.htm

Ohio
Richard Schottenstein, Regional Director
Ohio Office of Trade and Investment
Ohio Department of Development
1 Azrieli Center, Derech Petach Tikva 132
Tel-Aviv 67012
Tel: 972-3-609-6001
Fax: 972-3-609-6002
E-mail: ohiotrade@mail.com
Rick Personal: ohio1@barak.net.il

Oklahoma
Sherwin Pomerantz, Israel Director
Oklahoma-Israel Exchange (OKIE)
Atid EDI Ltd
Building 2, Har Hotzvim
P O B 45005, 91450 Jerusalem
Tel: 972-2-571-0199
Fax: 972-2-571-0713
Mobile: 972-53-825-641
E-mail: atidedi@netvision.net.il
Web: www.atid-edi.com/oklahoma.htm

Wisconsin
Sherwin Pomerantz, E Mediterranean Regional Director
Wisconsin Department of Commerce
Atid EDI Ltd
Building 2, Har Hotzvim
P O B 45005, 91450 Jerusalem
Tel: 972-2-571-0199
Fax: 972-2-571-0713
Mobile: 972-53-825-641
E-mail: atidedi@netvision.net.il
Web: www.atid-edi.com/wisconsin.htm

YEMEN

U.S. Embassy Trade Personnel
Barbara K. Bodine, Ambassador
Bradford Hanson, Deputy Chief of Mission
Donna Visocan, Economic/Commercial Officer
Darin K. Olson, Consular/Commercial Officer
Mohamed Khaleal, Commercial Specialist
Mohamed Sharaf-Aldin, Agricultural Specialist
P. O. Box 22347, Sanaa, Republic of Yemen
Phone: 967-1-303-156 through 162
Fax: 967-1-303-183

Washington-based U.S. Government Country Contacts
Department of State
Diane Shelby, Yemen Desk Officer
2100 C Street
NEA/ARP, Room 4224
Washington, D.C. 20520
Phone: (202) 647-6558; Fax: (202) 736-4459

Department of Commerce
14th and Constitution Avenues, NW
Washington, D.C. 20230
International Trade Administration
David Guglielmi, Yemen Desk Officer
Phone: (202) 482-1860; Fax: (202) 482-0878
Email: david_guglielmi@ita.doc.gov

Christopher James, Project Manager, Advocacy Center
Phone: (202) 482-3896; Fax: (202) 482-3508
Email: christopher_james@ita.doc.gov

The Multilateral Bank Office
Department of Commerce
Skip Jones, Director (On leave until January 2001)
Phone: (202) 482-3399; Fax: (202) 482-5179
Email: skip_jones@ita.doc.gov
Judy Sever, (Acting until January 2001)
Email: judy_sever@ita.doc.gov

TPCC Trade Information Center
Department of Commerce
Abdul Quadar Shaikh
Phone: 1-800-USA-TRADE
Email: abdul_shaikh@ita.doc.gov

U.S. Trade and Development Agency (TDA)
Henry D. Steingass, Regional Director, Africa & Middle East
1621 North Kent Street, Suite 200
Arlington, VA 22209-2123
Phone: (703) 875-4357; Fax: (703) 875-4009
Email: info@tda.gov
Website: www.tda.gov

Overseas Private Investment Corporation (OPIC)
Abed Tarbush
Business Development Manager, Middle East & North Africa
1100 New York Avenue
Washington, D.C. 20527
Phone: (202) 336-8799 or (202) 336-8400; Fax:

(202) 336-8700
Email: info@opic.gov
Website: www.opic.gov

Export-Import Bank of the United States (EXIM Bank)
Vernoique M. Cavaillier, Officer for the Middle East
811 Vermont Avenue, NW
Washington, D.C. 20571
Phone: (202) 565-3946 or (202) 566-8990; Fax: (202) 565-3380
Email: veronique.cavaillier@exim.gov
Website: www.exim.gov

U.S. Department of Agriculture (USDA)
Foreign Agricultural Service
Trade Assistance and Promotion Office
Phone: (202) 720-7420
Fax: (202) 720-3799
E-mail: hoffman@fas.usda.gov
www.fas.usda.gov

Yemen Chambers of Commerce
Sanaa Chamber of Commerce & Industry
Abdul Wahab Sinan Abu Lahom, Chairman
Mehdi Murshid Tarah, General Manager
P.O. Box 195, Sanaa, Republic of Yemen
Phone: 967-1-234-761/2/3/4 or 232-361/2; Fax: 967-1-232-412
E-mail sanaacomyemen@y.net.ye; Website: www.chamber-yemen.com

Aden Chamber of Commerce & Industry
Mohamed Omer Bamashmous, Chairman
Ahmed Hadi Salem, General Manager
P.O. Box 473, Crater, Aden, Republic of Yemen
Phone: 967-2-221-176 or 251-104 or 255-446; Fax: 967-2-255-660
E-mail: cciaden@y.net.ye; Website: www.yemnet.com

Hodeidah Chamber of Commerce & Industry
Abubaker Salem Shammakh, Chairman
Nabil Al-Wajeeh, General Manager.
P.O. Box 3370 Hodeidah, Republic of Yemen
Phone: 967-3-217-401/217-621; Fax: 967-3-211-528
Email: hodcci@y.net.ye

Hadhramaut Chamber of Commerce & Industry
Abdel Khalek Bamatraf, Chairman
P.O. Box 8302, Mukalla, Hadhramaut, Republic of Yemen
Phone: 967-5-353-258; Fax: 967-5-303-437

Yemen Government Agencies
Ministry of Electricity and Water
H.E. Eng. Yahya al-Abyad, Minister
Eng. Ahmad al-Aini, Deputy Minister
Eng. Abdul Moti al-Junaid, Acting Managing Director
Public Electricity Corporation
P.O. Box 11422, Sanaa, Republic of Yemen
Phone: 967-1-326-193/4 or 326-191/6; Fax: 967-1-326-198 or 326-214

Ministry of Oil and Mineral Resources
H.E. Dr. Rashid Ba-Raba'a, Minister
P.O. Box 81, Sanaa, Republic of Yemen
Phone: 967-1-202-309 through 13; Fax: 967-1-202-314
Email: momormastr@y.net.ye

Ministry of Communications
H.E. Eng. Abul-Malik Al-Mu'allimi, Minister
Yassin Mahmoud Ali, Deputy Minister
P.O. Box 17045, Sanaa, Republic of Yemen
Phone: 967-1-331-460/1; Fax: 967-1-331-473

Ministry of Industry and Trade
H.E. Abdul Rahman M. A. Othman, Minister
Dr. Jaffar Hamid Mohamed, Vice Minister (Industry Sector)
Mohamed Ahmed Al-Haimy, Deputy Minister (Industry Sector)
Ali Al-Siaghi, Vice Minister (Trade Sector)
Kaid Al-Herwi, Deputy Minister (Trade Sector)
P.O. Box 7296, Sanaa, Republic of Yemen
Phone: 967-1-252-471/9-252-340; Fax: 967-1-251-570
Website:www.most.org.ye:

Ministry of Planning and Development
H.E. Ahmad Muhammad Sufan, Minister
Abdul Rahman Mohamed Tarmoum, Vice Minister
Hisham Sharaf Abdallah, Deputy Minister for International Cooperation
P.O. Box 175, Sanaa, Republic of Yemen
Phone: 967-1-250-101 through 3; Fax: 967-1-250-665
Email: mpdminister@y.net.ye
E-mail: shaiban@yahoo.com

General Investment Authority
Abdul Karim Mutair, General Manager
Mohamed Ahmed Hussein, Chief, Promotion Sector
P.O. Box 19022, Sanaa, Republic of Yemen
Phone: 967-1-262-958; Fax: 967-1-262-964
Email: gia@y.net.ye; Website: www.giay.gov.ye

Commercial Banks (with U.S. correspondent banks)

Arab Bank PLC
Mehdi Alawi, Regional Manager (Tel: 276-582)
P.O. Box 1301 & 475, Sanaa, Republic of Yemen
Phone: 967-1-276-585, 276-592/3; Fax: 967-1-276-583, 276-475
E-mail: arabbank@y.net.ye; Internet:

www.Arabbank.com
(Arab Bank of New York)

Credit Agricole Indosuez Yemen
Francois Rivier, Regional General Manager
P.O. Box 651, Sanaa, Republic of Yemen
Phone: 967-1-274-370/1/2; Fax: 967-1-274-501
E-mail: hamid<caindosuezye@y.net.ye
(Citi Bank of New York)

International Bank of Yemen
Mohamed Mokbil Al-Amri, General Manager
P.O. Box 4444, Sanaa, Republic of Yemen
Phone: 967-1-273-273, 272-920 through 4; Fax: 967-1-274-127 or 272-925
E-mail: a.t.alabsi@y.net.ye
(Bank of America, Bank of New York, American Express)

National Bank of Yemen
Abdul Rahman Mohamed Al-Kohali, Chairman/General Manager
Queen Arwa Street, P.O. Box 5, Crater
Aden, Republic of Yemen
Phone: 967-2-253-606/253-484; Fax: 967-2-255-004 or 252-974
E-mail: nby.ho@y.net.ye
(Chase Manhattan, Bank of New York, Citi Bank)

Yemen Bank for Reconstruction and Development
Hussein Fadhl Mohamed, General Manager
P.O. Box 541, Sanaa, Republic of Yemen
Phone: 967-1-274-171 or 271-626; Fax: 967-1-271-630 or 271-635, 271-620
E-mail: ybrdid@y.net.ye
(Citigroup, Chase Manhattan)

Yemen Commercial Bank
Sikander Mahmoud, General Manager and Chief Executive Officer
P.O. Box 19485, Al-Rowaishan Bldg., Zubairi Street
Sanaa, Republic of Yemen
Phone: 967-1-284-272/3 ext. 242, 218-591, Fax: 967-1-284-656
E-mail: ycbho@y.net.ye
(Citigroup and others)

Yemen Kuwait Bank for Trade and Investment
Zaid Ahmed Al-Shami, General Manager
P.O. Box 987, Sanaa, Republic of Yemen
Phone: 967-1-214-315, 209-538/214-615; Fax: 967-1-206-148, 401-989, 202-085
ykb@y.net.ye
(American Express, Bank of New York, City Bank)

Yemen Gulf Bank Y.S.C.
Mr. Mohamed H. Al-Zubeiri, Chairman
P.O.Box: 100, Sanaa, Republic of Yemen
Al-Shokani Street, Near the Police Academy
Tel: 967-1-260-823, 260-825; Fax: 967-1-260-824
E-mail: ygbank@y.net.ye
(Bank of New York)

Al-Watani Bank for Trade & Investments
Dr. Ahmed Ali Al-Hamdani, Chairman
P.O.Box: 3058, Sanaa, Republic of Yemen
Tel: 967-1-214-459, 212-981, 206-613
Fax: 967-1-215-579, 205-706
E-mail: watanibank@y.net.ye
(American Express Bank, Bank of New York, Citi Bank)
Multilateral Development Bank Offices:

The International Bank for Reconstruction and Development (World Bank)
Gianni Brizzi, Resident Representative
P.O.Box: 18152
Street Number 40, off Damascus Road, Hadda Area
Sanaa, Republic of Yemen
Phone: 967-1-418-731/2, 413-708/ 710 or 418-166/7/8,421-623, 413-401; Fax: 967-1-413-709 or 418-733
www.worldbank.org

ISLAMIC LAW GLOSSARY

Adillah - (plural. of dalil) proofs, evidences, indications.

Ahadith - (plural. of hadith) narratives and reports of the deeds and sayings of the Prophet

Ahkam - (plural. of hukm) laws, values and ordinances

Ahliyyah - legal capacity

Ahliyyah al-ada - active legal capacity which can incur rights as well as obligations

Ahliyyah al-wujub - receptove legal capacity which is good for receiving but cannot incur obligations

Al-hukm al-taklifi - defining law, law which defines rights and obligations

Al-hukm al-wad'i - declaratory law, that is, law which regulates the proper implementation of al-hukm al-taklifi, such as by expounding the conditions, exceptions and qualifications thereof.

Dalalah al-nass - inferred or implied meaning of a given text

Dalil - proof, indication, evidence

Faqih - a person who is an expert on Islamic jurisprudence (law), fiqh.

Far' - literally a branch or a sub-division, and in the context of qiyas a new case.

Fard - something which is obligatory on a Muslim. It is sometimes used in reference to the obligatory part of salat.

Fard 'ayn - personal obligation - such as the fard salat (compulsory daily prayers)

Fard kafa'i - collective obligation - such as salat al-Janazah. If a group of the community fulfils this fard, then it is enough, and the duty is fulfilled.

Fatwa - Considered opinion given by a qualified scholar, a mufti (jurisconsult), or a mujtahid (one who is competent enough to conduct ijtihad) concerning a legal/religious issue; a religious edict

Fiqh - Islamic law as developed by Muslim jurists. The term is often used synonymously with Shari'ah; the main difference being that Shari'ah bears a closer link with divine revelation, whereas fiqh mainly consists of the works of religious scholars and jurists.

Fuqaha - plural form of faqih

Hadd - (plural hudud) literally. limit, prescribed penalty.

Halal - something that is lawful and permitted in Islam

Haram - something which is unlawful or prohibited in Islam.

Hudud - the limits ordained by Allah. This includes the punishment for crimes

Hukm - (plural ahkam) as in hukm shar'i: law, value, or ruling of Shari'ah.

Ibahah - Permissibility, being the verbal noun of mubah (permissible), which represents a value point in the Islamic scale of five values, coming next after wajib and mandub.

Ijma' - consensus of opinion

Ijtihad - literally. 'exertion', and technically the effort a jurist makes in order to deduce the law, which is not self-evident, from its sources

Ikhtilaf - juristic disagreement

'Illah - effective cause, or ratio legis, of a particular ruling

istidlal - Reasoning in general (istidlal) by methods other than the recognised sources

istishab - Accompanying circumstances to be taken into consideration

Istihsan - to deem something good, juristic preference

Istislah - consideration of public interest

Mahr - a 'dowry' given by the man to the woman he is about to marry. It is part of the Muslim marriage contract. It can never be demanded back under any circumstances

Majazi - metaphorical, figurative

Makruh - abominable, reprehensible

Mandub - Recommended, praiseworthy; a course of conduct which earns moral reward if followed; however a person who does not follow such a course of conduct is not open to punishment. It is also synonymous with mustahabb.

Mansukh - abrogated, repealed

Mubah - permissible.

Muhkam - perspicuous, a word or a text conveying a firm and unequivocal meaning

Mujmal - ambivalent, ambiguous, referring to a category of unclear words

Mukallaf - a competent person who is in full possession of his faculties

Mukhtasar - abridgement, summary, esp. of juristic manuals composed for mnemonic and teaching purposes.

Munasib - appropriate, in harmony with the basic purpose of the law

Mutashabih - intricate, unintelligible, referring to a word or a text whose meaning is totally unclear

Mutashabihat - (singular. mutashabih) Ambiguous, obscure, difficult to understand - the abbreviated letters which occur at the beginning of some chapters of the Quran are typical examples; the ambiguous passages in the Qur'an

Nahy - prohibition

Nass - a clear injunction, an explicit textual ruling

Nikah - Islamic Legal marriage contract.

Nusus. - (plural. of nass) clear textual rulings

Qadah - plural form of qadi

Qadi - Judge

qawl al-Sahabi - The opinion of a Companion of the Prophet. Also known as *madhhab al-Sahabi*

Qisas - retaliation in kind (eye for an eye). In Islam though, retaliation should be forgone as an act of charity sura 5, ayah 48

Qiyas - Analogical reasoning aimed at extending a given ruling of the Quran and Sunnah to a new case, on grounds of an effective cause common to both the new and th eoriginal case

Ra'y - Considered personal opinion, often used in contradistinction to nass (see above)

Rukhsah - concession or concessionary law, that is, law which is modified due to the presence of mitigating factors

Sadaq - same meaning as mahr

Sahih - valid, authentic

Sanad - basis, proof, authority

Shar'i - Juridical, legal

Shari'ah - Islamic law as contained in the divine guidance of the Qur'an and Sunnah. 'Islamic law' is the nearest English translation of Shari'ah, yet the latter is not confined specifically to legal subject matter and extends to the much wider areas of moral and religious guidance

shar' man qablana - Pre-Islamic divine laws

Shart - (plural. shurut) condition

Siyasah Shari'ah - Shari'ah-oriented policy; often refers to discretionary decisions taken by the Head of State or qadi in pursuit of public good, in response to emergency situations, or in cases where a strict application of the established law would lead to undesirable results

Sunnah - the examples of the Prophet's life, what he said, did, implemented, how he implemented, etc

Tahlil - an intervening marriage contracted for the sole purpose of legalising remarriage between a divorced couple

Tahrim - prohibition, or rendering something into haram

Tahsiniyyat - Embellishments, or things which are merely desirable, as opposed to daruriyyat which are deemed to be essential

Taklif - liability, obligation

Talaq - divorce initiated by the husband

Ta'lil - ratiocination, search for the effective cause of a ruling

Tarjih - Preference (of one legal opinion over others).

Tashri - legislation

Ta'wil - allegorical interpretation

Ta'zir - deterrence, discretionary penalty determined by the qadi.

Ulama - the learned, knowledgeble people in Islam. Plural form of alim

'urf - Custom.

Usul al-fiqh - Sources or roots of Islamic law and jurisprudence; refers mainly to the Quran and Sunnah as the principal sources of the Shari'ah, but also to a number of other sources and methods which are used in order to facilitatee the proper exercise of ijtihad.

Usul al-Qanun - modern jurisprudence.

Wajib - obligatory, often synonymous with fard

Wajib ayni - personal obligation.

Wajib kafa'i - collective obligation of the entire community

Waqf - charitable endowment

Wilayah - (walayah) authority, guardianship (of minors and mentally ill).

Wujub - obligation, rendering something obligatory

www.ingramcontent.com/pod-product-compliance
Lightning Source LLC
LaVergne TN
LVHW080034210926
848481LV00011B/3183